Desktop Witness

Desktop Witness

The do's and don'ts of personal computer security

Michael A. Caloyannides

Senior Fellow
Mitretek Systems
Virginia, USA

JOHN WILEY & SONS, LTD

Library of Congress Cataloging-in-Publication Data
(applied for)

British Library Cataloguing in Publication Data

A catalogue record for this book is available from the British Library

ISBN 0 471 48657 4

Typeset in $10\frac{1}{2}/12\frac{1}{2}$pt Sabon by Keytec Typesetting, Bridport, Dorset
Printed and bound in Great Britain by Biddles Ltd., Guildford and Kings Lynn
This book is printed on acid-free paper responsibly manufactured from sustainable forestry,
for which at least two trees are planted for each one used for paper production.

Dedication

This book is dedicated to my parents, Akylas and Etta, who considered the raising of their children to be their highest priority, and to my two infant children Melody and Brian whom I will not live to see as grown up adults as I am now battling lymphatic cancer. Hopefully, they will carry the torch of individual freedom in a world increasingly opposed to it.

Contents

Preface

When asked 'who are you?', people in different cultures tend to define themselves fundamentally differently in terms of what their respective culture considers to be most important. In cultures where one's professional and economic status is most important, people say 'I am an engineer', or 'a priest at St John's church', or whatever one's profession is. In cultures where family ties and ancestry are most important, people say 'I am John's son', or 'Hsiu's grandson'. Hardly anywhere does one answer the 'who are you?' question by asking 'in what context?'; societal pressures in most societies force most individuals to have largely one-dimensional personas.

The all too human yearning for security and for acceptance by others often makes some of us internalize and accept our immediate community's prevailing standards and beliefs as gospel without using any of our own judgment, and viewing with suspicion those that dare question those beliefs. Most in pre WWII Germany accepted Nazism because it was the 'in' thing; similarly, most ruthless dictators have a considerable number of followers, and so do most quasi-charismatic leaders of assorted oddball cults even if some of these leaders have mesmerized their followers into committing mass suicide – as has happened time and again.

The yearning by most people to have someone else 'spoon-feed' them what is 'right' and what is 'wrong', and to relieve them of the burden of deciding that for themselves, is, I believe, very strong for most people. It is no surprise, then, that the notion of privacy for others (as opposed to privacy for oneself) is very threatening to many; after all, it implies that someone else may have different views – God forbid – and that privacy may get in the way of the rest of the community knowing that!

For related reasons, citizen privacy is certainly threatening to most any government because it could keep dissent from being identified and being nipped in the bud. Even democratically elected governments that pride themselves in their purported respect for citizen privacy have a catch-all exclusion such as 'except as lawfully authorized ...'. In short, privacy is OK as long as you believe what the state (or the community) believes. Stated differently, you can choose any color as long as it is the one that is approved.

Having been born and raised in one culture, educated and lived my professional life in another, being married to a wonderful woman from a third culture, and having adopted a child from yet a different culture, I have come to appreciate the fact that a perspective that seems unpalatable to one culture (say, to law enforcers) makes perfectly good sense if seen within the logic framework of a different culture (say, freedom fighters in an oppressive regime). As such, I was not about to write a book preaching any party line, nor a book that is intended solely for one or the other point of view. Instead, this book is intended for anyone who is mature enough to value privacy. Sadly, this is not everyone, although most everyone values his or her own privacy – but not anybody else's.

Although this book deals with some fairly esoteric topics, it is intended to be understandable by anyone with intelligence. Quite simply, this book is for free-thinking, responsible, and mature people who want to write, store, and communicate their ideas with privacy. This includes businesspeople with proprietary documents, physicians with confidential data on patients, philosophers with new ideas, freedom fighters in oppressive regimes, and any person in need of privacy.

This book is for responsible people in need of safeguarding their privacy when using the twenty-first century's primary tool, namely, a computer of some sort. It is *solely* for responsible and mature people, and not for crooks; as with a kitchen knife or a screwdriver, a computer can be used for good and it can be used for evil. This book is emphatically not intended to facilitate the latter.

Gross abuse of anonymity is criminal, unconscionable, unethical, despicable, and shameful. There have been far too many documented cases when individuals' lives have been ruined as a result of anonymous malicious messages to their family, neighbors, employers, and friends. This conduct is positively not what this book is in any way condoning; quite the contrary, such malice should be hunted down and prosecuted.

No sane person is pro-arson or pro-murder, but one should not allow any oppressive regime's self-serving habit of criminalizing every act that it does not like to shape one's own judgment of what is really right or wrong. As an example of some 30 years ago, a military junta in Greece, the birthplace of democracy, banned the study of some ancient Greek philosophers because they talked 'too much' about freedom. Such practice is wrong regardless of what the self-serving laws in the oppressive regime say.

It used to be that the ultimate threat to privacy was some caricature of an authority figure in an oppressive regime, in or out of uniform. It also used to be that just as real a threat was the classical neighborhood 'busybody', that is, the immaturity and intolerance of our neighbors, of our social acquaintances, and of the people that we interfaced with. It was they who would feel threatened enough by our nonconformist views and conduct to consider it their 'obligation' (to whom?) to report to 'the authorities'. Today, conducting ourselves with discretion is not enough. Technology, such as interception of online traffic, makes the possibility of wholesale surveillance and automated screening not only possible but already in place. Unless one has nothing creative to offer beyond regurgitating the local dogma, one needs effective means of staying out of any oppressive regime's – and even out of one's neighbors – 'radar screens'.

One should also keep in mind that, even under the best of circumstances when one has done nothing wrong, law enforcement databases in even the most technologically advanced country often contain major errors. According to *Wired* reporter Julia Stevens on 11 May 2001 (http://www.wired.com/news/privacy/0,1848.43743,00.html), 'when Richard Smith got his FBI file, he learned . . . that he had died in 1976 and that he may have been previously married to a woman named Mary . . . [and] that he may be known [by] aliases he shares with a couple of convicts doing hard time in Texas'.

Perhaps unwisely, in this book I call a spade a spade, with no deference towards corporations or governments. Inevitably, this candor will offend some corporations and governments. I fully expect this book to be banned in some countries and attempts to be made to discredit it – and me.

In the final analysis, when we lie on our deathbeds we have to seek acceptance by a most critical and unforgiving evaluator of our lives who will see right through any excuse: our own individual conscience.

Michael A. Caloyannides
Washington, DC, January 2002

Acknowledgement

1

The Need is Very Real: Author's Perspective

Security is the means by which one makes it difficult for another forcibly to obtain information, whereas privacy is the means by which one makes information unavailable. Privacy and anonymity have been taken for granted in daily life since time started. We buy groceries and movie tickets with cash, we browse at store windows without showing any identification, and we look at newspapers without anyone knowing which particular article we are reading. Lovers have always whispered sweet words in each other's ears in private, and even some formal written and oral communications – such as privileged discussions between lawyer and client – have enjoyed legally sanctioned confidentiality in civilized societies.

This is all changing very rapidly simply because technology makes it easy to break confidentiality. The incentive to violate individuals' privacy exists both in commercial and in government sectors. Commerce has realized the cost-effectiveness of directed advertising to those already known to have an interest in what is being peddled, and has been deploying increasingly sophisticated technical means of identifying who likes what. Repressive governments, which have always feared any dissent, have availed themselves of even more intrusive technologies to create and maintain vast databases about people in order to identify any and all dissent so as to nip it in the bud; sadly, even democratic governments have played up citizens' insecurities and have done the same under the guise of protecting us from each other. One should not forget Montesquieu's words: 'there is no greater tyranny than that which is perpetrated under the shield of law and in the name of justice'. Nor should we forget the words of William Pitt, British Prime Minister, on 18 November 1783: 'Necessity is the plea for every infringement of human freedom; it is the argument of tyrants; it is the creed of slaves'. It is perilous to assume the position that 'I have done nothing wrong, so I am safe'. Holocaust victims had done nothing wrong either but had a lot to fear, and the same is true for numerous executed individuals who have been exonerated post-mortem as a result of DNA testing.

Furthermore, privacy is an essential element of freedom and does not imply any wrongdoing. We shower in private, we try to keep our medical records private, and we use curtains to keep others' gazes out of our personal and family lives. With the ubiquitous use of personal computers to which we entrust a lot of such private information, there is no reason why we should accept that our privacy ends the moment we touch the keyboard of that personal computer.

Prompted by the much-publicized open availability of strong encryption, many individuals have incorrectly assumed that encryption is the cure-all antidote to the increasing erosion of individual privacy. It is not. Just like a courier of expensive jewels would be ill-advised to stand out by advertising what he or she is carrying, one should not want to stand out by taunting an oppressive regime with encryption in a sea of unencrypted traffic; discretion and unobtrusiveness – without excluding camouflaged encryption – is often far better and more secure. Also, just like a fancy padlock on one's front door is counterproductive if the back doors and windows are not secured, encryption can give one a false sense of security that is worse than no security at all if one's electronic 'back doors and windows' are left unsecured.

The purpose of this book is threefold:

- to educate the average reader on the very real threats to one's online and offline privacy,

- to provide a 'how to' guide on securing one's online and offline privacy,

- to demystify openly available encryption while showing what not to do with it that would actually *reduce* one's privacy.

No technical background is required from the readers of this book beyond a working familiarity with personal computers. However, as with any serious matter, such as driving a car or skiing safely, the issues and fixes discussed require the reader's full attention; effective security cannot be achieved in a casual off-hand manner.

1.1   But Isn't This Book Helping Terrorists? No!

> *In coming months, politicians will flail about looking for freedoms to elminate to 'curb the terrorist threat'. We must remember throughout that you cannot preserve freedom by eliminating it.*
>
> Metzger, Wasabi Systems, September 2001

I worry about my child and the Internet all the time, even though she's too young to have logged on yet. Here's what I worry about: I worry that 10 or 15 years from now, she will come to me and say, Daddy , where were you when they took freedom of the press away from the Internet?

Mike Godwin, Electronic Frontier Foundation

As soon as men decide that all means are permitted to fight an evil, then their good becomes indistinguishable from the evil that they set out to destroy.

Christoper Dawson, *The Judgment of Nations*, 1942

No! This book is emphatically neither helping nor of any use to terrorists. This section would not have been part of this book prior to 11 September 2001 and the terrorist attacks on New York and Washington. It is an important part of this book now because there is a worldwide misconception promulgated by most law enforcers that being pro-privacy has shades of being pro-terrorist. This is patently false. Contrary to popular belief, countering terrorism is not a law-enforcement function but an intelligence function. Conventional law enforcement is mostly (though not exclusively) a post-mortem, after-the-attack, set of actions for finding the perpetrators, arresting them, and prosecuting them. If a terrorist attack gets to the point where it becomes a matter of finding the perpetrators, then we will have failed in counter-terrorism because the obvious need is to prevent a terrorist act from occurring in the first place. Prosecuting the perpetrators is an admission of defeat (that the terrorist act had not been prevented) and it is of no consolation to those whose lives were taken by the terrorist event.

What is badly needed is *effective* intelligence. But how? Indeed, it defies logic and common sense that the Western world has been underwriting the cost of massive systems that allegedly collect vacuum-cleaner-style just about anything that is communicated on earth when it is obvious that no machine can possibly realize that an e-mail that says 'the temperature at Joe's bar on Main street at 6 pm was around 75 degrees' could mean 'proceed with the pre-agreed main plan at 6 minutes after the hour using 75 kilos'. Double-talk has been around since time started; it is just as difficult for a human interceptor today to guess the hidden meaning of an innocuous-sounding phrase as it was a thousand years ago; it is impossible for a computer to do so. This means that vacuum-cleaner-style collection of telecommunications is highly unlikely to bear fruit in countering terrorism.

The fiery rhetoric against encryption is a case in point; the simplistic argument states that 'the terrorists may use encryption, so if we ban it there will be no terrorism'. In fact, the FBI has been extensively quoted in the press as having stated openly that encryption was *not* used by any of those hijackers or murderers of 11

September, and that they used plain language instead;[1] in fact, it appears that they used handwritten letters and not even e-mail. Similarly, the often-heard unsubstantiated allegation that terrorists have hidden their messages in pornographic images on the web seems like fiction too hard for tabloids to resist; indeed, a DARPA (US Defense Advanced Projects Development Agency) supported a University of Michigan study of some 2 million images on the world wide web failed to find even a single one that contained steganographically hidden content.[2] Noted British information security expert Ross Anderson of Cambridge University has stated very forcefully (see http://cryptome.org/al-stego-rot.htm) that:

> *It is unclear what national interest is served by security agencies propagating this lurid urban myth. Perhaps the goal is to manufacture an excuse for the failure to anticipate the events of September 11th. Perhaps it is preparing the ground for an attempt at bureaucratic empire-building via Internet regulation, as a diversionary activity from the much harder and less pleasant task of going after [terrorists]. Perhaps the vision of [accused terrorists] as cryptic pornographers is being spun to create a subconscious link, in the public mind, with the scare stories about child pornography that were used before September 11th to justify government plans for greater Internet regulation.*

Noted PGP (Pretty Good Privacy) creator, Philip K. Zimmerman, was similarly misquoted as stating that he 'weeps for the use of encryption that caused the tragedy', when in fact he said that he wept for the victims of the tragedy but continues to support secure escrow-free cryptology (see http://slashdot.org/interviews/01/09/27/0257248.shtml). As Rudyard Kipling said, the first victim of war is truth.

The demonizing of computer data protection (encryption and steganography) is a classical example of ineffective measures that give a false sense of security – or actually reduce security, as shown below – in the interest of promoting parochial agendas. The reasons are the following.

- A Western ban on encryption would not stop terrorists, domestic or foreign, or anyone else for that matter, from posting encrypted messages on foreign Internet servers such as foreign websites or usenet newsgroups whose contents are distributed worldwide.

---

[1] *USA TODAY* 1 October 2001, article by reporter Kevin Johnson, at http://www.usatoday.com/usaonline/20011001/3496196s.htm.

[2] Niels Provos and Peter Honeyman, 'Detecting steganographic content in the Internet'. Center for Information Technology Integration, University of Michigan; research supported by DARPA grant F30602-99-1-0527. Accessible online at http://www.citi.umich.edu/techreports/reports/citi-tr-01-11.pdf.

- Most substantive criminals (terrorists, organized crime, traffickers of narcotics, etc.) intentionally do not use encryption because it is too alerting. Instead, they use 'double-talk' in plain language. Even if encryption were made illegal this would not stop terrorists, organized crime, or traffickers from using it because they could easily hide the encrypted message inside an opaque electronic envelope (steganography, compression, etc.).

- Terrorism, trafficking, and so on does not need encryption to function and were around long before encryption became commonplace. It follows that banning encryption will not affect them, but it will affect the conduct of commerce, which requires confidentiality for such purposes as protecting corporate trade secrets, medical data, financial transactions, etc.

- In general, the logic behind the notion that 'Western legislation can eliminate international problems' is difficult to follow because foreign countries are not bound by any Western nation's law. This applies particularly to law violators such as traffickers, terrorists, and organized crime. Certainly there could have been no doubt in any hijacker's mind that flying a commercial jetliner full of civilians into a civilian building was very much illegal, yet they did so.

- Encryption is mathematics, and no one country has an exclusive on it. In fact, top-notch encryption in use today comes from all over the world, notably including the algorithm selected by the United States (NIST) as the new Advanced Encryption Standard (AES): 'Rijandel' (made by Belgians). The Israelis, Russians, Irish, Italians, and numerous others have developed top-notch encryption as well. As such, any imposition of 'back doors' on a Western nation's encryption-makers will have no impact, because encryption users will switch to non-Western encryption products (if they have not done so already).

- 'The danger in weakening encryption is that our infrastructure would become even less secure'. This is according to Bill Crowell, a former deputy director of the US National Security Agency, the organization charged with gathering electronic intelligence for the military and protecting the USA's own communications networks. Similarly, according to Republican Bob Goodlatte,

  Encryption protects our national security; it protects the controls of everything from nuclear power plants to the New York Stock Exchange, government communications, credit cards and the electric power grid. Encryption plays a critical role in our entire communication system, and to require that a backdoor be built into that system is just an incredibly dangerous thing to do.

In short, a backdoor for the government would quickly become a target for criminals and terrorists to hack; not to mention the governments' luckluster record of performance in guarding citizens' privacy evidenced through agents having sold secrets to foreign powers, investigations of people in Congress, leaks of corruption investigations, and so on.

So, why is the law enforcement community around the Western world now making such a fuss about encryption and privacy in view of the above? At the House Hearing (the House Judiciary Committee) in late September, Robert L. Barr Jr, the conservative Georgia Republican, asked Attorney General John Ashcroft,

> *Why is it necessary to rush this through? Does it have anything to do with the fact that the department [of Justice] has sought many of these authorities on numerous other occasions, has been unsuccessful in obtaining them, and now seeks to take advantage of what is obviously an emergency situation to obtain authorities that it has been unable to obtain previously?*
> (http://www.washingtonpost.com/wp-dyn/articles/A19559-2001Sep24.html).

In conclusion, and for the reasons stated above, this book is of no more help to terrorists than is any other tool used in everyday life, such as box cutters, airplanes, automobiles, pants, pens, regular mail, or anything else. Terrorism (defined as the attack of innocent civilians for political or religious reasons) is an affront to basic human decency and is not condoned by *any* religion. Nobody is seriously proposing to ban airplanes or box cutters or pants or pens just because they were also used by terrorists; nobody should seriously consider banning encryption and information about it either, especially as it was not used by terrorists anyway and is unlikely to be used either, since it can be alerting. Besides, banning encryption and steganography is about as likely to succeed as banning the wind; a Don Quixotean charge at windmills.

A reasonable person can readily support a nation's efforts to protect its citizens from terrorism; indeed, governments are obligated to do so just as they are obligated to protect their respective citizens from classical military aggression by foreign militaries. A reasonable person will also willingly accept numerous new rules and policies intended to protect citizens from terrorism; examples include enhanced police checks at airports, movie theaters, expanded background checks for employees of firms working at airports, and the like. A reasonable person will indeed support practically any new rules and policies intended to enhance citizens' safety from terrorism, as long as terrorism is not the pretext for enhanced police-state powers that have minimal impact in countering terrorism. A typical class of examples of situations where terrorism and state security is used as a pretext can be found in any dictatorship where charges of threatening the security of the state are brought on any dissenter, anyone who 'makes fun' of the state's leaders, and against any political or religious point of view that differs from the party line. It was very disconcerting, for example, when an effort was recently made in the USA to label as 'terrorists' any hackers, and to try to legislate mandatory life in prison without parole to anyone helping a hacker. This is, I believe, insanity run amuck because it would have meant that a person who identifies and publicizes a security flaw in some software can end up in prison for life as a 'cyberterrorist' because the government could claim that without that person's 'help' a subsequent hacking incident would not have happened. Fortunately, this legislation was modified so as to limit the 'terrorism' label to acts that are truly terrorist in nature and not to any old hacking by a teenager with extra testosterone.

I would like to underline that I deplore terrorism because it is a shameful abdication of even the most elemental human decency, and I would never knowingly do anything to facilitate it. As President George Bush stated to a joint session of Congress on 20 September 2001, 'enemies of freedom committed an act of war'. The last thing we would ever want is to react to this tragedy by attacking freedom from within and doing the terrorists' work for them. To quote Senator Robert Torricelli's Congressional Remarks on 26 September 2001:

> *If this Congress surrenders civil liberties and rearranges constitutional rights to deal with these terrorists, then their greatest victory will not have been won in New York but in Washington. Any administration can defeat terrorism by surrendering civil liberties and changing the Constitution. Our goal is to defeat terrorism, remain who we are, and retain the best about ourselves while defeating terrorism. It is more difficult, but it is what history requires us to do. The history of our Nation is replete with contrary examples, and we need to learn by them. They are instructive. For even the greats of American political life have given in to the temptation of our worst instincts to defeat our worst enemies and lose the best about ourselves.*

1.2 'If You Have Done Nothing Wrong, You Have Nothing to Hide.' Not True!

> *Why should you care if you have nothing to hide?*
>
> J. Edgar Hoover, former director of the FBI

I love my country but fear my government.
Anonymous

The greatest calamity which would befall us would be submission to a government of unlimited powers.
Thomas Jefferson, 1825

The assertion that 'if you have done nothing wrong, you have nothing to hide' has been popular with many in law enforcement positions. It is also factually wrong, for the following reasons:

- You might not be doing anything 'wrong' now, but in a few years the laws may – and often do – change retroactively with no statute of limitations, making what was not illegal before illegal now.

- History is full of example of entire populations of people who did nothing 'wrong' yet who paid with their lives nonetheless. The holocaust victims are one example, and so are the victims of any persecution based on religion, race, color, or whatever else.

- As DNA testing is being introduced in criminal forensics, numerous individuals who have been already executed have been found posthumously to have been innocent.

- Even in societies where an arrested person is presumed innocent until proven guilty, the arrested person has to spend a fortune in criminal legal defense fees to attempt to prove his or her innocence. Even if legally exonerated, an arrest record is a public record in most societies (e.g., in the State of California, among many other States and nations) and haunts the person proven innocent for ever after.

Who is to say what is 'wrong'? It is not as simple as saying 'wrong' is any violation of law in effect at any one time and place.

- Were Christ's or Mahatma Ghandi's acts 'wrong'?

- Was Joan of Arc 'wrong'?

- Was Galileo 'wrong' for violating local law and telling a very angry pope that the earth is not the center of the universe?

Additionally, the quest for privacy does not imply wrongdoing at all. The presumption that 'the only reason one may want to keep information and activities private is because such information or activities are incriminating' is factually false.

- There are many activities, such as visiting the restroom or engaging in conjugal relations, that civilized individuals want to keep to themselves.

- Civilized individuals invariably have things they do not care to share with others, such as whether or not they dye their hair, which medications they have been prescribed, a funny mole on their behind, the content of their love letters to their spouses, and so on. This does not imply any wrongdoing. All individuals form hierarchies of privacy: some things are shared only with family, other things with close friends, other things with one's medical doctor, and still other things (if any) with total strangers. None of these conventions has anything to do with wrongdoing.

- In most civilized societies, the privacy and confidentiality of many individual activities has long had the benefit of legal protection – often perhaps to the annoyance of some in law enforcement. Such activities include consultations with one's attorney, confessions to a priest, and some consultations with mental health professionals.

- Every individual has the right and indeed the obligation to protect himself or herself from such obvious illegal acts as credit card fraud, identity theft, and the like, or be denied insurance coverage for losses due to failure to take adequate precautions. Since what has to be protected is information, rather than objects, hiding the information is the only way to obtain such protection.

Privacy is not only about preventing access to some information to those who have no need to know it; it is also about *keeping things in the proper context* because some actions that are perfectly legal in one context may be illegal in another context. It is perfectly legal and appropriate for one to urinate in a private restroom, or to have sex with one's spouse in private, but the same acts in public are not.

Privacy and confidentiality are essential to the conduct of commerce; Western society would collapse without them. Every individual and company has to protect the confidentiality of its competitive developments (hence the legally protected notion of 'proprietary' information) from competitors or may face economic collapse.

We do not paste the content of our regular correspondence or personal diaries on our windows for the benefit of passers-by and policemen, and we do not publicize our credit card numbers. We expect full anonymity and privacy when we pay with cash to buy underwear at the mall, or a ticket to a show, or a book at the bookstore. It is perfectly legal (and perhaps highly advisable) to go to a different nearby town's store if one is an unmarried teacher wanting to buy birth control means (with cash), or if one is the local pastor wanting to buy a book extolling the virtues of another religion.

Yet, governments and law enforcement worldwide have embarked on what may be seen as a holy war to convince us that all of these privacy rights we have all enjoyed in our normal lives have to end the moment we involve our personal computers in these processes:

- Computer hard disks are being subpoenaed as 'evidence' with increasing frequency, not only in criminal investigations but also for civil 'discovery' for such matters as divorce cases, corporate attempts to silence criticism, etc. An entire cottage industry, that of computer forensics, has evolved that services the requests of law enforcers and civilian litigants to reveal others' thoughts entrusted to personal computers.

- Practically all nations are monitoring individual usage of the Internet by their citizens; what each citizen writes in e-mail and to whom (i.e., the equivalent of opening the envelopes of conventional private mail), what each citizen browses on the World Wide Web (i.e., the equivalent of standing behind us at the bookstore to see what we are actually looking at), and also what many citizens type on their computers that is never sent over the Internet (i.e., the equivalent of standing behind us all the time watching and taking notes when we type anything at all on our 'personal' computer keyboards).

The justification professed for this unprecedented governmental intrusiveness by practically all nations is 'to protect us from crime', as if crime did not exist before computers and the Internet. Why this massive electronic intrusiveness? It is simply because electronic surveillance is easy to do today – and will be even easier tomorrow.

When the Gutenberg press was invented by Johannes Gutenberg, royalty and people of influence felt very threatened that the general public could now document ideas and easily share them with others. This was an involuntary transfer of power from the state to the people. The Internet phenomenon is of equal if not larger social significance. Suddenly, anyone can proclaim anything he or she likes and reach an instant worldwide audience without requiring any approval or peer review; this is, I believe, anathema to any regime.

The concurrent availability of unbreakable encryption is the straw that has broken the camel's back. Now the general public not only can reach instant worldwide audiences but also can communicate in a manner that states cannot track or intercept. It is not surprising that regimes went into emergency high alert.

However, exorcising the Internet out of existence in a regime's own country is self-defeating because:

- a citizen can get around any local unavailability by accessing an out-of-country Internet service provider (ISP) by phone, cellphone, satellite phone, etc.;

- there is vast net economic loss to any country that opts out of the Internet.

As such, regimes have been spending vast fortunes (of their own citizens' tax money) to monitor all Internet traffic; luckily for the governments, it can be done with today's technology.

In my opinion, the requisite propaganda to make this intrusiveness palatable or even wanted by populations has been elevated to an art form by appealing to basic human fears as follows.

- 'Terrorists and criminals use the Internet': to support this truism, examples are cited where one of the elements used by a terrorist or a criminal was the Internet. By implication, if the Internet is controlled, terrorists and criminals will not do 'their thing'. But terrorists and criminals also use automobiles and shoes, and oranges, and telephones, and forks, and bandaids, and birthday candles.

- 'Foreign spies use the Internet and encryption': by implication, if the Internet and encryption are banned, foreign spies will not function, never mind that spies have been around since the times of Moses.

- 'The Internet is corrupting our citizens' morals with propaganda': Speaking of 'the pot calling the kettle black'! Guttenberg Press, round two!

Amusingly, less than a hundred years ago, Luis Brandeis, a soon-to-be Justice of the US Supreme Court, voiced strong objections to a local newspaper having published an account of a wedding reception; Brandeis had viewed this reporting as an unacceptable violation of privacy for invading 'the sacred precincts of private and domestic life'. Today, I imagine Justice Barndeis is rolling in his grave given the vast amount of violations of citizens' privacy that are sanctioned by the same Supreme Court of which he used to be a Justice. This constant creeping of violations of citizens' privacy reminds one of the frog syndrome; if you put a frog in water and raise the water's temperature suddenly, the frog will jump out to save its life. If, instead, you raise the water's temperature very slowly, the frog will stay in the water and die. As alredy mentioned, just like the automobile, the telegraph, electricity, pens, and pencils, the Internet, too, can be used in the commission of crimes. Is this reason enough to intercept and store every keystroke by every Internet user?

This book in no way condones, nor is it intended to facilitate, the use of the Internet for the commission of what is generally accepted to be a crime (such as murder, arson, fraud, etc.). At the same time, however, it is all too easy for any regime to define 'crime' to be anything it chooses, including criticism of the leader, discussions of freedom, etc. It is all too easy, unfortunately, to 'sell' an oppressive platform of 'law and order' to people by conjuring up images of unshaved savages roaming and looting neighborhoods. Every reasonable person wants to feel secure from others. It is also true that the most repressive regimes do have 'law and order'; but at what cost? Is that what we want? Certainly, a regime that monitors every act and every thought of every citizen so as to nip any dissent in the bud may have 'law and order'. But do we really want to surrender every human freedom as the price to pay for 'law and order'? The often-heard self-righteous assertion that privacy should be surrendered in the interest of preventing crime is, in fact, contrary to the US Constitution's 4th and 5th Amendments; the 5th Amendment, for example, specifically permits one to refuse to answer any question by law enforcement if the answer might incriminate oneself.

It is, indeed, far easier for any regime to treat all people as criminals and take everybody's privacy away than to try to identify the actual perpetrators of a crime. The main difference between totalitarian regimes and regimes that cherish freedom is the extent of freedom enjoyed by their respective citizens. That difference is not merely the presence of absence of voting or democracy; pre-World-War-2 Germany had a democratically elected government, yet we know what ensued.

As often said, 'freedom is not free'. It is all too easy to accept the demagoguery of those who thrive on controlling others under the color or 'law and order' and to surrender all freedoms as the price to pay for living in peace. It is also, I belive, an inexcusable admission of defeat of the human spirit.

This book's purpose is:

- To help the responsible individual regain privacy lost to technology.

- To help the responsible businessman protect his or her business proprietary information and competitive advantage.

- To help the professional (lawyer, medical doctor, hospital administrator, etc.) protect the confidentiality of information entrusted on that basis.

- To help the individual in any repressive regime from abuses by the state.

- To help push Orwell's *1984* or Aldous Huxley's *Brave New World* just a few more years into the future.

1.2.1 The Dilemma for law enforcement

> *There is no way to rule inocent men. The only power any government has is the power to crack down on criminals. Well, when there aren't enough criminals, one makes them. One declares so many things to be a crime that it becomes impossible to live without breaking laws.*
>
> Ayn Rand, *Atlas Shrugged*

In an honorable country, law enforcement is an honorable profession, the ultimate goal of which is to faciliate the tranquil environment that is conducive to raising a happy family of free people who can develop to their maximum potential. In a totalitarian country that is concerned more with the perpetuation of its leaders and less with the wellbeing of its citizens, law enforcers become instruments of the oppressive regime.

Paradoxically, the most technologically advanced societies have bestowed their law enforcement people with near absolute power, whereas more 'traditional' democratic societies have retained far more checks and balances on how their police conduct themselves.

The issue is whether or not a 'law enforcement officer' should or should not be exempt from the same legal procedures to which others are subject; namely, indictments and trials for actions taken as part of his or her official position. It is self-evident that a democracy that prides itself for its respect of the law cannot exempt anyone from it, least of all those tasked to uphold it. As such, there is hubris when policemen assert that they are immune from civil or criminal prosecution for actions done while 'on duty'.

Many of the gross abuses by law enforcers occur when police are called upon to enforce political agendas. The practical problem, however, is that a substantial number of laws themselves were enacted as part of some political agenda. In totalitarian regimes, many laws have a political agenda behind them: to keep the leader in power. In democratic regimes, too, laws do not come from 'The Mountain' but are the result of the machinations and relative forcefulness of assorted political or religious groups. The law-making week may be visualized as follows: Monday, the crowds make a huge fuss about 'moonshine' (home-made liquor) and voter-sensitive politicians promptly oblige and pass laws outlawing it; Tuesday, 'mothers against something-or-other' descend en masse on the state capital with their demands, and re-election-hungry politicians pass whatever new laws are needed to appease them; Wednesday, the agenda is about banning Mark Twain's

Huck Finn or the *Playboy* magazine in some southern little town; Thursday, the hot issue is laws about gay rights or about protecting the spotted owl; and so on. In another country there is religious pressure resulting in laws banning Salman Rushdie's *Satanic Verses*, or about banning Pokémon. In short, with the exception of obvious crimes such as murder or arson, most laws are politically motivated in every society. It is, therefore, very hard to make a distinction between 'actions driven by political agendas' and routine law enforcement driven by political agendas.

Then there is the issue of politically driven selective enforcement. In years past, the tax compliance offices of assorted countries have been routinely used by the regime in power against its political opponents whose tax declarations were no less and no more truthful than those of the upstanding pillars of the community. The law enforcer is thus reduced to being a pawn of the political machinery.

Today, most Western countries have enacted statutes that, in a strict sense, criminalize just about every conceivable act (including acts of omission, such as not wearing seat belts, not informing someone of something, not paying enough attention, etc.). A fully 'law abiding person' in such societies must, I suggest, drive from home to a mid-level position job thinking of nothing along the way (so as not to be distracted), must drive back home at 5 pm after stopping at the supermarket for milk, and watch *Mary Poppins* on Saturday on television.

A law enforcer, therefore, is forced to make constant judgment calls as to which laws to enforce, when, and against whom. Such judgment requires much more maturity than can reasonably be expected from the 20-year-old policeman on the beat, and much more social conscience than I suggest is likely to have survived in the mind of a cynical street-hardened policeman. It is certainly way beyond the grasp of those in law enforcement who sought their job because it would provide them with a legally-backed way to subjugate others; the adult equivalent of the classical high school bully.

Indeed, there *is* one fix for many of those ills: to have every law enforcement person held accountable for his or her actions, not in front of a sympathetic 'review board' staffed by people with ties to law enforcement, but in front of a civilian court of law like everyone else. This alone will do away with a lot of the arrogance and abuse by law enforcers who give that profession a bad name, and will result in a better police at all levels. Yet it is vehemently opposed by most police because they have been accustomed to being, at times, 'above the law'.

To be sure, the problem transcends law enforcement arrogance. Ultimately, the causes are societal. Specifically, in the West:

- As a society that values the 'macho' image of the self-reliant person, we have become accustomed to and numbed by violence. With the help of a steady diet of violent movies, we have been conditioned to tolerate violence by the police.

The police, too, have to face occasional violence in the general population who might think nothing of pulling a gun to settle a perceived injustice.

- Technologically advanced societies, with their decreased emphasis on strong family ties, have also surrendered their prerogatives to decide what is right and wrong to the courts and to the police. If a family dispute occurs, the police are typically summoned instead of the family sorting things out for itself. Whereas families in the past would ensure that their children were raised with a self-policing sense of shame or conscience, many modern parents today have no idea themselves what is right and what is wrong and expect some elected judge or some 20-year-old policeman to tell them.

But that is a whole different story.

1.2.2 The Internet undermines regimes' social order

Without censorship, things can get terribly confused in the public mind.
General William Westmoreland, taped interview in the 1960s

Initially, what held countries together was fear of real or imagined enemies and, in many places, a well-drilled indoctrination of what essentially amounts to chauvinism. As technology and travel exposed individuals in repressive regimes to the reality about other less-repressive regimes, the glue that has continued to hold most countries together has been shared ideas. Shared ideas as a unifier is a very unpredictable 'glue', however. Any society, whether democratic, autocratic, or anything in between, inevitably includes individuals, some of whose perspective on any one of many issues are very different from those considered to be 'appropriate' by that society. In the past, regimes and governments have always counted on the fact that these individuals would find it practically difficult to find each other and to 'reach critical mass' by banding together to the point where they could become a major irritant to the regime. The Internet did away with this 'fact' and made it eminently easy for geographically dispersed individuals holding extreme views on any one topic to find each other and to communicate efficiently and effectively thereafter; witness the existence of numerous usenet newsgroups on topics that espouse extreme positions; these groups serve as the virtual meeting place for individuals of any persuasion, deviation, fetish, or shared paranoia. As anyone who looks at the messages posted in some of those extreme usenet newsgroups can readily see, individuals who patronize them tend to feed upon each other's paranoia, be that about aliens from space, assorted conspiracy theories, PR, or what not. The same goes for numerous 'listserv' groups on extreme topics (as opposed to groups on strictly technical topics) where a message posted by any one subscriber gets received as e-mail by all of the other subscribers. A factually false message is often seconded by equally false testimonials by others with similar mindsets; soon enough, fiction becomes fact and the 'feeding frenzy' continues.

At the other end of the spectrum, an analogous situation applies to the case of perfectly rational virtual groups that are bound together by longings for and beliefs in such concepts as freedom, human rights, and other 'anti-establishment' topics (in the eyes of oppressive regimes). Indeed, even the most democratic regimes have topics that they consider taboo and off-limits.

In short, the Internet has made it possible and effective for individuals sharing any rational or irrational perspective to find each other, to organize, and to challenge established regimes. This is understandably very bothersome to every regime.

The other side of the same coin is that the Internet is the most surveillance-friendly medium ever devised. Any regime can readily keep tabs on who says what to whom, and who associates with whom, and when and how. On balance, it can be argued that the use of the Internet for subversion is a net benefit to a regime because individuals who would have met in, say, the catacombs of Rome in years past now meet in a manner that identifies them and allows their meetings to be fully monitored . . . until encryption and anonymity enter the equation.

Once individuals using the Internet can maintain their anonymity and can encrypt their communications and identity, then regimes lose all of the Internet's surveillance benefits and individual users win all of the Internet's virtual networking benefits. *That* is why encryption and anonymity is anathema to any regime; the sanctimonious official pronouncements about encryption and anonymity facilitating 'crime' constitute mostly official propaganda, as crime has existed since the dawn of humankind.

2

So You Want to Encrypt! Don't Hurt Your Own Interests by So Doing

The irony of the Information Age is that it has given new respectability to uninformed opinion.

John Lawton

There is a common misconception that encrypting files protects them from unauthorized perusal; the opposite may be true. If most computer users encrypted their data as a matter of course, then encrypting yours, too, would not be alerting. But, in fact, hardly any computer user encrypts files because it is not done automatically and users do not want to bother. As a result, the user who does elect to encrypt files will inevitably have to answer the question 'Why?' if apprehended, and – depending on in which country one lives – may be compelled to decrypt those files.

This means that one should go to great lengths not to draw attention to oneself, so that the presence of encrypted files does not become known in the first place. Advertising, or even allowing it to be known, that one has encrypted files amounts to taunting some regimes – a highly inadvisable act.

But then, if nobody looks at your files to begin with, why bother to encrypt them at all? The answer is that the encryption will still provide benefits in the following ways.

- It will keep casual snoops out (maids, friends, etc.)

- It will protect files from being compromised remotely when online if a hacker manages to penetrate one's online computer (see Chapter 5).

Figure 2.1

- It will give one some additional time to delay decrypting files if compelled, compared with having them unencrypted in the first place; during this time one can consult with one's lawyer, for example, on the best way to proceed.

- Instead of encrypting files for storage, encryption can be used only to transfer files and e-mail through the inherently insecure Internet, for confidentiality from hackers just as e-businesses use encryption to handle the portion of online ordering that involves giving credit-card information.

The point is that, no matter how one does it, encryption alerts others because it is still not commonly used. It is as if one elected to mail a letter in an envelope in a society where everybody used postcards with no envelopes. Given that essentially all countries' governments take a dim view of the use of encryption by citizens, and that many ban it outright, one has the following options depending on where one lives.

- If encryption is allowed in one's country, then one should be prepared to answer why one is using encryption, if confronted. Valid answers can include:

    ○ I have a personal technical interest in the field, as evidence by my subscriptions to these publications, my membership in this technical group, etc.

- In my professional capacity (as doctor, clergy, etc.) I am entrusted by others with data that I am required to protect from theft and compromise.

  - As a businessperson, my competitive edge is in my business plans and proprietary technologies that I use, and I have to protect those from thieves and competitors, especially when I travel.

- If encryption is not allowed in one's country and one still wants to protect the confidentiality of business and personal data, then by far the best protection is not to draw attention to oneself in the first place. Helpful answers if confronted could include:

  - I don't use encryption; I only experiment with it as an educational hobby as evidenced by my technical background. I would be happy to decrypt these files for you.

  - I merely want to protect my business files from hackers when online, or from my kids from changing them as a practical joke – you know how kids are these days . . . I have nothing to hide; here, let me show you . . .

One should be prepared by having ready encrypted numerous innocuous files which when decrypted support the above assertions of 'only playing'. There are still some ways whereby one can 'have one's cake and eat it':

- The exact same encrypted file can be decrypted into two totally different unencrypted 'originals': one that is the true sensitive file that is never shown to others, and another that is something perfectly innocent and appropriate that is intended to appease those who wish to see the file. This is done through the use of 'one time pads' that have been known since antiquity and is explained in detail in Section 2.5.

- The use of steganography (see Section 5.9). This amounts to hiding the fact that there is any hidden data to begin with. As a minimum one should not have the software that places steganography in plain view.

A related situation of concern is when one is traveling with a laptop from a country that permits encryption to one that does not and that also checks laptops at the ports of entry. This is discussed in Section 3.2.8.

2.1 Is Encryption the Answer to Your Problem?

If you think cryptography is the answer to your problem, then you don't know what your problem is

Peter G. Neumann, Computer Scientist, SRI International, Menlo Park, CA

Today, there is provably unbreakable encryption that is within anyone's reach; in fact, it has been around for a long, long time and it is known as 'one time pad'. Basically, one mixes ('exclusive-OR' in mathematical terms) the plaintext with a truly random string of symbols and the resulting ciphertext is provably unbreakable by anyone who does not have the exact same random string of symbols. The problem is that one has to somehow convey this random string of symbols to the intended recipient of your encrypted message in a manner than nobody else can intercept.

On 20 February 2001, the *New York Times* reported an announcement by a Harvard professor of computer science, Michael Rabin, that he had discovered a way to make a more practical implementation of what is basically the one time pad (see http://www.nytimes.com/2001/02/20/science/20CODE.html). Instead of the two communicating parties having to find a secure way to share the random string of symbols used to encrypt the plaintext, they both 'tune in' to the same source of data and, in complete synchronism, use that source of data as the random string. The security of this method is derived from the fact that there is a vast number of sources of data that two individuals can tune into; an interceptor cannot possibly record them all.

In a way, this method is very similar to the low-tech approaches used in the previous century when the two communicating parties would agree to use the same edition of the same book as their source of ostensibly random bits; that book could be a certain edition of the Bible or any other book. To enhance the randomness of the process, the agreement would usually entail some recipe as to which letters to use from that book, such as, first letter of the first page, then second letter of the second page, etc., or some other more sophisticated recipe.

In practical terms, however, the method suggested by Rabin, requires the following:

- The two communicating individuals must find a source of data that both can receive in synchronism. The synchronization issue is not trivial; if the source of data is at a rate of X bit/sec, then the required synchronization accuracy has to be better than $1/X$ s. If X is, say, 1 Gbit/sec, then the synchronization required is to within 0.000000001 s; this is realistically impossible if the two communicating parties are separated by a large distance. Even if they have a 'live' telephone connection going, the delays involved in the digitization and undigitization of speech will far exceed that short time, not to mention about a quarter second delay if a satellite is used in the communication and the difficulty of implementing a way to say 'start now' with an accuracy of 0.000000001 s (or even for a time a thousand times longer).

- The two communicating parties must find a way to agree on what source to use, on how to communicate the 'start now' command within a $1/X$ accuracy as per above, and also which recipe to use as to which bits of that 'random' source to select for their 'key' (e.g., every 10th bit, every 200th bit, or some other more elaborate recipe).

What is much more important, however, is the admonition given throughout this book and as implied in the opening quote to this section; namely, that encryption is *not* the problem; hardly anyone does cryptanalysis any more because there are far easier commercially available ways of getting to the plaintext than through usually fruitless cryptanalysis, such as commercially peddled keystroke capture (see Section 4.11.1), commercially available devices for the detection of Van Eck radiation (See Section 3.2.7.1), accessing plaintext files left behind in one's own computer (see Chapter 4), and so on.

As Dr Richard DeMillo, chief technology officer at Hewlett-Packard, has said, the open availability of provably unbreakable encryption merely 'reshuffles the policy deck' in the sense that cryptanalysis is no longer the issue (http://humboldt. sunyit.edu/553/The%20Key%20Vanishes-Scientist%20Outlines%20Unbreaka-ble%20Code.htm).

2.1.1   Encryption algorithms

Few false ideas have more firmly gripped the minds of so many intelligent men than the one that, if they just tried, they could invent a cipher that no one could break.

David Kahn, noted author on cryptography

The above quote means that one should shun any and all 'proprietary', 'novel' or 'secret' encryption schemes. The only trustworthy encryption schemes are the ones that have been subjected to the concerted scrutiny of many experts for a long time. This means that the encryption algorithm and its software implementation has to be 'open source', meaning, 'available to anyone to inspect'. This having been said, it is also true that a number of algorithms have, in fact, been subjected to such scrutiny and, as a result, have earned the respect and approval that has to go with any encryption algorithm before it can be used.

Practically any personal computer today can use any one of a multitude of such respected encryption algorithms (the accepted term for a mathematical recipe) that convert a plaintext into a cyphertext in a manner that brute force cryptanalysis cannot break in our lifetime. The reader is cautioned about the main point of this book which is that nobody tries brute force cryptanalysis any more these days precisely because it is near impossible to reverse the encryption; instead, there are numerous ways that an inexperienced encryption user can make mistakes that can be exploited by an interceptor to recover the plaintext very easily.

This having been said, the reader may wish to peruse through the extensive openly available literature on practically every commonly used encryption these days. The references in Appendix E, courtesy of John Ashwood on Usenet, will facilitate this (the list includes hashing[1] algorithms as well).

2.2 Common Sense is Not Common

We all tend to think from our respective vantage point and not from that of our 'adversary'; for a chicken to think like a chicken and not like a fox is an invitation to disaster: When you must protect the confidentiality of some computer document from a plausible threat, be that a hacker, a nosy neighbor, an overzealous investigator in a repressive regime, or from any other threat, you should try to place yourself in the shoes of that threat. How would you go after someone in your situation? What is the weakest link? How would you entrap? How would you exert the most psychological pressure to maximize the likelihood of a confession or, at least, of incriminating statements?

Give your adversary whom you perceive as a threat the benefit of intelligence, using both meanings of the word, of perseverance, and of limitless resources. Now how would you protect yourself from such an adversary? The dumbest thing to do is to assume that your adversary is dumb.

---

[1] In order for one to be able to detect if any change is made in a digital document, a mathematical operation known as a 'hashing alogorithm' is performed on the data of the document; this operation results in a short string of numbers (typically up to a few hundred symbols long) that constitutes the 'digital signature' (or 'hash') of that document. If any change whatever is made to the document, its digital signature (or hash) changes. In practice, the sender of a document computes this digital 'hash' and sends it along with the document; the intended recipient also computes the digital hash of what he or she received, and if the two digital hashes are the same then this is proof that the document has not been altered by anyone along the way.

Examples of unwise slips are too many to enumerate. If you are a happy retiree doing volunteer chores for local charities, you need only worry about hackings, theft of your identity, and the like. If you are a businessperson, you have the obligation to protect your company's equities. If you are an individual who is entrusted with details about a pro-freedom or pro-democracy group in a repressive regime, you have an unconditional obligation to protect that information with extreme measures because a slip could cause others' lives to end; the examples below pertain mostly to this situation [i.e., where lives (including your own) may depend on how well you secure confidential information in a repressive environment].

- Do not use a credit card traceable to you to buy any encryption or other sensitive software. Do not mailorder things to your house; walk into a store and buy off the shelf, instead, in cash. [In calendar year 2000, a US bookstore was served with a court order to produce its records to show which books were bought by credit card by a patron accused by the police of a crime (http://www.bookzone pro.com/newswire/showwire.cfm?wirenum=258).]

- Since most of the world's phone systems now have caller identification,even if the local telephone companies do not advertise it or allow customers to view who is calling them, do not use a telephone (including a cellphone) to make a call to connect your laptop to the Internet if you would rather not have that call traced to you. If you use a payphone to connect your laptop to the Internet, do not use a calling card traceable to you; for that matter do not use any payphone anywhere close to where you live or work.

- Do not think you have anonymity if you sign up for a disposable e-mail account online using your normal ISP or calling from a phone number traceable to you.

- Have a truly convincing and verifiable story as to why you are doing what you are doing, even if someone has been observing you – unbeknownst to you – for the past year.

- Do not put all of your eggs in one basket by, for example, entrusting your anonymity to a single go-between 'remailer' (see Section 5.4), and certainly not one in your own country.

- Do not trust any single 'disk wiping' software; use two or three different ones in sequence, instead. The only truly effective disk wiper is a very hot incinerator followed by the purchase of new hard disk. Better yet, my advice is not to use

Windows for anything sensitive; cleaning after all of its electronic litter, is a near impossibility.

- By all means, do not attract attention to yourself. Once you come under suspicion or, worse yet, under scrutiny, chances are you will slip up and will be arrested and convicted.

- Do not assume that 'it won't happen to me'. Many who did have come to regret it, and many have lost their lives.

- Oh yes, and do not publish a book like this one; it will not endear you to those in power.

In short, if you have to perform an act that you would rather keep confidential (e.g., sending an encrypted message to your business associate), think it through in its entirety *before* doing it. How to set it up, how to make it look normal and nonalerting, how to get the software or hardware to do it, where and when to do it, how to handle unexpected situations that could arise (e.g., you sprain your leg on the way to wherever while carrying your laptop, and someone else goes through your laptop), and so on. Again, your 'adversaries' are every bit as smart as you are, but have vastly more resources at their disposal than you do. Remember: encryption itself is only a very small part of the overall process of protecting the confidentiality of a computerized document; nobody really does cryptanalysis today because there so many other ways that you are likely to 'slip' that it is far easier to exploit those likely oversights instead.

2.3 Local Laws Against Encryption[2]

Numerous countries have laws against the possession and/or use of encryption. Since encryption used privately does not advertise itself, the main purpose of these laws is, I would suggest, to be used to provide the legal basis to prosecute after one has been found to possess or to have used encryption.

---

[2] For a country-by-country discussion of laws pertaining to encryption, see *Cryptography and Liberty 2000* (ISBN 1893044076), by the Electronic Privacy Information Center, http://www.epic.org/crypto&/.

Most other countries have been enacting laws that authorize each such country to be able to demand that an encrypted file in someone's possession be decrypted by that person. This clearly fails in those situations when it is mathematically impossible for one to decrypt a file for which one does not have the decryption key; this is the case, for example, in all public key encryption when the encrypted file has only been encrypted to the intended recipient's public key (see Section 5.8.3); the sender is mathematically unable to decrypt the file just encrypted.[3]

In the United Kingdom, the Regulation of Investigatory Powers Act received Royal Assent on 28 July 2000. It allows the police, intelligence services, or customs to demand that an encrypted file be decrypted. A person who knowingly fails to comply with the order is punishable with up to two years imprisonment [article 53 (1) and (5)]. It is also illegal to tip off anyone else; failure to keep the demand to decrypt a secret is punishable with up to five years imprisonment (article 54).

The USA is a notable exception in that its Constitution's 5th Amendment, which protects individuals from self-recrimination, appears to allow individuals to refuse to provide a decryption key that is stored only in the individual's mind. This same protection does not apply to information stored in any media, such as paper or magnetic media. In the case of public key encryption (see Section 5.8.3), where the keys are typically quite long and cannot be remembered, some implementations (such as PGP, see Section 5.8.4) require that the individual enter a 'passphrase' (that can easily be remembered) in order to 'activate' the decryption key each time it is to be used; this way, the decryption key can be surrendered without any loss of confidentiality (assuming that the 'passphrase' that activates it is not easy to guess and has not been written down some place).

Laws on encryption are changing very fast, almost invariably in favor of more controls on encryption. A reasonably current country-by-country version by Bert Jaap-Coops can be found online at http://cwis.kub.nl/~frw/people/koops/lawsur vy.htm. Another one, by the Electronic Privacy Information Center, can be found at http://www2.epic.org/reports/crypto2000/.

One interesting ongoing development has been the effort somehow to find a common ground between the strong privacy protection laws of the European Union and the relatively minimal privacy protection that exists in the USA so that e-commerce between these two continents can grow. See Chapter 7 for more details on the legal problems of uniformizing laws of different countries.

---

[3] In some implementations of public key encryption, such as PGP (Pretty Good Privacy; see Section 5.8.4), the sender has the option of also encrypting to his or her own public key as well, or of encrypting only to the intended recipient's public key. In other implementations (e.g. use of 'security certificates by Netscape Navigator/Communicator) the encrypted file is also encrypted to the sender's key by default.

2.4 But Isn't Encryption Used by Criminals Only? No!

There are three kinds of lies: lies, damn lies and statistics.
Benjamin Disraeli

'Statistics show that criminals use encryption.' Indeed, some do. Most crooks also use cars, and forks; they use clothes; and they perhaps use antacids for heartburn. So?

Encryption is already fully accepted worldwide in online ordering by credit card. Even so, as recently as May 2001, a software flaw was found in the software (PDG) used by some 4000 online merchants' web-sites, a flaw that exposed all customer records held by those merchants (see http://www.msnbc.com/news/574294. asp?0nm=T14Q&cp1=1). Numerous customers' credit cards have been subsequently used fraudulently by assorted hackers who had a field day exploiting this software bug.

One should not be swayed by pseudo-scientific prose that is self-serving through selective omission of key facts. One can present very true statistics about just about anything in a devious effort to mislead by suggesting a connection that simply does not exist (e.g., statistics show that 97 per cent of arsonists like chocolate ice cream; so what? most non-arsonists like chocolate ice cream as well).

Then there are the countless pseudo-scientific statements that try to imply a cause-and-broken-effect relationship that also does not exist. For example, law enforcement in most countries loves statements such as 'Most terrorists use encryption', and, by implication, if encryption is done away with, so will terrorism be eradicated. This makes about as much logical sense as stating that 'most rains occur after I wash my windows', as if washing the windows causes the rain to fall (or, as the Romans said, '*Post hoc, ergo propter hoc*'; i.e., 'after it, therefore because of it'). The world's societal ills, such as terrorism, violent crime, trafficking in narcotics, and the like, existed long before encryption (or cars, or forks, or electricity, or anything else) came into existence, and will continue existing in the future independent of any technical developments that will come about. If anything, the widespread use of encryption and anonymity by individuals act as a potent force to *reduce* serious crimes against humankind such as oppression, totalitarianism, abuse of authority, and the like.

The more totalitarian and oppressive a regime, the more intolerant it is of any ability on behalf of its citizens to communicate in a manner that it cannot monitor. Sadly, the fact that modern technology has made it so easy and inexpensive for any regime to monitor all of its citizens, the stampede to monitor citizens has also infected the most democratic regimes of the world as well; this is sold to the unthinking masses under the guise of a 'necessity to reduce crime' in yet another devious application of misleading logic.

Will the absence of any individual privacy 'reduce crime'? Yes, by definition, because if 'crime' is defined to be anything that a regime does not like and the regime can monitor all citizens' acts and communications, then it can zoom in and excise from such an Orwellian society anyone and everyone who even thinks of challenging the status quo. If, however, 'crime' is defined to include abuse of power, unreasonable search and seizure, and dehumanization of the populace, then the taking away of individual privacy through passive surveillance that denies citizens the ability to think and communicate beyond the reach of the state will *increase* crime to unprecedented rates. In that sense, the denial of encryption and of anonymity is a sure formula for the institutionalization of crime against humanity on a vast scale as the norm.

2.5 Applied Psychology

No person having power over another (such as any law enforcement 'authority' of a repressive regime, overzealous prosecutor, thief of data, malicious hacker, or whoever) likes to come out empty handed after a confrontation. This is just human nature.

If one has violated the cardinal rule of keeping a low profile and has unwisely managed to attract unwanted attention that has resulted in one being compelled to 'decrypt this file, or else', it would be even more unwise either to decrypt an incriminating file or to refuse to do so. This is where 'plan B' and common sense comes into the picture.

Good multi-engine pilots automatically assume that they may have an engine failure on each and every take-off, and are ready to respond to it in a matter-of-fact manner; such engine failures are, in fact, extremely rare, but they can be very deadly if the pilot is not ready to take the proper immediate corrective action, in which case they are not dangerous.[4] Similarly, even the most conscientious citizen

---

[4] I am an experienced multi-engine aircraft pilot. The reader may find it interesting to note that standard operating procedure during takeoff is to *anticipate* an engine failure (which has yet to happen, thank God) and to react extremely rapidly and in a way that is entirely counterintuitive: to assess the airspeed vis-à-vis the minimum speed needed to maintain directional control with a single engine and to actually *reduce* power on the remaining good engine, so that the asymmetry in the thrust can be removed, to *lower* the aircraft's nose (so as to avoid a stall and also to stay above the speed below which the airplane cannot maintain directional control with a single engine), to then increase power on the remaining good engine to maintain the airspeed which will allow the plane to maintain directional

of a repressive regime should be prepared for the worst and have a well-rehearsed plan on how to handle a knock on the door by overzealous law-enforcers demanding to decrypt files. As with an engine failure on take-off, if this preparedness never has to get put into actual use, so much the better.

In short, one should have:

- a good, well rehearsed, well supported, and believable explanation of why one has encrypted files floating about;

- encrypted files that will be decrypted, ostensibly reluctantly, for the pleasure of the visiting authorities of the repressive regime, that will actually support the above well-rehearsed story.

This means that one should actually create and encrypt files, the sole purpose of which will be to be surrendered and decrypted with strong *professed* displeasure. To justify the professed displeasure, yet not land one in jail, these files could contain, for example, somewhat embarrassing details (such as discussions of Viagra efficacy, of hair-growing potions, of amorous liaisons, etc.). One may be well advised to have created a track record of occasional e-mail and credit-card charges to lend credence to such details. Additionally, one should also encrypt routine business documents for the purpose of serving them unencrypted to repressive regimes on demand. Repressive regimes are unlikely to have a great interest in routine business matters anyway, and decrypting such files will only help establish one's innocence.

And what about the *real* encrypted files (such as membership lists in freedom fighter movements, freedom-related prose in a totalitarian regime, etc.)? Ideally, those should be invisible, using some good steganography (see Section 5.9); the problem is that one should also have a good explanation as to why one has software that does steganography in the first place.

Alternately, one can use a classical property of 'one time pads', which is a cryptosystem invented by Vernam and amounts to a one-for-one substitution of every symbol in the unencrypted text (the 'plaintext') into a symbol in the encrypted text (ciphertext); this is a provably unbreakable system[5] as long as the transforma-

---

control (hopefully without descending, which is often near-impossible in some low-end general aviation aircraft when fully loaded), to look for an emergency landing site just in case, and, time permitting, to notify the control tower of what is happening. All this has to be done within a second or two, hence the need for being prepared. A similar need for being prepared to handle a repressive regime's breaking down the door is called for.

[5] It has been quipped that 'As a practical person, I've observed that one-time pads are theoretically unbreakable, but practically very weak. By contrast, conventional ciphers are theoretically breakable, but practically strong' (Steve Bellovi).

tion table that is used for the one-for-one substitution is a truly random string of symbols that is never repeated and is never used again. This is easier said than done if one wants to use technology to mechanize this randomization process because any mechanized process is likely to be reapeatable and duplicatable by a savvy adversary. It is far safer to start mouthing off random runmbers and letters and jotting them down, or to use some other fundamentally unpredictable and non-repeatable physical source of randomness. One-time pads had their days of fame during the Cold War days, as shown in Figure 2.2 below, which depicts an actual Sovet one-time-pad reportedly (see http://web.ranum.com/pubs/otpfaq/) captured by the British in those days.

Figure 2.2   Soviet one-time pad allegedly of the Cold War days; see http://web.ranum.com/pubs/otpfaq/

The property of One-Time Pads that one can use to avoid decrypting a file while at the same time appearing to have complied with a request to do so is this: the same ciphertext (the encrypted version of the plaintext document) can be decrypted in two (or more) totally different plaintexts using an equal number of keys: the true plaintext, and one intended to appease the aggressive investigator of a totalitarian regime.

In simple terms, if the original sensitive plaintext results in a ciphertext C using a one-time pad O_1, this has happened as a result of the simple transformation:

$$C = [\text{sensitive plaintext}] + O_1 \qquad\qquad (2.1)$$

But the same ciphertext C can result from a different plaintext and a different one-time pad O_2:

$$C = [\text{different plaintext}] + O_2 \qquad (2.2)$$

where O_2 is intended to be 'reluctantly surrendered' and will result in the nonincriminating [different plaintext] above.

So, how does one go about doing this? After generating the ciphertext C with O_1, one finds a suitable 'different plaintext' that is:

- nonincriminating,

- warrants encryption (e.g., by virtue of relating to legitimate proprietary business processes),

- is about the same length as the sentitive plaintext,

- has the computer find O_2 from Equation (2.3):

$$O_2 = C - [\text{different plaintext}] \qquad (2.3)$$

This way, using O_2, the 'membership of the freedom fighter' encrypted text (ciphertext C) will decrypt into a proprietary recipe for making chocolate chip cookies. Unless a prosecutor from a repressive regime actually finds the one-time pad O_1 in one's magnetic media, it is mathematically impossible to prove that such an O_1 exists, or that the ciphertext C can be anything other that the proprietary recipe for making chocolate chip cookies (or one's Christmas card list, or whatever).

Unfortunately, although there is plenty of software that implements one-time pads that are openly available on the Internet, such as *Cassandra* from SmartSoft (Australia), there is no software that also implements this latter functionality of solving for 'what one-time pad could convert this innocuous text file into this given ciphertext'; one would have to write one's own; doing so is not very difficult at all, however, and might even be a fun project for an afternoon or two.

This underscores once more the importance of the key message of this book, namely, that encryption is only a very small portion of the overall problem of protecting the confidentiality of information.

3

Protect What and from Whom? The Answer Determines What you Should and Should Not Do

3.1 Protect What?

Electronic 'evidence' is better than paper evidence because, depending on what software was used, it also includes information that evidence on paper does not, such as:

- the date the file was created, by whom, using which software (including the specific serial number of one's particular copy);

- the date the file was last changed;

- the sequence of changes that the file underwent since it was first created (depending on the software and its configuration settings)[1]

---

[1] The default setting in Microsoft Word, for example, when saving a just-edited document is simply to append the changes to the version prior to them. While the document displayed and printed appears to correspond only to the final version, the digital version of that document includes all this historical information as well; a savvy adversary can therefore observe the historical sequence of most changes that the document went through prior to its final version. This default setting was done, presumably, in order to expedite the time it takes to save updates of a document. To disable this, merely uncheck the 'allow fast save' in the Tools/Options/Save menu. Also, ensure that the "track changes" option is not enabled.

- the name that the file was saved under.

As with any computer data, most of this information can be altered by a knowledgeable individual, but the fact is that the vast majority of individuals do not alter it.

Changing this 'metadata' (data about the data) of a document is not easy because each software maker uses his or her own recipe for inserting it in what is saved on the disk; some are mildly encrypted to thwart such manual changes. Also, some of this data (e.g., file name) is also saved in a separate file that sits in a separate portion of the disk than the file itself; removing all traces of the file by overwriting it (see Section 4.4) does *not* remove the file name itself unless the particular software used for the overwriting operation has this capability; see http://www.fortunecity.com/skyscraper/true/882/Comparison_shredders.htm for a comparison of file-wiping software openly available. Most such software does not remove the name of the file that it removes; if the name is too descriptive, it can be damning enough even if the file itself cannot be recovered by computer forensics.

Some things *are* straight forward (but tedious and time-consuming) to do, however.

- Wiping (overwriting) the information about the file along with wiping the file itself can be done by using some of the better 'wiping' software openly available (see Section 4.4). Since one should not trust any one of them it is recommended that the security-conscious user:

   ○ use one such 'wiping' program, *and then*

   ○ defragment the disk by using any of the existing defragmenting utilities, *and then*

   ○ use a different such 'wiping' program on the now defragmented disk.

- Since some software also stores the name (and occasionally a portion of a file) in a 'history' file that it creates, one needs to remove those traces as well. This is done easiest with the use of such recommended programs as the disingenuously named Evidence Eliminator, Eraser Version 5, NSClean/IEClean and Com-Clear; more on these utilities is discussed in Chapters 4 and 5.

- Since some software also stores some information about a user's activities in the registry, one must also 'clean' the registry from such information. This is quite tricky, for the following reasons:

- A mis-step in editing the registry can render the computer unbootable the next time around, unless one has taken special precautions by having made a full backup copy of the registry. It is far safer to use programs that clean up the registry, such as Evidence Eliminator, or, as a bare minimum, Microsoft's own REGCLEAN.EXE, which is downloadable directly from Microsoft at no charge.

- The registry is not a single file but a historical sequence of a few copies of those files that Microsoft keeps around in case the latest version gets contaminated. One must clean all of them (or remove all previous versions, which is a risky proposition if the last version becomes unusable). This can be done manually or through the use of a suitably configured Evidence Eliminator.[2]

It is quite apparent that even the above 'straight forward steps' are quite involved and, depending on the user's (lack of) experience, could be quite risky. This underscores yet once more the fact that Windows 95/98/NT/2000/XP was never designed for 'security' but for user convenience. If one wants more security, one can get it by booting a computer off a floppy disk with DOS and working within that DOS environment along with the benefit of a few 'utilities' for file wiping, file editing, file viewing, etc. For example, one can readily change the date that is associated with a DOS file by using the utility STAMPER.EXE.

Alternately, one can use Windows but with full-disk encryption (see Section 4.12), in which case one can adopt the attitude of 'I don't care about what is left behind because it is all encrypted anyway'. This is all well and good in the very few countries where one can refuse to decrypt a disk upon demand, but it is not fine at all in the rest of the world where one can be compelled to decrypt – 'or else'.

3.1.1 Protect the content

Information in one's computer can be stolen by any of the following means:

- direct physical access to one's computer by a third party: this ranges from casual snooping all the way to advanced computer forensics and it can be done

---

[2] Caution: there have been unsubstantiated allegations that Evidence Eliminator may pretend to perform its task but intentionally not do so if it suspects that the enabling code that is used to activate it is one that is not a genuine one that has been paid for; these allegations have been fueled by that product's own prose in its manual. Always be very careful with software designed to delete files. Check Leo Getz's list of allegedly booby-trapped software at http://lgbts.cjb.net/.

by anyone with physical access, and includes maids, friends, service personnel to whom the computer has been taken for repair, commercial competitors, law enforcers of repressive regimes, etc.;

- commercially available software that, depending on its sophistication, can intercept every keystroke, every screenful, every bit of incoming data, etc.: the intercepted information can then be sent out by modem, network connection, or by physical access by a third party;

- commercially available hardware that can intercept every keystroke (specifically including passwords and encryption and decryption keys), and store a substantial amount of such data until they are retrieved either remotely online or through direct physical access by a third party;

- interception of emanations from a computer by using commercially available devices and techniques openly discussed and detailed on the Internet: this is also referred to as VanEck radiation interception.

The techniques for protecting from each of the above threats are different. Accordingly, protecting from more than one of these threats involves correspondingly more protective measures.

Contrary to popular belief, and to the delight of computer forensics investigators, protecting the confidentiality of a document created and/or stored in a computer is very hard; simple schemes invariably trap one into a false sense of security, which is worse than no security at all because one is more cautious when knowing that there is no security at all.

The procedures and steps for properly protecting the information in a computer are shown in this book; they are tedious, but there is no shortcut that works other than not using a computer in the first place.

If, in addition, one needs to protect information also that is being sent to someone else (e.g., by e-mail) the process is even harder and requires its own set of steps; those procedures and steps are also shown in this book and they involve additional steps that are also tedious.

Protecting stored content from forensic investigation

At first glance one could say, 'encrypt it'. That is emphatically inadequate and applies even to the most unbreakable encryption on earth. Practically every computer in the world today uses a graphical user interface (GUI) on the screen. In the old DOS (disk operating system) days about 15–20 years ago, users had to know 'computerese' to type obscure commands to get a desired result. Then the Apple Macintosh came out with a GUI and stole the show. Microsoft then developed 'Windows' as an alternative to Macintosh. Mostly as a result of a series of what can be seen as management miscalculations and wrong decisions at Apple Co., Windows became the de facto operating system.

In its quest to be user friendly, Windows has tossed confidentiality and privacy out the . . . ahem . . . window, in the following ways:

- If one is typing a document or other file and the computer 'crashes' for any one of many reasons, most software applications ('programs' of yesteryear) allow one to resume where one has left off, even if one has not actively 'saved' the file. This is because such software periodically saves the file that one is working on 'for good measure'; this file is saved with an odd name at an odd location on one's disk, and that saved file is often 'invisible' to normal searches. It follows that, even if one were to remove every trace of that file, the duplicate file saved under an odd name will still exist.

- The file name as well as *metadata* (i.e., information *about* the file (such as date of creation, date of revision, serial number of the particular copy of the software that created it, etc.) are also saved on a different place on the disk. Even a full 'wiping' (overwriting) of the original file itself does not remove this separately saved file name and metadata. If that file name is too descriptive ('letter to paramour.doc'), forensic discovery of the file names and the meta data can be unwelcome news to a user.

- Unless one uses special software that is not part of either DOS or Windows, neither of these operating systems ever truly deletes information from a disk. The 'delete' command merely instructs the computer to treat the space occupied by a file as 'available' if needed; the file stays very much intact.

- In the Windows 3.1x days, there were two reasonable length files, win.ini and system.ini that contained a lot of information about a user's preferences and settings. With Windows 95/98/NT/2000/XP, these files have been replaced with a very long set of files known as the 'registry' that routinely stores a lot of information about what one has been doing with the computer. This information often includes names of files, metadata, location on disk, etc., long after the files themselves and even their file names and metadata have been truly removed. Editing the 'registry' is not for the fainthearted: it is often very hard to find and remove the tell-tale traces one should be concerned with; a single mistake can also render the computer unusable unless one has taken specific precautions before tinkering with the registry.

- Since random access memory (RAM) used to be very expensive and users wanted to make do with as little as possible, Microsoft® implemented the notion of a 'swap' (also known as 'paging') file in a disk: the software determines what absolutely has to be in RAM at any instant in time and stores the rest on the hard disk in a file called the 'swap' file; a fraction of a second later, the software may need something stored in the swap file and not need something else in RAM, and promptly 'swaps' them in a manner that is invisible to the user. This is all well and good except that information that was never intended to be saved onto a disk (such as secret passwords, financial data, and even entire portions of documents) end up on the hard disk.

- Because of the way information is stored on disk, it can have a far longer life than one would have expected. In both Windows and DOS, any disk is divided into a number of invisible bins, each of which holds a fixed amount of data. No bin is allowed to hold data that correspond to more than a single file even if that file is far smaller than the bin size. The problem that results is as follows: if a long file that occupied a bin is 'deleted' (which, as stated above, does not really delete anything) and a small file was saved on a portion of that same bin later, the space between the end of the new small file and the end of the bin will contain the information from the old long file; that data will never be touched because no additional file can be written on a bin partially occupied by another file. This area is known as the 'slack' and is a goldmine of information for a forensic investigator.

It follows that the process of 'cleaning up' one's computer from all evidence that could be used against one is a complex task that requires special and elaborate sequences of steps. These are discussed in Chapter 4. It is *far* easier:

1. not to have any confidential information in one's hard disk in the first place, or

2. to have the entire disk encrypted (as opposed to using individual file encryption, which is vulnerable to the Windows security weaknesses identified above; this has its own problems in countries that can compel a user to decrypt files under penalty of automatic jail sentence for refusing to comply.

Implementing option (1) above implies foregoing most of the convenience of Windows:

- Use the old venerable DOS (not as a Windows option but genuine DOS with no Windows); this goes a long way towards enabling a computer user to control what data gets stored where and to remove it by overwriting it as desired.

- If one absolutely refuses to use DOS and is willing to take one's security chances with Windows, at least disable the 'swap' or 'paging' file altogether (see Section 4.3.2).

- Additionally one must use RAM-disk to enter all data. What this amounts to is that the user tells the computer to appropriate a portion of the RAM and treat it as if it were a disk (hence the name RAM-disk). This way one writes and stores files on that RAM-disk with the convenient command of using a disk, yet when power is switched off the contents of the RAM evaporate into thin air.

- One is well advised to use as much RAM as one's computer will allow. This eliminates the need for a 'swap' file and allows one to have a large RAM-disk as per above.

- Given how difficult it is to clean up one's disk (contrary to popular belief, neither the 'format' nor the FDISK commands overwrite a hard disk), one should start with a clean disk to begin with. With disk prices being as low as they are these days, one can readily buy a second internal hard disk and start clean.

Implementing option (2) above involves using any one of a handful of security programs that facilitate entire disk encryption. If this is done, one no longer has to worry about 'temporary files', 'slack', 'registry' or 'swap' files, as everything is encrypted. A severely watered-down alternative is to use openly available software that allows one to have *a portion* of the regular hard disk be encrypted. Anything saved to it is encrypted. This, however, does not solve the many security weaknesses summarized above, such as temporary files, slack, swap file, and so on.

Detailed 'how-to' information on how to implement the items discussed in this section is provided in the corresponding sections below:

- disabling or wiping the 'swap' or 'paging' file: Section 4.3.2 and Appendix C

- establishing a RAM-disk: Section 4.3.2

- full disk encryption: Section 4.12

- encrypted disk partitioning: Section 4.10

- protecting data being entered in a computer from interception of emanations through the use of commercially available devices: Section 3.2.7.1

- protecting data entered in a computer from commercially available hardware and software that intercept every keystroke: Section 4.11.2

3.1.2   Hiding the 'subject': entry

Regardless which encryption program one uses to hide the content of an e-mail or of an attachment, the words in the 'subject' go out unencrypted. This is true even if one uses the encryption provided by either Netscape Navigator/Communicator or Internet Explorer; the security certificates used encrypt only the content of the message.

   The only ways to hide the words used in the subject line from anyone other than the intended recipient are:

- don't type anything there

- Type something generic, innocuous, and appropriate

If one is connected using SSL (secure sochet layer) encryption (see Appendix B), then there is end-to-end encryption between one's computer and the remote website that one is connected to; in theory, the entire communication is secure, but it may not be so, for the following reasons:

- one places one's faith in the security of the remote website one is connected to with SSL

- the website one is actually connected to may not be the one that one thinks one is connected to; this can happen through a typing error, a faulty DNS lookup, through a compromise of one's computer, or through a number of other more esoteric hacks. Also, the SSL security certificate may belong to the website hosting the information and not to the entity providing the information.

The use of anonymous re-mailers (see Section 5.4) hides (parts of) the connectivity of who is sending a message to whom, but it does not necessarily hide the words entered by the sender in the subject line.

3.1.3   Protecting the information of who communicated with whom

In addition to the content of e-mail or other communication (e.g., connecting to a website, connecting with Telnet, etc.), one often needs to hide the connectivity itself.

The local dentist may not want others to know he or she is web-browsing for AIDS information; a freedom fighter in Outer Slobovia may not want that country's repressive regime to know that he is exchanging e-mail with a friend in a free country.

The real problem is hiding both 'what is happening' and, especially, 'who is doing it'. Ideally, one wants to hide both. Hiding only the 'what is happening' part (e.g., through a visibly encrypted connection) alerts a repressive regime that a particular user who can be readily identified may be up to no good; this is unwise. Hiding only the 'who is doing it' part is also unwise because it taunts and challenges a repressive regime to identify the perpetrator in a 'catch me if you can' game.

The threat can come from two different places:

- what goes down the phone line (or xDSL, cable, or whatever other means is used to connect to the Internet) that can be seen by the ISP or by anyone with access to that line;

- what traces are left in one's computer setup (this includes buffers in commercially available hardware and software devices that intercept every keystroke).

As far as the first threat is concerned, one is referred to Chapter 4. Chapter 4 is a long chapter because removing *all* traces from one's computer is a very difficult and tedious proposition. Unless one is a specialist on the matter, chances are that one will always leave enough traces behind for a 'creative' forensics investigator to be able to make a believable case to a hostile judge; just remember the words of Cardinal Richelieu:

> *If you give me six lines written by the most honest man, I will find something in them to hang him.*

As far as the second threat above is concerned, as with most complex problems there is no general purpose solution that applies to all situations. Common sense can suggest any of the approaches listed below, either in isolation or in combination, depending on the specifics of one's situation, the trouble that one is willing to go through to 'hide', the expected frequency of the activity to be hidden, and so on. The one 'golden rule' that should be used is that the observable act has to be nonalerting and be readily explainable and nonincriminating. As already stated, running off to an Internet Café after dinner when one has a perfectly good Internet connection at home could be hard to explain (but not impossible: 'I wanted to surprise my wife with a Club Med vacation and did not want to do the browsing of Club Med's options from home'; of course, the netscape.hst file at the Internet Café should better show that one *did* in fact access Club Med there). The options are, then:

- Use someone else's Internet connection, as long as no records will exist of who did what and when. Then send or receive encrypted e-mail using encryption software in a floppy disk in your pocket, and finally, wipe clean the contents of that floppy disk and add some innocuous stuff to it from the web.

- Use a secure (SSL) connection to a website that allows you then to branch off to a web-based e-mail site, realizing that the fact that a connection was made to a secure website will be readily visible and a matter of record.

- Use anonymous re-mailers (see Section 5.4), realizing that the fact that if an encrypted e-mail is sent to (or received from) an anonymous re-mailer, this act will be readily observable.

- Assuming that one has had the opportunity to work out a pre-agreed 'code' with the intended correspondent, one can engage in innocent-looking activities such as *occasionally* posting an innocuous looking message on a Usenet forum, such as 'why do I get a blue screen (BSOD) on my computer when I do [thus and so]?'

Given the reports one reads in the news media about the massive resources that some countries are devoting to monitoring the Internet wholesale, one may also want to seriously consider *not* using it for anything that the local repressive regime may take exception to and using it, instead, to build up one's profile as a 'goodie goodie'. This is not much different, in essence, than the standard social practice we all use when we leave our house: we shower, shave, dress well, and, all-in-all, behave in a manner that we want others to think is our real persona; to the extent possible, we try to hide from others any signs of aging, any physical or emotional difficulties, and any medical problems. Internet connectivity is far less private than using postcards in place of mail in an envelope.

For 'how-to' details on the topics discussed above, the reader is referred to the corresponding sections below:

- SSL connections: Appendix B

- anonymous re-mailers: Section 5.4

- removing 'evidence' from one's computer: Chapter 4

- anonymized web browsing: Section 5.5

What is noteworthy here is the realization that 'encryption' is only a small part of the overall picture and that it may not even be desirable because it could be alerting.

3.1.4 Protecting oneself from inferences from observables

Just because the e-mail content is encrypted, the sender has set his e-mail software to show that the e-mail ostensibly came from God@Heaven, and the intended recipient's e-mail address is obscured by using one or more anonymizing re-mailers as go-betweens does not mean that the sender is 'secure'. Quite the contrary.

Let us look at what is observable in the above assumed scenario:

- The e-mail is encrypted. This, in and by itself, is likely to taunt almost any regime.

- The sender's e-mail address is faked. This is silly because it is extremely easy for the recipient to find the true identity of the originating ISP; a call to the ISP can readily show additional detail as to which of that ISP's account-holders sent the e-mail.

- An anonymizing re-mailer was used. This is likely to antagonize local authorities even more. Armed with the information from the ISP, local authorities can easily identify who is trying to avoid them and focus resources on that person's future actions.

- The time of the event. This can further narrow down which of a number of possible individuals with access to a given computer identified from the ISP could have sent it. It can also correlate the sending of e-mail with some external event.

- If a pattern is observed in e-mails such as the above (e.g., every Friday at 6 pm), this is likely to give further hints to the observing regime as to what may be going on.

Clearly, this conduct is hardly advisable for a businessperson on travel in a repressive regime or in a regime where there is the possibility of kidnapping, nor for a freedom fighter, and certainly not even for a tourist who wants to vacation outside a local jail. Instead of scheming on how to be secretive, the aspiring user of the Internet must see things from the perspective of 'how would my act look to a suspicious third party that may be watching all aspects of it?' Once this is done, the desired course of action will become evident; it will also become evident that there is no one recipe that fits all scenarios, and that the right course of action will depend entirely on the situation at hand. The essential ingredients are:

- to be nonalerting,

- to be able to explain any act in simple and believable terms,

- to have no smoking gun in one's computer that can make a fool out of one ('And, tell us again, why is it that your Christmas card list includes so many known members of the opposition party?').

These ingredients are relatively easy to have for a single occurrence if one has common sense *and* follows the technical advice in this book. As an act, such as sending e-mail, becomes repetitive, however, it may be next to impossible to continue having those ingredients.

3.2 Protect From Whom?

It makes all the difference in the world from whom one is trying to oneself. About a century ago, sociologist Georg Simmel noted what most instinctively have always known and practiced; namely, that people tend to confide more in strangers than in friends and relatives. This is part of the reason why we tend to 'confide' in what we mistakenly believe to be anonymous, the Internet; we confide in Internet strangers, we foolishly place our confidence in our respective Internet service providers (who see all), we foolishly place our confidence in the administrators of assorted websites that we visit when we think that nobody is watching. All in all, we place our confidence in vast numbers of individuals who have every incentive to betray our confidence. This is utter foolishness.

3.2.1 Protecting from casual snooping

Some of the most enterprising hackers are teenagers. Coupled with youth's propensity to take risks, this means that a person who may seem like a casual snoop may in fact be very well versed in such effective techniques as:

- installing an 'adaptor' on your computer's keyboard cable, which can be a commercially available keystroke recording device (see Section 4.11.1.1);

- installing one piece of software out of many that do the same thing (see Section 4.11.1.2); even suspicious spouses have been offered such software from numerous commercial vendors;

- inserting (intentionally or not) malicious code (a virus, Trojan, or worm) in your computer;

- copying or modifying some of your files.

As such, making a distinction between a 'casual' and a 'sophisticated' snoop is pointless and dangerous. Even so, as a bare minimum that is of use when one is away from one's computer for just a few minutes, one should have:

- a screensaver that one activates when stepping away from one's computer that requires a password to get out of, and

- a CMOS boot-up password, and

- a password to log in to Windows NT or 2000 or XP (sorry, Windows 95/98 is hopelessly insecure).

- a software-based disabler of the floppy drive.

These measures are only useful to thwart against software attacks that can be carried out within a couple of minutes. They will not protect against adding the 'adaptor' to a desktop's keyboard; laptops are clearly far less vulnerable to such 'adaptor' attacks but are more vulnerable to theft of hard drives, since the hard drives of most laptops can be swapped within a minute.

3.2.2 Protecting from disgruntled or nosy insiders

This section applies only to those who share their computing resources with others, either by virtue of being connected to a local area network (e.g., employees in a business) or by virtue of sharing stand-alone computers with others in a group (this specifically includes the repairperson of one's computer, which means that it applies to everyone).

The systems administrator or 'SysAdmin'

The systems administrator [or sysadmin (also known as 'sysop' in less fomal settings)] holds the keys to the kingdom of any organization using networked computers. This person can walk out with an entire organization's database (including e-mails, deleted e-mails, proprietary designs, everything) in a digital tape that fits in a shirt pocket. And he or she can certainly cause the network he or she administers to crash or the databases to be irretrievably wiped clean, even days or months after he or she leaves your employment disgruntled; it has happened time and again.

By far, most sysadmins are honorable professionals. As with any profession, however, be that law enforcement, priesthood, or anything else, there are a few 'bad apples'. It is also not too uncommon for even an honorable person to get into such dire straits (or be blackmailed) to the point of engaging in such criminality against an employer.

Contrary to popular belief, the situation is not hopeless if the following protective measures are taken. One should:

- take extreme care in hiring such a person, checking background, etc.;

- take extreme care in monitoring such a person's behavior for any changes in attitude;

- take steps to keep the sysadmin happy; a salary that is higher than what one's sysadmin can get elsewhere, along with other fringe benefits, is a very small price to pay for having a loyal sysadmin;

- insist that no activities can be undertaken unless two such persons are present and concur; this means having at least three sysadmins (to allow for vacations and other unavailabilities);

- record all of a sysadmin's computer activities in unerasable media (e.g., CD-ROMs) in a manner that is inaccessible to the sysadmin (either physically or electrically); this will act as a disincentive to misbehave to even the most enterprising sysadmin and it will also help prosecution;

- have automatic backups of all databases in unerasable media and store them off-site; this will minimize the time to recover;

- have all sensitive databases encrypted 'on the fly' prior to anything being saved, specifically including e-mail; the sysadmin needs no access to the content of databases and hence needs no access to such decryption keys.

A word to the wise employee: do not do anything inappropriate with your employer's terminal. The sysadmin can see everything. In the USA, and in most other countries, the employer is legally entitled to see anything you do with the computer (and telephone, and office) with which he or she provides you. In the

United Kingdom, the recently enacted Regulation of Investigatory Powers Act empowers a large number of individuals from the police, customs and security services to demand that you decrypt a file under penalty of a two-year jail sentence; additionally, all Internet traffic is intended to be monitored by the local security service; finally, there, too, employers can legally monitor employee use of computer resources.

The shared computer (including the inevitable sharing with a repairperson)

This is the situation that most of us are in. We do not live in a cave by ourselves, we do not sleep and shower with our computer, and we often send it out for repair. In short, our computer is accessible to others. Unless we have taken the protective measures shown in Chapters 4 and 5, our data are likely to become accessible to others.

Even if we were to lock the computer in a room guarded by Kerberos,[3] the moment we connect the computer to the Internet or any other network, security is tossed out the window unless we have taken all of the protective measures of Chapters 4 and 5. It must be emphasized here that even the 'ultimate weapon' of full-disk encryption (see Section 4.12) that protects from unauthorized access a computer that has been turned off does *not* offer any protection when online (at which time the computer is 'on') because the data are decrypted 'on the fly' as they leave the hard disk.

3.2.3 Protecting from the Internet service provider

The Internet service provider (ISP) can observe and – if motivated by any reason or compelled by a court order – record every bit of information that flows to and from anyone that ISP extends Internet access to.

ISPs are mostly commercial entities that want to maximize profits. They have no economic incentive to spend time and/or devote resources to any individual subscriber unless they suspect that a particular subscriber is a threat to them by virtue of:

---

[3] The two-headed dog that guarded the gates of hell to make sure no dead person sneaks back out, not the similarly named encryption and authentication protocol by the Massachusetts Institute of Technology.

- hacking into the ISP's databases (e.g., to steal other users' passwords, to try to obtain 'root access',[4]

- giving the ISP a bad reputation by virtue of what a user is alleged to have done while online,

- using excessive amounts of the ISP's technical resources,

- having been particularly obnoxious in interacting with the ISP's staff.

Additionally, to the extent that it is technically possible, any ISP has to comply with the host country's legal system if served with a court order to monitor a user's (or more users') online activities. In many countries, this requires a court order; in others it may require only an unofficial request by someone with 'clout' or law enforcement credentials.

Additionally, an increasing number of countries are installing automated equipment of varying sophistication that can trigger for any one of many causes, such as particular words (e.g., 'Taiwan' in Mainland China, 'nude' in neo-prudish countries, 'bomb' or what-not in other countries), access to particular Usenet newsgroups or websites that a local regime deems as being unacceptable, e-mail addresses to and from particular countries, and so on.

Since one has usually no way of knowing if one's online activities are being monitored by the ISP, one must assume that they are and not provide any evidence that can either be used against one or that can trigger an unwelcome interest by a local repressive regime on an individual who has never come up on that regime's 'radar screen' before.

There are numerous options available to one, depending on the particular circumstances.

- One can use a stranger's Internet access, such as through a public Internet café, through a local public library, through a hotel's pay-by-the-hour Internet terminal, through a local university's Internet terminals, etc. In all cases, what is important is that there be no records of who was at the terminal at any one time. It is emphasized yet once more that one's observable behavior must make sense and pass the 'giggle test':

---

[4] This term comes from Unix, an operating system that most ISPs use, but amounts to an unauthorized individual becoming able to grant himself or herself the same privileges as a fully authorized system administrator of a computing system; such privileges include full access to every file in the system, authority to create and to delete any file (including evidence of the intruder's intrusion), and so on.

And would you tell the Court, why you left your house in the rain to go use an Internet Café when you have a perfectly good computer and Internet connection at home?

And would you tell the court why is it that you had a floppy disk with encryption software in your pocket when apprehended at the Internet café that rainy night?

- One can use SSL (secure socket layer) connection (see Appendix B) to a remote website that offers such connectivity that can act as a jumping point to whichever other website one *really* wants to connect to. In a nutshell, SSL provides end-to-end encryption between one's terminal and the remote website one is connected to. All that the ISP can 'see' is that there is an encrypted connection (which may be annoying and alerting to an ISP in and by itself), who connected to which SSL site, when, and for how long; this can be alerting enough to an oppressive regime, however, and only the user can determine if this risk is acceptable or not. For obvious reasons, the remote website that one connects to with SSL encryption should not be in the same country that the user is connected to the Internet in.

- If available in one's country, one can use the new two-way Internet service available direct to and from satellite by Hughes Network Systems. This makes one's ISP US Hughes Network Systems, which, for a user from outside the USA cuts out all in-country ISPs.

- If one's lifestyle and business interests warrant it, one can use a briefcase-like personal Inmarsat M+ terminal (see Chapter 6) that can access any telephone number anywhere in the world from practically anywhere in the world. This, too, eliminates the local ISP concern.

- One can dial an ISP that one has established a relationship with in another country that is not under the control of one's local oppressive regime. In this case, one must make the judgment call as to whether or not this act is in and by itself alerting to a totalitarian regime. Unless the connection is encrypted with SSL, every bit going to and from the user can be intercepted by the local oppressive regime. If a conventional telephone is used, the local regime will know instantly where the call is coming from. If a cellphone is used, the local regime will also be able to know where the call is coming from within a few hundred feet. If the cellphone is a GSM phone (see Chapter 6) with a foreign home base (e.g., a Swiss cellphone in a third country), the local regime will not know who that cellphone is registered to[5] and – depending on the country – may or may not have difficulty deciphering the content of the Internet communication even if no encryption is used.[6]

- If one's Internet communications needs are minimal and have been pre-arranged, than one can use innocent-looking preagreed signals where 'having a beautiful time in the evenings, wish all seven of you were here' may have been preagreed to mean 'meet you in the evening on the seventh of the month'. The variety of such schemes is limited only by one's imagination and they amount to what is collectively referred to as 'steganography', discussed at length in Section 5.9, that can handle even moderate communications needs.

Protection from the search engine used

Have you ever wondered who pays for the very convenient service provided by 'search engines' such as Yahoo!, Google, or any of the others? Certainly, they are not providing the massive amount of computer horsepower required out of the goodness of their heart! Some get their revenue from companies that pay them to steer you to them first when you are looking for something. Others get their revenue from on-screen advertisers. Still others get their revenue from selling your browsing habits so that customized advertising can be placed on your web browser's screen or, if they are bold enough, sent to your e-mail address, extracted behind your back from your browser's configuration.

Accoding to ZDNet on 28 June 2001,

Akamai's EdgeScape surfer tracing technology will let Yahoo! figure out where you are surfing from and which ads to deliver to you ... in order to

---

[5] The design of the GSM cellular system was deliberately made to prevent foreign GSM cellular service providers (meaning, ones in countries other than the country that a GSM phone is registered in) from knowing the identity of a GSM user whose 'home' registration is from another GSM country. All that a foreign GSM cellular service provider can know is that the aspiring foreign GSM user is registered with country X and that country X vouches that the bills that will be incurred by that out-of-country GSM user will be paid.

[6] The encryption referred to here is what the Internet user deploys (e.g., SSL, PGP, etc.). It is not referring to the GSM encryption which is deployed at the local GSM service provider's option and which is invisible to that GSM service provider. The difficulty of 'reading' GSM cellphone traffic comes from the complex signaling scheme being used by GSM and pertains *only* to interception of the GSM radio signal by a receiver; it does *not* apply to the country's GSM service provider because it routinely demodulates all GSM signals into conventional audio signals anyway, and can readily comply with a request by that country's legal and law enforcement apparatus to record any communication to and from any given GSM cellphone number.

more finely tune the advertising delivered across its service by comparing their IP address to a table compiled by the company's edge servers which are located in 650 networks worldwide. This information is used by Akamai's clients to adapt their pages according to the surfer's location.

There are easy countermeasures to all this:

- do not use Microsoft Internet Explorer because it is too intimately tied to the operating system,

- obtain and use the free 'junkbuster' software (http://www.junkbuster.com) and configure it to provide false 'referral' information (i.e., the name of the website you visited last),

- obtain and use SurfSecret (http://www.surfsecret.com) and configure it to clean the records in your computer every minute,

- use anonymizing proxies (see Sections 5.3 and 5.5),

- Do not stay on prolonged single sessions with any search engine; instead, start a new session every minute or two after cleaning up your Netscape browser's caches and other data in-between sessions by using ComClear, available at no charge from http://www.neuro-tech.net.

3.2.4   Protecting from a remote hacker

The spectrum of mischief that can be caused by a remote hacker is vast, but the degree of such hackers' success is entirely in the hands of the individuals who wants to protect themselves from such mischief. One cannot connect a new computer 'out of the box' to the Internet, browse, possibly even download and run assorted files, and then expect not to get hacked in numerous ways. To be protected from remote hackings one has to do all these *before connecting even once online*:

- start with a computer that has not been hacked into already;

- install all existing security updates to the operating system software as well as to assorted applications software in it;

- configure the computer to eliminate all *known* remaining vulnerabilities;

- install a current version of a good antivirus software and run it to ensure that the computer does not have a virus, Trojan or worm already;

- install a good 'firewall' and configure it in its most conservative setting. Zone Alarm Pro (http://www.zonelabs.com) alone or in conjunction with either Black Ice (http://www.networkice.com) or Norton's Internet Security firewall or Signal 9's Conseal is recommended (http://www.signal9.com and http://www.consealfirewall.com);

- install and run an 'ad-ware' detection program, 'Ad-aware' from www.lavasoft.de/aaw is recommended;

- install and run an application that will alert the user if a new program starts running in the background behind the user's back; WinPatrol (http://www.winpatrol.com), Who's Watching from www.trapware.com and SpyCop (http://www.spycop.com) are recommended for that purpose;

- if web-browsing is planned, install and use a local proxy program; Junkbuster (http://www.junkbuster.com) is recommended (this requires some configuration of the web browser as well; it is recommended that one does not use Internet Explorer because of its use of ActiveX and the seemingly endless litany of security problems associated with it);

- if e-mail is planned, it is recommended that one avoid Outlook and Outlook Express; despite their conveniences, they have been associated with a vast number of serious security problems;[7] If Eudora is to be used it is recommended that the user attend to the security fixes acknowledged by Eudora (see Appendix A);

- never ever open e-mail from a total stranger at all – delete it unread if it looks suspicious (e.g., 'Subject: the information you requested', when you never requested any, or from a sender that has an obviously fake address); if the e-mail has any attachments, do *not ever* open those attachments – find them and delete them unopened;

---

[7] Among other fatal problems, most versions of Outlook and Outlook Express since 1997 do not check buffer overflows and allow a sender to execute arbitrary code of the sender's choice on the recipient's computer when the recipient opens the vCard sent by the sender. Equally troubling is the fact that one could not configure either of these programs to ignore HTML code in incoming e-mail. When Microsoft released Outlook Express it knew very well that most Windows users would just go along with the masses and use it with its insecure default settings. And most, unfortunately, did and were enamored by the fact that their HTML/RichText e-mail would display 'cool graphics' in an e-mail, while being clueless to privacy threats and vulnerabilities introduced in the process.

- open all e-mail (from known senders) *after* going offline, never while you are still online; this is to negate 'e-mail web bugs'.

3.2.5 Protecting from a commercial competitor

This threat can be quite formidable, as was made apparent a few years ago when a highly placed employee of a major US automaker accepted employment with Volkswagen and allegedly took with him a lot of his original employer's proprietary secrets (see http://www.brinkshofer.com/resources/tradesecrets.cfm and http://www.swiss.ai.mit.edu/6805/articles/crypto/nrc-report/nrc0j.txt). As recently as May 2001, senior employees of Lucent (which used to be AT&T's highly respected Bell Labs) were arrested and accused of stealing proprietary information and passing it on to contacts in China (see htpp://www.cybercrime.gov/ComTriadarrest.htm and http://www.cipherwar.com/news/01/cybercrime_0507.htm).

Protecting from a trusted insider is extremely difficult; the threat goes as far back as recorded history. The threat is of particular concern today (and tomorrow) because most commercial concerns store their proprietary data in a single place: databases. A trusted employer can walk off with all a company's crown jewels – and then some – in his or her shirt pocket; a tape that can hold rooms full of printed documents can fit in a shirt pocket. In many commercial cases, the same data can be – and has been – removed electronically.

3.2.6 Protecting from an untrusted recipient of your e-mail

You may take all of the security precautions in the world about your in-house security but you really have no control over what the authorized recipient of a sensitive e-mail from you does with it. A number of companies are selling assorted schemes that promise to protect your outgoing e-mail. Some prevent the recipient from printing or forwarding incoming e-mail, prevent the incoming e-mail from being viewed more than once, etc. The bottom line is that there can never be a protection from the intended recipient snapping a photograph of his or her screen that displays your e-mail, carrying out OCR (optical character recognition) of the photograph, and ending up with a totally unprotected copy of your superprotected outgoing e-mail.

3.2.7 Protecting from overzealous authorities in a repressive regime

For all practical purposes, any nation state has infinite resources to direct against an individual who it considers to be a threat. Even in the most democratic nations, let alone in totalitarian and oppressive regimes, is most unwise openly to challenge or taunt the government of the country that one lives in. If, for whatever reason, a citizen feels compelled to engage in computer-related activities that the local regime disapproves of, the only way to do so is with the utmost discretion.

When it comes to online computing, it is no longer true to assert that a regime 'cannot track all the people all the time'; it can, and many do. (Offline computing is a whole different story; it is a mostly passive activity and, unless one's profile has surfaced on a regime's radar screen for *other* reasons, offline computing is nonalerting.) It follows that using the Internet to handle the communications of a 'freedom fighter' in a repressive regime is about the most unwise choice of means for regular communications precisely because it is so easy for a regime to monitor all online communications. The same holds for online activities involving anything that a particular regime objects to, be that connectivity to websites dealing with sensitive national issues about disputed sovereignty, to sites associated with political opposition groups, etc.

About the best one can do is not to attract attention and to give oneself some 'elbow room' in online communications by: developing a legitimate profile as an Internet service provider or a company with foreign affiliates; a local commercial representative of an international charity organization; being a student in a university doing research in a field (such as Physics) where one normally needs to access foreign publications, etc.

If a government, especially one with few true legal restraints, decides to take a strong interest in one of its citizen's activities, then no amount of technical means of protection deployed by the targeted individual will preclude that government from knowing precisely what that person does with his or her computer. It is that simple. Even law enforcers in governments with full legal protection of individual rights have been known to engage in blatant violation of these rights when collecting information; they simply do not bring such information to a court of law where it would be dismissed but use it instead as a source of information of where to find 'evidence' that can legally be obtained and which *would* be admissible in court.

What computer forensics can find in your magnetic media and how

The first order of business for someone wanting to do forensics on your computer is to photograph the inside and outside of your computer in order to:

- notice any existing unconnected hard disks; this is a common 'trick' by individuals who merely do not want another member of their household to access files, presuming that such other members of the household will not open the case of the computer;

- jot down the BIOS data.

The next order of business is to copy your harddisks (and floppies) in their entirety after disconnecting them from your computer. A digital hash value (essentially a souped-up version of a 'checksum') is computed for the original and for the copy in order to ensure that the copy is an exact copy of the original so that legal defense cannot claim that it was altered. A typical digital hash value is a 128 bit MD5, which means that it has 340 billion billion billion billion possible values, and the likelihood that two files will have the same MD5 hash is one in 340 billion billion billion billion, (i.e., there practically no such possibility).

The next step for the analyst is to identify all 'known' files (such as the executable portions of commercial software) by comparing the digital hash values of such known files with ones found in your magnetic media; this is done to reduce the investigator's workload so that he or she does not have to bother any more with such 'known' files. Note that renaming a file you want to hide 'word.exe' or 'something.dll' will not fool any investigator because its digital hash value will not match with that of the known files; if anything, such shenanigans will result in increased scrutiny.

Next, the investigator will look for 'notable' files. This is the term used to denote files known to be contraband in a given country. Again, the checking is done on the digital hash value and not on the name, so renaming a file has no effect.

Link (.lnk) files are then checked. A link to an external drive (e.g., E:\) alerts the investigator that external magnetic media existed at some time, whereupon he or she will tear your place apart to look for them.

Printer spooling files are checked next. There are two such types – .SPL and .SHD files. (shadow files) – for every file you have printed in the past. Shadow files include information about the owner of the file, printing method (RAW or EMF),[8] printer and file name. Although while these files are 'deleted' after printing, they really stay on the harddisk until and unless they are overwritten. In a network environment (e.g., your computer at work) they also stay at the network server's magnetic media.

Folders (even deleted ones) are checked next. Microsoft records the date and time each folder was created, last accessed, and modified. Windows NT/2000 also records the time a folder was last accessed. When a file in a folder is moved or is renamed, it retains its original date/time stamp, starting cluster, and file size.

The forensics investigator can plot a history of a file's travels from folder to folder in your disk; this can convince a court that you knew of the file's existence and that you treasured it enough to move it around.

---

[8] RAW and EMF are the two alternative file types used to store printer spool files in a Windows-based computer's hard disk.

As with folders, so with the recycle bin.
Amateurish countermeasures to defeat forensics analysis do not work.

- Screensaver passwords are worthless. In the case of Windows 95/98, one can use ss95deco.exe to get around any such password. If the screensaver password is also used in other situations, such as encryption, the damage will be far worse.

- BIOS passwords are worthless. There exist many backdoor passwords for most BIOSs; additionally, many new motherboards include two test points that, when shorted, disable the BIOS password without erasing the rest of the BIOS data.

- FDISK does *not* render data unrecoverable, contrary to popular belief. It touches only the 64 bytes of sector 0.

- FORMAT does not render data unrecoverable, contrary to popular belief. When, during formatting, one sees the indications 10 per cent complete, 20 per cent complete, etc. this is *not* overwriting anything but merely checks disk integrity. It does return the root directory to zero, however, meaning that subfolders can no longer be associated with their parent folders.

- Repartitioning (e.g., taking a 10 Gbyte disk with data and repartitioning it to show that it is only, say, 1 Gbyte) does not fool any forensics investigator.

- Using Adobe Photoshop's ability to sandwich multiple layers of an image into one where the top layer is opaque in order to hide another layer below it with a contraband image (e.g., an image of currency for counterfeiting) does not fool a competent investigator.

In short, if the information is in magnetic media, and chances are that it will be, a competent forensics investigator will find it. Very few people would even think of getting rid of .LNK files, .SPL files, past versions of the registry, swap files, etc. Even fewer know that FDISK, FORMAT and repartitioning do not remove data from their hard disks.

Van Eck radiation interception with commercial technology and know how

It is basic physics that every wire that carries alternating current (AC) of any frequency radiates some of the signal that it carries. This applies to powerlines that bring electricity to one's house, and it also applies to all wires carrying AC, including wires coming out of one's computer. Indeed, as far back as 1985 Wim van Eck published a paper called 'Electromagnetic radiation from video display units: an eavesdropping risk?' in the journal *Computers and Security*. Electromagnetic radiation as a computer security risk was mentioned in open literature as early as 1967.[9]

'Data security by design', an article by George R. Wilson (http://jya.com/datasec.htm) asserts that such emissions can be picked up 'as far away as half a mile' using 'a broad band radio scanner, a good antenna and a TV set – all

Figure 3.1 Screen display of encryption key setup on targeted computer. Reproduced with permission from Kuhn and Anderson, 'Soft tempest: hidden data transmission using electromagnetic emanations', Computer Laboratory, University of Cambridge, Cambridge, UK

---

[9] Harols Joseph Highland, (1986) 'Electromagnetic radiation revisited', *Computers and Security* **5**, 85–93 and 181–184.

available at electronic stores such as Radio Shack for a few hundred dollars'. This is further verified with experimental results published by Kuhn and Anderson.[10]

The two Figures 3.1 and 3.2 from Kuhn and Anderson lend credence to the foregoing conditions.

Figure 3.2 Encryption keys: intercepted image of encryption keys using VacEck radiation. Reproduced with permission from Kuhn and Anderson, 'Soft tempest: hidden data transmission using electromagnetic emanations', Computer Laboratory, University of Cambridge, Cambridge, UK

So how does one protect oneself from this security threat? Again, basic college physics and standard techniques used by amateur radio operators over the past few decades to shield transmitters can be used:

- use ferrite cores, available at most hobbyist electronics stores, and wrap each cable leaving your computer a few turns around such a core;

- ground the computer chassis to a good ground (such as the nearest cold water pipe);

---

[10] Kuhn, M.G. and Anderson, R.J., 4 soft tempest: hidden data transmission using electomagnetic emanations', Computer Laboratory, University of Cambridge, Cambridge, UK; available online at http://www.cl. cam.ac.uk/~mgk25/ih98-tempest.pdf.

- since laptops, which have to conserve battery power, use much less energy, it stands to reason that correspondingly much less energy is radiated.

Amusingly, a freely available piece of software, Tempest for Eliza (named after Bethoven's 'Für Elise' popular piano masterpiece; go to (http://www.erikyyy.de/tempest/) is a program that claims to use one's computer monitor to send out an AM radio signal that can be heard on one's radio. It does so by displaying the 'correct image' on the screen into a radio frequency signal – in this case, resulting in the music 'Für Elise'.

3.2.8   Protecting from customs agents of foreign repressive regimes' customs agents at border crossings

Practically every country on earth has some written material that it forbids within its borders that is perfectly legitimate in the country of origin of a traveler. Some ban prose they consider threatening to or critical of the regime, some ban assorted definitions of nudity, some ban material associated with banned political movements, some ban material related to politically sensitive topics, some ban personal encryption, and so on. Additionally, many countries target the laptops of business-people from other countries as a potential goldmine of information that could help them leapfrog ahead or gain a competitive advantage in competitive international procurements. In all of these cases, a responsible traveler has every justification to take measures to keep the contents of his or her laptop computer confidential. The issue is 'how', given that a traveler arriving at country X's port of entry is subject to that country's laws and can be compelled to have his or her laptop's stored data scrutinized at length.

Antagonizing any country's customs inspectors is likely to backfire and land one in jail in addition to having one's belongings searched with even greater vigor. Common sense dictates discretion. Given how inexpensive laptop harddisks are nowadays, replace the hard disk in your computer with another one that has nothing even remotely inappropriate or interesting, and be very cooperative when asked to have the laptop 'examined' then.

Depending on the circumstances, one may want to encrypt the entire original hard disk using any one of the few existing commercial products that allow one to encrypt the entire harddisk on a track-by-track and sector-by-sector basis. At the same time, one must be aware that the mere presence of encryption on magnetic media can bring a lot of unwanted attention, especially since some countries have laws that compel travelers to decrypt files or face an automatic lengthy jail term. Decrypting a harddisk on demand in those countries that have the laws to allow this will be no worse for one than providing an already decrypted harddisk to every snoop that wants to look at a traveler's data. The options at this stage include, but are not limited to, the following.

- The original laptop hard disk, now encrypted, which can fit in a shirt pocket, can be hand-carried by a friend with a different last name who clears customs well ahead of yourself.

- The original laptop hard disk, now encrypted, can be mailed ahead by using a commercial express courier.

- The sensitive data and software can be put in encrypted form in a CD ROM before leaving home, and the CD ROM can be carried among a number of music CD ROMs – ideally by someone else. The original hard disk can then stay home. Do *not* attempt to remove files from the original hard disk and bring it along unless you are well versed in the ins and outs of computer forensics (see Section 4.2.10); tell-tale evidence is invariably left behind for a hostile investigator to find and to haunt you.

- Sensitive data can be e-mailed ahead to oneself in encrypted form either for one to download on arrival or, better yet, can be e-mailed to an in-country friend. Both alternatives are risky in that many countries take a dim view of encrypted files and may elect to follow up what they might perceive as an affront.

- Have no customs-alerting laptop at all when entering a particularly repressive country, and buy one of the desired manufacturer and model from the local economy. Have only the (encrypted) small harddisk when entering the country and swap it with the one in the laptop after it is purchased locally.

The one piece of advice that should be remembered is *never* to antagonize customs inspectors, nor to assume that they are any less intelligent than you are. They can be quite well trained in identifying amateurish attempts at deception, and they have the full authority to cause you to end up in jail. Your story must stand well on its own two feet against a very savvy questioner. Spending an important business trip – or one's dream foreign vacation – in a foreign jail is most unappealing.

- For encrypting an entire hard disk: Section 4.12.
- For a detailed discussion of computer forensics: Section 4.2.10.

3.2.9 Protecting from adware and spyware

Maybe your audience hears it – Maybe they don't. But what if you could whisper in their ear, talk to them, know them? Now that is power. Real Power. Discover that power through software advertising. That's right, software. Users want it and we give it to them for free. In exchange, they give us information about themselves that you can use to target your market

Extracted from the official Radiate web page, http://www.radiate.com

FBI turns to private sector for data
ChoicePoint turns a profit by selling personal information

By Glenn R. Simpson, *The Wall Street Journal*, Washington, 13 April 2001

Give me Liberty or give me . . . well, whatever you think is best for society

Slashdot.sig

Adware and spyware is the collective name for the increasingly common practice whereby software makers include a usually hidden functionality in their respective software that causes one's computer to send varying amounts of information through the Internet behind one's back.

The practice started innocuously enough when software vendors thought of allowing users to 'register' software over the Internet; the only information sent was what the individual user had entered. Shortly thereafter, software makers took it on themselves to retrieve varying amounts of information about the user and/or the user's computer (such as the name stored in the registry, the names and even the serial numbers of other software stored in one's computer). Once on that slippery slope, the practice degenerated to theft of information from unsuspecting individual users' computers. For example, some highly advertised (and used) software intercept, store, and later send to a third party through the Internet every keystroke that a user has made and/or every screenful of data that the user has seen. This is quite legal in many cases, such as employee monitoring of employee computer usage at work, parents' monitoring of underage children's online activities, and so on.

By and large, the incentive for spyware and adware has been mostly a profit motive: information about individuals is a commodity with a value, and the more information is collected the more it can be sold for. In a purely marketing sense, adware provides sellers with an accurate database of names and (e-mail) addresses of individuals who are most likely to want to buy what a vendor wants to sell; more than that, if the information sent to these vendors (behind the unsuspecting user's back) is detailed enough, it can certainly help the vendor understand the actual needs of would-be future customers (for a description of the most common spyware and adware and how to get rid of it, see http://cexx.org and http://home.att.net/~willowbrookemill/spylist.pdf).

'So, what is wrong with that?', one can argue. What is wrong is that it is not much different from having a camera[11] in one's house that has been secretly installed by total strangers. It is a violation of privacy, pure and simple. It is trespassing. It is voyeurism with a commercial motive. It is also a substantive threat because such data can cause one irreparable harm. Let us suppose that an online bookstore records the fact that you have purchased D.H. Lawrence's *Lady Chatterley's Lovers* and feeds it into a typically simplistic software that infers that you would likely be interested in sexual or even lesbian themes and starts bombarding you with e-mailed ads for such books; since e-mailed attachments stay in one's computer even after the e-mail has been removed, a forensics investigator would readily find lots of those explicit references in your computer and it would be very hard for you, then, to convince a nontechnical judge or jury that you are not 'into' such themes. Such 'evidence' could then easily support prosecutors' claims of one being unfit as a parent; it could also support the opposition attorneys' claims of just about anything in a divorce case.

There is no clear distinction of where online registration ends and where data theft and adware and spyware start. It is strongly recommended that you avoid the entire spectrum of online registration, even if you feel that you are dealing with a reputable company. In particular, do not place any faith whatever in 'privacy' policies by any company. If that company is bought by another, merges with another, and especially if it goes bankrupt, its assets (notably including the 'private' database of its customers), the so-called private information, becomes yet another tangible asset that will be bought and sold at will. To its credit, EBay came up with an announcement in mid-April 2001 that its privacy policy may not survive a merger or acquisition in the future. If only all companies would state the same up front.

There is no clear distinction where adware end and where spyware starts. As of early 2001 there has been a plethora of commercial software that performs different overlapping spyware functions of one type or another. They are not illegal and often serve very legitimate functions. I makes no claim that the list in Table 3.1, which is compiled from unverified Internet sources, is correct.

Some software tools are available that detect the *known* adware and spyware in one's computer. As with a virus (human or computer), one can only detect what one knows how to look for. The best is Lavasoft's Ad-Aware, which is free from http://www.lavasoft.de shown in Figure 3.3. A very good complementary package is Spyblocker from Spyblocker Software at http://noads.hypermart.net/index.htm;

---

[11] There is a plethora of commercially available concealed video cameras available to anyone online at such places as http://www.spybay.com/products.html.

Table 3.1   Adware and spyware

007 STARR	Flyswat	Remote Control PC
007 Stealth Activity Monitor	Freewhack	Remote Explorer
AOL Recorder	Ghost Keylogger	Save Keys
AppsTraka	GoHip!	SentryCam
ASCII Spy	GuardPuppy	ShadowNet Remote Spy
Aureate	IAmBigBrother	Silent Watch
Big Brother	I-Gear	Smart Alex ICU
Blackbox 6	I-SeeU	Snapshot Spy
Boss Everyware	ISpyU	Spector
Canary Settings	Internet Detection 1	SpyGraphia
ChatNANNY	Internet Filter Suite	Spytech Shadow
Cheater Beater	Internet Watchdog	Spytech SpyAgent
Comet Cursor	IntraSpy Manager 2	Spy Tool
Compu-spy	Keyboard Monitor	Stealth Keyboard Intereceptor
Computer Cop	Key Interceptor	Stealth Spy
Conducent	KeyKey Statistics	Surfing Spy
Cyber 007	keylogger 97	Surf Spy
CyberSentinel	KeySpy	TimeSink
CyberSitter	Kid control	Triple Exposure
Cyber Snoop	LookSpy	Web3000
Cybersurveillance	Message Inspector	We-Blocker
Cyber-track	MiniSpy	Webhancer
Cydoor	Net-rated	WebPI Control
Desktop Detective	NetSpy	WinGuardian (User Monitoring Utility)
Desktop Surveillance	Parents Friend V	WinWhatWhere
Disk Snoop	PC Spy	
Disk Tracy	ProBot	
DSSAgent	Prudence	
eBlaster 2	Radiate	
FamilyCAM	RedHand Pro	

Source: unverified Internet sources; the author makes no claim that this list is correct.

it is compatible with Windows 95/98/ME but not with NT and 2000. It, too, is free. Another is PC Investigator (also known as Hookprotect) from http://www.geoci-ties.com/SiliconValley/Hillis/8839/utils.html.

An excellent spyware-detecting software is SpyCop – corporate version – from http://www.spycop.com; it is not free (see Figure 3.4). Yet another very good one is Who's Watching, from http://www.trapware.com. It is particularly good at detecting some keystroke capturing and transmitting software (Figure 3.5). Finally, a very good spyware-detecting program is Spy-Detect, from http://www.spydetect.com.

Since adware and spyware and keystroke recording software evolve all the time,

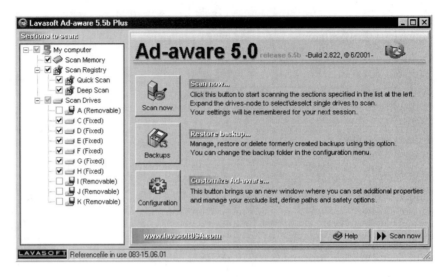

Figure 3.3 Ad-aware: adware-removing software

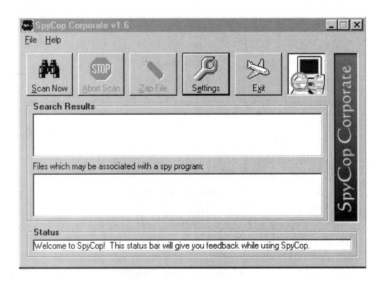

Figure 3.4 SpyCop software for detecting some software that 'calls home'

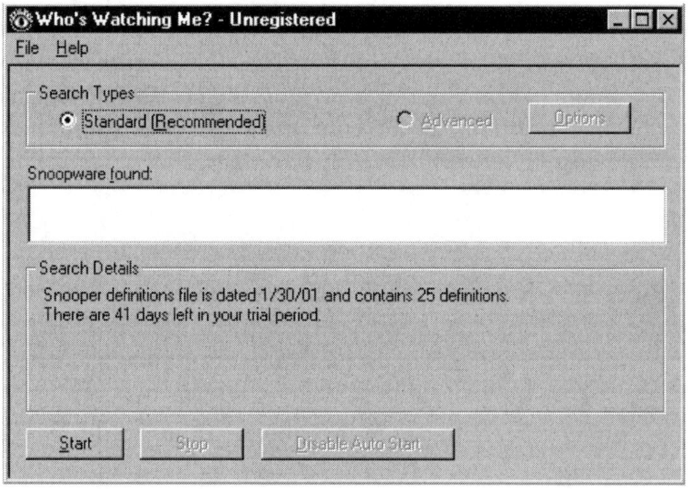

Figure 3.5 Who's Watching: software for detecting software that 'calls home'

the software that detects them has to have regular updates to stay current too. The first such adware-detecting software, at www.grc.com is no longer available (and would not be very useful even if one were to use an old version). It has been superceded by Ad-Aware (see above) from www.lavasoft.de. For a detailed comprehensive site that deals with adware, see http://www.alphalink.com.au/~johnf/spyware.html.

An actual layer of protection is provided by the highly recommended 'firewall'[12] Zone Alarm Pro from http://www.zonelabs.com. It will alert the user most times when software within one's computer attempts to access the Internet and ask for permission to allow it or not. It works with all versions of Windows. At the same time, be advised that some adware/spyware can get around Zone Alarm Pro and communicate undetected.

Finally, some computer motherboards themselves are alleged to contain spyware in their BIOS. PhoenixNet's manual states:

---

[12] A 'Firewall' is a misnomer perpetuated by the software industry that makes them. At best, they are porous membranes. The best of the software 'firewalls' intended for noncoproprate use is ZoneAlarm Pro from http://www.zonelabs.com. Even so, one should never leave the computer 'online' any longer than one absolutely must. Additionally, the computer that gets connected online to anything should *never ever* have had anything even remotely sensitive in it. The computer that you use to store your sensitive files should never be connected online to any network; no ifs, buts, or howevers.

PhoneixNet is a service that provides PC users with best-of-breed, free software services to support their PC hardware and software and to turn their computer into a powerful tool. These services are delivered to the user as hotlinks on the desktop and in the web browser or, as applications that PhoenixNet automatically packages, downloads and installs.

3.2.10   Protecting from worthless 'privacy policies'

A company's 'privacy policy' is, quite frankly, not worth anything because:

- it can be (and often has been) changed by the company and is applied retroactively; the cases of amazon.com and Ebay are classical examples;[13]

- once a company goes bankrupt, its 'confidential' list of customers and the data they provided to that company in confidence becomes just another 'asset' that is sold to satisfy the bankrupt company's creditors who, in turn, are not bound by the bankrup company's privacy policy.

Typically, on 1 August 2001, Essential.com, a company that retailed communications services, arranged to sell its customer list of 70 000 customers for $1 million and close down (http://www.boston.com/dailyglobe2/214/business/Essential_puts_on_fire_sale+.shtml).

3.2.11   Protecting from databases where you posted your resume

A resume that is posted online to any of the many companies that act as online 'middlemen' between aspiring job applicants and job seekers is certainly not a private matter.[14] What *is* a private matter, however, is:

- information provided to resume services that is provided with the explicit mutual understanding that it is not to be disclosed; such information could be, for example, an applicant's home address or current employer;

---

[13] On Amazon's change in policy, see http://www.pcworld.com/resource/printable/article/0,aid,18458,00.asp.
   On Ebay's change in policy, see http://www.news.cnet.com/news/0-1107-200-346336.html.

[14] See http://www.wired.com/news/print/0,1294,46559,00.html.

- resumes removed and deleted from such online services after it has been removed and deleted, certainly, the poster has a reasonable expectation that the online service will not sell that information after it has been removed by the poster.

The Privacy Foundation accused Monster.com, the world's largest job seeking site, of

discussing the sale of users' private data to marketers, failing to completely remove resumes after job seekers deleted them and sending user information to America Online to satisfy the terms of a business agreement' (http:// www.privacy foundation.org/privacywatch/monster.asp)

An author of many books on online job seeking, Pat Dixon, submitted a test resume to H&R Block and was subsequently able to pull that same resume at numerous other 'private label' job sites such as Tyco, Sony, Blockbuster video, and even Monster.com. The upshot of this is that you should never trust any online job seeking firm's assurances that it will protect the privacy of any information you provide. Given the fact that the percentage of job applicants that actually do end up with a job as a result of online job postings is extremely small, you may be well advised not to post your resume online in the first place. By far the largest percentage of successful job applicants result from personal introductions from former fellow employees and other professional and personal contacts, and not from online postings of anything.

4

Effective Protection for Computers that are Not Connected to Networks

Most security failures are due to failures in implementation, not failures in algorithms or protocols.

The National Security Agency

4.1 Trusting your Computer with your Life and (Relative) Freedom

When using a personal computer to store and/or transmit a sensitive file, security inevitably involves a considerable amount of trust. If the consequences of a compromise are serious (e.g., a freedom fighter in a totalitarian regime storing the names of other freedom fighters in a file – a very reckless act to begin with), one would want to rely less on trust and more on verification. But the complexity of software and hardware today, as well as the sophistication of ways of compromising them, is such that even the most motivated individual lacks the skills and time to verify most of what needs verifying.

How do you know, for example, *for a fact*:

- that the computer hardware you just bought has not been pre-compromised in any of the commercially available ways discussed in Chapter 3?

- that, unless you sleep, shower, and dine with your computer under your arm, it has not been compromised during times when you had no direct control over it?

- that any of the software used, including the operating system, has not been compromised from day one, or at any time thereafter, using any of the many commercially available ways discussed in Chapter 3 and later in this chapter?

- that the encryption software used, that seems to be working fine, has not been doctored so as to be selecting an encryption key from a population of only 100 possible keys instead of from a population of a quadrillion possibilities, thereby making cryptanalysis trivial?

- that the digital signature vouching for the integrity of the document you just downloaded is indeed trustworthy?

- that if you elect to compile the source code of an encryption program yourself, the compiler itself that you are using has not been compromised?

- that a file has not been added to your computer that records your activities for later retrieval by a third party?

- that the 'public key' of the intended recipient of your e-mail does, indeed, belong to that person and not to someone else ('man in the middle', see Section 5.8)?

- that the recipient of the sensitive file will secure it appropriately (what you send can incriminate you far more than what you receive)?

- that nobody is picking up the Van Eck radiation from your computer, using the commercial devices and techniques discussed in Section 3.2.7?

- that none of your passwords can be guessed or found with an exhaustive dictionary attack (see Section 4.5)?

- that your premises have never been entered in your absence to install any one of a number of possible sensors in the room where you use your computer?

- that the repair facility that worked on your computer did not add means to make interception easier before returning your computer to you?

- that no member of your family has ever played a computer game or run any of their own software in your computer that could have unwittingly compromised its security?

- that the printer and monitor that you use have never been compromised ever since you bought them – or even before?

- that any and all of the peripherals connected to your computer (e.g., SCSI drives, scanners, CD ROM writers, etc.) have never been compromised?

- that not a single unauthorized person ever could have wandered in your absence into where your computer is located (this includes maids, plumbers, telephone repair people, painters, social acquaintances, etc.)?

- that all the recommendations made in Chapter 5 about being online have been religiously followed and that during each and every online connection of your computer, no remote entity could *ever* have retrieved information from your computer?

And the list can go on and on.

Although some things are easier for an individual user to verify than others, the point is that one needs to do the impossible task of verifying everything above if lives are at stake. An average person who has not been targeted either by competing commercial interests or by security services, needs only to worry about:

- run-of-the-mill hacking;

- criminality such as identity theft, cyberstalking, fraud, etc., all of which are increasing at a very rapid rate;

- subpoenas by hostile civic actions that can lift words and sentences from one's computer media out of context in an attempt to incriminate in any one of many possible legal actions (divorce proceedings, employment-related issues,[1] etc.);

- entrapment by rogue law enforcement;

---

[1] Recently, a Northwest Airlines flight attendant hosted a message board on his personal website on the Internet. Among the messages posted in it by others were a few anonymous ones by other employees urging co-workers to participate in sickouts (which are illegal under US Federal labor laws) so as to force that airline to cancel profitable flights during the 1999 Christmas season. Indeed. Over 300 Northwest Airlines flights were cancelled during that time. Northwest Airlines obtained a court order from a federal judge in Minneapolis to search 22 flight attendants' hard drives in their computers located not only in union offices but in their homes as well, so as to find the identities of those who had urged the above sickouts.

- slander or libel by others; anonymity and pseudonymity on the Internet can be – and has been – abused with impunity to slander others;

- theft of confidential or other sensitive information;

- being inadvertently caught in others' illegal acts.

With the exception of entrapment, the resources likely to be deployed against one in such situations are typically minimal, though quite effective nonetheless, unless one has taken extensive active measures to protect oneself.

A person who has been targeted by competing commercial interests must be content with the likelihood of much more extensive and expensive resources being used against him or her. The target is usually theft of proprietary data.

A person who has been targeted by security services, such as a freedom fighter in a repressive regime, is in a whole different class, since the resources that can be directed against him or her are, for all practical purposes, limitless. About the best thing one can do is never to be identified as a target by local security services. If one has already surfaced on a repressive regime's local security service's radar screen, the best advice is not to do *anything* observable that is even remotely incriminating; any computer-related activity is readily 'observable', as shown throughout this book. Better yet, such a person would be well advised to use the computer to advantage by projecting an image that is squeaky clean in the hope that security services will get bored, lose interest, and be unable to justify any further surveillance downstream.

The point of all of the above is that *encryption is not a cure-all*; worse yet, it may give a false sense of security. Encryption is only a very small part of a process of protecting sensitive files, and the overall process of hiding something has to protect from numerous additional threats that have nothing to do with breaking one's encryption.

In view of all of the foregoing, the emphasis on 'strong encryption' is really a fetish and not a defensible goal. Hardly anyone will ever bother to 'break' your encryption through cryptanalysis simply because there are far easier ways to get to your sensitive files. Unless you have 'covered your bases' to protect yourself from all those easier (to the thief) ways, such as the ones listed above, encryption will provide no protection whatever.

4.1.1   File confidentiality in your computer

Protecting the confidentiality of documents in your own computer brings in a totally differed set of issues from the problem of confidential communications (e-mail). The key question that has to be answered by each user up front is: protect from whom?

- From a casual snoop with no technical sophistication who gains access to one's computer for a short time?

- From industrial theft by technologically savvy competitors?

- From an investigator of a totalitarian regime with access to sophisticated computer forensics expertise?

- From the security services of a technologically backwards country that tries to steal advanced technology when businesspeople from a technologically advanced country visit it?

- From an investigator of an oppressive totalitarian regime who is trying to identify potential dissidents through their computer activities?

- From the customs inspector of a country that has unusual laws as to what is not allowed in that particular country (e.g., one country has recently banned the possession, in any form, the popular cartoon character 'Pokémon'; another bans Playboy images and their digitized images; others ban this or that religion-related book and its digitized versions; most ban any criticism of their respective leaders in any form, including digitized; and so on.)?

- From an online hacker who can access your files behind your back?

One cannot 'protect from all of the above for good measure' because different protective techniques apply to different situations. For example, 'encrypting the files' (assuming it is done well, which is easier said than done as this entire book is showing in great detail) may be effective against some threats but is certainly not effective where encryption is banned and one can be compelled to produce the decryption key – or else!

This section will dwell only on the key aspect of hiding in a data storage media *even the existence* of a file, whether encrypted or not – and one would be well advised to encrypt a sensitive file before hiding it, just in case.

There is a lot to hide besides the sensitive file itself. One would need:

- to hide all indications that the file was ever created, including:

  o its name that it may originally have been saved under,

- its metadata (when it was created, using which application software, etc.),

- any and all temporary files that may have been created along with it, behind one's back, by the application software that created it (e.g., Microsoft Word),

- any reference to that file's creation or even mere viewing in any of many 'history' and 'most recently used' (MRU) lists;

- to consider the possibility that information from or about that file may have leaked into the swap/Paging file. (see Appendix C);

- to consider the possibility that a 'sector' in the computer's disk that housed that file may have been deemed of marginal dependability by the hard disk and may have been substituted for by a different sector, marking the first sector as 'unusable' but without 'wiping' the sensitive data in it – such ostracized sectors are beyond the reach of most 'disk-wiping' utilities that claim to sanitize one's disk;

- to remember, in the event of an all too frequent computer crash, there are numerous .chk files created by scandisk; they contain recovered data clusters that have no corresponding entry in the file allocation table; these clusters could well contain segments of precisely the file(s) that you may have wanted to disappear.

It is evident that doing all this is a very tall order that most individuals cannot (or do not want to) bother with. But what if the file in question is Coca Cola's much-heralded secret recipe or the list of proactive dissidents in a highly repressive totalitarian regime? What if one's life depended on that file remaining hidden? What if that file contained the names of informants used by an anti-drug enforcement operative? Or, on a different level, what if that file contained a digitized Pokémon cartoon and one could be jailed for having it while touring with one's family the country that bans it? What if that file contained information that an aggressive divorce lawyer might use out of context to sway a court in favor of denying you custody of, or even visitation rights to, your children?

4.1.2 A highly recommended solution

In a nutshell, making a Windows-based computer immune to hostile computer forensics is an impossible task unless you do this for a living, day and night. The recommended solution below acknowledges this fact of life and shows you how to have a computer that *is* immune to computer forensics.

1. Get a very inexpensive computer (some are free) and remove its hard disk. Create a number of DOS bootup disks for it with some minimal text editing software in it. An old laptop is much preferred as there is very little room for modifications and also because you can lock it up when you are away.

2. Inspect it very carefully to ensure that it has no odd adaptors in its keyboard or other cables. If it is a desktop, rather than the recommended laptop, buy a new keyboard from the store. Mark its screws and cable in a manner that will show you in future if it has been opened or if the cable has been changed in any way. An exaggerated example is shown in Figures 4.1 and 4.2 below; your markings should be more discrete. Make sure you physically check them prior to each use. This is to detect any commercial keystroke-capturing device.

Figure 4.1   Marking of desktop case screws to detect surreptitious entry

3. Set the time and date of that computer to some ridiculous value such as noon on 1 August 1965.

4. Add to each of those disks a DOS-based encryption program, such PGP 2.6.3i (or any of the older DOS-based PGP versions). Keep the keys in a different floppy disk. DOS version of PGP are available from numerous sources, such as http://www.ipgpp.com.

5. Make each such bootable disk create a RAM disk by adding the following line in its CONFIG.SYS file:

DEVICE=C:\WINDOWS\RAMDRIVE.SYS 1024/2

Figure 4.2   Marking of desktop retainers to identify surreptitious entry

using any text editor. This will create a 1 Mbyte RAM drive whose letter designation will most likely end up being D:\. If you have a CD ROM drive, its drive letter will now change, and you want to know that when software asks you where to look for the CD-ROM.

6. Boot from any one of those floppy disks. Start creating your sensitive document in RAM disk. Save it in RAM disk only.

7. Encrypt the document and save it into RAM again.

8. Now use the STEALTH utility (DOS-based and available from numerous PGP-related web sites) to remove the tell-tale headers and footers of a PGP-encrypted file and save the result in RAM.

9. Now zip-compress that file so that it does not look encrypted at first glance, and save the result (i.e., the compressed version of the encrypted file) with a nondescript name on the floppy disk.

10. Use the STAMP.EXE DOS-based utility to change that document's file-creation date to whatever you like.

11. Turn that cheap computer off. All 'evidence' is gone!

12. Physically destroy that floppy disk to be on the safe side; it only costs a few pennies anyway. No, cutting it in two is not destroyed enough.

13. Now go to your 'real' computer and copy that compressed encrypted file from a floppy (on which there has never been stored any unencrypted data) to the RAM disk on your 'real' computer.

14. Rename that file to something suitable for inclusion into a folder unlikely to attract any attention. For example 'terrain.dat' would be a good name if you have a game installed in your computer that uses terrain maps; save that file in the folder used by that game. Alternatively, you may want to consider using Scramdisk's (see Section 4.10) steganography option to hide a file. First, record a few minutes of music from an old scratchy LP (long-play) record (no, not from a compact disk (CD); they are too perfect and any change can be detected) and use that as the carrier or cover file to hide things in. If you do this, make sure that:

    (a) you first establish credibility as an LP record enthusiast, or the scheme will look 'fishy' to any intelligent investigator;

    (b) you use Scramdisk in its 'traveler' mode so that its existence in your computer is not evident.

As with any discrete act, the above ritual should not be overused. Having 500 terrain1.dat, terrain2.dat, etc., files is not good form, for obvious reasons; having one is most likely OK though; likewise for having too much music from scratchy LPs taking up space in your hard disk.

Granted, the above process seems a bit tedious but it really isn't; once it is streamlined and you get used to it, it can be completed in a minute or two. And by all means do not brag, or even hint, to anyone else what you do and how you do it.

4.2 A (Readable) Tutorial on Hard Disks

Given that all computer forensics people exploit what is left behind on hard disks, a working familiarity with the ins and outs of hard disks is essential to any serious attempt to minimize the dangers of unscrupulous hostile analysis of one's hard disk (e.g., thieves of businesspeople's laptops, overzealous investigators in repressive regimes, unscrupulous lawyers fishing for dirt in civil divorce and other cases in subpoenaed hard disks, etc.). Even if you are allergic to techie-talk, you may well want to go through this section. It is easy to follow and informative.

4.2.1 The basics

A hard disk rotates at a constant speed, typically 4500, 7500, or 10 000 rotations per minute (rpm). The faster it turns, the faster the information can be read from or written to the disk – all else being equal. But the hotter the disk gets, and a cooling fan blowing air on the disk case will help increase the hard disk's lifespan.

Data on a disk (floppy or hard) is not strung out in a long spaghetti-like manner like the music on an LP record. A disk's magnetic surface is divided in concentric circles (called 'cylinders', each of which is divided into 'sectors', each of which can fit a fixed amount of data (typically 512 bytes to 4096 bytes each).[2] Since the circumference of the outer tracks is longer than that of the inner tracks, outer tracks can have more sectors than the inner tracks.

A 'cluster' (of sectors) is the smallest building block that the disk considers in writing data. Since a disk allows no cluster to contain data from more than a single file, this means that if a cluster is only partially filled with data, the rest gets unused. *This is a security problem.* It means that if the file occupied an entire cluster before, was subsequently deleted (which merely tells the disk the space is available now but does not remove the data), and is now occupied only partially by a new file, the space between the end of the new file and the end of the cluster will contain the data from the precious file that filled that cluster; this will continue for ever unless one uses a utility to 'wipe the cluster tips' (see Section 4.4).

If data are in consecutive or nearby sectors, the magnetic heads that try to find and read them have to do less searching and the same operation can be completed faster (ergo: defragment your disks regularly).

To speed up disk access, disks usually read more than you ask them to just in case you will need what you have not yet asked for, and will store it in a 'cache' memory, which is kind of a 'purgatory'; it is also a security headache because things that you did not ask for can be read or written.

It used to be that each physical (or real) sector had a number, and this number corresponded to the exact physical location of that sector. No longer. Hard disks nowadays have a vast capacity compared with those of even a couple of years ago. Accepting the fact of life that some of the sectors will be defective, they all include

---

[2] A 'byte' (often abbreviated to B) is a term to denote 8 bits (zeros or ones) of data.

numerous more unallocated sectors. As soon as one formerly good sector is sensed by the disk to become suspect and 'flaky', its data are moved to one of these unallocated spare sectors and this new sector is now renamed to have the name and address of the disowned one; the user is totally oblivious to this. As such, what the disk tells you is 'sector 12' is really a 'logical' rather than a 'physical' sector number; the actual physical sector that corresponds to that number may well be a long distance from 'sector 11'. *This is a security disaster*; it means that the disowned suspect physical sector whose contents have been moved over to a spare physical sector that now bears the number previously held by the suspect sector *is inaccessible but still contains data that can be incriminating*. As a user, you have no way of knowing that this has happened. A forensics investigator with the proper tools can get to that data. *No disk-wiping software in the world will wipe that disowned sector because the hard disk pretends that it does not exist.*

The 'boot sector' is important. This is where the disk stores information such as how many sectors it has, the code to load system files needed to continue the boot process (e.g., IO.SYS and MSDOS.SYS), etc. If the boot sector is contaminated (and some viruses do exactly that) or is physically damaged (unlikely) the disk will not boot.

4.2.2 EIDE versus SCSI

There are two commonly used hard-disk types and associated interfaces: EIDE [the most common; shorthand for enhanced intelligent (or integrated) drive electronics, from Western Digital Corp.] and SCSI (small computer system interface). Each EIDE controller interface has a primary and a secondary channel, and each can connect two devices, a 'master' and a 'slave', such as hard disks, floppies, CD-ROMs, and even some tape backups as of late. If you connect a CD ROM put it on the secondary channel, because it can slow the hard disk down when the system waits for a CD ROM command to finish.

If you get a new hard disk, making it a 'master' is a chore because it does not have an operating system on it (yet) and will not boot; you have first to reinstall the operating system on the new drive. The easiest way is to first install the new drive as a slave, copy all the files from the old one to it, turn off the computer, and switch the master–slave status. Be careful not to reverse the connector of the cable and how it connects to the hard disk; whoever designed the standard for these connectors was in my opinion a lousy engineer for not making it impossible to connect the cable in the wrong way.

SCSI hard disks typically require you to buy and install a card that implements the driver software to read and write on those disks, because most motherboards do not include that function. Adapter cards from Adaptec Co. are the best (http://

www.adaptec.com; Adaptec Inc., 691 South Milpitas Boulevard, Milpitas, CA). SCSI disks are about quadruple the price of equal capacity EIDE disks but, depending on the interface card and the disk, can be considerably faster and reach transfer speeds of up to 80 bit/sec (in the case of 68-wire data cable Wide SCSI with a 40 MHz Fast-40 Ultra-2 SCSI bus clock). By comparison, EIDE disks top out at 16.6 bit/sec (with a much-heralded option of 33.3 Mbit/sec for 'MA mode 2', which still has technical problems).

You can connect up to 8 (or 16 depending on the interface card) SCSI devices on a chain. Getting the SCSI chain to work well is a bit of an art; in theory, you should only have a 'terminator' at the end and at the beginning of the chain and nowhere else. In practice, you may have to experiment with different relative positions of the peripherals along the chain to get them all to work well. A short total length of the cable helps and so does having an 'active' rather than a 'passive' terminator; good cable quality is a must.

If you have both EIDE and SCSI disks in your system, you cannot boot from a SCSI disk; if you only have SCSI disks you can. The boot SCSI disk should be assigned identification number 0 and the interface adaptor number 7. You will also have to configure the CMOS information in your motherboard about whether or not you have EIDE disks in your computer.

4.2.3   Security aspects of the FDISK command

This information should be of security interest because it can help render any previously stored information on a hard disk unreadable. There are different 'flavors' of FDISK and you should use the proper one for the operating system you have in your computer.

- DOS 6.22 FDISK cannot handle drives larger than 8.4 GB.

- Win95 FDISK supports drives larger than 8.4 GB if the BIOS can support INT14 Extensions; to use it correctly, boot to the 'command prompt Only' on Startup, or choose 'Restart in MS-DOS Mode' on shutdown or boot from a Win95 startup floppy disk.

- Win95 OSR2 also supports FAT32 (see Section 4.2.6) but you must answer 'yes' to the question 'Do you want to enable large disk support?' (Answering 'no' still enables access to large drives but not to FAT32). Do not use the /X option.

- Win98, WinNT, Win2000. Use the FDISK that comes with those systems.

Use the /MBR option if a virus has infected your mater boot record (MBR).

4.2.4 Security aspects of the FORMAT command

The FORMAT command writes marks on the disk to indicate the beginning and end of tracks and sectors. There are two kinds of formatting: 'low level' and 'conventional'. The former is done by the disk manufacturer and does wipe out any previous data on the disk. The latter (conventional formatting) does *not* wipe the disk clean; any data from before can still be recovered easily forensically. There is an exception in the case of a floppy disk, in which case the FORMAT command does both low-level formatting and conventional formatting. Even so, do not count on that to remove all forensic evidence from a disk; given that it costs only pennies, open it up, cut it up in as little pieces as possible, and burn it or flush it down the toilet.

The reason why the FORMAT command does not do the much desired (for security reasons) low-level formatting on hard disks, is that there are far too many different hard disks, and FORMAT does not know how to handle them all (or any); for example, the number of sectors per track varies on hard disks but not on floppies.

4.2.5 FAT (file allocation table)

This is merely a directory, invented in 1977 for floppy disks, that tells a disk controller where (which track and sector) a stored file is stored and in what order; it also holds information about that file's name, size, date/time stamp, whether the file is supposed to be 'hidden', 'archived', and so on. It can support up to 65 525 files and is limited to 2 GB. It is about 2 per cent faster than FAT32 (see below) for small drive sizes, and its performance for large drives drops dramatically.

4.2.6 FAT32

Basically, FAT32 increases the efficiency of how large hard disks store data by minimizing wasted space. It does so by using smaller 'clusters'; it also has the ability to relocate the root directory and to use a backup copy of the file allocation table (FAT) in place of the main one. Security warning: wiping the FAT on a disk for security purposes achieves nothing since there is a backup; also the files are still on the disk and can be painstakingly reassembled without any FAT.

Disk size and cluster size and the corresponding efficiency for FAT32 disks are given in Table 4.1.

Table 4.1   Disk size, cluster size, and efficiency of FAT32 disks

DISK SIZE (bytes)	CLUSTER SIZE	EFFICIENCY (%)
$< 260 \times 10^6$	2000	98.4
$> 260 \times 10^6$	4000	96.6
$> 8 \times 10^9$	8000	92.9
$> 60 \times 10^9$	16 000	85.8
$> 2 \times 10^{12}$	32 000	73.8

Unlike FAT16, the boot sector of FAT32 drives needs two sectors, not just one. Also, the file allocation table is larger in FAT32 since each entry requires 4 bytes rather than 2 bytes: also there are many more clusters to keep track of.

4.2.7   NTFS (new technology file system)

This, basically, is intended as a survivable system in that it uses the 'master file table' (MFT) rather than FAT to keep multiple copies of files so as to protect against the possibility of data being lost. Because MFT takes a lot of space (around 400 Mbytes), it is not intended for small hard drives.

From a security-from-forensics perspective it can be disastrous precisely because it keeps multiple copies of files, and also because it supports 'hot fixing', which allows the disk to replace bad sectors with good ones without wiping the data on the bad sectors.

4.2.8   Security implications of cluster size

The smaller the cluster size, the less room there is between end-of-file and end-of-cluster and hence the less likely that much data can be found forensically even if one does not wipe the cluster tips. Note also:

• the more clusters in a disk, the slower the disk access;

• the smaller the cluster size (and hence the more the clusters, all else being equal), the better the utilization efficiency of the available storage size of a disk.

4.2.9   Which operating system can read what?

- Windows 3.1x and DOS cannot read FAT32 or NTFS.

- Windows 95 OSR2, and Windows 98 can read FAT32 but not NTFS.

- NT4 can read NTFS but not NTFS5 (Windows 2000).

4.2.10   Forensics issues

This small section does not take the place of the extensive information spread throughout the rest of this in Chapter 5 but complements it. From a data confidentiality perspective, it is important to retain the following thought.

- The DELETE and FORMAT commands do not remove data from hard disks. The FDISK command makes it somewhat more difficult for knowledgeable, competent, and experienced forensics examiners, but not necessarily impossible unless one does low-level formatting, which is not usually a manufacturer-provided option to disk owners.

- Most modern hard disks automatically assign new physical sectors to replace marginal ones without informing the disk user. When doing so, the data in the physical sector that has been mothballed remain in it for the benefit of forensics examiners using software such as Tiramisu.

  ○ Tiramisu can also read drives with no good boot sector, no good FAT, and no good file directory. It can nondestructively read lost directories and copy them to a virtual drive in RAM memory. It also can put fragments found together. Versions exist for DOS, 16-bit Windows, FAT32, NTFS, and even Novell.

  ○ Stellar (http://www.stellarinfo.com) is another excellent piece of software, this one made in India, that can be used for forensics and data recovery and can handle hard disks that seemed 'destroyed' as far as conventional software is concerned.

  ○ REPO2000 is yet another good piece of software that can recover data even from damaged hard disks as long as the master boot record is intact. It can handle FAT12 (floppies), FAT16 (DOS, Windows 95A and NT4), FAT32

(Windows 95B and Windows 98 and Windows 2000) and NTFS (Windows NT and Windows 2000).

- Data can 'hide' in the space between end-of-file and end-of-cluster, in the space occupied by ostensibly deleted files, in decommissioned sectors as per above, and, of course, in actual files that were never wiped because the user forgot to or did not know that they existed.

Unless you are a specialist on all the ins and outs of Windows as well as of all of the applications software that is in your computer, chances are that a determined and competent forensics analysis of your hard disk will uncover information that you had hoped had long been laundered clean. ENCASE (by http://www. guidancesoftware.com) is the forensics package used by most (though not all) US law enforcement groups at the State and local levels. It sells for about $2000 and training classes in its use are offered all the time in the USA as well in the United Kingdom.

4.3 Starting Clean

This describes how to start (or restart) with a computer that has nothing even remotely incriminating in it. Difficult as it may be, this is the easy part.

The difficult part is to decide if that is what is really best for your particular situation and the threats you are concerned with. It may well be better for you, for example, to be at least on record of having bought a used computer (or at least a used hard disk) so that you can credibly claim that many files (that may be found by a forensics investigator) were placed there by the previous owner of that hard disk and not by you. Unless you know exactly what you are doing, however, blaming your own files on a previous user is not that easy because many such files and/or their attributes are date/time stamped; unless you know how to manipulate those dates and times, you may dig a bigger legal hole for yourself.

This chapter assumes a worst-case scenario, namely, of a freedom fighter using a computer in a repressive totalitarian regime. You might dismiss this as being too far removed from your own reality, but do not be too quick. A typical divorce lawyer can subpoena your hard disk; a few adult image files found can be presented by a skillful opposition attorney as showing a 'wanton pattern of emotional alienation from his family, proclivities towards pornographic imagery that would clearly make him unsuitable to retain custody of the children,' and so on. Similarly, snippets of text lifted out of context from your hard disk can be used by a skillful opposition attorney to sway an unsophisticated jury of just about anything; for example, evidence of seeking a job and of being a volunteer worker in a youth organization can be presented as 'he is jobless and hangs around with kids'.

Walk into a store and buy a computer you like. Do not let the store 'customize it' nor 'set it up' for you. Buy it, and take it with you right then and there. Do not buy by mail order if there is the possibility that your order can be intercepted by the totalitarian regime you may live in and cause the computer your receive to be pre-bugged. If you cannot pay cash for it or if you have unwisely managed to get yourself on a regime's list of individuals it keeps an eye on, have someone else buy it for you on their credit card, and have them give it to you as a present on the day the local regime holds sacred, such as the local independence day, 'day of our glorious leader', or whatever. As with hardware, so with software to the extent possible.

Buy additional RAM memory for the computer to bring it up to no less than 256 MB so that you can completely disable the SWAP/Paging file (see Section 4.3.2) and its serious security implications. Forget about Windows 3.1x/95/98; they are hopelessly insecure. Make sure the computer you buy has Windows NT or Windows 2000 installed in it already and has all the requisite 'drivers' for it (meaning, the software that allows the operating system to access your screen, your sound card, the modem, etc.).

Since Windows installation is customized to each user (meaning that each user is expected to enter their respective names during installation), make sure you do *not* enter yours when the time comes. Enter something like 'Mr Good User' or some such, along with fictitious other information wherever asked. The reason is that most software you subsequently install will read that data you entered (name, etc.) from the registry where it is saved in numerous places and will most likely send that information behind your back through the Internet to their respective databases.

After installing Windows NT or 2000, make sure you do all of the following:

1. Require that Alt–Control–Delete must be manually pushed before you can 'log in'.

2. In the case of NT, rename the administrator account to anything you like that is not guessable by anyone else.

3. In both NT and 2000, create a second user profile and give it limited user privileges. Use *that* account all of the time, and not the administrator account, especially if online; the reason is that most hacking software and remote attacks will be limited to the limited privileges of the 'user' and not have the unlimited privileges of the administrator.

4. Make unobtrusive markings to the screws that hold the computer together, to the cables, and to the connectors (keyboard, monitor, etc.), and to the keyboard, and document someplace what these unobtrusive markings are. Keep that document in a safe place. This is so that you can detect if your hardware is ever compromised in your absence (see Section 4.11). If it is, do not panic (see Section 4.11.3).

5. Convert to NTFS using the command

    convert C : /fs : ntfs

    If converting a drive other than C:, put the appropriate letter.

6. Consider seriously using entire disk enryption (see Section 4.12). It is your only powerful protection against physical computer forensics (meaning, someone getting hold of your hard disk), but it does not protect from hardware keytroke interception (hence item 4 above) nor when you are online (hence the strong admonition never to connect the 'good' computer online but to have a cheap second computer that has nothing even remotely exploitable in it and that you use only for connecting online).

7. Disable virtual memory (SWAP/Paging file) altogether (see Section 4.3.2), assuming you have at least 256 MB of RAM. If you absolutely have to have virtual memory because your work involves image processing of large files, at least make it a fixed amount – rather than letting Windows determine the amount – and also specify that Windows is to wipe the swap file at shutdown every time as follows:

    (a) Use Regedit and go to HKEY_LOCAL_MACHINES\System\Current ControlSet\Control\Session Manager\Memory Management

    (b) Find ClearPageFileAtShutdown REG_DWORD

    (c) Set it to 1

    For the case of Windows 95/98/Me, see the specific step-by-step instructions in Appendix C.

8. Go to an electronics store and buy a handful of clamp-on ferrite cores and wrap a few turns of each and every cable leaving you computer (power cable,

monitor cable, keyboard cable, mouse cable, modem cable, printer cable, etc.): ideally, one at each end and one in the middle.

9. Get a good surge protector and uninterruptible power supply (UPS). No, this is not just for the run-of-the-mill protection of the computer. It is for sound security reasons: crashes cause sensitive data that you may have planned to wipe to end up in hard disks, causes bad hard disk sectors to occur and to be marked as 'off-limits' to your disk-wiping software (see Section 4.4) *along with the sensitive data inside them*, and related security problems. Given that UPS batteries tend to become useless after a year or two, find a local electronic store that carries such batteries and buy a couple. It is scandalous that computer stores and UPS manufacturers – and even mailorder stores – do not sell those batteries but seem to expect the hapless user to buy an entire new UPS every year or two just because the battery needs changing.

10. Do not, under any circumstances ever register online, despite the strong pressure tactics of vendors of operating systems and software. No ifs, buts, or howevers. If the software gives you no option to not register, opt for a mailed registration; this will cause the printer to print one out and you should shred it (you do have a shredder, right?) and trash it.

11. Install all of the security updates and patches to the operating system you have. To its credit, Microsoft has made this relatively easy to track by going to http://www.microsoft.com/technet/security/notify.asp and subscribing to its free notification service. I strongly advised you *not* to install Microsoft Office SR-1 or subsequent upgrades to Office 2000, because they require you to contact Microsoft to get an activation key. See Section 4.6 on this security problem. I advise against installing Windows XP or Office XP for the same reason.

12. Install the various software you want. Again, given how low the cost of computers is these days and how unpleasant and expensive (and life-ruining) a run-in with a local oppressive regime can be, do not give in to the temptation *ever* to connect your 'good' computer online; use a cheap one with nothing inappropriate in it for just that purpose.

13. Install the many security updates to the software above.

14. If using NT, disable the task scheduler MSTask by renaming it. Details are provided at http://www.securityfocus.com/templates/archive.pike?list=1&msg =3.0.3.32.20001216120830.006b6e20@mail.sover.net

15. Disable Scrap Files (see also Section 4.13.1 on SHS and SHB):

    (a) Start/Settings/Folder Option

    (b) Select View tab.

    (c) Disable 'Hide Extensions for known file names' option.

    (d) Use Regedit to find the value 'NeverShowExt' and rename it to 'Always-ShowExt'.

16. Install means for making full backups and for storing these backups out of the reach of uninvited guests.

17. Install a RAM disk (i.e., specify that a portion of your RAM memory, say, 1.4 MB out of 256 MB) will pretend to be a disk that you can write to with the assurance that all of that data will vanish when the power is turned off (as long as you do not have a SWAP/Paging file enabled and as long as your software does not create temporary files on the physical hard disk).

18. Remove any association with Visual Basic Script Files:

    (a) Go under 'File Types' and delete VBS (virtual basic script) from the registered list.

    (b) Any **.vbs** file you can find, rename it so that it cannot be run.

19. Disable windows scripting host:

    (a) Start/Settings/Control panel

    (b) Click on Add/Remove Programs

    (c) Select Windows Setup

    (d) Double click on Accessories

    (e) Ensure that 'windows scripting host' is disabled.

20. Disable unused features. In particular NETBIOS; see Section 5.10.

21. Install and properly configure a number of security software now, as per Section 4.3.1.

22. For the computer that goes online, follow the recommendations in section Chapter 5.

4.3.1   Security software[3]

It is emphasized that, as with any tool, and especially in connection with security-related tools, what tools you have is insignificant in impact compared with knowing how to use them. Each of the tools listed below takes a considerable amount of time to learn to use effectively and securely. Familiarize yourself well with each before bothering to go to the next one.

Even though some tools listed below have overlapping functions, it is still recommended that you get and use them all. The reason is that you really cannot fully trust any one item of software (e.g., to do disk wiping), when it is a good idea to use at least two different tools in sequence.

For a computer that never goes online

- ZapEmpty: a DOS-based free disk-wiping utility to be used before installing Windows; from http://www.sky.net/~voyageur/wipeutil.htm.

- Scramdisk: excellent free software for making encrypted partitions on your hard disk; from http://www.scramdisk.clara.net.

- BestCrypt, version 6: a very good competitor to Scramdisk; from http://www.jetico.com. It has an undocumented feature that allows you to have a hidden encrypted container inside the normal encrypted container; this way you can have some mundane files in the normal encrypted container to justify

---

[3] Here, again, good judgment has to be used. Sure, you can make your computer something akin to a fortress. But can you explain to a suspicious visitor from the local Ministry of Conformity (or police, or State Security, or whatever it is called at your place) as to why you have done all this 'if you have nothing to hide'? You should seriously consider having a believable and well-supported answer to this question that will not antagonize the local oppressive regime. Options could be, for example, 'I am teaching information security at the local womens' club and have to research what I teach', or 'I am employed in this line of work and I live my work', or 'this is a hobby of mine as evidenced by my technical publication in the thus-and-so magazine', and so on.

its existence if questioned, plus the real files of interest to you in a hidden container.[4] It includes a disk-wiping function (See Section 4.4).

- Evidence Eliminator: a controversial disk-wiping utility;[5] from http://www. evidence-eliminator.com.

- Scorch, and Scour: free utilities for wiping the SWAP/Paging file; from http:// www.bonaventura.free-online.co.uk/. See Appendix C for a specific step-by-step procedure for using Scorch effectively.

- Secure Clean: to wipe a hard disk; from http://www.accessdata.com.

- Eraser: an excellent free disk-wiping utility; from http://www.tolvanen.com/ eraser/.

- ACDSee: to view files; from http://go.acdnet.com.

- Encase: to check that your hard disk has been cleaned (to the limited extent that one can do that); from http://www.guidancesoftware.com.

For a computer that goes online to the Internet or any other network

For a computer that goes online to the Internet or to any other network, install the following security-related software in addition to the ones for a computer that never goes online (described above).

- ZoneAlarm Pro: excellent firewall; from http://www.zonelabs.com. I advise against using the free (non-Pro) version as it leaves port 113 open Knowledge Systems'. Set it up for the highest security levels allowed. Configure it to disallow *any* software acting as an Internet server.

---

[4] The procedure, thanks to 'Dr Who', is quite tedious for setting it up but well worth it.

[5] The controversy results from the admonition in the documentation that came with that software that states: 'If stolen or banned keycodes are entered, the program may silently and without warning at any time cease to perform as advertised even though it may appear to be working correctly'. The problem with this is that if a legitimate user inadvertently mistypes the legitimate keycode and happens to enter the wrong one, then (according to the software's own brochure) the program may fool the legitimate user into thinking that it works. If true, this would be totally unacceptable, and this software is not recommended.

- Norton Antivirus: a very good antivirus software; from http://www.symantec. com. You may want to get the 'package' that includes the Norton firewall, as it is compatible with and works harmoniously with Zone Alarm Pro above. Check for and install updates at least weekly.

- Subscription to the anonymity services of www.cotse.com or to those of http:// anon.inf.tu-dresden.de

- Junkbuster: an ad-filtering and privacy-enhancing adjunct to web browsing working harmoniously with Freedom 2; from http://www.junkbuster.com.

- PGP: for high-grade encryption of e-mail. It can also be used inside a Freedom 2 message for additional privacy. I recommend version 6.02CKT,[6] release 7 (see Section 5.8.4).

- Quicksilver: free software for advanced anonymous encrypted e-mail and Usenet posting through Mixmaster re-mailers; from http://quicksilver.skuz.net/ (see Section 5.4).

- JBN2: (Jack B Nymble), and Private Idaho: competing free software for advanced anonymous encrypted e-mail and Usenet posting. JBN is excellent but not for the novice. Private Idaho is also very good but seems to have some annoying quirks. JBN is available from http://www.skuz.net/potatoware/jbn/ index.html; Private Idaho is available from http://www.skuz.net/Thanatop/ down.htm.

- Forte Agent: for Usenet and even e-mail. Positively do not use a Web browser for either Usenet or e-mail; from http://www.forteinc.com.

- SecureCRT: to be used in conjunction with Freedom 2 for enhanced anonymity and privacy when reading from and posting to Usenet; from http://www. vandyke.com. This combination is an alternative to the use of Quicksilver above (see Sections 5.3.4 and 5.6.2).

---

[6] In mid-July 2001, CKT versions of PGP abruptly stopped being available at their developer's site (http://www.ipgpp.com). They do exist, of course, and can be found through a search on the Internet. One source for PGP6.5.8CKT, for example, is ftp://ftp.zedz.net/pub/crypto/incoming/. The versions with the 's' suffix have the source code for anyone wishing to inspect it and compile it, whereas the ones without that suffix have the executable code one can run.

4.3.2 Controlling memory bleed: Swap file and RAM-disk setting

Fixing the Swap file security problem

The swap file (also known as the 'paging file' or 'virtual memory') is a major source of forensic information for a computer investigator. To an individual interested in maintaining the privacy of his or her computer files (e.g., an attorney with clients' privileged files, a physician with patients' confidential medical data, a businessperson on a trip with a laptop containing his or her company's proprietary designs, etc.) it is a relatively easy threat to remove, although most users are only vaguely aware of it.

Basically, the swap file is a large space on one's hard disk (typically a few hundred megabytes; (i.e., a few hundred million alphabetical letters' worth) where Windows places anything that currently resides in RAM memory (the electronic memory that 'evaporates' when the power is turned off, as opposed to disk memory, which stays) that Windows does not need at any particular instant, so as to make room in memory for other data that are needed at that same instant. An instant later, different data may be needed in memory, and Windows will juggle what is in RAM and in the swap disk file so that it has in RAM memory what it needs at any one instant in time. This way, a user with limited physical memory (RAM) can 'run' more with less such memory.

From the perspective of the security-conscious reader, this file is an unmitigated disaster because it can end up including just about anything, such as passwords typed on a keyboard and never intended to be stored on disk, copies of sensitive files, etc. Even if a user securely deletes all evidence of a sensitive file (see Appendix C) the swap file – if not specifically 'wiped' – may well contain a copy of that same file or portions of it.

The amount of space allocated to the swap file on a disk is determined by Windows itself (in the default situation), but can be altered by the individual user. One would reasonably think that the more physical RAM memory one has, the less swap file size is needed; amusingly, Windows feels otherwise and assigns more swap file space when one has more RAM.

One can specify exactly how much swap file size one wishes to have (if any). Go to Start/Settings/Control Panel/System/Performance/Virtual Memory and specify what amount one desires to have (if any). One can ignore admonitions by Windows about not allowing Windows to decide this. In general, one would be well advised to have as much RAM memory as possible (at least 128 MB for Win3.1x, at least 256 MB for Win95/98/NT/2000/XP), and to disable completely any virtual memory. Doing so still leaves the hard disk with the last version of the swap file (called win386.swp). This must be securely removed. If one has elected to allow numerous programs to run in the background (e.g., virus checkers, software firewalls, etc.)

then one's RAM requirements can exceed the minimums suggested above; a good way to find just how much RAM one is actually using under normal circumstances is to run a small utility called SWAPMON by Gary Calpo of Flip Tech International, and widely available from the Internet at http://www.pinoyware.com/swapmon/index.shtml.

Even if one elects to have some disk space allocated to the swap file (not a good idea from a security perspective, as per above), it is strongly recommended that this amount be fixed by the user and not by Windows (which is the default setting), despite the admonitions to the contrary by Windows. This is so because it is far easier for security utilities that 'wipe clean' the swap file to do this on a fixed-size swap file than on one whose size changes all the time. The reason for this is obvious: if the size of the swap file is fixed, then 'wiping it' (that is 'overwriting it') is straight forward; if its size changes all the time, then it is quite possible that its last size is smaller than the size at the previous time the computer was used; wiping the smaller sized swap file will leave the evidence contained in the disk space that accommodates the difference between the smaller last swap file and the bigger previous one untouched and available to any forensic investigator.

The procedure for setting a fixed swap file is similar to that shown below for setting no swap file: the user simply selects the same value for minimum and maximum size of the swap file.

Wiping the swap file can be done *only* from DOS and *never* from within Windows. When starting Windows, it opens up the swap file with exclusive access and prevents any other application from accessing it so as to prevent the system from crashing.

Do *not* trust any wiping software that runs under Windows and claims to wipe the swap file; many such programs try to do this by allocating very large amounts of memory and hoping that the operating system will write it to the disk, thereby – it is hoped – overwriting the swap file; this is unacceptably insecure. Some well-written disk-wiping files, however, wipe the swap file well because they 'drop down' to DOS before wiping the swap file. Examples include Secure Clean from Access Data Corporation (2500N University Avenue, Suite 200 Provo, UT 84604, USA; http://www.accessdata.com).

Since no one wiping program can be entirely trusted, a security-conscious user is well advised to use two different such programs in tandem, preferably one of them from within DOS. Possibilities for wiping the swap file from DOS include the following.

- Using a DOS version of pgp. Type:

  pgp–w win386.swp

- Using RealDelete, (available from http://www.bonaventura.free-online.co.uk/ realdelete/). Type:

  realdel [win386.swp]/per/garb

  The brackets are needed to wipe a file as a foreground task, and the additional switches select personal security level – just one overwrite in this case – and a random data overwrite.

- Using Scribble. Type:

  SCRIBBLE/A/K c : \windows\win386.swp

  The /K switch allows the file to remain as an entity after it is wiped clean. Since a swap file is typically a few hundred megabytes long, this wiping will take a few minutes to complete.

- Using Scorch in Windows 95/98. This is both more effective and more involved. Appendix C has a detailed step-by-step procedure for doing this.

Windows NT allows one to delete and overwrite with zeros the swap file automatically as part of a shutdown. According to Microsoft's own Resource Kit, one must edit the registry (type regedit at the 'run' blank space) and go to:[7]

HKEY_LOCAL_MACHINE\System
\CurrentControlSet
\Control
\Session Manager
\Memory Management
ClearPageFileAtShutdown REG_DWORD

---

[7] **Caution:** back up the registry first before doing any editing. How to do so depends on which version of Windows one is using. For Windows 95/98 for example, one can do so with Start/Run **SCANREGW**. In Windows NT, one can do so by creating an emergency backup disk with Start/Run **RDISK /S**.

Range 0 or 1

Default 0

Set it to 1.

Note that Windows NT will *not* overwrite the entire swap file because some of it is being used by NT. To overwrite the entire file one must do so outside Windows (whether NT or any other). This can be done manually or through the use of any one of many disk-wiping software commercially and freely available (see Appendix C).

Do *not* change the size of the swap file by editing the registry. To create a new paging file or to change the size, go to Control Panel/Performance/Virtual Memory/ Change.

As of mid-to-late-2001, a convenient alterantive has been made available to the security-conscious computer user: BestCrypt, version 7, by Jetico (http://www. jetico.com) offers the option to have the entire swap file encrypted on the fly using essentially unbreakable encryption (256 bit Rijandel, for example, Figure 4.3). This is highly recommended for all users.

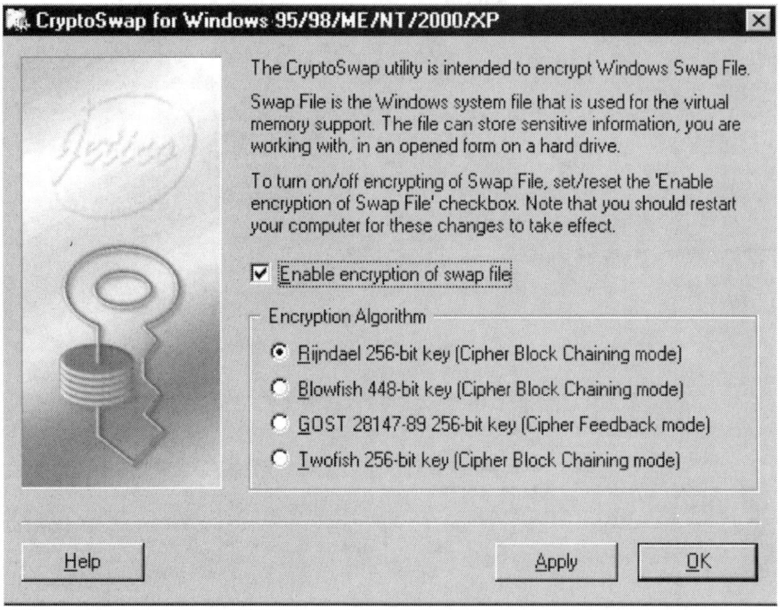

Figure 4.3 Background swap file encryption from BestCrypt, version 7

Making a RAM-disk

A RAM-disk is RAM pretending to be a disk. This way you read from and write to this nonexistant disk. The security benefit is that, unlike a disk, whose contents can haunt you if stolen by an unscrupulous competitor or thief, a RAM-disk's contents 'evaporate' into thin air the moment you turn the power off. It is an ideal 'disk' to use to compose text that you plan to encrypt, so that only the encrypted text will be written onto a real disk.

Creating a 1 MB RAM-disk in DOS and Win95/98 amounts to entering the command

DEVICE=C : \WINDOWS\RAMDRIVE.SYS 1024 /2

in the CONFIG.SYS file using any text editor.

Creating a RAM-disk in WinNT/2000 requires custom software. The best of the bunch in my opinion is Install and use a RAM-disk, such as the one depicted in Figure 4.4, from http://www.jlajoie.com/ramdiskNT. A free trial version is available from that source.

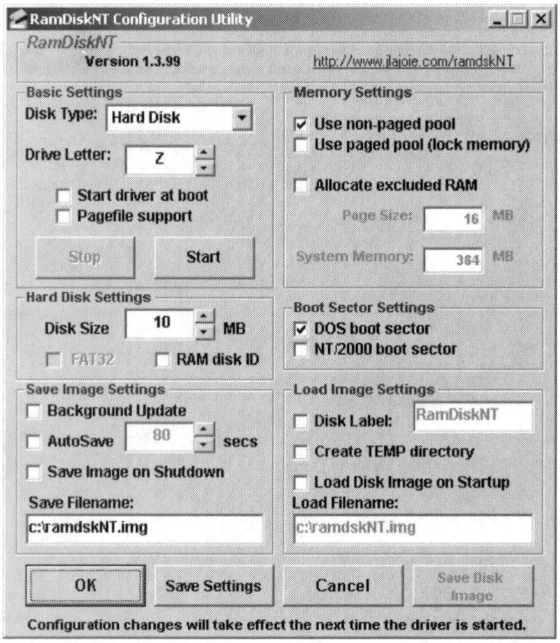

Figure 4.4   RAM-disk for Windows NT/2000; do not enable any of the 'Save image' settings

Do *not* enable the option, shown in Figure 4.4, whereby the RAM-disk is saved onto the physical hard disk just before shutting down; doing so would negate the security benefit of having a RAM-disk in the first place.

Warning: a RAM-disk in Windows is far less secure than a RAM-disk if you have booted from a floppy disk and are using DOS. For real security, forget about Windows and use DOS with no hard disk anywhere in the computer that you use for secure work.

An alternate source for a RAM-disk function is Dynamic RAM drive from Hurricane98 (see http://www.musicgraveyard.com/hurricane98.html).

4.4   Secure Disk Wiping

Contrary to the 'hype' associated with a number of software products available that claim to wipe one's disk, secure disk wiping is a very complex proposition, full of traps for the unaware. This is so because the data that one should want to get rid of include *all* of the following:

1. temporary files created by assorted software and saved under nondescript names, and often as 'hidden' files not normally visible from within Windows Explorer;

2. history and activity files created by assorted software (e.g., netscape.hst in the case of Netscape Navigator/Communicator, assorted .dbx files in the case of Internet Explorer, etc.) that detail some of one's computer activities that relate to the corresponding software; additionally, Windows may mislead you into thinking that a file has been removed when it has not;[8]

3. registry entries that do likewise; (recall that Windows keeps multiple copies of the registry so that editing the last one does not undo the previous ones): securely deleting the previous ones is a dangerous proposition because if the current registry version happens to be corrupt, then the computer will not be able to be booted again until all the software has been reinstalled from scratch – a very unpleasant proposition;

---

[8] Try this: open Explorer and right click on the History folder and delete it. Shut down Explorer, and then reopen it and navigate to the History folder again. Although the icon is no longer there, there is a folder with Content.ie5 and index.dat in it.

4. cached files stored in one's hard disk by web browsers; these files and images, which can get one in legal trouble in many countries, may never have been knowingly solicited by one but were provided by the remote website as part of its advertising-supported revenue scheme;

5. the 'cluster tips', namely, the data between the 'end of file' and 'end of cluster' in one's hard disk; this space is not accessed by the operating system but is very much accessed by forensic and investigative software;

6. the 'free space' of the disk (which contains ostensibly deleted files);

7. the file names of deleted and even securely deleted (wiped) files; these are stored separately from a file in a disk (if one were unwise enough to name one's files with foolish names – even in jest – such as forgery.txt, lethal.doc, etc., those names could come back to haunt one if presented to a humorless jury or judge).

There are other points to bear in mind.

8. One should consider the fact that data stored in RAM from a previous application software (say, a word-processing program), is *not* usually removed from RAM before a new application program writes onto that same region in RAM.[9] The problem occurs when the 'new' application software saves its data from RAM onto the hard disk; data from the previously run software (the word-processing software in this example) ends up on the hard disk. As such, practically everything on RAM at the time when a new application is run becomes part of the data of that new application if the areas in RAM used by the old and the new applications overlap.

9. One should consider the fact that when modern hard disks determine a 'sector' (see Section 4.2) to be marginal, they copy the data from it to one that had been reserved as a 'standby', assign the same logical sector number to the new sector, mothball the old one *without removing the data in it*, and do all this without informing the user.

10. One should consider the fact that Windows uses a swap file in the disk that swaps data between RAM memory and the disk, thereby saving onto disk data that were never intended to be saved (such as passwords and encryption keys). Even if one uses any of the numerous software for 'wiping' the swap file, data

---

[9] This sad state of affairs is the result of the fact that older computers used to be very slow and no execution cycles of the microprocessor were 'wasted' on such niceties as security.

are still leaked all over one's hard disk if one uses the default Windows choice of making the swap file size variable (i.e., determined by Windows itself).

A disk-wiping utility takes care only of items 5 and 6 above, as it has no way of knowing which of the other files (e.g., history files, temporary files, etc.) one wants to keep or not. Some (emphatically not all) also take care of item 7. None take care of threat 9 above, not even a utility from AccessData Corp. (www.accessdata.com) called Cleandrive (WIPEDRV.EXE and CLEANDRV.EXE) which is intended to overwrite each and every portion of a hard disk. To find and overwrite the physical sectors of a hard disk that have been 'mothballed' by the disk would require a detailed technical knowledge of every different manufacturer's ways of implementing this 'intelligent' way of removing sectors from any further consideration. Also, nothing solves problem 8 above as long as the legitimately saved file is kept on the disk. Some custom software (such as Window Washer from http://www.webroot.com) take-care of items 1 and 2. Still different software (such as ComClear from http://www.neuro-tech.net/; Figure 4.5) take care of item 4. Evidence Eliminator does too, but seems only to be able to handle one 'profile' in Netscape. There have been allegations on the Internet that Norton WipeInfo may give a false sense of security.

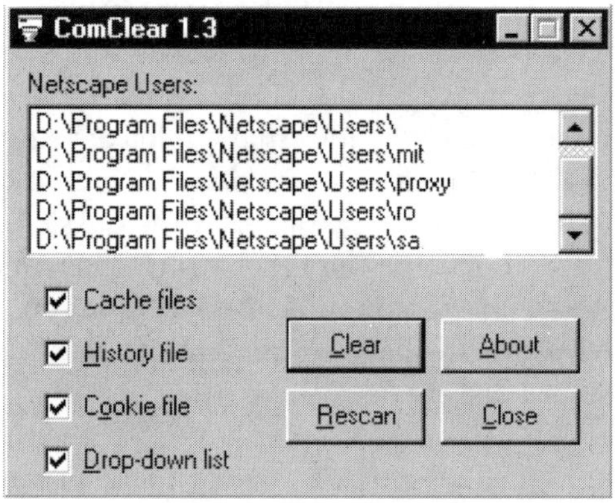

Figure 4.5   ComClear for cleaning up after Netscape

Still different software (such as Evidence Eliminator, from http://www. evidenceeliminator.com) optionally take care of item 3 as well. This software, which in my opinion is reasonably good, seems to have a persistent black cloud hanging over it as a result of repeated allegations in Usenet postings that, if it thinks that the copy being used is a bootlegged one instead of a properly paid one, it allegedly only pretends to wipe some files without doing so in fact. If this allegation is true, it would be enough immediately to disqualify this software from any consideration because of the concern that the software might 'think' it is not paid for when it is, and mislead the legitimate user into a false sense of security.

And, if all of the above complexity were not bad enough, there is a remaining problem that *none* of the disk-wiping software handle at all: the bad disk sector. When a magnetic disk develops one or more flaws on its surface – as all eventually will – the software is smart enough to realize it during a disk scan (done from Start/Programs/Accessories/SystemTools) and marks that sector, *including all of the data that is in it*, as 'off-limits' as if it did not exist any more. Those 'off limits', ostensibly no-longer-existing, sectors can be readily viewed by forensics software.

Formatting a disk does *not* remove the information in its tracks and sectors. Low-level formatting (which creates the invisible magnetic markers on a disk) does, but it is rarely, if ever, included as a user-exercisable option.

In view of all of the foregoing, you have the following choices.

1. If a hard disk has potentially sensitive or proprietary information in it (e.g., a businessperson's corporate plans, or sensitive information that could expose an undercover US drug law enforcement official overseas to traffickers), it should ideally be physically trashed and replaced with a brand new one from the store (never a used one from a swap meet or from another friend). 'Trashing' involves more than throwing it in the trash; it means physically opening the screws of the cover to expose the hard disk, sandpapering and otherwise damaging the magnetic surfaces, and then throwing it away, preferably at a location that will not be searched – actions that could cast suspicions on the user in and by itself. Hard-disk prices are so low these days that cost should not be a consideration any more. The only real issue is the hassle of installing operating systems and software. If one does buy and install a new hard disk, it is *highly* recommended that full-disk encryption be used from that point on; this will basically eliminate the need ever to have to go through this tedious process of securely cleaning one's hard disk again.

2. If one is in the situation where there just is no new hard disk available for purchase where one happens to be, but one does have *all* the software needed to reinstall things from scratch (specifically including system software, software drivers provided by the computer manufacturer for screen, sound, modem, etc., and all application software, encryption and decryption keys if any are used, etc.), then:

    (a) create a huge file of nonsense (it must be huge so that it does not result in many cluster tips being left empty) and copy it a few times over (with different names each time) onto the hard disk until the disk fills up;

(b) wipe it with conventional means (I recommend Eraser 5.0 from http://
www.tolvaren.com/eraser/; note, however, that although Eraser is an excellent disk wiping program it has difficulty handling Scramdisk; if you
have Scramdisk installed, remove it first and then use Eraser 5);

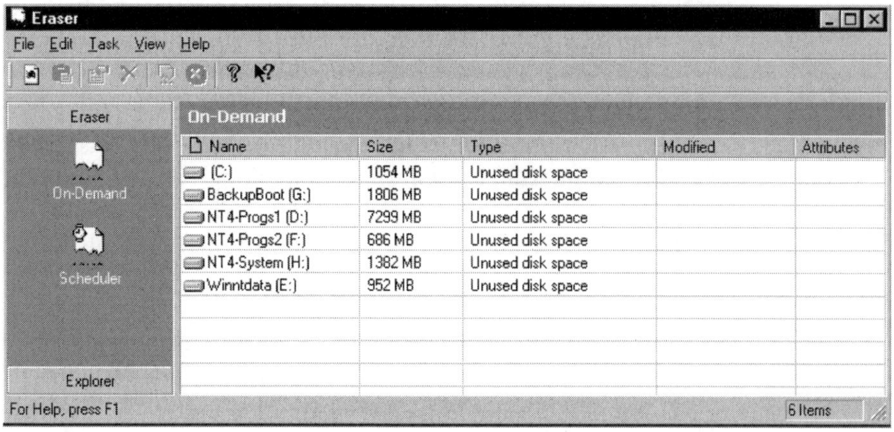

Figure 4.6   Eraser

(c) use the WIPEDRV.EXE $30 utility from Access Data Systems that claims to
wipe an entire hard disk. (It can be obtained from http://www.accessdata.-
com/Product07_Overview.htm?ProductNum=07);

(d) boot from a floppy disk which has the FDISK and FORMAT utilities;

(e) use the FDISK utility and go through the process of partitioning the disk,
creating an active partition, secondary partitions – if any – and, finally,
formatting. *Before* doing so, review the ins and outs of using that utility by
typing 'FDISK /?' (without the quotes) from the command prompt; also
write down the configuration of your soon-to-be-wiped hard disk so that
you can recreate it from scratch; to do so, go to the command prompt, and
type FDISK /STATUS, or boot from a floppy with FDISK, type FDISK and
use the option that allows you to view your settings on your current hard
disk.

3. If the disk in question is a floppy disk, physically destroy it by cutting the
magnetic surface in as many little pieces as possible and flushing them down

the toilet.[10] If one is concerned about the appearance of having physically destroyed floppy disk covers in one's trash do not flush those down the toilet as it will plug it up. One could also use the magnetic bulk erasers sold at stores worldwide and spend a couple of minutes per floppy disk.

4. If one is fairly convinced that the hard disk in question has been 'clean' ever since it was installed and merely wants to make sure that there are no surprises in it, then the following sequence of steps is recommended, in the order shown.

   (a) Use *two separate* utilities in tandem to clean up browser-collected information. Such utilities include ComClear, Window Washer, NSClean, IEClean (if using Internet Explorer; not something I would recommend), etc.

   (b) Install and use the registry-cleaning RegClean.EXE utility available at no charge from Microsoft.

   (c) Use *two separate* utilities in tandem to clean up after the trails left behind by most other software. Such utilities include Window Washer, Evidence Eliminator, and others. In the case of Window Washer make sure you have all the 'plug ins' that correspond to the applications software in your computer. In the case of Evidence Eliminator make sure that you first configure it correctly; it does *not* come preconfigured right out of the box.; for example, you have to tell it where RegClean.exe is if you want it to use that utility – as you should.

   (d) Use a registry cleaning utility from the commercial sector, such as "JV16 Power Tools" from http://www.jv16.org

   (e) Defragment the disk using either the built-in utility in Windows or a faster one made by Executive Software called, not surprisingly, Defragmenter.

   (f) Use the system utility ScanDisk.

   (g) Use *two separate* utilities in tandem to erase your hard disk's 'cluster tips' and 'free space'. Use the excellent Eraser (Figure 4.6), available at no cost from http://www.tolvaren.com/eraser/, and Secure Clean from Access Data

---

[10] There have been statements made on Usenet newsgroups to the effect that, if the individual is under enough scrutiny by a totalitarian regime, it is possible that the sewer system may have been tapped to detect documents being cut up and flushed down the toilet. This seems quite extreme for the vast majority of individuals, though.

Systems (http://www.accessdata.com). This will take a couple of hours at least.

(h) Again defragment the disk as in step (e) above.

(i) Use *two separate* utilities in tandem to wipe the swap file. This can only be done from within DOS. Recommended utilities include Scorch (see Appendix C for details; SwapWipe, from http://www.kagi.com/vfstudio/, which is available at no cost; and Secure Clean, from Access Data Systems). If using Windows NT or Windows 2000, you should already have enabled the option to wipe the swap file on shutdown by carrying out the steps shown at the beginning of Appendix C.

(j) Run the application software Encase (from http://www.guidancesoftware. com) and have it look for whatever you do not want to have anyone else find in the disk. Hopefully, you won't find anything.

In view of the propensity of Windows to create temporary files behind one's back, one may also want to consider creating and running on startup the following batch file in AUTOEXEC.BAT, as recommended by 'Ron' on Usenet on 26 May 2001. It uses the earlier mentioned free software Eraser. To add a batch file to AUTOEXEC.BAT add the line C:\eraser.bat in AUTOEXEC.BAT with any text editor and create a text file with the exact lines below and save it with the name eraser.bat in the C:\directory.

```
if exist %winbootdir%\smartdrv.exe %winbootdir%\smartdrv.exe 2048 16

d:\progra~1\eraser\eraserd -file c:\winzip.log -passes 35

d:\progra~1\eraser\eraserd -file

d:\progra~1\acd\acdsee\imagedb.ddf -passes 35

d:\progra~1\eraser\eraserd -file d:\progra~1\opera\vlink4.dat –passes 35

d:\progra~1\eraser\eraserd -file c:\windows\cookies\index.dat –passes 35

d:\progra~1\eraser\eraserd -file

c:\windows\temp\cookies\index.dat -passes 35

d:\progra~1\eraser\eraserd -folder

c:\windows\history -subfolders -passes 35

d:\progra~1\eraser\eraserd -folder
```

```
c:\windows\temp\history -subfolders -passes 35

d:\progra~1\eraser\eraserd -folder

c:\windows\tempor~1\content.ie5 -subfolders -passes 35

d:\progra~1\eraser\eraserd -folder

c:\windows\tempor~2\content.ie5 -subfolders -passes 35

d:\progra~1\eraser\eraserd -folder

c:\windows\temp\tempor~1\content.ie5 -subfolders -passes 35

d:\progra~1\eraser\eraserd -folder

c:\windows\temp\tempor~2\content.ie5 -subfolders -passes 35

d:\progra~1\eraser\eraserd -file c:\win386.swp

exit
```

This is still not enough to take care of Internet Explorer's propensity to litter your hard disk with data about your web browsing, hence my strong admonition against using Internet Explorer; you need to wipe all the **.dbx** files, or, better yet, place them all in an encrypted partition (see Section 4.10), but this requires considerable tinkering with the registry so that Internet Explorer knows where to look for those files or it will not load.

It is quite evident by now that disk cleaning is not a 'quickie'. It takes concentration and a lot of time to do properly; sloppy cleaning is worse than no cleaning at all as it will give a false sense of security, which is worse than no security. It follows that disk wiping is not the sort of thing that one can do when someone from an oppressive regime is knocking on the door. It has to be done on a regular and continuing basis on the assumption that the knock on the door will come sometime.

Alternatively, one can use full-disk encryption (see Section 4.12), keeping in mind that it protects only against computer forensics when the computer is off; it provides absolutely no protection when the computer is on, and also no protection when the computer is online. One must be extremely careful with 'encrypted partition' software such as Scramdisk, E4M, and BestCrypt. Although they indeed do encrypt what is in the partition, there is a likelihood that – since one is operating within Windows – sensitive data will leak into the swap file for the benefit of the hostile forensics examiner. If one is enamored with the above 'encrypted partition' software, one would be well advised to have enough RAM in the computer (over 256 MB) to be able to disable the virtual memory altogether (see Section 4.3.2) before using such software.

Finally, one should not forget that 'cleaning' is always much harder than not having to clean in the first place, meaning that nothing incriminating should be on one's hard disk to begin with. If one must use a computer to compose a dissertation the local oppressive regime is likely to find unpalatable, it is best to do it in RAM only and to save on disk only the encrypted version. To do this:

1. Have RAM disk enabled (see Section 4.3.2).

2. Have swap file (virtual memory) disabled.

3. Compose text using a dumb text editor. Do not use a Word Processor.

4. 'Save' the completed file onto the RAM disk.

5. Encrypt (e.g., using PGP, whose keys are on a floppy disk).

6. Save only the encrypted file on the hard disk if encryption is allowed wherever one is.

7. Double and triple check that what was saved was indeed only the encrypted file. It is all too easy to be distracted and save the unencrypted file, instead, in its full glory.

4.5 Password Protection is Worthless

Unlike full-blown encryption, the term 'password protection' has come to denote a number of very weak security schemes the intent of which is to protect a document from a minimally competent casual passerby. In short, such schemes are not worth a great deal.

A very reputable Utah-based company, Access Data (http://www.accessdata.com) sells a large number of individual password-breaking modules 'that help you recover lost passwords for almost every product in the industry'. Needless to say, the passwords in question could be for someone else's documents. The modules are sold as part of the company's Password Recovery Tool Kit and can break the passwords of, among others:

Access	MS Money	Quickbooks
ACT!	Organizer	Quicken
Ami Pro	Outlook	Scheduler+
Approach	Paradox	Symphony
Ascend	Pro Write	Versacheck

BestCrypt	WinZip nd & Generic Zippers	Word
DataPerfect	Q&A	Wordperfect
Excel	Quattor Pro	WordPro
FoxBaseLotus 1-2-3		

Additional utilities are sold to bypass network administrator passwords for Windows NT 3.51 and 4.0 file servers and Novell 3.x and 4.x servers in the event of an unknown supervisor password.

Access Data guarantees its password modules on a money-back basis if they fail to let one get into a password-protected file. It also offers 'in-house' services for $35–$50 per file whereby one can send the company the password-protected file to break it; again, no charge if the company is not successful.

For fun, they even show how to break Quicken 3.0 and Money 2.0 passwords (see Box 4.1).

Box 4.1 Free password breakers, from Access Data

QUICKEN 3.0

Quicken stores the data in *.QDT files. The default is QDATA.QDT. You can password protect either the File or the Transaction. The password protected transaction prevents you from changing or deleting any transactions prior to a certain date. This generally does not affect our analysis, but the file password prevents us from accessing the file through Quicken. The simple fix is using a copy of the *.QDT file (NEVER TRY IT ON THE ORIGINAL). Use your favorite editor and zero out the offsets 445, 446, 447 (Change whatever hex value is there to '00 00 00'). Now go back to your copy of Quicken and the password should be gone.

DIRECT ACCESS

Direct Access tells me that by deleting the MENU.CNF file, all passwords (as well as color setup) will be deleted, however the menu will be intact.

MONEY 2.0

The Back Door – Recovery of Microsoft Money 2.0 passwords.

While most password protection schemes Access Data encounters require a great deal of complex analysis to break, some password schemes are easily broken with nothing more than a pencil, paper, a good hex editor, and a little bit of creativity. MS Money 2.0 is an example of the latter type.

> *To recover an MS Money 2.0 password open the data file (the file with the MNY extension) with a disk editor like Norton Utilities DiskEdit. Move to offset position 444. This value is the number of characters in the password. Starting with offset 445 is the hash of the password. The generation of the hash value is very simple. The password simply XORed with a portion of the string 'Microsoft Barney'. The result is then padded with hex 0xFF to make 16 bytes and stored at offset 445. To recover the original password simply re-XOR the hash value with the string 'Microsoft Barney' for a second time and the password simply falls out.*
>
> *As an example: this is the hex values starting at offset 444 of an MSMONEY.MNY file locked with the password 'ALEXANDER'. Note that the HEX value at offset equals the number of characters in 'ALEXANDER'.*
>
> 09 0C 25 26 2A 2E 3D 2B 23 26 00
>
> *If we start with offset 445 and XOR this string with the Hex representation of the string 'Microsoft Barney' we get a result as following:*
>
> 0C 25 26 2A 2E 3D 2B 23 26
>
> ^4D 69 63 72 6F 73 6F 66 74
>
> 41 4C 45 58 41 4E 44 45 52
>
> *The resulting string is the Hex representation of the password 'ALEXANDER'.*
> Source: Access Data, http://www.accessdata.com

4.6 Office-XP and Windows-XP: Don't![11]

> *Money is at the root of all evil; but without evil there would be no good. You decide.*
>
> Unknown author

---

[11] This admonition is my personal advice. For a different perspective, please see http://www.microsoft.com and navigate to the keyword of interest to you.

Microsoft shouldn't be broken up. It should be shut down.

Bruce Schneier, Cryptogram, 15 May 2000,
http://www.counterpane.com/crypto-gram.html

OSR-1 update of Microsoft Office 2000 introduced a little-noticed security disaster: the fact that individual users' legitimately paid Office 2000 installations have to be 'enabled' after 50 or so uses by contacting Microsoft, which issues an individualized serial number that brands the particular legally owned copy of that software. The details of the activation ritual are provided by 'Fully Licensed GmbH', Rudower Chaussee 29, 12489 Berlin, Germany, at http://www.licenturion.com/xp/.

The first step in activating Windows XP involves providing Microsoft with the installation identification number (ID) obtained and displayd by msoobe.exe, which is the utility that guides a user through the activation process. That number consists of 50 decimal digits that are divided into groups of six digits each. (Interestingly, if msoobe.exe is run more than once, one gets a different installation ID every time.) Microsoft then provides a confirmation ID number that matches the given installation ID, which, when entered, completes the activation process.

The obvious question then is, 'how much information is sent to Microsoft through this "installation ID" and how is it generated?' The installation ID is the encrypted result that is based on the product ID and also the hardware configuration of your particular computer; more specifically, on:

- CPU serial number

- amount of RAM

- CD ROM

- serial number of system volume

- network interface card serial number

- graphics card

- SCSI card

- IDE controller

Clearly, more than one computer can have the same hardware configuration.

Given that, in the past, Microsoft had individually serial numbered each copy of Office 97 to the point where every document created with one's Office 97 included the electronic serial number of the particular copy of Office 97 that created it (a 'feature' that was removed in the early releases of Office 2000), any individual serial numbering or other means of identification of individual copies of any Microsoft product is to be avoided.

Any civilized person respects a vendor's right to be compensated for the intellectual property being offered for sale; this writer specifically does not condone theft of software. The approach taken by Microsoft has failed in this endeavor as evidenced by the unfortunate fact that unlicensed copies of XP are reportedly being sold for a couple of dollars in the Far East (http://www.zdnet.com/zdnn/stories/news/0,4586,5099511,00.html).

The approach taken by Microsoft in this case is also, I believe, inappropriate, for the following two reasons. First, Microsoft's argument that this is a means for preventing unpaid copies is perhaps interesting but to a user of fully paid Microsoft products it is Microsoft's problem and should not become the legitimate user's problem. The so-called solution that Microsoft has come up with affects legitimate users of such software adversely: when (not if) your computer crashes and you have to reinstall the software, or you sell the computer and buy another one and, a year or so later, buy yet another one, you will *not* be able to use your fully paid Microsoft software until you have contacted Microsoft and convinced them that you really are not a thief. Try doing this from a remote overseas site with a poor telephone connection at, say, $10 per minute for the call every time this happens.

Second, with Office XP and Windows XP, Microsoft will, reportedly, sell software on a subscription basis, ostensibly to combat unpaid copies but in reality, I would suggest, to increase its revenue. Already available worldwide on the Internet is a 'recipe' posted by a British online news company that asserts that it shows how to defeat the Microsoft protective scheme. I do not condone this, but the truth of the matter is that large-scale distributors of illegally duplicated software are highly likely to avail themselves of this and related future schemes to counterfeit software, whereas individual users are mostly unlikely to do so. It follows that the Microsoft scheme will, therefore, not reduce the real problem (wholesale illegal duplication of its software). One then wonders what the scheme is really intended to achieve. One logical inference, I suggest, is that it is intended to amass a large database of which individual user is using which particular legally purchased copy of such software; if so, this would be a privacy threat that individual users may wish to keep in mind.

Having any software on a subscription basis is unacceptable from a security viewpoint and is to be avoided simply because it allows the software-maker access to too much information about who has which serialized copy of legally purchased software. Given the volume of traffic that will result from serialized subscriptions, Microsoft will almost certainly have to do this over the Internet, which makes it technically possible for much *more* information to leave your computer without your knowledge.

Even from a purely financial perspective, numerous users (e.g., the Netwerk Gebruikersgroep Nederland, that unites 3700 IT professionals in the Netherlands, and others) have criticized Microsoft's new licensing scheme, which amounts to a forced upgrade every 18 months vis-à-vis the common four-year upgrade cycle.

Furthermore, even from a purely technical perspective, 'Windows XP Will Make Internet Unstable', according to top security expert Steve Gibson. (http://www. theregister.co.uk/content/4/19332.htm). This is because all Windows up to Windows 2000 would not allow someone to 'spoof' the source of Internet packets (by comparison, Unix-based computers always could).

It is therefore recommended that you:

- stay with Office 95 or 97, but make sure you apply the patch available from Microsoft that disables the individual serial number for them, or

- stay with Office 2000 but not using OSR-1 or any later 'upgrade'.

In either case, do not 'upgrade' or use Windows-XP or Office-XP unless they are released on a standard nonsubscription basis. Also, do not get *any* other subscription-based software from any vendor, with the possible exception of reputable antivirus software, which by their very nature require weekly updates online.

On a related note, some have found that Microsoft's Windows (XP) sometimes cripples open source software (OSS), including earlier versions of PGP (see Section 5.8.4). I quote *Information Age*, April 2001, without comment:

Gates feels more threatened than ever by anarchic software developers who seem happy to share their work for little more than prestige. This was clearly conceded by Microsoft in the now infamous 'Halloween documents', a series of memos sent to Bill Gates by two of his senior staff.

'OSS [open source software] poses a direct, short-term revenue and platform threat to Microsoft, particularly in the server space. Additionally, the intrinsic parallelism and free idea exchange in OSS has benefits that are not replicable with our current licensing model and therefore present a long term developer mind share threat', they wrote.

Their recommendations on how to deal with this threat involve 'decommoditising' common open protocols and applications. 'By extending these protocols and developing new protocols, we can deny OSS projects entry into the market', concludes the document.

In addition to all of the foregoing, Office XP acts with absolute assurance as if it knows better than you what you want. Using Office XP's 'Word', if you are using

Outlook (not a good idea for security reasons because of the plethora of viruses that have exploited Outlook and Outlook Express), type the unusual looking link

$$http://www.fred.com/trial//2345$$

where the double slash is intentional. If you hover the cursor over this link, it will show a single slash; if you edit it back to a double slash, Office XP will change it back to a single slash!

In addition to the above, Microsoft had plans to include 'smart tags' in Windows XP; these 'smart tags' would direct users to Microsoft's favored websites, according to the *Wall Street Journal* of 27 June 2001. This idea has been shelved for the time being as a result of massive criticism. Jim Allchin, Microsoft's group vice-president in charge of Windows and the Web browser said that he made the decision to eliminate 'smart tags' because 'we got way more feedback than we ever expected' and that 'we hadn't balanced the legitimate concerns of the content providers with the benefits we think Smart Tags can bring to users'. (*MSNBC*, 28 June 2001).

In yet another strike against Microsoft's XP, US Senator Charles Schumer (Democrat, New York) released on 24 July 2001 a long list of complaints over antitrust issues involving Windows XP and asked the Justice Department to include discussions on XP in its settlement talks with Microsoft that began mid-July 2001. (see http://newsbytes.com/news/01/168286.html).

Along related lines, numerous privacy groups sent a letter to Federal Trade Committee (FTC) Chairman Timothy Muris and to congressional oversight committee members to convince them to take action against Microsoft. The letter asserts that Microsoft's 'passport' authentication service, which is bundled with Windows XP, violates Section 5 of the FTC Act, prohibiting unfair and deceptive practices. Specifically, the concern is about how personal information will be stored and used in view of Microsoft's less than stellar record in security. [For more information, see http://junkbusters.com/new.html, http://www.newsbytes.com/news/01/172050.html, and http://www.att.net/~distanceed/privacy.htm.]

Even (temporarily) overlooking the problems with Windows XP discussed above, Windows XP 'out of the box' has most of its security features turned off; unless the buyer takes the time and has the know-how to activate them, that buyer ends up with a very insecure system. Specifically:

- It automaticallty comes with an 'administrator' account that has no password!

- During setup, one is asked for the names of the users of the computer. It then creates such accounts with, again, no passwords!

- The built-in mini-firewall is not nearly as potent as established software firewalls such as Zone Alarm Pro (http://www.zonelabs.com) or PC Conceal (http://www.consealfirewall.com and http://www.signal9.com). For one thing, it is not turned on as a default and one must search through 'Help' for the somewhat obscure steps for activating it.

In addition, a 'feature' introduced in Microsoft's Windows XP requires users to establish an account with Microsoft 'Passport authentication service' to use the new instant messaging and telephony features (see http://news.cnet.com/news/0-1003-200-6343275.html), thereby further violating a user's privacy. 'There are very real consumer issues with Passport, HailStorm and Net taking away consumer choice',[12] according to John Buckley, a corporate vice-president for AOL Time Warner, in the same article referenced above. ProComp, (Washington, DC), a trade group, issued a 61-page paper contending that 'Windows XP is designed to force adoption of Microsoft's Web services' (see http://news.cnet.com/news/0-1003-200-6343275.html or http://business.itspace. com/policy/wp_passport2.asp; for the full text of the paper see http://www.procompetition.org/headlines/ WhitePaper6_21.pdf). Passport sign up may not be included in the installation of the October 2001 release of Windows XP.

In October 2001, the US Department of Energy's CIAC (Computer Incident Advisory Capability, http://www.ciac.org) issued a warning about XP (see http:// www.ciac.org/ciac/bulletins/m-004.shtml or http://www.newsbytes.com/news/01/ 171293.html). Finally, in mid-October 2001 it was revealed (http://techupdate. zdnet.com/techupdate/stories/main/0,14179,2818129,00.html) that Microsoft.com error reveals IDs and passwords for passport users who sign on to Microsoft.com. Passport is an integral part of XP.

4.7   Microphones and Cameras in your Computer

Most laptops come with built-in microphones; some even come with built-in cameras, and those that do not can accommodate an external one just like one can (and often does) connect a microphone and/or camera to a desktop computer.

---

[12] '.Net is considered to be a strategy for Microsoft selling software over the Internet as a service or on a subscription basis. Passport is envisioned by Microsoft to be a gateway into numerous services (may for a fee_ that Microsoft will deliver to third-party service providers. HailStorm is the first ".Net" building block and it relies heavily on Passport.' (John Buchley;).

Since the operation of cameras and microphones is software-controlled and since others can doctor your software unbeknownst to you either directly or through the Internet (or any other network), it is strongly recommended that you disable the camera and the microphone until such time you specifically want to use them (e.g., to use the microphone to communicate by fully encrypted voice using Speak Freely; see Section 6.5.1).

1. To disable the camera, merely put some black tape over it; make sure it does not have its own built-in microphone.

2. To disable an external microphone, unplug it.

3. To disable an internal microphone in a laptop takes some easy trickery:

    (a) Fool the laptop into thinking you have an external microphone, instead, by plugging the appropriate plug in the laptop jack that corresponds to an external microphone. You can easily get such a plug from any electronics store; in fact, it is just as inexpensive to get a cheap microphone with the right plug, in which case you should simply cut the cable leaving the plug.

    (b) Short out the two places to which a microphone cable would normally have been soldered. If you get a cheap microphone, cut the wire and short out the two conductors: the braided external shield and the center conductor.

    (c) Test the result by using some software that records voice and make sure that no sound is recorded even if you shout loudly.

    (d) Make a habit of having such a microphone-disabling plug in place whenever you use your laptop.

A microphone in a laptop is particularly insidious. It can record for many hours and store the recorded sound on hard disk, or it can relay it 'live' online to whomever has configured your computer to do so.

4.8 Windows Knows Your Name

Indeed it does, because you foolishly volunteered it when you installed Windows (or any other software bought since). That ended up in the registry at:

HKCU\Software\Microsoft\MS Setup (ACME)\User Info\

HKLM\Software\Microsoft\Windows\CurrentVersion\RegisteredOwner

HKLM\Software\Microsoft\Windows\CurrentVersion\RegisteredOrganization

Getting it out is not easy because numerous software packages that you installed afterwards took it on themselves to look up your name in the above registry entries and to copy it over to their entries in the registry. So, your name is now all over the place. Worse yet, given that remote sites you connect to can usually look at anything they like inside your computer (unless you take the specific defensive steps shown in this book), your name and anything else you have volunteered to Windows and/or to other software is a commodity that others far away have availed themselves of.

The cleanest fix is to 'bite the bullet' and 'start clean' (see Section 4.3) and reinstall everything from scratch, but properly this time. Yes, it is tedious and you may well have lost a number of 'key codes' that 'enabled' shareware or other software that you may have bought online.

A poor 'second' choice is to:

1. Run REGEDIT.

2. Edit/Find your name (look for the first few letters of it), your company name, etc.

3. Change them to something else. Be careful here; some software purchased online that use the 'activating code' scheme to convert from free trial to paid mode have a serial number that is derived from the name that you registered the software under, and if you change *that* name in the registry for *that* software, then *that* software will no longer work in the paid mode.

4. Realize that any editing changes you make in the registry *do not*, in fact, remove what you edited out. The registry is edited to show that it was changed from the old to the new, and the old still remains there for the benefit of any computer forensics investigator.

5. Exit REGEDIT.

6. Run RegClean (you can download Regclean.exe from Microsoft).

7. If using Win95/98, run SCANREGW a few times.

8. Reboot your computer a few times so that all backup copies of the registry get replaced by the new one that you just edited *and* subsequently cleaned with RegClean. This is so because Windows keeps a number of them just in case the last one or two become contaminated and your computer would have otherwise refused to even boot.

Also, run regedit and do a search for your name, and try X-Setup from http:// www.xteq.com.

4.8.1 Microsoft Word knows and stores your thoughts?

When we draft and save a document using Microsoft Word, most of us go through a number of updates before the final version. Unless you have modified a 'default' setting in Microsoft Word, what you have actually saved includes the original version and all subsequent changes. Although this is not evident in what gets printed, this record of all previous versions can be retrieved by anyone to whom you either e-mail or hand it out to in a diskette. This can be quite embarrassing if the original version of what now says 'My dear Mrs Smith' started out as 'You miserable witch'. It can also be quite devastating to a businessperson if the document in question is a cost proposal.

Encryption has nothing to do with it. Even if you had encrypted the final version, the unencrypted version would still contain the history of the revisions of the document.

What you need to do is to go to Tools/Options/Save (in Microsoft Word) and uncheck the 'Allow fast saves' option that is checked by default. This is depicted in Figure 4.7. 'Fast' in this case means to save only the changes to the previous version and to leave the previous version alone.

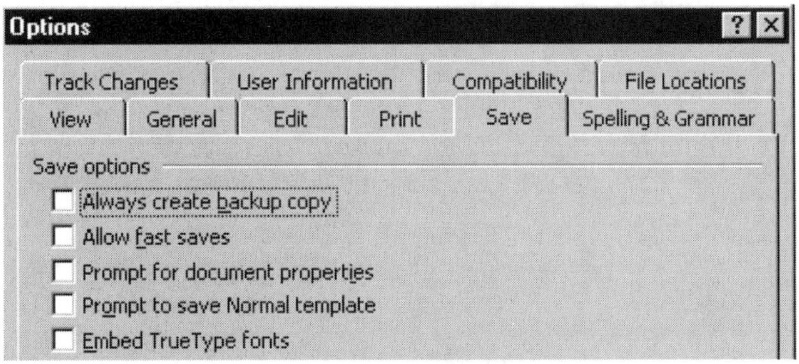

Figure 4.7   Preventing compromises in Microsoft Word

4.9   The Security Problems of Backups

If you wish to find a competing company's crown jewels you should not bother with approaching its chief executive officer or its president. Go for the fellow who runs and maintains its computer network and try to get a backup tape; it will contain *everything*, and it will also fit in your shirt pocket; nobody will miss it, either, if it is an extra backup copy. As with the company's crown jewels, so with yours. Your backups contain everything.

4.9.1   The problem of making effective backups

Your hard disks *will* crash; it is only a question of when. As a bare minimum (not recommended for the reasons below) you should back up all of your data on a regular basis and keep at least two generations of it (i.e., the last two backups). As someone who has had his own hard disks crash as a result of malicious commercial software that overwrote some of my system files with theirs, I had to spend the better part of a few days reinstalling the software. Here is the problem.

- A typical computer has some 30 000–60 000 files in it; this includes DLLs (dynamic link library files), system files, data files, etc., etc. That represents some 100–400 software packages, most of which have had the benefit of assorted 'upgrades' (bug fixes) obtained over the Internet that often had to be installed in the right order to work right. Trying to redo this installation of not just the software but also all the updates (and you do not remember which software had which updates, when, and where from) is an unpleasant proposition that is highly likely to fail partially.

- Most software purchased and downloaded online came with a 'key' that was also e-mailed that you had to enter to make the software work. Unless you kept all of those keys in a file 'just in case', chances are that you will have to do a lot of work to find them – if you can find them at all. If you cannot find them, you will have somehow to convince the seller (if you can find it) that you really did pay for that software at some unknown time in the past using a credit card number that might have changed since then and you do not know anymore, and using an e-mail address which has also changed since them and you do not remember any more.

In short, you are far better off backing up *everything* (executables and all) so that, when your hard disk crashes, you can simply restore everything, including all system files, from a single backup *in a single step*. This is not easy, and, amazingly, not common because you cannot back up many Windows system files while you are *inside* Windows. And if you get outside Windows into DOS, chances are that you cannot save many things either, such as long-name files, NTFS-formatted sectors in Windows NT and Windows 2000, encrypted partitions (e.g., with Scramdisk or other encrypted partition-making software), and so on.

Any of the following solutions are recommended, because they work.

- Get a dedicated piece of hardware, the sole purpose of which is to let one make identical copies of hard disks; these are advertised in computer magazines and are intended for use by small businesses but would also serve the individual. They are quite costly, but he cost is far, far less than the combined cost of your time to try (unsuccessfully) to reinstall everything from scratch, as per above, plus the cost of not having the use of the software that you cannot reinstall for the reasons stated above. Buy a hard disk of identical (or larger) capacity to the one(s) you now have, and periodically copy your hard disk(s) to the backup(s); hard disks are cheap these days. When (not if) your hard disk(s) crash, yawn rather than panic, and install the backup(s).

- Buy another computer to use exclusively for backup-making. I suggest you buy SafeBack from http://www.sydex.com, which is intended as a court-accepted means of making backups of suspects' confiscated or subpoenaed hard disks for forensic analysis, and use that for making your own 'forensically identical' hard-disk backups.

- If you are using a laptop, the same situation and solutions above apply; you will simply need an adaptor from the standard desktop computer hard-disk connector to that of a laptop. They are quite cheap and are available from computer parts vendors. Well worth the minimal investment. If you are using Windows 95/98 you can, instead, use a cute and effective solution, 'Disaster Recovery From Notebooks', from Agate Technologies, at http://www.agatetech.com/products_drs.html that allows you to make a full backup of your laptop's hard disk without even removing it from the laptop; it has a PCMCIA (Personal Computer Memory Card International Association) card adaptor that connects to a housing where you put in a blank hard disk of the same size as the one you want to back up, and the software to make that possible. I have tried it and it works; the only additional step you have to do to make the backup a fully bootable one is a one-time step of booting from a floppy and entering the command

SYS C:

to transfer the system files to the new disk and make it fully bootable. The manufacturer expects to have a version for Windows NT and 2000 soon. Another competing product is ABS+, from CMS Products, at http://www.cmsproducts.com/ which is depicted in Figure 4.8. Although this product is easier and faster to use, it appears to be very finicky with hard disks that are not purchased from CMS Products at a premium price.

Figure 4.8   Laptop backup, by CMS Products, http://www.cmsproducts.com

- Create an altogether separate logical disk drive in your system; buy and install a multi-operating system utility such as System Commander from http://www.v-com.com/product/sc2_ind.html; create a second system installation of your system, say, Windows NT. In that second installation, merely install a means for making backups of other disks in your system. One convenient one comes with any installation of Iomega's Jaz drives. To make a backup of any and all of your disks that you use, specify when you first turn on your computer and system commander asks you which operating system you want to use that time that you want to use the one intended for backups as per above. When there, simply run the backup utility to backup all of your 'real' disks. This will copy everything, *including* the system files (which cannot be done from within Windows) because you are not using the system that you are backing up but another one!

4.9.2   The problems of protecting the security of backups

Quite simply, these backups should be where they cannot be found by anyone other than yourself. You can send them by courier to a *trusted* friend in another country, you can put them inside the coffee can that says 'sugar' on the outside, but, whatever you do, realize that they constitute one of your largest security vulnerabilities, so treat them accordingly. Just do not put them anywhere close to strong magnetic fields (such as inside television cabinets) unless you specifically want them to be erased if you take a deliberate action should the roof cave in – figuratively speaking – which is an option to keep in mind.

If you have been using fully encrypted hard disks inside your computer (see Section 4.12), which is a very good idea to begin with, then the backups may or *may not* be encrypted depending on how they were made. If the backups were made from within Windows of the operating system that would have been encrypted in your hard disk if it had not been 'active', your backups will *not* be encrypted. If the backups were made using a track-for-track and sector-for-sector copy approach using the first two options above, then the backups will be identical copies of the originals; if the originals are encrypted, the backups will be too.

Many companies offer 'online backups of your data for a nominal fee'. In a word, don't! The problem is threefold:

- Under US law, the remotely stored data do not enjoy the same legal protection from unauthorized search and seizure as the data in your premises. This applies more so in countries that have less legal protection for any data stored anywhere. Basically, you will not even know if your remotely stored data are being examined.

- As the data transits to the remote online site, it will be vulnerable to interception unless the connection is fully encrypted [e.g., a secure socket layer (SSL) connection; see Appendix B].

- Even average home users of computers have far too much data to upload for storage online. Even a single 5×7 photo of the baby, in typical 300×300 dots per inch, is a few megabytes that would take forever to upload. Many Internet service providers (ISPs, e.g., the major Cable Modem Service company Cox.rr. com, refuse to allow customer to upload any one file that exceeds even as little as 10 MB).

One viable solution that takes care of the first two problems but not final problem is to pre-encrypt all of the data you upload before you upload it. If you do so make sure that the file names used are nondescript; make triple sure that all of what is uploaded is encrypted before uploading it. Time and again I have received an e-mail which was intended even by sophisticated senders to have been encrypted but was not because of a 'silly mistake'.

4.10 Encrypted Disk Partitions

Rather than bothering to encrypt individual files that are intended for yourself only, it is more convenient to have an 'encrypted virtual disk', in your own computer; in other words, a disk drive letter (say, K:\) where everything in it is encrypted; this way you only need to type a single passphrase to get into anything in that encrypted virtual disk, and not a passphrase for each and every file in it. (Of course, if that passphrase is compromised, then every file in that encrypted virtual disk will be compromised as well; this makes it *extremely* important for you to ensure that your computer does not have a keystroke recorder installed, whether hardware or software; see Section 4.11) nor a camera overhead.

All that someone without the passphrase will see is:

- a large single file (whose size is the size of the encrypted virtual disk partition that you have elected to create) of apparent gibberish;

- depending on which software is used to create and access the virtual encrypted disk, tell-tale files (e.g., .dll's, executables, etc.) that give away the fact that an encrypted partition exists. For obvious reasons, you would not want any such tell-tale files at all in your computer, so that you will not be faced with the possibility of being compelled to decrypt the virtual encrypted disk; instead, you would want any such files to be in a floppy disk that you can carry separately and discretely.

Some of the most common software that allow you to have virtual encrypted disks are:

- BestCrypt
- E4M ('encryption for the masses')
- FlyCrypt
- F-Secure FileCrypto (part of the F-Secure Workstation Suite)
- Invincible Disk with Data Lock
- PGPDisk (not recommended because of continuing compatibility problems with many versions of Windows).
- SAFE Folder
- SafeHouse

- S to Infinity

- McAfee PC Crypto

- ScramDisk

An informative comparison of most of these can be found in the article 'On-The-Fly Encryption: A Comparison', by S. Dean, at http://www.fortunecity.com/skyscraper/true/882/Comparison_OTFCrypto.htm.

4.10.1   Scramdisk

Scramdisk, by a talented British programmer, Shaun Hollingworth, is in my opinion the best of the bunch. The Windows 95/98 version is freely available worldwide from http://www.scramdisk.clara.net/ and its source code has been made available for review and scrutiny. Until October 2001, when Scramdisk was merged with E4M and BestCrypt to form DriveCrypt (see Section 4.10.3), the Windows NT/2000[13] version was available for $20 from:

Shaun Hollingworth

Stoney Corner,

Moat Lane,

Wickersley,

Rotherham S66 1DZ

UK

As with any encryption software, purchase should be anonymous or pseudonymous. This is not a reflection on any vendor's trustworthiness; it is merely good security practice. The vendor has indicated that he is even amenable to being asked – upon receipt of pseudonymous payment – to post the 'enabling key' encrypted on a news server with a pre-agreed encryption key; in this case, you, the recipient, should download a number of posted messages and not only the one of interest.

Scramdisk can use any one of a large number of established reputable encryption algorithms, and it is recommended for other reasons as well (see below). Figure 4.9 depicts the user interface to Scramdisk.

---

[13] My Windows 2000 laptop refused to work with it until I removed SD.SYS and disabled that software; the software author maintains that he has had no such complaints from others, however.

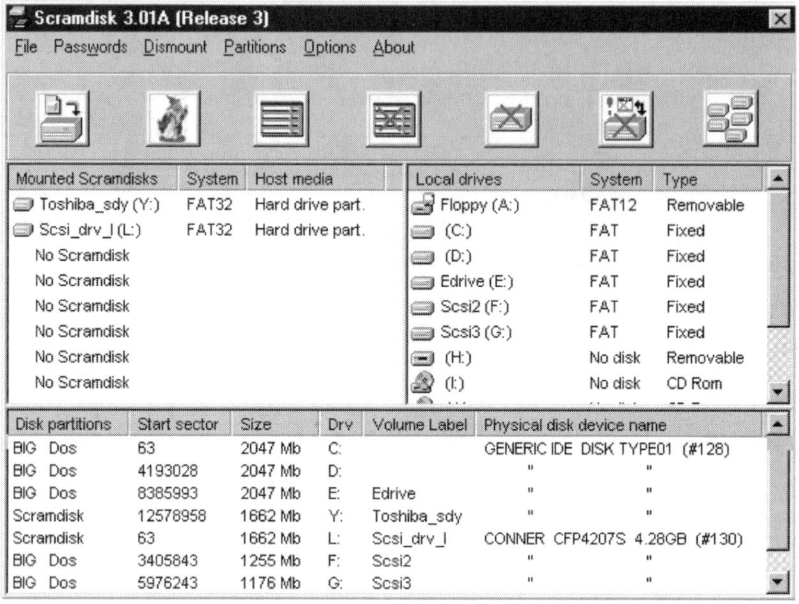

Figure 4.9   ScramDisk user interface for encrypted disk partitions

Scramdisk goes considerably beyond the conceptually simple task of merely encrypting files for oneself by including all of the following two functionalities intended to conceal the fact that it is being used. First, it is computationally infeasible to prove that a large file held on a drive is a Scramdisk virtual disk container without knowing the passphrase. The Scramdisk container files do not have to have a standard file extension and contain no file headers which indicate the file is anything but random data.

Caution: although the above is true, the registry of a computer on which Scramdisk has been installed has unmistakable evidence to that effect. Also, the presence of the file SD.SYS in one's computer is yet another indicator that Scramdisk has (or had) been installed in it. Also, any ScramDisk encrypted partition has an ID 0×74 which is used to scan and mount ScramDisk partitions. This means that an informed investigator of your computer can readily figure out that you have a ScramDisk partition even if there is no Scramdisk software in your computer.

Second, unlike the Windows versions of PGP, some of which are about 8 MB long, the Scramdisk executable program is very small and can be carried on a $3\frac{1}{2}''$ floppy disk.

To Scramdisk's credit, the following key points show the care that has been taken in the program's creation:

- Passwords are protected from ending up on the swap file.

- Scramdisk files cannot be identified as being such. They look like random data.

However, the user should take the following precautions:

- A user should have a plausible story as to what the random data are. One could, for example, create a digitized long file of, say, an old 33 rpm audio disk,[14] and seamlessly append the Scramdisk file to it. *Regardless, one must have a believable reason as to why there is a large file of random data in one's hard disk.*

- To obscure the tell-tale evidence of Scramdisk, one should rename the device driver (SD.VXD) to something plausible, such as DRV45GX.DLL. Likewise for the executable portion of Scramdisk. Also, make sure that there is no Scramdisk.ini anywhere; this is created only if one alters the standard configuration of Scramdisk, in which case that file, too should be suitably renamed.

- Scramdisk volumes have the .SVL filename extension, but one can name them anything at all.

- Since Scramdisk counts the number of times that a volume has been mounted along with the time and date that this occurred (albeit in encrypted form), the user may well wish to prevent this by making the volume file a 'read only' file.

- Do not use the 'fast shutdown' option in Windows 98 Second Edition. Disable this option if using Windows 98 Special Edition.

- Use the 'Red Screen' option for password entry. It defeats some (but not all) keyboard sniffers openly available. This works only for the standard QWERTY keyboards and not others (such as Dvorka, French, German, or other).

- Use the latest version of Scramdisk. Older versions have a security weakness that allows one to reset the passwords of an encrypted volume to the original ones when the volume was created.

- Do *not* leave the computer 'on' unattended after dismounting a Scramdisk volume.

---

[14] Not from a CD because of the identifiable high quality of the CD recordings.

- Consider availing yourself of the security benefits of a companion utility (free) called SecureTrayUtil, from http://www.fortunecity.com/skyscraper/true/882/SecureTrayUtil.htm.

- If you use Scramdisk's steganography option, select the 4/16 bits option and not the 8/16 bits option. Do *not* use a '.wav' (sound) file from a CD; use one that you yourself have digitized, preferably from a scratchy old LP or 78 rpm disk. This is so for two reasons: an interceptor would not have the digital original with which to compare your version, and the scratchy record would not have moments of 'digital silence' (all zeros) where steganography-created data would stand out like the proverbial sore thumb.

As of late October 2001, ScramDisk, E4M, and BestCrypt (see Section 4.10.2) have agreed to merge their efforts into a single joint product, 'DriveCrypt', discussed in Section 4.10.3.

4.10.2   BestCrypt hidden folder undocumented feature

BestCrypt, from http://www.jetico.com, is recommended because of an undocumented feature that it has that is explained below. BestCrypt's standard configuration panel, shown in Figure 4.10, is quite intuitive.

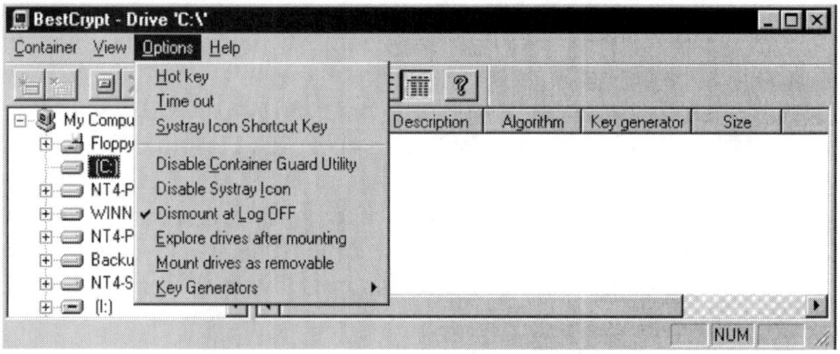

Figure 4.10   BestCrypt: an intuitive and effective configuration panel

BestCrypt version 6 has the undocumented feature whereby you can have a hidden encrypted volume inside a normal encrypted volume. This way, you can decrypt the normal volume upon demand and this will show only some routine files that would justify having the encryption, such as credit card numbers; it will not show the hidden file inside that encrypted volume.

The procedure below is tedious but well worth the effort. My thanks to 'Dr Who' who spelled it out in his 'Security and Encryption FAQ'.

1. Create a BestCrypt container in the normal manner.

2. Run 'command' to get into DOS.

3. Change directory to wherever the BestCrypt executable file is; it is usually in C:\Program Files\Jetico\BestCrypt. Keep in mind that in DOS you cannot type long names, so the command

   CD Program Files

   will likely have to be typed as

   CD Progra~1

4. Type: bestcrypt.exe debug

5. In the BestCrypt screen that opens, click on the drive that has your BestCrypt container from step (1), where you want to put your hidden file, and right-click on that encrypted file.

6. Select Properties from the drop-down list.

7. Enter your passphrase when asked.

8. Look for the box that opens that is titled 'Change Container Properties', and look for the box titled 'Create hidden part' below the 'Change algorithm and password' box. Click on that button and click on OK.

9. A new screen will appear that that asks you to confirm. Click on Yes, and then on Next.

10. In the next screen, which asks you for the size of the hidden container, enter some reasonable number (make it no larger than you need so that its presence will not be noticed) and enter a new and totally different passphrase for it.

11. You are done. To access this hidden container, merely use that new passphrase. To access the main container use the passphrase for that main container only.

12. Put some files in the main container that can justify you having it (such as tax records, credit card numbers, etc.).

13. To destroy the hidden container unobtrusively, merely place a large file in the main container that takes up all of the space of that main container – and that in the process squeezes out the hidden container and makes it impossible to mount again.

14. Note that you can use the above approach to create a hidden container in a floppy disk, a Jaz disk, or even a CD-RW disk, although you may have to make a cold reboot before being able to format the hidden container.

Caution: Now that the above trick is in the open, expect those who might confront you to know about it just as well. As such, do not put all of your eggs in one basket and use other approaches discussed in this book as well, as appropriate.

4.10.3   'DriveCrypt'

ScramDisk, E4M ('encryption for the masses'), and BestCrypt seem to have joined forces as of late October 2001 to create a single joint product called DriveCrypt.

On the positive side, such a product could be expected to have the benefit of the expertise from three different sources. The negative is that it will be a close-source product and the buyer will have to depend on the assurances of the sellers that the product has no 'back doors'. The big claim to fame of pre-Windows NT/2000 ScramDisk (and PGP, for that matter) has been that the source code has been openly available to anyone to inspect.[15]

A demo version of DriveCrypt can be downloaded from http://www.drivecrypt. com/update/home.asp using the login ID 'e4m' (or 'scramdisk' if one prefers) and password 'freedownload' (without the quotes). This is encouraged by DriveCrypt's makers.

ScramDisk's main claim to fame was that its source code was open for inspection. DriveCrypt is closed source and, as such, is just as suspect as any closed source security software. This is unfortunate because it resulted from the efforts of individuals, such as the creator of ScramDisk, who had earned the respect of many users. It pains this writer not to be able to recommend DriveCrypt.

---

[15] For a detailed presentation of the debate between proponents of open source and proponents of closed source (such as Microsoft and most sellers of software), the reader is referred to 'Does open source improve system security?', by B. Witten, C. Landwehr and M. Caloyannides, in *IEEE Software*, (September/October 2001).

4.11 Keystroke capturing

The commercial sector has seen the profits to be made by marketing keystroke capturing to suspicious spouses, parents, employers, and others. Commercially available products come in two classes: hardware and software. These are discussed in turn below.

4.11.1 The threat

There is a large number of commercial devices available all over the world to anyone who wants them that capture keystrokes as they are entered.

Hardware keystroke capturing

Keyghost is openly available worldwide from Keyghost Co. (http://www.keyghost. com); it looks like a small adaptor on the cable connecting one's keyboard to the computer. It requires no external power (and hence lasts indefinitely) and no software installation (and hence cannot be detected by any software). Numerous versions are available, as shown in Table 4.2. The device itself is shown in Figure 4.11. When installed, the commercial keystroke capturing device looks as shown in Figure 4.12. It is also available as built-in equipment in a standard keyboard, in which case it would be undetectable by the vast majority of users. The captured keystrokes are stored in the device encrypted with strong (128 bit) symmetric encryption.

Software keystroke capturing

Numerous software are openly available on the Internet, some for a fee and many for free, that record all keystrokes. A number of them that are downloadable from http://www.cotse.com/winnt.htm are:

- Playback.zip
- Win95pwgrabber.zip
- Keycopy V.1.01
- Keylogger V. 1.5

Table 4.2 Various version of keystroke capturing by the Keyghost device

Model	Capacity (keystrokes)	Ghost playback?	Encryption (bit)	Fast download adapter?	Casing
Keyghost II Professional SE	2000 000	Yes	128	Yes	EMC Balun
Keyghost II Professional	500 000	Yes	128	Yes	EMC Balun
Keyghost II Standard	97 000	Yes	None	No	EMC Balun
Keyghost Mini Covert	120 000	No	N/A	Yes	PS-2 Plug
Keyghost II Security Keyboard (Pro)	500 000	Yes	128	Yes	Keyboard
Keyghost II Security Keyboard (Std)	97 000	Yes	None	No	Keyboard

N/A Not applicable.

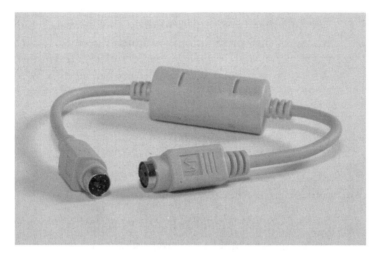

Figure 4.11 Keyghost keystroke-capturing device

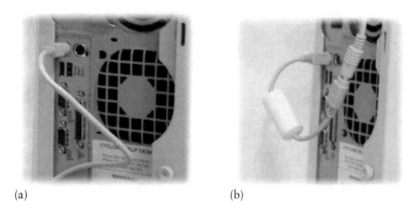

(a) (b)

Figure 4.12 Keyghost keystroke capturing device: (a): unmodified keyboard cable; (b) modified keyboard cable

- 9x_int09.zip
- achtung.zip

Other openly available keystroke-logging software include the following:

- Internet Tracker 2.1: this is intended to track stolen computers. It reports on a computer's activities by e-mail).

- The Investigator 3.0: this records all keystrokes and sends the data out to whoever the surreptitious installer specified (available from http://www.wugnet.com/shareware/spow.asp?ID=195). It is sold for $99 by WinWhat-Where. It is popular with employers for monitoring employees. According to CMP's Tech Web (http://www.techweb.com/), this software has been purchased, among others, by the US State Department, the US Mint in Denver, Exxon, Delta Airlines, Ernst and Young (accounting firm), US Department of Veteran Affairs, and Lockheed Martin.

One can also obtain the following software-based keystroke capturers from http://winfiles/cnet.com/apps/98/access-control.html:

- Got your Keystrokes: freeware, developed as a tool for parental control of children; many other software products peddle comparable capabilities.

- SpyAgent Professional: shareware for $34.95; poweful full-featured software;

- NetSpy: shareware for $19.95; this also allows the snoop to see what websites were accessed by the targeted computer, as well as e-mail even if that mail is subsequently deleted; it currently supports Netscape Navigator, Internet Explorer, AOL and Prodigy;

- Desktop Detective: shareware for $29; full-featured snooping utility;

- Spytech Shadow: shareware for $29.95; this emphasizes visual screen monitoring rather than text capture and records full visual screens every few seconds.

Other lesser known software-based keystroke capturers include:

- Silent Watch, by Adavi, Inc.

- KeyCount, by Paul Postuma

- Silent Guard, by Adavi, Inc.

- Winmag.com Snooper, by Winmag.com

- Cyber Snoop (Personal), by Pearl Software

- LittleBrother, by Kansmen Corporation

- Cyber Snoop Enterprise, by Pearl Software

- surfCONTROL, by JSB Software Tech.

- ChatNANNY, from Tybee Software
- ViewForAll, by InFORAll, Inc.
- IamBigBrother, from Tybee Software
- Disk Tracy, by WatchSoft Incorporated
- WinGuardian, by Webroot Software Inc.
- StealthSpy, by Andrei Birjukov
- Investigator, by WinWhatWhere Corp.
- Stealth Logger, by Andrei Birjukov
- SafeNet, by SafeNetCorp.com
- Stealth Logger ProBot, by Andrei Birjukov
- SafeNetPro, by SafeNetCorp.com
- Stealth Logger Core, by Andrei Birjukov
- Spector,[16] by SpectorSoft Corporation
- Probot, by NetHunter Group
- PC Activity Monitor Pro, by ANNA Ltd
- System Detective, by Harris Digital Publishing Group
- PC Activity Monitor, by ANNA Ltd
- eNFILTRATOR Black Box, by BSSCO, Inc.
- Stealth Keyboard Interceptor AutoSender, by ANNA Ltd
- Omniquad Desktop Surveillance Personal Edition, by Omniquad Ltd
- Stealth Keyboard Interceptor for Windows NT/2000, by ANNA Ltd
- Omniquad Desktop Surveillance Enterprise, by Omniquad Ltd
- Stealth Keyboard Interceptor Pro, by ANNA Ltd
- Snapshot Spy, by Virtual Imagination Inc.
- Stealth Keyboard Interceptor, by ANNA Ltd

---

[16] There is a free program available to disable the spying software spector, at http://www.wilders.com/free_tools.htm.

- Resource Monitor, by Strategic Business Solutions Inc.

- SnapKey, by SnapKey, Inc.

- Analyzer, by Hybridware Corporation

- MoM, by A Value Systems

- Spysoft, by Baysite Plus Publishing

- SilentRunner, by Raytheon Company

- Keyboard Monitor, by Tropical Software Corporation

Additionally, one can purchase keystroke captures such as *Keykey* from http://www.keykey.com/index1.html and from http://cyberdetective.net/keykey.htm, for Windows 95/98, NT, 2000, and XP. Keykey asserts that it hides itself from antimonitoring software, records date/time stamps; it currently sells for $19.95.

Keykey's versatility is evident from Figure 4.13 below that shows the reporting options available to the installer of that software; notice that these options include e-mailing the captured keystrokes.

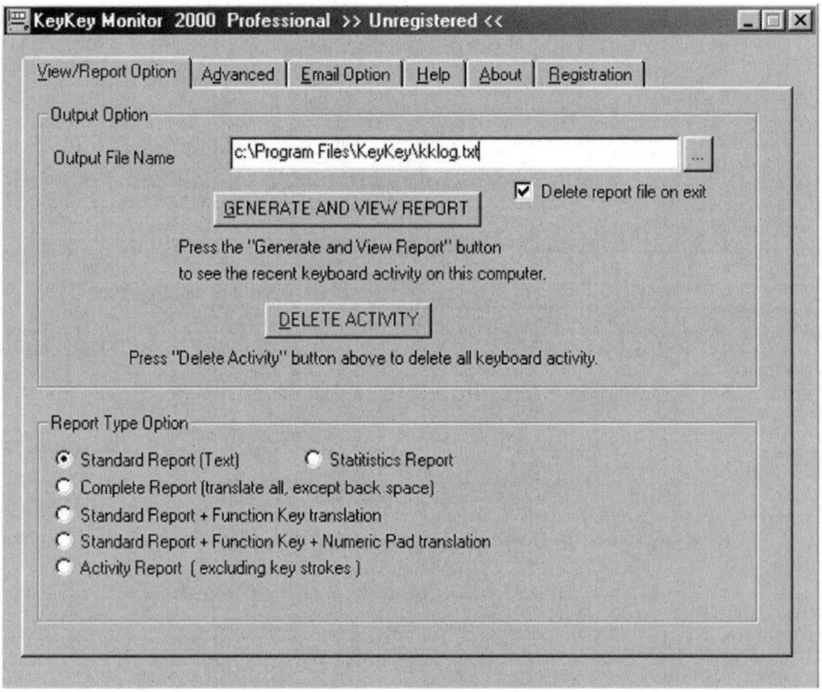

Figure 4.13   Keykey: keystroke-capturing reporting options

Keykey's higher priced Professional version also comes with a screen capture package; it surreptitiously captures, stores and can transmit what someone is viewing on the screen as well, as shown in Figure 4.14. Notice that the options include capturing screenfuls at preset intervals of time, or when the mouse or keyboard is used in any mode defined by the installer.

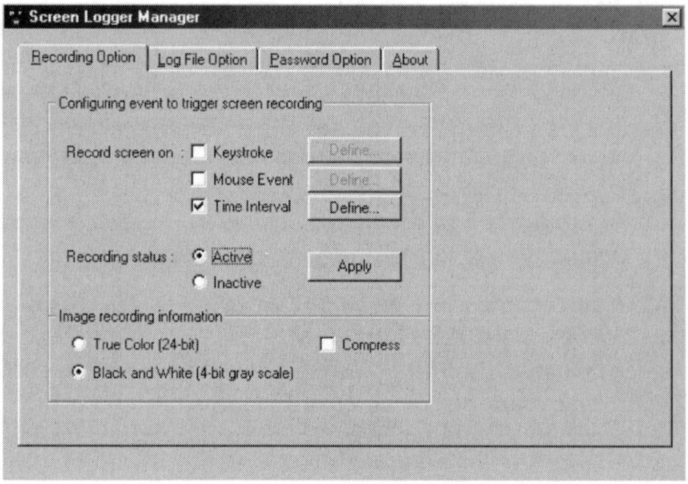

Figure 4.14   Keykey: screen-capturing reporting options

DIRT   What I regard as a particularly offensive commercial software package is DIRT (Data Interception, by Remote Transmission). It is a tool that claims to provide remote monitoring of one or more targeted computers without the need for any physical access and is sold by Codex Data Systems (http://www.codexdatasystems.com/menu.html) . According to that company's own website:

> *all that someone with DIRT needs to know is your e-mail address. Period. All he has to do is send you an e-mail with the imbedded DIRT-Trojan Horse and he is home free, and you are a clueless victim.*

It can be installed remotely without the targeted individual's knowledge and without the need for physical entry into the targeted person's premises. For that to happen, however, the targeted user has to have his or her guard down, namely, he or she has to have allowed hostile software to enter his or her computer in the first place by, for example, executing incoming attached files from strangers, allowing malicious mobile code to get in by not having disabled Java/Javascrip/ActiveX/VBScript, or by not having abided by the security procedures outlined in this book. See the subsection below on detecting and removing this product.

Sadly, according to an article in http://cryptome.org/riaa-secret.htr dated 8 October 2001, DIRT is alleged to have been purchased by such reputable organizations as the Recording Industry Association of America, the Motion Picture Association, and, the International Federation of the Photographic Industry, who allegedly 'routinely use it to monitor servers which are suspected of infringing content'.

DIRT is marketed by Codex Data Systems (http://www.codexdatasystems.com) as follows.

> *DIRT TM – Data Interception by Remote Transmission is a powerful remote control tool that allows stealth monitoring of all activity on one or more target computers simultaneously from a remote command center. No physical access is necessary.*
>
> *Application also allows agents to remotely seize and secure digital evidence prior to physically entering suspect premises.*

An investigative report by the British site *The Register* (http://www.theregister. co.uk/content/4/19480.html) has some very uncomplimentary allegations about the chief executive officer of Codex Data Systems and the product, referring to it as 'a loathsome scam run by an equally loathsome con artist'. Even less complimentary is the prose at http://www.cryptome.org, which referred to this product as 'criminal'.

Detecting and removing DIRT

It is not currently detected by antivirus software. However, its default configuration (which can be changed) installs DESKTOP.EXE and DESKTOP.DLL in the C:\WINDOWS directory. Look for them and get rid of them post haste. Additionally, you should check your registry for any reference to these two files at:

HKEY_LOCAL_MACHINE\SOFTWARE\MICROSOFT\WINDOWS\CurrentVersion

HKEY_USERS\SOFTWARE\MICROSOFT\WINDOWS\CurrentVersion

HKEY_USERS\DEFAULT\SOFTWARE\MICROSOFT\WINDOWS\CurrentVersion

or anywhere else in the registry.

Not finding these two files or any references to them is no assurance that this odious software has not made it into your computer; this is so because whereas the default names of the files it adds to your computer are DESKTOP.EXE and DESKTOP.DLL, it can be configured to name them anything else desired by whoever caused that program to be installed in your computer.

DIRT allegedly uses 'unused space' in the file system, so high-level-formatting will not remove it. To remove DIRT you will actually have to wipe the entire disk at the device driver level. This allegation is disputed by the software's original writer, Eric Schneider, who reportedly left Codex Data Systems on ethical grounds.

[On the conviction record of Codex's president, see http://cryptome.org/dirty-jones.htm; on the alleged connection with the FBI's forthcoming capability, see http://crytome.org/dirty-lantern.htm.]

4.11.2 The countermeasures

As with any affliction, it is far easier to prevent it than to detect it, let alone to cure it.

Hardware

Devices such as Keyghost (from www.keyghost.com) can either be 'add ons' (e.g., to cables, such as the commercially available 'keyghost' devices) or replacements for keyboards or other devices; the latter are obviously even harder to detect. Common sense dictates that one should use computers than are not amenable to 'add ons' or replacements. Laptop computers are exactly that because they do not need any external cables or attachments to operate; there is precious little room inside them for any additional components. Desktop computers, by comparison, have all sorts of cables and attachments connected to them (keyboard, mouse, monitor cable, etc.) before they can function at all.

If you must use a desktop computer and there is a plausible reason it may be targeted for a hardware device that could record your keystrokes, common sense again dictates that the prudent course of action is to provide for a way that you can detect these.

- Given how low the prices are for powerful desktop computers these days, and given the incalculable cost of compromise, go to the store and buy a new one in a box; do *not* order one by mailorder. Do *not* use the one that has been at home or at the office for a while.

- On opening it, make visually imperceptible marks on:

  - the screws that would have to be removed if one were to open the computer or its peripherals,

  - all the cables connecting to it and their connectors on both ends,

○   the peripherals themselves (keyboard, mouse, etc.),

and document those marks in a manner that can easily be accessed by you and by nobody else. Periodically check them to ensure that nobody has taken any liberties with your computer. In the unlikely event that you find that the computer has been compromised, consider it a godsend: do *not* acknowledge the find to anyone: instead, take advantage of the opportunity you now have to feed whoever is monitoring you with what *you* want them to know.

Software

Given the multitude of ways that such different keystroke capturing software works, detecting them all is a practical impossibility. Even a device driver could be logging key presses, and such device drivers typically do not show up in autostart lists. A software program that can detect *only some* software snoopers is called "who's watching" and is available from Trapware Corp. (http://www.trapware.-com). Another software product that can detect *some* software snoopers is Spycop (http://www.spycop.com). It is a little quirky in that it does not distinguish if the keylogger or program is monitoring you, or if it is merely present in a hard drive. If you elect to use either of those products, keep in mind the following:

- if it finds nothing, it does not mean that there is no snoopware in your machine; all it means is that it found nothing. Do not get a complacent false sense of security from it.

- after installing it and running it, uninstall it and remove all traces of it from the registry. This is in case someone were to check for its presence before installing a snoopware product that would be detected by it. Reinstall, run, and re-uninstall periodically as needed.

Since not even a laptop can be under one's continuous physical control at *all* times (including dinner, shower, church, etc.), accept the fact that the computer you use may be compromised. Even so, the following commonsense measures may help minimize the likelihood of a software compromise, or at least detect it once it has occurred:

- Use a laptop rather than a desktop. Select a model where it is easy to remove the small shirt-pocket-sized hard disk from within it and take it with you (yes, to dinner, to church, everywhere). Instead of leaving the laptop with the tell-tale evidence of the hard disk having been removed, insert another fully functional bland one (to be purchased from the manufacturer for a couple of hundred dollars) for the benefit of whoever takes an interest in it. Mark the screws or plastic so that you can tell if someone does take an interest in it. Do not let anyone else use it. Do not run any suspect software in it, specifically including downloaded executable files or free software. Do not have the screen visible from the window. Periodically reorient the laptop. Operate it from battery power. Abide by all of the precautions detailed in this chapter and in Chapter 5.

- Carrying the hard disk with you does not, obviously, protect from having you arrested along with that disk in a repressive or totalitarian regime. Consider using full disk encryption (Section 4.12) if a compromise of the contents of the disk can be catastrophic (e.g., membership list of a freedom movement or human rights group in a totalitarian regime); a few years in jail for failing to decrypt a file on demand is better than a number of individuals who may have entrusted their identities with you losing their lives.

- Do not connect that computer to the Internet or any other network. If you must connect a computer to a network, use another one (buy a cheap new one from a store) that you must take pains to ensure it contains nothing even remotely inappropriate. See Section 4.3 on cleaning up a hard disk if you elect, instead, to use an older computer with its own used hard disk drive in it. If you need to send or receive documents created in the sensitive laptop, transfer them back and forth using some magnetic media (e.g., a floppy disk) after ensuring that only encrypted documents enter and leave both the network-connected computer and the floppy disk that acts as the go-between. For all Internet connectivity, abide by the precautions detailed in Chapter 5.

Defeating keystroke capturing altogether

The following simple techniques devised by this writer will defeat keystroke capturing; unfortunately neither has been implemented yet in software:

- Create a screen that provides a one-to-one mapping of actual keys pressed to the symbols they are translated to. For example, to get A push F; to get S push 6, and so on. This mapping must be random and be different each and every time a password is asked for.

- Create an image of the keyboard on the screen and select the letters with the mouse. The keyboard will not be used at all.

One would hope that these techniques will soon become standard features in future versions of encryption software. Better yet, do the following. To encrypt and decrypt files, use a cheap computer that is *never* connected online and is *always* kept under lock and key; this is much easier to do if you have a laptop for this purpose, the hard disk of which is easily physically removed and is placed in a demonstrably safe place where you can at least detect if, despite your best efforts, it is accessed by anyobody other than yourself. Transfer only encrypted files between that protected computer and the one that you use online. It is that simple.

4.11.3 What if you find your keystrokes *are* being captured?

If you find any keystroke or screen capturing software or commercial hardware, you really do not want to remove it because by so doing you tip your hand. Keep it there. It is a godsend in the sense that you now know something your adversary does not: that you have discovered that your adversary (e.g., the local dictator's secret police) is monitoring you. Use that knowledge to feed your adversary whatever *you* want him or her to think of you; praise the regime in anything you type, proclaim your admiration for and support of the regime's goals, order pictures of the 'great leader' to decorate your walls (preferably visible from the outside), etc.

If encryption is tolerated in your regime, go buy another computer to do your real work; follow the advice in Section 4.3 about starting clean, and install and use full-disk encryption with Safeback, from http://www.controlbreak.net.

If encryption is not tolerated even among such open admirers of the local 'great leader' as yourself, then you may seriously want to consider not doing anything even remotely suspicious or inappropriate while you are under surveillance. Instead, make some plans for a short family vacation abroad; and stay abroad if you want to stay alive.

4.11.4 How about 'official' keystroke capturing?

'Officials' may exempt themselves from laws applicable to mere mortals, but everybody is subject to the same laws of physics. The one significant practical difference between 'official' and criminal interception of keystrokes is that a sufficiently influential entity may try to strong-arm major virus detection software-makers deliberately 'not to detect' that entity's software keystroke capturing trojan, citing higher principles (see http://www.wired.com/news/conflict/0,2100, 48648,00.html and http://www.theregister.co.uk/content/55/23057.html).

It is unlikely that this will succeed; it is more likely to backfire with unpleasant political consequences for all concerned, for the following three reasons. First, virus-detecting software-makers have an international market; are they expected to play along with the 'lawful' request of any one of the countries they have a market share in or just with that of their home base?

Second, the moment this is discovered and it is almost inevitable that will happen – the software vendor might as well declare bankruptcy as its worldwide customers will abandon it en masse. This is highly unlikely to be palatable to its stockholders who will sue en mass. If the exploit were to be done through the active help of the operating system maker, Microsoft stock will tumble overnight – a situation that is highly unlikely to come about with the concurrence of its top management.

Last, most computers use at least two different, complementary softwares in tandem for detecting viruses and trojans. Norton's virus detection software, for example, is reputed to be not as strong in detecting trojans as Moosoft Software's The Cleaner, shown in Figure 4.15. A 'sufficiently influential' entity will have to convince all such vendors to play along, an unlikely possibility given that not all such vendors are in the same country. For example, Agnitum Software's Tauscan, shown in Figure 4.16, is made in Ireland; other popular competing virus and trojan detecting software are made in Australia, India, and elsewhere.

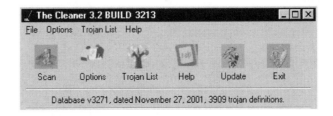

Figure 4.15   The Cleaner: trojan detection software from Microsoft (http://www.Microsoft.com)

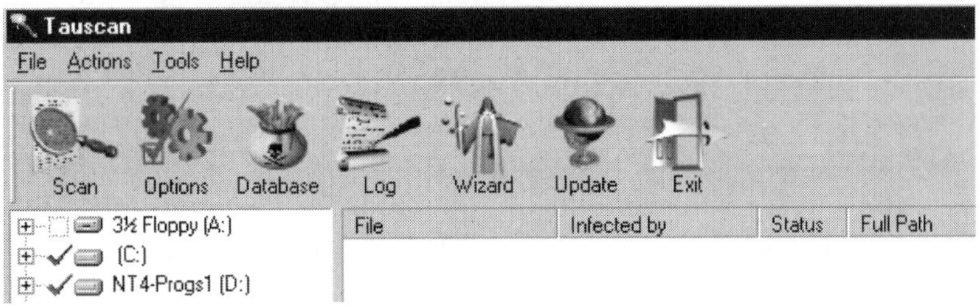

Figure 4.16   Tauscan: trojan detection software, from http://www.agnitum.com

This all having been said, most countries have enacted laws that permit their respective security services to implant technical means for capturing the keystrokes of the individuals they target. This trend has accelerated since the tragedy of 11 September 2001, with the terrorist attacks on New York and Washington (see http://www.epic.org). (On the use of keystroke capturing, see, for example, http://www.members.tripod.com/sludge/2001.htm, (http://www.nylawyer.com/news/01/09/091701f.html, and http://www.infowar.com/iwftp/risks/Risks-13/risks-13.90.text.)

4.12   The Ultimate[17] Solution: Full Disk Encryption

As I am attempting to emphasize throughout this book, encrypting a file is almost pointless because of the many other threats posed by Windows (temporary files, swap/paging files, history files, file names stored separately from the files themselves, marginal sectors in large hard disks being remapped to other sectors without removing the data from the ostracized bad sectors, etc., etc.). In fact, mere file encryption is actually inadvisable because of the false sense of security that it generates.

The next step 'up' is the use of encrypted disk partitions, such as one can have through the use of ScramDisk (http://www.scramdisk.clara.net/dload.html) or Best-Crypt (http://www.jetico.com) (see Sections 4.10.1 and 4.10.2). This is fine but it still does not get away from many of the fundamental security problems of Windows listed above, such as what happens if the disk crashes while working on files intended to be saved in the encrypted partitions, use of software such as Microsoft Word and its propensity to make temporary files, etc.

The ultimate solution is to have the *entire* disk encrypted on a sector-by-sector basis. In that case, all the above-listed security problems of Windows would result only in encrypted electronic trails that would be unreadable by an adversary. Such solutions are, in fact, commercially available and highly recommended. The best commercial implementations are:

- SafeGuard Easy, by Utimaco (http://www.utimaco.com),

- Safeboot, from Contrl Break International in the UK (http://www.controlbreak.net).

---

[17] It is 'ultimate' in the sense that it protects from any forensics analysis of the magnetic media. But it emphatically does *not* protect from keystroke capturers nor from anything you do while you are online.

I have also tried a competing product, PC Guardian (http://www.pcguardian.com), but that company's technical support department was unable to get my installation to work on a Windows 98 laptop – the only platform it was tried on – despite considerable effort.

Caution: full disk encryption does *not* defeat keystroke capturing. It is also useless if one is online because at that time one's files are directly accessible.

4.12.1   Technical details

Because of the potential seriousness of what could happen if a reader were to entrust his or her highly sensitive data to software, especially in those cases when lives could be at stake, this section will dwell on more technical detail than the rest of the book. It can if wished be skipped, but it should be of great interest to those who are technologically inclined and want to assess for themselves if the encryption software is good enough for them.

Safeboot uses RC5 encryption algorithm at 1024 bits. It also allows the option of using Blowfish with 448 bit key length, and the new advanced encryption standard, Rijandel, with 128 bit, 192 bit and 256 bit key lengths. It uses CBC (cipher block chaining) based on the sector number and then chains the data as blocks within the sector. The passphrase is stretched to 1024 bits using 2000 rounds of PKCS5 with a 32 bit salt. There is a unique key for the encrypted disks which is protected by the logon token which can be a password, a smartcard (optionally sold by that company as well), an encrypted floppy disk, etc.; this way, each installation uses a different sector encryption key.

The manufacturer asserts that there is no 'back-door' key. This may well be true. However, one must appreciate that no manufacturer of encryption software would ever admit to a back-door key even if there were one. Indeed, it is very easy for any encryption software manufacturer to provide for a back-door key that would be impossible to find without one having access to the entire source code and the time and competence to review that code; witness the fiasco with the additional de-cryption keys in some versions of PGP (See Section 5.8.4).

The economic viability of a company that makes its living from security products would be totally undermined, however, if it were to be discovered (e.g., through a disgruntled former employee with access to that information) that there is, in fact, a back-door key to some encryption software.

The safest approach is to assume that there may be such a key, even though there is no indication that there is. Even if the source code were to have been made available, it is reported to be about 600 MB long and consisting of in excess of 3700 files, including Assembler, MFC, Borland, Microsoft, C++, device drivers, vxd files, etc. Realistically, it is unlikely that anyone would find anything in such a complex package.

One needs to treat the hard disk, then, with the same collection of techniques described in this entire book for disks that are not encrypted, such as having enough RAM not to need a swap file, disk-wiping, use of encrypted partitions (in this case within the fully encrypted disk), and so on. In short, do not trust your life on any single thread.

An equally valid concern is the following: even if Safeboot is fully secure and has no back-door key, could an adversary install a keystroke logger? The answer is:

- yes, in the case of desktop computers, where commercially available hardware devices can readily be installed (see Section 4.11);

- with extreme difficulty in the case of a laptop or with any software keylogger because it would require

  - writing (or getting) the code for the attack,

  - physical access to one's computer,

  - installing the code somewhere on the disk (remember that the drive is encrypted, so one would need to find sectors that happened to be empty and not used for something that the user would readily notice),

  - getting the machine back to the user, undetected,

  - stopping the user booting to the operating system (Safeboot self-repairs), and so on,

  - taking care of the use of the smart card if one is being used;

- yes, easily, with any computer if the user goes online and is conned into downloading an executable file that installs a software keystroke logger.

4.12.2   Recommendations

- Get, install, and use Safeboot, but do not place all of your faith in its integrity. Also get and use the smart card option.

- In addition to Safeboot, treat the disk as if it were unencrypted and use all of the specific techniques discussed in this book as well, including file wiping, file encryption, encrypted partitions, periodic defragmenting, and so on.

- Do not connect the computer to any network *ever*. Transfer files that need to be sent or received over a network to another computer that is used for online activities, using removable media (floppy disks, Jaz/Zip disks, etc.).

- Do not run, let alone install, any software of suspicious or uncertain origin.

- Use a laptop. Lock it up securely when not in use, even for a short time. Do not allow its screen to be visible to any unauthorized eyes or possible lens.

4.12.3   Biometrics: do not use unless . . .

One of the latest 'bells and whistles' making frequent headlines these days is biometrics. DNA is used 'definitively' to identify crime perpetrators;[18] palm prints are used by the US Immigrations Service in place of other identification for 'frequent travelers' at some port's of entry; and iris scanners are coming down in price to a couple of hundred dollars.

  Fingerprint readers will start being integrated into laptop computers ostensibly to 'enhance the security' of the laptop. They emphatically do not. All they do is to replace the drudgery of having to enter a password with placing one's finger on the fingerprint-reading portion of the laptop. A computer forensics analysis of the hard disk does not require either a password or a fingerprint, and will uncover just as much information regardless. In fact, biometrics in computers are patently undesirable, for the following reasons:

- they give a false sense of security which is worse than no security;

- *they deprive you of the option of deniability*; this alone is reason enough to reject the use of biometric authenticators in one's computer;

---

[18] Although every human's DNA is indeed unique, the DNA profiling used for police forensics is based on only a small portion of the information contained in a human's DNA and it also quantizes that partial information. As a result, there is a very small probability (which is, reportedly, less than one in a million or so) that two individuals on this earth could have the same 'quantized representation of the small portion of the information contained in a human's DNA'. For police forensics purposes, this is good enough because they are interested in the question 'did he/she or didn't he/she?' and not 'who among all of the world's living people did it?'.

- if using a fingerprint, which is the least expensive biometric, they deprive you of access to your computer if your finger is severely damaged;

- if using a fingerprint, it can be spoofed since you leave your fingerprints all over the place, specifically including all of the surfaces of your laptop computer itself.

- Unlike a remembered password, which can be changed, a stolen biometric such as your stolen fingerprint can never be changed.

There is, however, one variation of the biometric schemes that would be a benefit; it has not been commercialized yet. Whoever does commercialize it will likely become a rich person. The biometric should be used as the encryption key itself (in place of a manually typed key that can be intercepted by a keystroke recorder as per Section 4.11) in conjunction with full disk encryption. In other words, the entire hard disk will be encrypted, thereby rendering it invulnerable to all computer forensics; in addition, the encryption key will be one's strong biometric (such as iris scan).

4.13 Troublesome Microsoft Windows Files

4.13.1 The shell scrap object security problem

Along with Windows 3.1, Microsoft correctly felt that individuals need to have multiple application software on the same screen and to share information. That resulted in object linking and embedding (OLE). It allows, for example, to insert an Excel spreadsheet into a Powerpoint document. Clicking in the Excel Spreadsheet inserted in Powerpoint invokes Excel and allows one to manipulate that spreadsheet. The imbedded file ('object') carries with it its own data about itself (date it was created, its own type, etc.) in a wrapper called 'shell scrap object' and has the suffix .SHS.

The security problem comes about because double-clicking on an .SHS file causes it to be executed. In other words, a nonexecutable file can carry in it an executable (.SHS) file. Such 'execution' could include, for example, deleting the contents of one's disk, copying password files into an innocuous-looking file that would not alert the affected user, etc. To the unsuspecting user, the execution is hidden. This is a sneaky way of doing just about anything on the targeted computer. The .SHS extension, by the way, is usually hidden from being viewed with Windows Explorer (but will show up in DOS listings that most younger users have never had to learn to be comfortable with). This is controlled from within the registry under the key

HKEY-CLASSES-ROOT\ShellScrap

A similar situation exists for files with .LNK suffixes and with .SHB files, for which the 'never show' registry value is in

HKEY_CLASSES-ROOT\DocShortcut

Be very concerned about loose .SHS and .SHB files in your computer. After changing the never-show status in the registry as per above, search for them and convince yourself that they serve a useful (to you) function that you know about. If you do not want to touch the registry, search for them from within DOS by booting the computer from a DOS floppy disk.

Such files typically enter your computer through your web browser and your e-mail software from the Internet. If you want to see if your web browser alerts you to incoming .SHS and .SHB files, as a test download two safe ones from

http://www.pc-help.org/security/shs_demo.shs

and

http://www.pc-help.org/security/shb_demo.shb

If you are using Eudora for e-mail reading, you need to add one line to its Eudora.ini file (search for it using the Find option from the desktop). Open that file with a text editor (no, not a word processor but a plain old text editor such as Notepad) and modify the line that looks like the one below to include all of the symbols shown, making sure that it ends with the '|' symbol:

WarnLaunchExtensions=exe|com|bat|cmd|pif|htm|do|hta|xl|reg|lnk|vbs|js|shs|shb|

There is a Microsoft-provided patch for Outlook, but it is strongly recommended not to use Outlook nor Outlook Express because of the seemingly endless string of documented security vulnerabilities that they have; you really should not be using application software that is intimately integrated into the operating system when you do anything online. (On these vulnerabilities, see http://www.guninski.com/javaea.html, http://www.mimesweeper.com/support/messages/ThreatLab%5C44.asp, or http://www.slipstick.com/outlook/esecup.htm.)

To disable scrap files completely use regedit and remove calls to shscrap.dll (or rename that dll file if you do not mind the loss of functionality and the occasional error messages). You may want to do this on the computer that you use for Internet access but not necessarily for the 'good' computer that never gets connected to the Internet.

4.13.2   Other Microsoft Windows vulnerabilities you should fix

Negate VBS script

This is at the root of most of Outlook's and Outlook Express's security problems; namely, their propensity to open executable code attached to incoming e-mail. In addition to applying the security patch made available by Microsoft, you should:

1.   Run/Settings/Control Panel/Internet Options/Security

2.   select custom level.

3.   select 'disable' for everything in the list, specifically including all items on 'scripts'.

Independently, for Win98:

> Start/Programs/Windows Explorer/View/Folder Options/File Types/
>
> Registered File Types

for WinMe:

> Start/Programs/Accessories/Windows Explorer/Tools/Folder Options/
>
> FileTypes/Registered File Types

for WinNT:

> Start/Programs/Windows NT Explorer/View/Options/File Types/
>
> Registered File Types

for Win2000:

Start/Programs/Accessories/Windows Explorer/Tools/Folder Options/

File Types/Registered File Types

1. Then, find VBScript and highlight it.

2. Edit (in Win98) or Advanced (WinMe).

3. Click the 'Set Default' option.

The last sequence of steps will prevent a VBS file from running; instead, it will appear as text in your Notepad editor. If you find it is safe to run, save it and then right click on it and choose 'Open'.

Independently, to avoid being 'had' by VBScrip malicious code that masquerades as another type of file (e.g., picture.gif.vbs), you want to set your computer to show the complete and full name of each and every file in your computer, as follows (Figure 4.17):

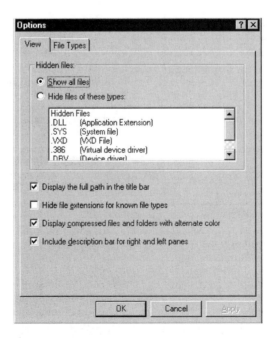

Figure 4.17   Opting to show all files and extensions

1. Start/Programs/Windows Explorer/View/Folder Options (for Win98) or Start/ Programs/Accessories/Windows Explorer/Tools/Folder Options (for WinMe).

2. Advanced Settings/Show All Files (for Win98), or Advanced Settings/Show Hidden Files and Folder. Set that. Apply.

3. Remove the default check on hide file extensions for known file types.

    Independently, to display the extensions of scrap files (the fix above for displaying all files will still not display scrap files):

1. Run/REGEDIT.

2. Look in HKEY_CLASSES_ROOT to fine ShellScrapFolder.

3. Highlight this. If you see 'NeverShowExt' key on the right panel, delete it. If not, count your blessings and exit.

Disable print sharing over TCP/IP connections

1. Run/Settings/Control Panel/Network/File and Print Sharing: uncheck all.
2. Run/Settings/Control Panel/Network/TCP/IP ->Dial-Up Adapter/Properties/ Bindings: uncheck all.

3. Run.Settings/Control Panel/Network/Dial-Up Adapter/Properties/Bindings: make sure that only TCP/IP adaptor is checked.

Protect from a Java virtual machine, from a WebDAV, and from a web extender client vulnerability

1. Download and install http://www.microsoft.com/technet/security/bulletin/ MS00-081.asp.

2. Download and install http://www.microsoft/com/technet/security/bulletin/ MS01-022.asp.

3. Download and install http://www.microsoft.com/technet/security/bulletin/ MS01-001.asp.

Preventing passwords for password-protected folders from being stored in your computer behind your back

1. Download and install a patch from http://www.microsoft.com/tehnet/security/bulletin/MS01-019.asp.

2. Find and securely wipe (not just delete) C:\Windows\Dynazip.log.

3. Create a new file in that same location with that same name (dynazip.log).

4. Right click on it, and under 'properties', make it 'read only'.

Malicious use of Media Player 7

Download the patch from http://www.microsoft.com/technet/security/bulletin/MS01-010.asp.

Use of Internet Explorer

As recommended numerous times in this book: do not. This is because of the endless amount of security problems associated with it that even Microsoft acknowledges in its regular e-mailings on security patches to its software (e.g., http://www.microsoft.com/technet/security/bulletin/MS01-027.asp). Even if you do not use Internet Explorer – and especially if you do – the settings in your computer should still be changed as recommended below because some of these settings affect other functions of your computer:

1. Download and install all security patches, specifically including http://www.microsoft.com/technet/security/bulletin/MS01-015.asp.

2. Apply the fix of the first item (1) on negating VBS scripts (page 144).

3. Use the latest version of Internet Explorer.

4. Change the location of INDEX.DAT from the default location, from C:\Windows\Temporary Internet Files to another location of your choice, by going to Start/Settings/Control Panel/Internet Options/Tools/Temporary Internet Files/Settings/Move Folder.

5. Start/Settings/Control Panel/Internet Options/Content/AutoComplete: disable it

and clear both 'forms' and 'history'. Since this will not 'wipe' the data already there, defragment the disk afterwards, followed by a wipe operation with Eraser version 5.1 (http://www.tolvaren.com/eraser/) or a later version. (Figure 4.18).

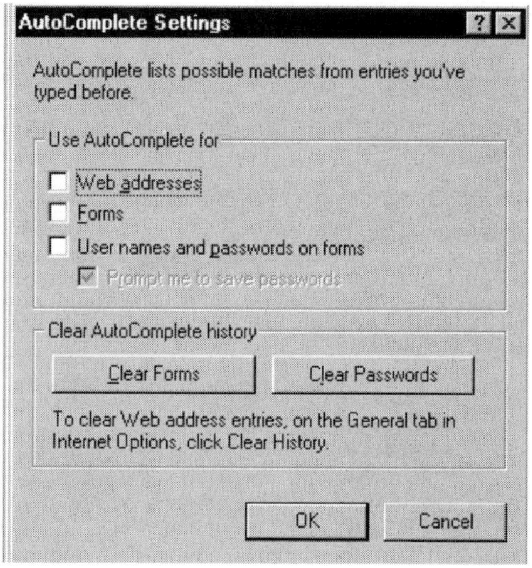

Figure 4.18   Disabling Internet Explorer's Autocomplete security vulnerability

Guard from faked Microsoft security patches

Most web browsers do not check the 'certificate revocation list' of security certificates. Have your browser check for the dates of any certificates issued to Microsoft; if they are shown to be 29 January or 30 January 2001, do *not* accept whatever is being peddled. If you use Internet Explorer, get patch http://www.micrtosoft.com/technet/security/bulletin/MS01-017.asp and install it.

WinNT/2000/XP

Unless you are specifically using such options as logging or Telneting into your computer from afar, running a Web or an FTP or a domain name server (DNS), or other such uncommon services for individuals not in the server business, turn them off. Go to:

Start/Settings/Control Panel/Administrative Tools/Add-Remove Programs

and remove the services you do not use.

4.14 Keeping Tabs on which Programs are Running Behind your Back

There are numerous ways whereby executable programs can be installed and run in your computer without your knowledge. Such ways include, but are not limited to:

- adware and spyware (see Section 3.2.9),

- hackers' files (e.g., BO, BO2K, etc.),

- self-appointed vigilantes looking for files they do not want you to have (e.g., DIRT, see Section 4.11.1),

- keystroke capturing software (see Section 4.11) placed by spouses, commercial competitors, overzealous members of oppressive regimes, etc.

You should certainly know which software are supposed to run in the background and which are not. This is a very difficult task to do if you decide to do it 'right now' because, unless you are a specialist, you really have no idea which of the many ones that are running and have legitimate-sounding names are supposed to be running and which ones are not.

Getting a list of which software are running in the background is relatively easy. Get, for example, Floke Integrity (freeware under the general public license framework) from http://www.angelfire.com/wi/wickman/floke.html as well as from ftp://ftp.simtel.net/pub/simtelnet/win95/security/fi002jwi.zip. The archive is 822 011 bytes long. It goes through your drive looking for all .com and .exe files and it records their names and locations, along with a 'hash value' for each (SHA-1, RIPEMD-160, or MD5) so that you can tell subsequently if they are doctored in the future. If you run it at a later time it will report any changes in the hash value, thereby alerting you to the fact that they have been changed; it will also alert you to any additions and removals from the list of executable files.

It is important to configure your system so that the list of executables it finds includes *.vxd and *.dll files as well because these too are executable files.

Caution: Although Floke Integrity finds all the files it is supposed to find, it does not always report them all.

Since, realistically, you will not know if many of the files identified should be there or not, this process should be done shortly after you first install Windows (any flavor), and then be redone every time you install additional software as well as any time when there are reasons to suspect that someone may have taken liberties with your computer.

4.15   Beware of Devices with Infrared Ports

It is strongly recommended that if you use portable devices (laptops, Palm Pilots, or what not) that have infra-red (IR) ports that you disable them. This will prevent them from being remotely interrogated.

A program called Notsync was created by a security consultant to show one such vulnerability: when the portable device with the IR port tries to 'sync' with one's desktop computer, the Notsync software fools the Hotsync standard application software into thinking that the hacker's device is the desktop computer so that the hacker's device can capture the password and all other files.

4.16   Encryption for Personal Digital Assistants such as Palm Pilot

Personal digital assistants (PDAs), such as Palm Pilots (http://www.palm.com), are already widespread enough that users should be concerned about the consequences of having all the confidential data in them ending up in the wrong hands. Unlike computers that store gigabytes of information, only a small fraction of which is usually sensitive, PDAs by nature store information which is almost entirely sensitive. Such information often includes:

- all of one's passwords;

- all of one's personal contacts, their addresses, phone numbers, and e-mail addresses;

- one's schedule of past and future meetings;

- e-mail content (in the case of Palm Pilots used for e-mail, either with the built-in modem of model VII or with the add-on modems for other models).

There are a few choices:

- Use PGP for Palm Pilots. This is *not* recommended because the version sold is compatible only with PGP 7.x, which is shunned by the security-conscious computing community because of security concerns that, among others, stem from the fact that NAI is not releasing the source code for it.

- Use Certicom's new software for this purpose; see http://www.informationweek.com/story/IWK20010608S0010.

- Use the German product Secret!, from http://www.linkesoft.com. It uses the 128 bit IDEA algorithm that is *very* secure if implemented correctly. Unfortunately, it does *not* encrypt what you already have in your Palm Pilot; instead, it allows you to create a new file that is encrypted in which you place whatever information you consider sensitive. It uses about 40 KB of RAM and is compatible with all versions of the Palm Pilots.

- A small assortment of home-brewed implementations of DES (data encryption standard).

If you use a Palm Pilot or other PDA, you may seriously want to consider encrypting sensitive data in it. PDAs are notoriously easy to lose, and the loss of sensitive data, even to a prankster, can be quite unsettling.

5

Effective Protection for Computers Connected to the Internet or Other Networks

Virus checkers and firewalls notwithstanding, the fact is there is a very large number of threats to one's computer by being online. The long list of threats includes, but is not limited to, adware and spyware that 'call home' (Section 3.2.9) and can upload information about one's data and software complement, software and hardware keystroke capturers (Section 4.11) that can also 'call home' and relay a few million of one's keystrokes (including encryption keys and passwords), and so on.

Since it is unrealistic to expect that one can be in full control of one's computer at all times of the day and night, the most prudent solutions – from a privacy perspective – is for one to have two computers: the 'real one' that never gets connected to any network, and an inexpensive one that has never had anything even remotely sensitive in it that gets connected to networks.

The days when this can still be done are rapidly coming to an end as more and more software manufacturers, motivated by a 'cash inflow maximization' drive, require software buyers to 'register' their newly installed software online – or else. Microsoft's Office 2000, SR1, and SR2 service releases are typical examples; Office 2000 software stops functioning after a small number of activations if one has not 'registered' it. Microsoft's Windows XP requires one to register online. Although software vendors' efforts to reduce the problem of unauthorized software copies is understandable, the requirement for online registration is making it much harder to prevent exposure of one's sensitive data to the multitude of constantly evolving online threats.

On the question of whether to use desktops or laptops, a desktop is considerably more vulnerable that a laptop because:

- it is much more susceptible to interception of its radiation (see Section 3.2.7) simply because it consumes more power and has long cables hanging between it and the monitor and keyboard;

- it is much easier for an adversary to add a commercial keystroke capturing 'adaptor' on any other hardware device to a desktop than to a laptop because the laptop is very compact and has no empty space in it;

- a laptop's hard disk is usually very easy to remove and carry in one's pocket or to hide away someplace; doing so for a desktop's hard disk involves considerable work.

5.1 Beware of Traps

The Internet and the commerce that has been created around it includes numerous traps for the unaware.

5.1.1 Beware of free Internet connectivity offers

Common sense shows that no commercial for-profit company can possibly survive for long with no source of income, yet there are some companies that offer free connectivity to the Internet to anyone who wants it. If they do not collect any revenue from their Internet subscribers, and many indeed do not, they *must* collect it from someone else. There are four main sources of alternative revenue – and they are not mutually exclusive – for such companies. First, they may gain revenue from advertising. Just as the source of revenue for many free trade journals are the fees paid by advertisers, many companies that offer free Internet access can afford to do so by charging advertisers for the right to send unsolicited ads to these companies' Internet subscribers. This is perfectly legitimate and it is a desirable option for many would-be Internet users.

Second, they may collect information from their Internet subscribers – with or without these subscribers' knowledge – and sell that information to commercial entities that want it for such purposes as directed advertising to recipients that have already been identified as having an interest in what will be peddled to them. This is also perfectly legal if the 'small print' in the subscriber's agreement makes it clear that the Internet user consents to this collection of data.

Third, they may actually bill the subscriber. A recent investigation by the authorities in the USA found that a number of 'free' Internet subscription services may have deceived the subscribers who were subsequently presented with bills.

Last, they may use the subscribers' computers to run unspecified software of interest to the company that provides the free Internet connectivity. This is a very recent trend introduced in late January 2001 by Juno company http://www.juno.com 18 January 2001 Service Agreement states, among others:

> 'You agree to provide Juno with accurate, current and complete information ... You Agree in your enrollment and in your use of the Service not to impersonate any other person or entity' (paragraph 2.1).

> 'You expressly permit and authorize Juno to (i) download to your computer one or more pieces of software (the "Computational Software"), designed to perform computations which may be unrelated to the operation of the Service, on behalf of Juno (or on behalf of such third parties as may be authorized by Juno, subject to the privacy statement), (ii) run the Computational Software on your computer to perform and store the results of such computations, and (iii) upload the results to Juno's central computers ... In connection with downloading and running the Computational Software, Juno may require you to leave your computer turned on at all times, and may replace the "screen saver" software that runs on your computer' (paragraph 2.5).

As with any commercial service, this service may well appeal to some individuals, even though the benefit of a free Internet connection may well be offset by the increased costs of electricity for keeping the computer on at all times and by the associated increased wear and tear of the computer. From a privacy and security perspective, however, the notion of agreeing to run someone else's unspecified software in your computer while online is contrary to every security practice in information security. Amusingly, software has been peddled through the Internet underground for the purpose of altering the information sent back to Juno for the purpose of convincing the consumers of that information that it may not be reliable and hence to terminate their support of this effort.

This is not to imply that free Internet connectivity is technologically any more intrusive of a user's privacy than paid Internet connectivity; the difference is that a provider of a commercial product or service that is alleged to be free is guaranteed to be getting paid by someone else, such as the revenue sources identified above, whereas a provider of a paid service may or may not be collecting any information from or about an Internet user's computer and/or online activities.

5.1.2   Beware of Internet installations that come only in a CD ROM

A number of large Internet service providers (ISPs) refuse to provide would-be subscribers with the information needed to set up one's Internet connectivity and absolutely insist that the new user load the CD ROM these ISPs provide. Do not! Not even if the CD ROM comes from a big name company such as AT&T.

The problem is that a large number of such installations done through a CD ROM also install 'spyware' that allows the ISP to monitor much more about your computer and what you do on the Internet than you should want to share. It is all very legal; somewhere in the fine print they state that you accept the terms which include such snooping; to make it sound 'proper' they use such content-free phrases as 'and such other activities as permitted by law', which means only that they will not do something illegal; the problem is that current laws allow a massive amount of snooping by companies as long as you have agreed to it by clicking 'yes' somewhere in the installation ritual.

Insist that any ISP you associate with merely provide you with the information needed to us your account that you can set up yourself with Windows, namely:

- Name of the POP, SMTP, and NEWS servers.

- Number to dial.

- Your user identification (ID), and your password (that you should change afterwards).

- Whether or not the server will provide the IP address of the DNS to you automatically or, in the unlikely event that it does not, the IP address you should enter when configuring your account with Windows.

Any ISP that tells you that you 'must' use its CD ROM should not be used. Period.

5.1.3 Beware of assorted 'Security-enhancing services'

The Internet is full of offers that, for a fee, promise security, anonymity, and the like. Although a minuscule percentage are good, most are either rip-offs or have some parochial agenda (e.g., collecting names and e-mail addresses, or being operated by some countries' security services, etc.,). Some of these offers, for example, promise 'secret and secure offshore mail drop addresses'; a number of them – curiously, coming from Angola – promise rapid wealth if you would only provide them with your banking information (bank name, account number, etc); sadly, it does not take too many gullible fools for a scheme like that to become profitable for the con artist that promotes it.

Before you respond to an ad for a service that promises to protect your equities, ask yourself:

- Why should you trust them?

- What would be the loss to you if, unbeknownst to you, they were to be operated by your worst enemy?

- Could it be a variant of a 'pyramid scheme' that would get you in legal trouble and cause you to lose your money? These schemes usually promise 'rewards' if you sign up more members.

In short, trust nobody unless you have a *very* good reason to.

5.2 Is it What You Send or What You Receive That Matters?

There are two separate issues here: one issue is legal culpability in civilized societies where governments have to abide by the laws; the other is 'popping up on a repressive regime's radar screen as someone to watch'.

In a country of laws, you cannot be held legally liable for the prose that someone sends to you, unless it includes contraband, in which case you can also be held accountable for possessing what was just sent to you (e.g., unpaid software, seditious material, or whatever your country considers 'illegal').[1]

It follows that you should be far more concerned with protecting what you send out (to the extent that it can be shown that you were the individual person who composed and sent it and not someone else with access to the same computer) than what you receive.[2]

---

[1] Along those lines, as an online user one must be extremely careful about what one receives by e-mail or while web-browsing, even though one may never have solicited it. Since incoming data get stored in one's computer regardless of whether they has been solicited or not, any online user will have a very expensive and uphill battle to prove that data found by forensic analysis in his or her computer was not willingly obtained. This can be a real problem while web-browsing, since numerous legitimate websites are peppered with assorted nudes; likewise, attachments of incoming e-mail (notably including 'spam', i.e., unsolicited e-mail) can include anything that is locally illegal, be that nudes, bomb-making plans, or what-not; since most users who delete incoming e-mail do not 'wipe' (overwrite) the e-mail attachments, and most users also do not overwrite the 'cache' files that store unsolicited web graphics, an individual can readily find himself or herself in jail through no personal fault, even in a democratic society.

[2] Given how easy it is for a totally innocent person to find himself or herself accused – and possibly even convicted – on the basis of faulty 'evidence' as per the footnote directly above, it behooves one never to state that one is the only user of any computer. The importance of this cannot be overemphasized.

This presumes, of course, that what you receive does not quote you 'chapter and verse'; hence the importance of never committing in electronic mail (or on paper) anything that would not look good to your mother or on the front page of your local newspaper. You just cannot control how the recipient of your e-mail will protect (or not protect) the confidentiality of what you sent; encryption is irrelevant since the intended recipient can always save the decrypted information. The art of being oblique and circumspect is a necessary skill unless your communication is oral and is only whispered to the other person's ear.

5.2.1   ICQ and other instant messengers: never!

ICQ (I seek you) gives you quick and convenient access to anyone online that you want to contact right now who is also using ICQ. It is precisely for that reason that anyone else can find you, nag you, and stalk you. Using ICQ removes all privacy you may have wanted.

ICQ will make one's IP address available to other users, regardless of whether one allows such other users' software to display that IP address; this is self-evident because unless this information is sent out, nobody can reach you and ICQ is pointless. At the same time, however, it is very important, if you elect to use ICQ despite the admonitions to the contrary in this section, that you at least take the standard security precautions against remote hacking, such as:

- disabling NetBIOS file sharing,

- shutting down all open port services (FTP, Telnet, etc.,)

- using a good firewall, properly configured. (I recommend ZoneAlarmPro),

- having encrypted any and all sensitive data in your computer.

Unless you have configured it to 'accept messages only from users on [your] contact list' and to 'not accept multi-recipient messages', nor 'WWPager messages', nor 'Email Express' messages, it is likely to waste a lot of your time as assorted others try to get your attention, and it is also likely to result in a lot of unsolicited junk e-mail to you downstream. All anyone needs to e-mail your ICQ account is your ICQ number, and there is no way selectively to filter some 'WWPager' or 'Email Express' messages; you either get all or none. Opt for none.

A trick that lets one archive all of one's instant messaging 'conversations' through Yahoo is available at http://news.cnet.com/news/0-1005-200-6333967.html. AOL's ICQ has had an archiving capability since day one. In Microsoft's Windows Messenger, which will be part of Windows XP, archiving is also an easy option. In short, you never know if the 'other person' (not to mention online interceptors, ISPs, etc.) you are communicating with is archiving the content of what goes back and forth.

If you still want to use ICQ, at least do not publicize your e-mail address. Click on the ICQ button, select Add/Change Current User, then View/Change My Details, then click the Main tab, and finally check the 'Don't publish my primary e-mail address' box. Keep in mind that this will only hide your *primary* e-mail address; any other e-mail addresses you may have unwisely entered will still be visible.[3]

Being stalked is another concern, and this risk is part and parcel of what any instant messaging system, such as ICQ or its AOL or Microsoft Messenger variants. Note that, in addition to any information you provide, such as your primary e-mail address, names, or ICQ number, the two web pages associated with your ICQ account show your online status to anyone with a web browser (unless you change some privacy settings). You can selectively blind another ICQ user (who will not know that you are doing so) from seeing you by:

1. clicking on the ICQ button,

2. selecting Preferences & Security,

3. selecting Security and Privacy,

4. clicking on the Ignore List tab,

5. adding the stalker's details, filling the fields of at least one of the search tabs (this will prevent messages from that person from coming to you),

6. double clicking on that name (if the person is in your contact list, you can merely drag and drop that name on the Ignore List window),

7. clicking 'save',

8. clicking on the Invisible List tab and add the person there also (this will list you as 'offline' in that person's ICQ even if you are online),

9. going back to step (3) above, and clicking on the Security tab,

10. finding the 'web aware' section and clearing the option 'allow others to view my online presence on the web'.

---

[3] You can always enter a fake primary e-mail address but that is pointless as you might as well follow the procedure above to prevent that from being accessible by others.

The foregoing will not help against someone who can hack into ICQ's privacy and security features. In that case, you may want to stop using that ICQ account and start another one (or, better yet, stop using any instant messaging system).

While you are at it, to prevent the presumptuous ICQ habit of forcing your web browser always to start with the http://www.mirabilis.com home page:

1. click on the ICQ button,

2. select Preferences and Security,

3. click on the 'connection' tab,

4. uncheck the 'launch default web browser when connection is detected' box,

5. click OK,

6. go the your web browser and change the startup web page to what you had before (in the case of Netscape, go to Edit/Preferences/navigator and make the appropriate changes),

7. in Internet Explorer (not recommended for security reasons), go to Start/Tools/InternetOptions and change the URL of the home page you want, then go to the Windows Explorer, go to the Windows/Favorites folder, right-click in the ICQ folder, click on the Hidden box under the General tab and click OK. This won't make it go away but at least it will hide it from view.

Ideally, you want to ensure that ICQ does not go through your computer's firewall. Unfortunately, this is not all that easy because ICQ has many ways to connect and many servers with different names, such as login.icq.com, icq.mirabilis.com, etc. It can use high ports above 1024 and it can also use privileged ports such as 21. The only real 'fix' is to remove all ICQ client software and make sure that none is installed behind your back.

At the risk of seeming repetitious, it is strongly recommended for security reasons that you never use any of the instant messaging capabilities or software.

5.3 Proxies and Maximum Online Security

5.3.1 Basics

A proxy, quite simply, is an intermediary between one's computer identity and whatever remote site one is connecting to. The whole point is to:

- prevent the remote site one wants to connect to from knowing your IP address; if you think about it, this is like wanting your cake and eating it too because practically every activity you do on the Internet, (e.g., sending e-mail, web-browsing, etc.) involves an immediate confirmation of information to be sent to you by the Internet, which means that the Internet has to know where to send that data to; about the only thing you can do is to set up a go-between to launder your identity (that is, your IP address), or to send in the blind with no confirmation.

- defeat those network censors who block access to any remote site in their 'disallowed list' by connecting to an allowed go-between proxy and having *that* connect to the site in the disallowed list; this includes websites, Usenet news-groups, etc.

- defeat those regimes that block one from accessing Internet-based telephony (e.g., through http://www.net2phone.com) to protect their revenue from government-owned local telephone companies.

Initially, proxies started as a means for small networks to minimize access to larger networks by locally storing ('caching') frequently accessed material; such networks would intercept individual users' request for connectivity to select sites and files and redirect them to locally stored copies if indeed these were locally stored copies.

5.3.2   What are you really trying to do and why?

One may be trying to:

- prevent a remote website from collecting information about you,

- get around censorship by a regime, but not worrying about the regime figuring out that you are doing so because you have assessed that the penalties are minimal, if any,

- get around censorship by a regime in a manner that the regime does not realize what you are doing, because you have assessed that the penalties for getting caught are severe.

The first is trivial. The second is easy. the third is extremely difficult and dangerous to your health if you slip.

Preventing a remote site from collecting information about you

The 'proxy' can merely be software inside one's computer that assumes the role of denying a remote site *some* (though not all) information about the true user. An excellent example is Junkbuster (http://www.junkbuster.com). This software, among other things:

- blocks incoming ads,

- provides fake information about the web browser being used,

- provides fake information about the 'referring page' (i.e., the identity of the last website visited prior to the current one),

- blocks cookies

Junkbuster does *not* alter the IP address of your computer, which is really the main reason for using a proxy.

Circumventing local censorship when the penalties are minimal or none

By far the easiest and arguably the most secure way of doing so was through the use of the Freedom 2 package from Zero Knowledge Systems (see Section 5.8.6). However, Zero Knowledge Systems has ceased to provide this service. Alternatives are shown in Section 5.8.6.

A free alternative is to use free proxies. Web-based 'cgi proxies' are websites that act as such 'go-betweens' and, depending on which such proxy is being patronized, replace or do not replace your IP address with their own when accessing the website of interest. Some can be accessed with full end-to-end SSL encryption between your computer and them, so that local regime censors cannot see what website is ultimately being contacted; clearly, a regime that does such checking will take a very dim view of such blatant countermeasures by an in-country person.

One ought to exercise a lot of caution when using anonymous proxies as *some proxies are actually operated by governments* and some by hackers. Almost all do keep logs. This makes it that much more important, from a security perspective, to concatenate ('chain') proxies; information on how to do this can be found at http://www.all-nettools.com/privacy/. In the simplest case, you can set up your web browser to use proxy1 and, if you know the addresses and port numbers of 2–3 more proxies, say proxy2, proxy3, and proxy4, you can type the URL as: http://proxy2:port/http://proxy3:port/http://proxy4:port/http://www.whatyouwant.com/, keeping in mind that not all proxies allow such concatenation. Also, keep in mind that your ISP will be able to see (and record, if so inclined) the entire transaction above and all that follows it. About all that such proxies will do is to hide your geographic location from the www.[whatyou want].com that you visit, and that is only if you do not violate any law and you do not antagonize www.[whatyou want].com to try to subpoena logs of the preceding proxies to try to identify you.

Caution: never forget that *all* anonymizers, proxies, and what-nots will comply with a court order or other official coercion from the country that has jurisdiction over them. This means:

- do not use an anonymizer, proxy, etc., more than once or twice;

- do not place all of your faith in any one of them; concatenate a few, preferably in different countries from your own and from each other;

- do not access anonymizers, proxies, etc., from the same IP address, nor send traffic to the same IP recipient or IP address;

- do not use anonymizers, proxies, etc., from home or office, nor at the same time of day or the same day of the week or month; in short, do not be predictable.

Never forget, however, that any anonymizer or proxy may be operated by or for a government. Exotic proxies (described below) are especially undependable in the sense that they are 'here today, gone tomorrow'.

To check a bit on the seriousness of a proxy so as to minimize the likelihood that they are hacking you, you can check to ensure that it has a domain IP status and is not a dial-up IP; such checking can be done at http://www.all-nettools.com/pr.htm and by using the smartwhois at http://www.all-nettools.com/tools1.htm.

Examples of proxies include:

- http://www.anonymizer.com: widely but with no substantiation suspected to be affiliated to US law enforcement;

- http://anonymouse.home.pages.de: free and reasonably fast;

- http://www.jmarshall.com/tools/cgiproxy/: text only, cannot handle cookies, and is free. (username is 'free', password is 'speech');

- http://www.idzap.com.: free for non-SSL (non-secure-sochet-layer) connections; paid mode for SSL;

- http://www.rewebber.de.: a German site with different levels of protection (and prices ranging from $12 to $50 per 3 months);

- https://lesser-magoo.lcs.mit.edu/px.html: a free SSL proxy at the Massachusetts Institute of Technology;

- http://www.webfringe.com/anon/: free;

- http://www.siegesoft.com/services/siegesurfer.htm: offers SSL service as an option but has a Javascript pop-up with every page accessed;

- www.magusnet.com: offers ftp. wais, and gopher service for free, but SSL and SSH connection is not free;

- www.topsecretweb.com.

Most of the above can be accessed through http://proxys4all.cgi.net/web-based.shtml. Additional proxies include:

- http://www.noproxy.com/
- http://www.fairagent.com/
- http://www.websperts.net/
- http://www.besilent.com/
- http://www1.webincognito.com/
- http://www.cyberarmy.com/portal.shtml
- http://www1.freeweb.ne.jp/~yzz/cgi-bin/startproxy.cgi
- http://www1.freeweb.ne.jp/~yzz/cgi-bin/startproxy.cgi
- http://www.leader.ru/magic/
- http://www.chenxq.webprovider.com/startproxy.cgi
- http://www.tag4tag.com/scripts/tools/anonymizer/startproxy.cgi
- http://modulus.freeshell.org/cgi/startproxy.cgi
- http://www.cotse.com/COTSEServices.htm

- http://www.df.lth.se/~nh/cgi-bin/s.cgi

- http://www.df.lth.se/~nh/cgi-bin/nph-proxy.cgi

- http://www.wotsthestory.com/nph-proxy.cgi/http://

- http://sticky.custard.org/nph-proxy.cgi/http://

- http://aixs.net/aixs/

- http://www.in.tum.de/~pircher/anonymouse/

- http://www.jasper.force9.co.uk/Rphh/Services/

- http://www.cotse.com/anonimizer.htm

- http://hyperarchive.lcs.mit.edu/telecom-archives/secret-surfer.html

- http://fr0.idzap.com/

- http://www.whois.com.au/content/jump-nongovau.html

- http://www.io.com/~jsm/cgiproxy/startdemo1.cgi username/pwd: free/speech

- http://sigint.978.org:8802/

- http://www.cast.org/bobby/

- http://ians.ml.org:8801/

- http://978.ml.org:8801/

- http://bluebox.ml.org:8801/

- http://ians.loyalty.org:8801/

- http://www.osiris.978.org:8802/

- http://www.InformationSecrecy.com ($8.95/month for SSL)

Additional proxies can be found at http://mvlad.newmail.ru/proxiesn.htm as well as at http://tools.roseinstrument.com/cgi-bin/fp.pl/showlines?lines=200&sortor=0. You can find even more by going to a search engine and searching for proxy +server+configuration+port.

Alternatively, one can set up one's web browser to connect to any one of many remote sites that act as go betweens, merely by setting the web browser as follows:

- very.elastic.org:8000

- macaroni.unix-ag.uni-kl.de:8000, 8001, 8002, 8003

- www-cache.unix-ag.uni-kl.de:8000,8001,8002, 8003
- kleinbonum.ethz.ch:8000
- olympus.eclipse.net:8000
- ad-proxy.eclipse.net:8000
- yoho.uwaterloo.ca:8000
- proxy.rhein-ruhr.de:8000
- rena.zfn.uni-bremen.de:3128
- junkbuster.rz.uni-karlsruhe.de:8000
- alpha.fact.rheim-ruhr.de:8000
- fax-bior.sozwi.uni-kl.de:8000
- ns2.clearstation.com:9000
- snoopy.bndlg.de:8000
- ls-andromeda.mmedia.is:81
- shoemaker.mmedia.is:81
- cornpops.cx:5050
- lys.eurecom.fr:18080
- ns-internal.clearstation.com:9000
- proxy-01.evesta.com:7854
- proxy1.interpacket.net:21
- lys.eurecom.fr:18080
- term-1.spb.sitek.net:8000
- sp-5.sto.telegate.se:8000
- edinburgh-88.edinburgh.k12.in.us:8801
- datacentre.chass.utoronto.ca:5680
- ns1.guetali.fr:880
- dns.guetali.fr:880
- proxy.guetali.fr:880

- mx-old.guetali.fr:880

- invest.nnov.city.ru:9000

- squirrel.owl.de:33434

- rtr-22.capcollege.bc.ca:82

- cvs.ul.com:82

- rtr-22.capcollege.bc.ca:82

- proxy.turboline.be:1234

- office.ompages.com:5860

- office.ompages.com:5860

- bess.cusd.claremont.edu:8310

- 156.63.41.8:7036

- 202.96.140.66:4147

- 206.153.33.11:9003

- ns.escorts.co.jp:8000

- 156.63.41.8:7036

- filter.netfilter.net:83

- 195.146.218.10:880

- irafs1.ira.uka.de:82

- somebody.net:666 (username is 'free', password is 'free')

Additional lists of free proxy servers can be obtained from http://tools.roseinstrument.com/proxy/. They are categorized by port number, by domain (e.g., .edu., .org., .com, etc.,), by connect method (e.g., SSL, http, https, etc.,) and so on.

A list of anonymous 'exotic proxies' that is updated up to a few times per day (!) can be found at http://www.cameleon.org. These are proxies in such countries as Malaysia, Taiwan, Argentina, Singapore, Uruguay, Emirates, Turkey, Guyana, and so on.

Keep in mind that some regimes block some ports (such as 8000, which is often used for such proxies) entirely. This is possible because all TCP/IP packets (including web-page affiliated ones) have a destination port (such as 8000) and can be censored out by a regime. This censorship is in addition to destination censoring (e.g., censoring access to, say, http://www.cnn.com). Usenet access can be blocked entirely by a regime by blocking packets to port 119. For that matter, e-mail (ports 25 and 110) could also be blocked.

Finally, you may want to consider a user-friendly go-between service, such as Multiproxy (http://www.multiproxy.org) which can hide your IP address by dynamically connecting to nontransparent (effective) anonymizing public proxy servers; it listens on port 8088, and it is free for personal use.

Before doing much of anything with any of the above proxies, connect to any of the many websites that display for you what they think is your own IP address and make sure that it is not, well, your own, but that of the proxy. One such possibility is http://www.multiproxy.org/env_check.htm. A much longer list of some hundred-odd 'environmental variable checkers' that show what any server can receive from you is available at http://proxys4all.cgi.net/env-checkers.shtml.

Circumventing censorship and interception when the penalties are harsh

Do not attempt to do this unless you have a very good reason *and* you are willing to become *very* well informed on the ins and outs of how to do it, *and* you are willing to take considerable risks just in case you inadvertently slip. Keep in mind that a nation state has vast resources compared with you, plus the full weight of the local law behind it. Once you pop up in the state's radar screen as 'someone to watch', you will have lost the game, as considerable resources can be brought to bear by the state to find just exactly what you are up to and why; about the best you can do then would be to become a model citizen. The real danger is that, most likely, you will *not* know if and when you pop up on the State's radar screen as

Figure 5.1   You may not want to circumvent some countries' Internet censorship

someone to watch and that you will continue doing whatever you were doing in the presumptuous belief that nobody has caught on to you when, in fact, you are being carefully watched; that is when you will likely live to regret thumbing your nose at the state (Figure 5.1).

5.3.3 Practical proxy tools

For those cases when you believe that a remote site has a proxy capability but you do not know which ports to use, Proxy Hunter by Zhang Feng will scan any IP range that you specify and will look for open proxy ports and report its results to you. It can be downloaded from http://proxys4all.cgi.net/tools.shtml. Two related tools from the same source above are AutoProxyChecker 1.0 and Auto Proxy Env Checker 2.2; they inform you of features of the proxy server being considered, such as whether it is anonymous or not.

Assorted Web-based CGI proxy scripts that act as http proxies can easily be set up with the aid of CGIProxy 1.1 by James Marshall from the same source above. Other comparable tools are CGI-Proxy 0.03 by Maurice Aubrey and Cyber Anonymizer CGI Script by CyberArmy, also from the same source above.

5.3.4 Advanced privacy

The basic idea is for you to connect dependably to some remote site that *you* control *and* that is beyond the reach of the local regime. Commercial anonymizer web-browsing remailers are all well and good except that you really ultimately depend on their willingness to protect your equities.

You will Telnet (remotely connect) via SSH (fully encrypted connection) to that remote site that is under your control on whichever port you like and hence will get around the port-blocking censorship that some countries use. At the same time, you must realize that your encrypted connection will be readily visible to the local country's Internet monitors, unless you have also taken the additional measures of bypassing the local country's communications by using direct satellite access, or other schemes discussed in Chapter 6. Unless you have taken those other measures, the encrypted connection could be enough to get you noticed by the local regime and targeted for in-depth investigation, something that would most likely not be in your best interests.

This is a multistep process; the initial setup is a bit of a hassle, but subsequent usage is streamlined and fast.

1. Obtain SecureCRT from Van Dyke technologies for about $100. This is the software that allows you to connect with SSH encryption.

2. Install and use any one of the many ways detailed in this book to anonymize your e-mail connections.

3. Using the anonymized e-mail connection, contact a commercial provider of a 'shell account' (see below) in a free country (I recommend Switzerland, or any other country that respects its citizens' rights to privacy). Expect rates of $10–$20 per month. Make sure it offers SSH connectivity. Pay with a credit card of some friend or, better yet, with cash or some form of postal money order for a year's subscription. Possible providers to consider include:

   • http://www.panix.com/

   • http://www.eskimo.com/services/shells.html

   • http://www.kirenet.com/shells.html

   • http://www.cyberspace.org/member.html

   • http://www.nether.net/

   More can be seen at http://www.angelfire.com/wy/0waynes/recommendedISP Accounts.html.

   To use this setup:

1. Connect through an anonymizer supporting SSH protocol with Secure CRT (encrypted SSH) to your above server. Your connection to it is anonymized by the anonymizer and encrypted by SSH connection. That server operator has no way of knowing who you are.

2. From the remote server now go to an anonymizing proxy (see the long lists above in Section 5.3.2) for an additional layer of insulation.

3. Now connect to wherever you want to end up, be that a website, Usenet, or whatever. Keep the connection reasonably short (5–10 minutes). Next time you connect use a different time of day, a different proxy in step (2), and a different 'nym' anonymizer, in step (1).

The procedure for accessing your news server through SSH is a bit more complex.[4]

If the local regime blocks the port you use, reconfigure your remote gateway to use another one, realizing that by so doing you would be thumbing your nose to the regime – not a wise course of action.

And yet once more: since any encrypted connection in a totalitarian oppressive regime may well irritate that regime, have a very good explanation why you are doing it should investigators knock on (or break down) the door. Frankly, unless you can credibly show that it is a hobby with no seditious implications, a credible explanation will be the hardest part of all to come up with. So, do have one just in case.

5.4 Remailers

5.4.1 Why use them?

It is easy to get carried away by the intuitive appeal of a remailer. It is also pointless because, unless it is done in a sophisticated manner, it really does not improve any security and could actually harm one's long-term interests.

A remailer takes incoming e-mail from you, substitutes its own 'from' information in place of yours, and passes it on to the intended destination you specified. In this simple form, no security has been enhanced because:

- Unless your outgoing e-mail to the remailer is encrypted, it can be observed by your ISP and through a legal or illegal telephone tap. If it is encrypted, the fact that you are sending encrypted e-mail to a remailer can be observed and get you added to the list of individuals that your country will keep an eye on from now on.

- Unless you trust the remailer (how? why?) the remailer knows both where the e-mail came from and where it is going. Even if you trust the remailer, someone

---

[4] To set up your SSH connection to access your own news server:

- set up your SSH client to listen to 127.0.0.1 port 119;

- on the server side, include port 199 and the news server.

This will tunnel port 199 requests from your news client software, attempting to contact 127.0.0.1:119 across the SSH tunnel to your SSH server; then it will go to the news server and make the connection, sending the requested information back the other way.

with sufficient resources could be monitoring everything going into and out of the remailer so as to correlate what goes in with what goes out and make inferences. Unless the remailer actively changes the size and looks of incoming e-mail before forwarding it, and also holds incoming e-mails for a random amount of time, the anonymity provided is nonexistent.

About the only benefit that *might* result from the use of a remailer is that the intended recipient (individual or Usenet newsgroup) may not know that the message came from you; is this minimal benefit worth the high price of getting on your country's 'to be watched' list?

Sure, the technical problems associated with the second point listed above can be – and *partially* have been – fixed. This has been done and is openly available to anyone. The 'fix' amounts to using a string of encrypted concatenated remailers. You encrypt your message with the public key of the intended recipient, then re-encrypt it with the public key of the last remailer, then with the public key of the next-to-last remailer, and so on. This way, the first remailer (the one you send the end result to) decrypts the outer public key encryption layer (the only one it can) and sees the address of the next remailer that it should forward your creation to; this process gets repeated until your message (hopefully, but not assuredly) gets to the intended recipient.

In a partially successful attempt to defeat traffic analysis, each Mixmaster[5] remailer pads the incoming message so that what goes out looks a bit different from what came in (it does, anyway, by virtue of having removed one public key encryption layer), and delays it by a random length of time. This is depicted in Figure 5.2.

Formating e-mail to a remailer is quite straightforward and can be done manually, if desired, as follows, using your regular e-mail program. Follow this format, exactly as shown below; the '::' and ## symbols and blank lines should be just as they are shown below:

```
::
Anon-To: recipient@wherever.com [substitute your recipient's e-mail address]

##
Subject: This is a test message [Put whatever subject you want here]

[Enter your message here]
```

---

[5] Mixmaster remailers are the latest step in the security evolution of remailers. Older, less secure, types have only historical interest and will not be discussed here.

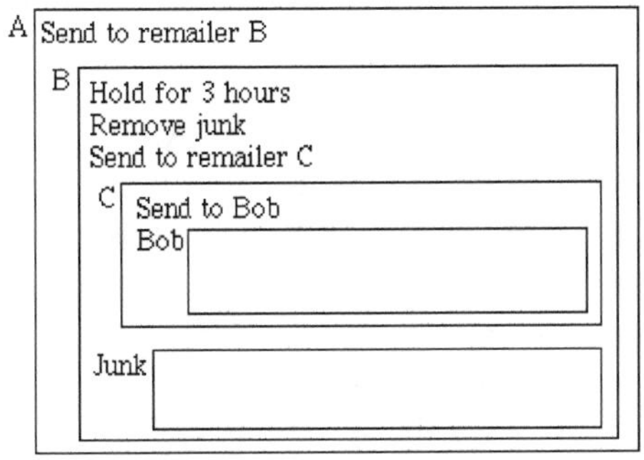

Figure 5.2 Mixmaster anonymous remailer concept; each rectangle denotes a different layer of encryption

That is all there is to it. For sending anonymous Usenet messages use the following format:

::
Anon-Post-To: misc.test

Subject: This is a test message [Your subject goes here]

[Enter message text here.]

For a message to a Usenet newsgroup, try e-mailing it to frogremailer@bigfoot. com.

If the remailers will not accept your messages then you probably must encrypt them first using PGP and the remailer's public PGP key. In this case, encrypt the whole message (including the :: and ## directives) to the remailer's public key, copy the ASCII block into your e-mail window, and then preface the whole thing with:

::
Encrypted: PGP
[and a blank line]

In this case, you might as well use an automated, rather than a manual, way of doing things, as discussed in Sections 5.4.2–5.4.4 in connection with Private Idaho, Jack B. Nymble, and QuickSilver software.

5.4.2 'Private Idaho'

This is one of the three main free software packages that automates the process of routing a message to an e-mail recipient or to a Usenet newsgroup through a chain of remailers, all of which use public key encryption. You do need to have a standard SMTP e-mail server, such as always provided as part of any Internet access (e.g., through an ISP).

Private Idaho is not a full-featured e-mail program such as Eudora but is a free rudimentary one intended to simplify the tedious process of preparing an e-mail for Mixmaster remailer transmittal. It has a long evolutionary history, having its roots in DOS and Windows 3.1x. New 32 bit versions are available at http://www.itech. net.au/pi/.

An excellent source of step-by-step information on setting the software up as well as a list of frequently asked questions (FAQs) is available at http://www.skuz.net/ Thanatop/preface.htm. Detailed setup information for the earlier Private Idaho versions (2.8) is available at http://www.eskimo.com/~joelm/pihelp.html. Be forewarned that the initial setup is a bit convoluted, but once it is set up and streamlined its use is very easy.

Since remailers come and go (mostly because they have been abused by spammers and advertisers) and their public encryption keys change you need a current listing of the ones that are active. This is available, among other places, at

- http://www.cs.berkeley.edu/~raph/remailer-list.html
- http://kiwi.cs.berkeley.edu/mixmaster-list.html, http://www.jpunix.com
- http://students.cs.byu.edu/~don/mail2news.html

To send messages through Mixmaster remailers you need several files that are included in MIXMASTE.ZIP:

- MIXMASTE.EXE
- MIXMASTE.COM
- PUBRING.MIX
- TYPE2.LIS
- MIXMSTR.TXT
- MIX.PIF

and you also need to add the following line to the AUTOEXEC.BAT file:

SETMIXPATH=C:\PIDAHO

assuming that is where you put PIDAHO.

Mixmaster client software is also available by anonymous ftp from ftp.obscura. com and from ftp.jpunix.com.

5.4.3 'Jack B. Nimble'

Jack B. Nymble version 2 (JBN2) is a Windows e-mail client that facilitates the use of anonymous remailers for anonymous e-mail and newsgroup posting. It is easy to use for beginning users, and it also allows sophisticated control of remailer messages for more advanced users. Support is included for PGP encrypted messages, Mixmaster, attachments, and MIME (multipurpose Internet mail extension) mail.

JBN2 also includes a mini web browser used for downloading remailer reliability statistics, keys, and web pages. Support is included for PGP versions 5.5.3x and 6.x, in addition to DOS version 2.6.x. Mixmaster 2.0.4 is also fully supported. For detailed information see http://www.press.nu/leiurus/filez/docs/JBNH-en.htm. It can be downloaded from many sites, including http://www.skuz.net/potatoware/jbn/ about.html.

5.4.4 'QuickSilver'

QuickSilver, by Richard Christman of Benchmark Software, is a free and relatively new e-mail client program that uses the Mixmaster remailers it also facilitates anonymized posting to Usenet newsgroups; these are considered to be the most secure remailers in the evolutionary scale of remailer development. QuickSilver does not contain any cryptographic algorithms itself but serves as a graphical user interface to Ulf Möller's Mixmaster version 3, which is also free.

Although QuickSilver does not require Mixmaster to run, it needs it to run in the secure mode and to concatenate remailers; these are the two primary reasons for Quicksilver's existence anyway. It can be found at: http://quicksilver.skuz.net amd http://www.skuz.net/quicksilver.

In its present form, it works only with Windows 95/98, which is odd for a security and anonymity software, given that these are far less secure operating systems than Windows NT and 2000.

The easiest way to get Mixmaster 2.9 is to Click 'Help|Update ...' on the QuickSilver main menu. The Update Wizard will then get Mixmaster for you and begin the installation. All other QuickSilver (QS) plugins (e.g., QSpop3, QSpgp) can be handled in the same manner. Alternatively, one can get Mixmaster version 2.9 from ftp://mixmaster.anonymizer.com and from ftp://skuz.net/pub/quicksilver.

After downloading Mixmaster in this manner, the zip file must be put in the QuickSilver home directory. The next time one starts QuickSilver, Mixmaster will be installed. A Windows registry key for Mixmaster will also be created and Mixmaster's home directory ('MixDir') will be stored there.

5.4.5   Security vulnerabilities of even sophisticated remailers

Despite their relative sophistication, Mixmaster remailers are still vulnerable to some security attacks by sufficiently resource-rich organizations. For example:

- If an adversary has enough capacity to record all traffic going into and out of a remailer, and if the attacker can also send a number of messages to the remailer and observe their transit, the attacker can figure out which incoming message results in which outgoing message. If this process is repeated for other remailers in the chain, then a sufficiently resource-rich security organization can negate the remailer anonymity.

- An adversary that controls the communications paths into and out of a remailer can selectively prevent some messages from reaching their destination.

- If the remailer does not reorder the sequence of outgoing messages to be different from the sequence in which came, then the random delay introduced in each message's handling is pointless.

- Despite 'padding' of some messages to change their size a little, a huge incoming message will still cause a huge outgoing message, thereby identifying which incoming message resulted in which outgoing message.

- If an incoming message is captured by an adversary on its way into a remailer and is replayed back into the same remailer many times, this will cause the next remailer in the chain to show a sudden increase in traffic volume, thereby identifying which remailer is the 'next' one in the chain for that letter. The same technique can be used against that 'next' remailer, all the way to the destination remailer. This negates the entire remailer concept, but requires an attacker with considerable resources; if the remailers are scattered all over the globe, as opposed to all being in a single country, then the attacker's job becomes impractically large. For a remailer to negate this threat it must keep copies of all incoming traffic and refuse to handle incoming duplicates; this implies an amount of computational capacity and storage that is often beyond the means of typical remailers paid for and operated by volunteers.

5.4.6   Gross abuse of remailers and of anonymity

Abuse of online anonymity, whether through remailers or otherwise, comes in three basic flavors:

- Abuse by advertisers (spammers) who do not want to be identified.

- Out-and-out criminality, such as in the case of death threats, extortion, etc., This is the modern version of the 'handkerchief over the telephone's microphone' of movies of yesteryear (which never worked, by the way, because all that it does is to attenuate a little the high-frequency content of one's voice without altering the voice in any significant manner).

- Malicious defamation and libel with impunity. Unfortunately, many of us are all too eager to believe malicious rumors and statements about someone we do not know – especially about someone we do not like – even though such rumors may be totally false. This does not hit home until everybody starts avoiding *you* – or even tries to kill you – because someone posted a pseudonymous message falsely informing the world that you have AIDS or that you eat ham sandwiches in a Moslem country, or what-not. Such messages get picked up by search engines and become available to anyone forever after even long after the original libelous message has been removed.

Law enforcement routinely cites the above abuses as reason enough to do away with anonymity. In fact, what many law enforcers and regimes do not say is that what they really want to go away is not libel, defamation, and unsolicited advertising, but untraceable criticism of the regime in power, as well as untraceable communications.

Anonymity for truly criminal purposes was not invented after the Internet came to life. We have all seen the movies of yesteryear when kidnappers would send ransom demands using letters cut from assorted newspapers. If anything, there was *far more* anonymity possible (and practiced) in the past than there is today.

- Until about a decade ago, a short phone call was very hard to trace whereas today it can be traced instantly.

- In the past there was far more use of cash than of traceable credit cards for practically all purchases. This includes the purchase of travel tickets. Try to buy a one-way ticket to anywhere with cash today and see how soon it will be before police stop you to find out why.

- Until about a decade ago there were hardly any video cameras in public places, whereas today one is hard pressed to find a public place without a video camera.

This having been said, the reader must appreciate what was stated in the preface to this book, namely, that gross abuse of anonymity is criminal, unconscionable, unethical, despicable, and shameful. There have been documented cases when individuals' lives were totally ruined as a result of anonymous malicious messages to individuals' family, neighbors, employers, and friends. This conduct is positively not what this book is in any way condoning; quite the contrary, it is emphasized yet once more that such malice should be hunted down and prosecuted with the full weight of the law, and then some.

5.5 Secure and Anonymous Web Browsing

Anonymous from whom?

- From the remote website being browsed?

- From someone tapping the phone line (or cable line, ISDN line, xDSL line, or other network connection line) you use to connect to the Internet?

- From your own Internet service provider (ISP)?

- From someone obtaining physical access to your computer after you are through web browsing? (Someone wanting to do computer forensics on your computer?)

- From someone who has installed a keystroke (and/or screenful-capturing) device or software on your computer?

- From someone exploiting Van Eck radiation from your computer from across the street?

- From the owner of the computer terminal you are using (if you are using a terminal at a hotel or Internet café or other public place)?

One *must* answer the above questions before even beginning to devise solutions to the problem of anonymous web browsing, because the process of obtaining anonymity from each of these threats requires a different set of protective measures.

Even the relatively simple case of being anonymous to a remote website being browsed is not a black-or-white proposition; do you want the remote website *not* to be able to know:

- Your name?

- Your IP address?

- Any information about your computer (e.g., web-browsing software used, which version of Windows you use, which website you visited immediately prior to the present one, any information stored in your registry)?

And even if you answer the above follow-up questions do you want your anonymity to exist even if you make repeated accesses to that same remote website from the same computer, or just for a single access?

The reader can begin to appreciate the difficulty of unconditional anonymity. Each situation has to be assessed individually, just as each patient must be individually assessed by a good physician before a prudent course of action is prescribed; there simply is no 'one size fits all' solution. You *can* afford to be sloppy with anonymity when merely trying to minimize the likelihood that a remote website will end up sending you junk e-mail. You *cannot* afford to be sloppy with anonymity if you are a drug enforcement administration (DEA) officer overseas and want (most unwisely) to access your federal credit union's account at home to see what your bank balance is or what are the latest interests being charged for various types of loan.

Providing a detailed 'how to' set of recipes for each of the seven threats outlined at the opening of this section can take the better part of an entire book if all the 'ifs, buts, and howevers' are addressed, as they should be. Instead, this chapter will summarize the issues so that the reader will have the tools with which to proceed to make a custom solution to his or her own unique set of circumstances.

As a bare minimum when setting up a web browser, follow the recommendations below.

- Do not use Internet Explorer; it is too intimately connected with the operating system, has had a vast number of security-related problems that have been acknowledged by Microsoft, and it obtains its configuration information (such as your name) from the operating system;[6]

- Assuming you opt for the lesser evil – Netscape – then:

  o do not enter your name, e-mail address, or ISP information in it; since you should not use it for either e-mail or newsgroup posting, your true name and ISP identity should not be volunteered to the world;

  o disable the 'smart download' option; even that will not prevent the vulnerability this feature has (see http://www.theregister.co.uk/content/18450.html);

  o download, install, and use the free ad-filtering software Junkbuster, from http://www.junkbuster.com;

  o disable Java, Javascript, Cookies, and Smart Update;

  o use any of a number of software items that cleans up after the many files left back by Netscape; a good one, which is also free, is ComClear, from http://www.neuro-tech.net; also obtain and use SurfSecret, from http://www.surfsecret.com.

5.5.1 Technical issues

There are three basic approaches to online privacy offered commercially:

- Use of proxies: (see Section 5.3): proxies basically forward data packets and do not add encryption. They are also often unusable from within controlled environments (such an intranets, corporate terminals, etc.,) that have their own proxies. They require some amount of technical know-how, however minimal, to set up correctly.

---

[6] See, for example, 'People surfing the web incognito may want to think twice before using Internet Explorer', in http://news.cnet.com/news/0-1005-200-2751843.html?tag=st.ne.1002.bgif.ni. Microsoft has acknowledged that ID redirects its various web server visitors through a very small number of routers, which is the reason why Microsoft experienced a major outrage and was inaccesible when one of its routers experienced problem in mid-2001 (see http://news.com/news/0-1005-200-2768545.html).

- Web-based: this chapter is concerned with the web-based approach that allows one to use it even from someone else's computer (e.g., Internet café, public library, hotel, etc.).

- Fully encrypted end-to-end connection, such as that afforded through any of the many commercial implementations of VPN (virtual private networks).

Which web browser?

Users are advised to avoid Internet Explorer; it is too intimately connected with the operating system and it leaves far too many electronic trails all over one's hard disk in locations that are far more difficult to identify and remove than in the case Netscape, which is also free software. Additionally, the list of security-related bugs in Inernet Explorer that even Microsoft itself has publicly announced and provided fixes for is embarrassingly long.

The many security alerts associated with Internet Explorer can be found at numerous websites such as that maintained by CERT, the Computer Emergency Response Team at http://www.cert.org. Microsoft itself maintains in its own website listing the various security problems of its Internet Explorer; one needs to navigate through Microsoft's site (www.microsoft.com) to find them, as they are often relocated to different URLs.

If you are determined to use Internet Explorer despite the admonitions above, then at least follow the specific guidelines given in this book for cleaning after the electronic trails that it leaves behind.

As a minimum, download, install, and use a free piece of software that cleans after some (though not all) of the evidence left behind by Internet Explorer: Spider (http://www.fsm.nl/ward). The latest version at the time of writing is v1.16. Appendix F gives a long and detailed recipe for cleaning up after Internet Explorer's security-compromising litter left in one's hard disk.

5.5.2 The fundamental logical problem with all web-based 'Anonymizers'

All anonymizers are fundamentally intended only to hide your identity from the site you browse. Some of the better ones also:

- use SSL encryption (see Appendix B) between your computer and the anonymizer's computer so that your ISP and anyone tapping your line cannot see what is going through it.

- do not forward your IP address to the website you are browsing.

The logical problem is this: the anonymizer website you are connected to and which is acting as the 'go-between' knows both who you are (knows your IP address, and hence can find through your ISP which authorized subscriber ID it corresponded to at the time of any one connection) and what is the eventual website that you are browsing 'anonymously'. If the anonymizer website is in the same country as you are, it can be compelled by a court order or subpoena to record and retain any and all activity by you, and/or any and all activity by anyone accessing this or that eventual website (e.g., a site associated with the political opposition in a repressive regime).

It follows that, at the very least, one should never use an anonymizing website that is within the legal jurisdiction of one's own country. At the same time, the mere act of using an anoymizing website in a foreign country may be reason enough for a repressive regime to direct unwanted special attention to you.

Ideally, you would not want to have any *one* entity know both 'who' is using web-browsing anonymity and 'what' is being browsed anonymously; ideally you would like to concatenate two different anonymizing services, preferably located in two different countries, where the first anonymizing service knows *only* who you are (but not what you are accessing, other than 'another anonymizer') and the second one knows *only* what is being accessed anonymously (but not by whom, other than 'by an anonymizer in another country').

Unfortunately, this is technically not possible with means within the purview of any average user of the Internet. This is so because, even though one can concatenate SSL encryption connections (e.g., one SSL encryption from you to anonymizer 1, a different one between anonymizer 1 and anonymizer 2, etc.,) this would *not* serve the intended purpose of keeping anonymizer 1 in the blind as to what anonymizer 2 is seeing because anonymizer 1 would still be able to see what anonymizer 2 is seeing.

Consider Figure 5.3. As can be seen from this figure, there is no practical way of concatenating two different anonymizers for the purpose of preventing any one of them from knowing both *who* is accessing a remote website and *which* remote website is being accessed. It follows that all one can expect from even the best web-browsing anonymizers is:

- if the anonymizer is using SSL encryption, prevent one's ISP (and any taps on your connection to the Internet) from seeing what remote website is being accessed;

- preventing your IP address from being forwarded to the remote website;

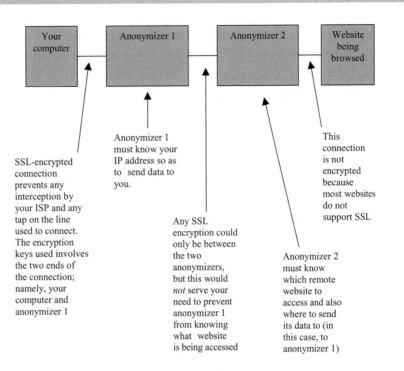

Figure 5.3 The fundamental problem of preventing any one anonymizer from knowing both who is accessing a remote website and also the identity of that website

- to the extent that the particular web anonymizer chosen does this, prevent some dangerous mobile code (notably Java, ActiveX, plugins, etc.,) by the remote website from reaching your computer.

SSL-supporting anonymizers worthy of consideration include:

- http://www.safeweb.com: introduced October 2000; no registration needed; free;

- http://anonmouse.is4u.de; offline recently;

- http://www.the-cloak.com/;

- https://www.rewebber.com;

- https://anon.xg.nu/;

- http://www.freedom.net: by subscription only; needs $49.99 custom software purchase; generally considered a standard against which others are judged;

- http://www.siegesoft.com/;

- http://www.privacyx.com: this site, although technically still in existence, is out of business for the time being; PrivacyX has been purchased by another company which states that it plans to reinstate it.

Caution: any anonymizers that require you to have enabled Javascript or ActiveX are not recommended because the remote site could snoop into your computer through either of those paths. A fairly good list of anonymizers can be found at http://www.webveil.com/matrix.html.

It must be kept in mind that *every* anonymizer will have complete access to the data stream you send or receive through it and could abuse this privilege. The argument can be made that a privacy company would not be inclined to violate privacy because it would lose its business. This argument is very flimsy, however, for the following two reasons. First, any anonymizer would have to comply with a court order or subpoena by a court having jurisdiction over it to intercept and retain all traffic to or from you or to or from any one of a list of remote websites. If the anonymizing service charges users, then the anonymizer will certainly have records of who paid what and when and how. If it is free, it has minimal financial incentive to retain the 'business' of a nonpaying customer. It follows that one should use out-of-country anonymizer services; even that, however, provides no assurance of any privacy. Second, some anonymizers are reportedly operated by some countries' law enforcement organizations, for obvious reasons.

Furthermore, and again for obvious reasons, one should be very careful with and suspicious of web anonymizers that require one to register one's name, address, and e-mail account before being allowed to use that service; many will not accept 'throw-away' free accounts that one can create on the spot. One should be even more suspicious of web anonymizers (and all privacy-peddling entities) that will not function unless the user enables the dangerous options of Java, Javasctipt, cookies, stylesheets, ActiveX, specific plug-ins, etc., To be fair, a web anonymizer has to have *some* way of causing the remote website's information to appear on your screen in a manner similar to the way it would have appeared if you had not used an anonymizer go-between; this comes back to the issue of how much you trust the anonymizer. The following suggestions may be of use.

- Do not browse only what you are interested in; browse much more what you are not interested in so as to hide what you are *really* interested in.

- Do not use always the same anonymizer; use different ones.

- Do not web browse with a pattern (e.g., same time or same day of the week).

- Have numerous ways of accessing the Internet (e.g., from home, from an Internet café, etc.,) and numerous accounts; spread your browsing among them but do not establish the same pattern with all of them either.

- If you use different Internet accounts, as recommended above, do not have them all in the same hard disk or even in different disks that are on at the same time on the same computer. Either use a different computer for each (e.g., a laptop for one account, a desktop for another), or at least different bootable removable hard disks for each. This is to prevent any remote user with the appropriate hacking skills from seeing that all the accounts you have correspond to one and the same person.

5.5.3 Specific web anonymizers worthy of notice

Freedom 2 from ZeroKnowledge Systems (http://www.freedom.net) was a good product.[7] It did not, however, work with MacOS, Windows NT, Windows 2000 or Linux. This is odd because the company claimed that the reason why it shut down the Freedom network was lack of enough customers, yet did not make its product available to enough customers to begin with. Also, it did not work in some managed networks (such as corporations) because it used some high-numbered ports that may be blocked. Also, it required the installation of software that may also be blocked by some managed networks. In addition, it had some incompatibilities with some firewall products. Even so, it was recommended with the proviso that it was purchased in an anonymous or pseudonymous manner and not directly from the manufacturer using one's own credit card and mailing address.

SafeWeb (http://www.safeweb.com) was one of the better web-browser anonymizers until it ceased offering its services to individuals in late 2001.[8] It required, however, Javascript and StyleSheets to be enabled in one's web browser, so as to

---

[7] **Caution:** I experienced a number of incidents when Freedom 2 failed to pseudonimize the outgoing e-mail and sent it, instead, with the sender's true e-mail address. This can be catastrophic in some cases. This is academic, however, since Zero Knowledge Systems shut down the Freedom networks as of mid-October 2001 under what can be viewed as suspicious circumstances, because the shutdown was so shortly after the tragedy of 11 September. The official reason for the shutdown was lack of users (the text above). See http://www.wired.com/news/business/0,1367,47337,00.html.

[8] Even though it is one of the better free web anonymizers, it is not recommended for anything other than hiding your IP address from most of the commercial websites that you may visit. Its use of Javascript is unacceptable from a security viewpoint.

implement its navigation bar (i.e., to control the layout and make its toolbar look as close as possible to the original without taking more than a few vertical pixels from the original content area). The user is cautioned that Safeweb had stated that it retains its records (of who accessed what) for a week – more if it has been served with a notice to preserve evidence.

Under its URL bar, there was a 'configure' button that allowed one to customize one's preference in terms of convenience or privacy. One could turn off all Javascript (except that from SafeWeb direct, which draws the Safeweb toolbar) or just dangerous Javascript, such as 'evals', 'doc.write', and other dynamic potentially self-modifying code on which most Javascript malicious code is based.

Since Safeweb was free to its users, one could justifiable suspect that the cash inflow came from some form of directed advertising based on Safeweb users' browsing preferences. According to its president and co-founder, Mr Jon Chun (personal e-mail communication), Safeweb has

> built [its] own unique non-invasive targeting engine that is more accurate than DART's targeting engine at DoubleClick ... If you are reading the front page story of New York Times, Safeweb parses that article in real time to identify all key words and does a real-time analysis of frequency, separation, etc., and plugs these into a targeting formula weighted by adaptive neural networks trained by crawling over the top 100 sites in each content category.

A new arrival to the scene (May 2001) is http://www.topsecretweb.com and it allows end-to-end SSL encryption. It is one of the few that anonymizes advertisers' 'click through', which is a means whereby advertisers could defeat conventional anonymizers. Unfortunately, it requires Javascript to be enabled; in my opinion this is an automatic disqualifier for any anonymizer. One should also consider the services of http://www.cotse.com ("church of the swimming elephant") in the Boston area.

5.5.4   So what is the bottom line?

It is technically possible, as per above, to prevent a remote website from knowing who you are. It is quite easy (but alerting) to prevent one's own ISP from knowing what remote website you are accessing through a web anonymizer. It is technically *not* possible to hide any and all evidence of one's online browsing from the web anonymizing site that one elects to use if such web browsing is done from one's own premises using one's own computers and/or Internet access accounts. If that is what you need, then technical means have to be augmented with procedural steps such as the ones suggested above; this will require a significant level of effort, commitment, and discipline on your part.

For those in Australia

A site dedicated to ways to circumvent Broadcasting Services Amendment (Online Services) Act of 1999 is http://www.2600.org.au/censorship-evasion.html.

5.5.5 Preventing your web browser from contacting select remote sites

Various versions of some browsers take it on themselves to contact assorted remote Internet sites, sometime for banner ads and sometimes for reporting on browser users' online activities. Netscape 4.77, for example, reportedly likes to connect to home-v4.websys.aol.com (207.200.89.226). Also, some adware and spyware try to defeat detection when 'calling home' by doing so through web browsers' legitimate ports (namely port 80). There is an easy fix that takes advantage of the fact that, when you want to access a remote site, say www.cnn.com, Netscape checks a local file in your own computer called 'hosts' that serves as a local 'telephone directory' to find what the IP address for that site is; if it cannot find it listed there, then it goes to the Internet [a domain name server (DNS)] to find it. The fix amounts to telling your computer that the IP address for the offending site is your own computer (whose IP address is always 127.0.0.1) so that it never connects to that site.

One easy fix for Netscape is as follows:

- Start/Find 'hosts' (without the quotes);

- Add the following line using the spacing as shown; chances are that there are already other sites in there, so make sure that your addition conforms to the format of those other sites:

    127.0.0.1   home-v4.websys.aol.com

    substituting whatever site(s) you do not want Netscape to visit. Note: there are five spaces between 127.0.0.1 and the following text.

- While you are at it, modify the IP address of any other site that you find in that file that you do not want to have your browser visit, and make it 127.0.0.1 as well.

A comprehensive version of the hosts file can also be found at http://www.smartin-designs.com.

The above steps will redirect the IP address of the offending site to your own computer; be prepared for a small delay. This is very tedious and requires a lot of manual labor on your part to keep the list (which can run into many tens of type and written pages) current, especially since identifications for ad-related websites change *very* rapidly. A typical case is Akamai Co. (http://www.akamai.com); it is not spyware itself but does host ads and distributed applications services for its client companies; there is a vast number of servers that sport the Akamai name with all sorts of different prefixes and suffixes. There were numerous postings in 2001 in the alt.privacy newsgroup in Usenet to the effect that one of Akamai's goals to pinpoint the city block in which you live.

Alternately, one can use Junkbuster from http://www.junkbuster.com. This also offers some useful ancillary functions that further enhance one's privacy online.

Detecting what your computer is doing online behind your back

To see, at regular intervals, who is connected to you, Start/Run

NETSTAT 10

This will show you every 10 seconds who is connected to your computer; be prepared for the corresponding slowdown in other computing functions you may be going through.

A fancier version of NETSTAT (which is built-in in Windows) is Xploiterstat from http://xploiter.com/tambu/totostat.shtml for Windows 95/98/NT/2000. It comes in both a freeware version ('Lite') and a more powerful paid for version. The Lite version has been reported to have problems with Windows 2000. If you ask for a 'ping' display, the Xploiterstat looks as shown in Fig. 5.4. It allows you to monitor *all* ports of your system.

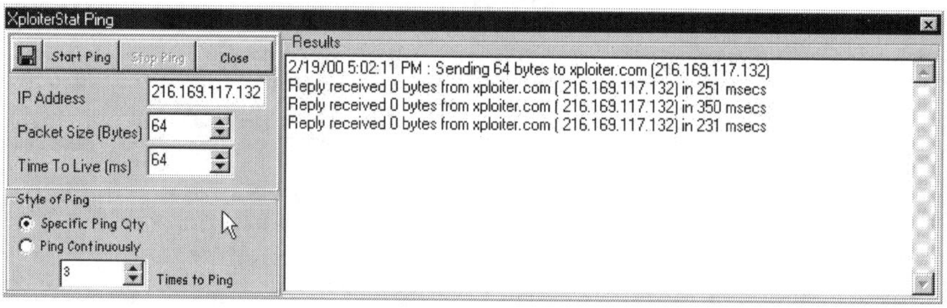

Figure 5.4   Xploiterstat Network status display

An alternative is PortMon (Port Monitor) for Windows NT/95/98/2000, from SysInternals (http://www.sysinternals.com/ntw2k/freeware/portmon.shtml). It also has advanced filtering and search capabilities, seeing how different applications use ports. Version 3.x allows remote monitoring even across the Internet; this is clearly very dangerous and you should make sure that your installation does not accommodate remote monitoring by anyone else. The thoroughness of its coverage is evident from Fig. 5.5.

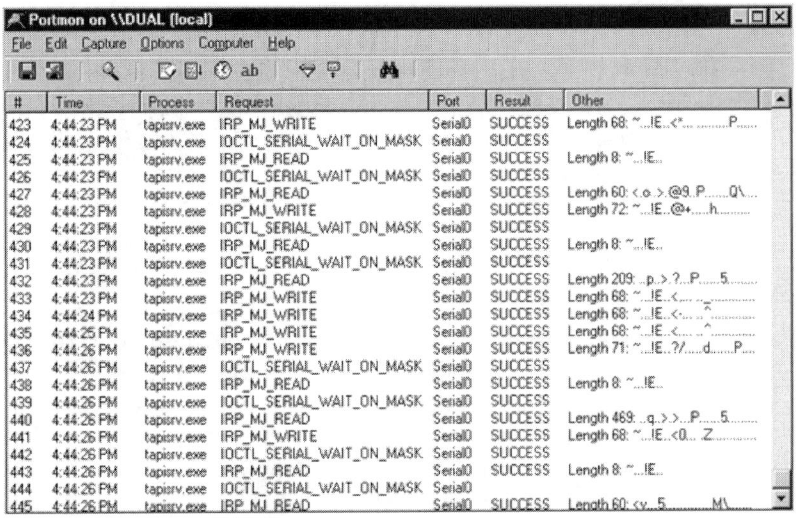

Figure 5.5   Portmonitor display

SysInternals also provides free monitoring tools such as Regmon (a useful utility to monitor the registry and how it is accessed and by which software), FileMon (file system monitor), Tdimon (a TCP/IP monitor), and Pmon (a process and thread monitor), and Diskmon (a hard disk monitor).

A further another complementary product is CommView, from http://www. tamos.com/cv.htm. It is intended to monitor network activity and is capable of capturing and analyzing packets on Ethernet networks. It allows a full view of all traffic going through one's PC or local area network (LAN).

Removing advertisements from websites you visit

A number of software packages exist, most of them free, that remove ads. The issue here is far more than mere annoyance: given that all ads that show up on the screen are almost always 'cached' in your disk for the benefit of a forensics investigator, you could end up in jail if such material were to be found in your disk in those countries that prohibit it. The likelihood that you would be able successfully to convince a nontechnical and unsympathetic court that you did not 'knowingly and willingly' obtain such material is slim to none. A good source of such ad-filtering software can be found at http://www.flourish.org/adremove/.

5.5.6 Cookies

The short message is 'never accept cookies from a stranger' – or even from a friend for that matter, as they not good for one physically or metaphorically.

Cookies is the cute name for a string of data (typically up to a few thousand symbols but usually much shorter) that a website you visit sends to your computer and expects your computer to store in your hard disk. These data often contain personal information that you have yourself provided to a remote website, such as name, address, credit card number for a purchase, and what was ordered. Although there is no evidence that these data can bring in a virus or other malicious mobile code, the problem is that your hard disk ends up collecting a history of what you saw and when you saw it; this history can be retrieved remotely by practically every site that you subsequently visit – not to mention by forensics examination of your subpoenaed hard disk (see Section 4.2.10).

Many websites refuse to deal with you unless you accept their cookies. To be sure, there are some plausible benefits from nonmalicious cookies:

- cookies allow you a convenient way to shop online in that the information of what is in your online shopping basket is stored in your computer as cookies until you 'check out';

- cookies allow you to revisit a website that is accessible only to those who have 'registered' (e.g., for-pay information sites, limited-access sites, etc.,) without having manually to type your name and password each time.

You can use an assortment of software that permit you to select which websites to accept cookies from and which not to. This does not solve the problem of the history file building up on your computer that can be used against you when you least expect it ('Ladies and gentlemen of the jury, his cookies file shows conclusively how often he accessed [whatever] rather than associate with his wife, as further evidence of my client's assertion in these divorce proceedings that he was not a loving husband').

The recommended approach is to fool remote sites into thinking that you accept their cookies by accepting them into RAM memory, but never to allow them to be written on your hard disk. In the case of Netscape Navigator/Communicator, simply make the cookies.txt file *for each and every profile you use* a read-only file. To do so:

1. Go to Program Files/Netscape/Users/Default (or the profile name instead of default).

2. Find cookies.txt.

3. Delete it.

4. Create a new text file at the same folder with the same name (cookies.txt).

5. Save it.

6. Right-click on it.

7. Select Properties.

8. Select the Read Only option.

9. Periodically check that file's size to make sure it is still zero. Netscape often takes it on itself to undo the read-only status of that file behind your back.

10. For good measure, before shutting the computer down each time, run any one or more of the many programs that clean after web-browsers' litter, such as ComClear from http://www.neuro-tech.net, NSClean from www.wizvax.net/kevinmca/, or Window Washer from http://www.webroot.com.

The only disadvantages of the above approach are as follows.

- For those websites that require you to sign in every time, you will have manually to sign in every time. (**Caution:** do not keep a list of user IDs and passwords in a file in your computer; it is far safer to keep such a list on a sheet of paper in a safe place.)

- You are still vulnerable to remote sits retrieving the cookies stored in RAM during your current online session. To remove this vulnerability, exit your browser, run any of the programs identified above for cleaning after web-browsers' litter, and re-enter your browser.

It is not recommended that you use Internet Explorer for web browsing or anything else (specifically including e-mail with Outlook or Outlook Express as well as any Usenet newsgroup reading or – God forbid – posting). Consider, instead, using Netscape or Opera.

Microsoft is inserting Platform for Privacy Preferences, or P3P, into the new version of Internet Explorer 6. The intent is to enable automatic reading of each accessed website's privacy policy so that you can pre-specify how you want to deal with that site based on its stated policy. Do not use it. As it became apparent when Amazon.com changed its privacy policy midstream from one of protecting its customer-provided data to one of far less such protection, some companies' stated privacy policies are not trustworthy.[9] Another example to keep in mind is that when a company goes bankrupt, its ostensibly private database of former customers' data becomes an 'asset' and the creditor that gets it or buys it is usually not bound by any privacy guarantees made by the now-bankrupt company to its then clients.

You would be well advised to reject all cookies as the default policy. When (not if) you come across a website that refuses to deal with you unless you enable cookies and that you want to deal with, go to Netscape's Edit/Preferences/Advanced setting and enable 'cookies sent only to the originator' after having first made the cookies.txt file a read-only one as per above so that the cookies will still never end up on your hard disk anyway. If you are also using Junkbuster (highly recommended), you will also have temporarily (for that website only) to deactivate it by going to Netscape's Edit/Preferences/Advanced/Proxies setting and selecting 'direct connection to the Internet'; make sure you return it to the previous proxies option when done with that one website.

5.5.7   Stealth cookies[10]

This amounts to a timing attack. The remote website looks at the visiting user web browser's 'cache' of recent activities (a log that all browsers compile to increase their apparent speed). The remote website then times how long it takes the visiting user's browser to respond to queries about other sites; a quick response indicates

---

[9] Interestingly, the Federal Trade Commission (FTC) decided on 25 May 2001 that Amazon.com did not deceive its customers when it made changes to its privacy policy. The FTC investigation was done in response to a complaint filed by the Electronic Privacy Information Center and Junkbusters Corp. Jason Catlett, president of Junkbusters, has responded to this decision of the FTC with a letter asking the FTC to order Amazon to submit to a privacy audit, and has stated that the FTC has traditionally been lenient on Amazon when it comes to privacy (CMPS Tech Web, 31 May 2001, 'Is FTC too forgiving of Amazon's privacy violations?').

[10] This privacy vulnerability was presented by Edward Felten and Michael Schneider in the *Proceedings of the Association for Computing Machinery Conference on Computer and Communications Security*, 1-4 November 2000, Athens, Greece; see http://www.sciencedaily.com/releases/2000/12/001208074325.htm.

that the particular site being queried was recently visited. No known counter-measures exist for current web browser designs other than exiting the web browser after each site visited, deleting the cache, and reopening the web browser.

5.5.8 Searching the searcher

Nothing done online is private, and that certainly includes any form of searching or looking; whereas nobody knows that particular article you may be looking at in a newspaper, this same privacy does not extend to 'just looking' at anything on the Internet (or any other network). This specifically applies to search engines on the Internet, such as http://www.altavista.com, http://www.google.com, http://www.excite.com, http://www.hotbot.com, http://www.lycos.com, http://www.metacrawler.com, http://yahoo.com, http://www.webcrawler.com, or any of the many others in existence.

An excellent paper that summarizes which search engines in the Internet collect what information is called 'Search Engines and Privacy', by Marc Roessler in Germany; the paper can be downloaded from http://www.franken.de/users/tentacle/papers/search-privacy.txt.

As with everything else discusssed in this book, you must first answer the question of what are you trying to hide and from whom. If all you are concerned with is to prevent remote websites from connecting you to what is being searched, you can simply:

- block cookies, and

- do not use Internet explorer, and

- block Java/Javascript/VBScriot/ActiveX/What'sRelated, and

- use SurfSecret (from http://www.surfsecret.com), and

- use Junkbuster, and

- set up your web browser with fake or no identifying information, and

- suppress or take the 'referrer' option (Junkbuster does this for you as an option).

Contrary to popular belief, all of the above will do precious little, however; your ISP will certainly know what you are doing, and many ISPs supplement their income by selling that information to companies that have lost their patience with users doing the above.

Plurimus Corp. of Durham, NC, (see http://stacks.msnbc.com/news/555017.asp), which formerly used the name Foveon Co., claims that it monitors 3.5 million

Internet users by getting the data from their ISPs. *Plurimus* means 'many' in Latin. Plurimus asserts that the data it collects are anonymized. Information about the Plurimus Program Overview is at http://www.plurimus.com/ISP/index.html.

Unless you use encryption to some go-between proxy, your ISP and any telehone tap will know what you are looking at, when, for how long, etc., If you use a proxy or other anonymizing site, *that* site will also know. What you need is some means of concatenating two (or more) go-between proxies in a manner that the closest proxy (that knows who you are) has no idea what you are looking at, and the proxy furthest away from you (the one accessing whatever you want to access) knows what is being accessed but has no idea by whom. Even that is not fool-proof because if those proxies keep records (and you really have no way of knowing if they do), their records could be subpoenaed (or confiscated in the case of totalitarian regimes), and a correlation of times will show who really accessed what and when. About the only way to get around that is to concatenate proxies in numerous different countries, preferably countries that hate each other and will not cooperate with each other.

And even that is not good enough if you live in a repressive regime, as the mere encrypted connection to your first proxy will irritate the regime you are in and prompt them to visit you and take a real good look at your hard disk. This means that, in addition to the use of concatenated proxies (see Section 5.3 earlier), you also have to ensure that nothing remains in your hard disk that can be used against you. Since it takes only seconds for a door to be broken down, this, in turn, implies that nothing should ever even enter your hard disk that could be used against you. This, in turn, means that you must either operate with no hard disk (I am unaware of any web browser that works off a floppy or even any of the new 100 MB super-floppies) or that you use full disk encryption (see Section 4.12) *and* be able to handle the likely demands that you decrypt that disk. And/or you must make the first connection to the Internet in a manner that totally bypasses the local regime, such as by using direct satellite connectivity, by connection to the Internet and to a website with SSL encryption using a GSM phone registered in another country, etc., (See Chapter 6).

The security pitfalls of being too modern

If you live in a totalitarian regime and decide to track an express package you sent by courier to the USA (Figure 5.6), be advised that this is rather unwise, for two reasons. First, your online tracking of the package could easily be monitored by the country you are in. If you track early enough, that country may become motivated to inspect the contents of your package under the guise of some local law (to check for the possible exportation of currency, etc.,) before it even leaves the country.

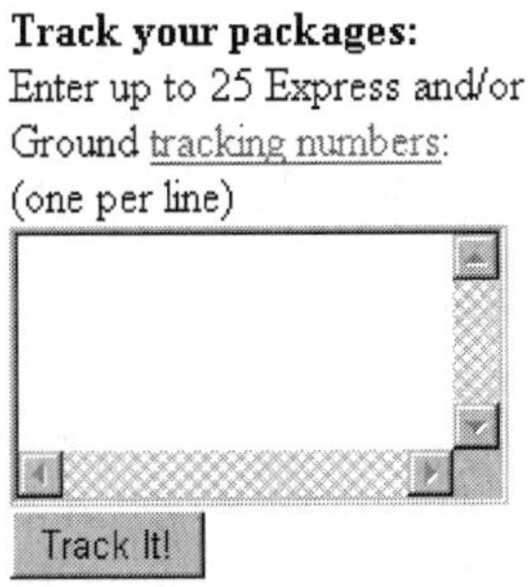

Track your packages:
Enter up to 25 Express and/or
Ground <u>tracking numbers</u>:
(one per line)

Track It!

Figure 5.6   FedEx dialog box enabling one to track a package online

Second, express courier services log all aspects of Internet-based tracking of packages (including the IP address that the tracking request originated from, which is readily traceable to you personally unless you went through anonymizing proxies and remailers as per Section 5.4). It is true that a US-based express courier service is most unlikely to capitulate to another country's desire for this information; it is also true that the Convention on Cybercrime, which has been proposed as a treaty by the Council of Europe, a 43-nation public body, and which, curiously, is allegedly the brainchild of the US Federal Bureau of Investigation (FBI), would obligate US law enforcement to force US couriers to comply with a member foreign country's request for that very same data, especially if that foreign country represents that request as 'terrorism investigation' or some such.

If you *must* check on the status of an express courier package that you either sent or are expecting, have someone else do it from within a free country and communicate back and forth with that someone else by encrypted e-mail or encrypted voice, if such communication would not get you in political trouble.

Again, at the risk of being repetitious: do not be alerting and do not pop up on a repressive regime's radar screen; once you do, you have lost the game and you might as well pack your bags before you contaminate your friends with your newfound status.

5.6 Usenet Newsgroup Security and Anonymity

There are some 100 000 electronic bulletin boards on as many topics,[11] also known as 'Usenet newsgroups' on the Internet. Topics range from very useful (medical

---

[11] Actually, this number is inflated by roughly a factor of three because it includes newsgroups that are dead (and many more than are 'brain dead') that have not been removed from existence.

information, suicide prevention, users' comments about software and hardware, factual travel information, etc.,) to the mundane. With such a large number of topics to pick from, and given that anyone can start a new topic – and many do – it is inevitable that the list includes topics that are revolting to some people, topics that are in poor taste, and even topics that are taboo in this or that country.

It has often been said, correctly, that the Internet mirrors life in many ways. Some ancient temples in India included in most tours have ornate carvings of just about every conceivable sexual variation; likewise with imagery in some Usenet newsgroups. Pauline Reage's *Story of O* that shocked France a century ago with its sadomasochistic theme has its counterparts in some Usenet newsgroups too. Fiery prose in favor of or against just about any human activity, such as drug use, anarchism, this or that religion, pro or con anything has always existed in 'real life' and exists in Usenet newsgroups as well.

It is not surprising, therefore, that most regimes take strong exception to a number of Usenet newsgroups. This manifests itself in censoring (which is technically impossible since one can access uncensored newsgroups through numerous ways discussed in this book) and in banning the viewing, posting, or possession of any material related to this or that topic; this is partially enforceable through online monitoring of all local ISPs and/or individual users, and through computer forensics on the computers of individual suspects who have become 'suspects' mostly through online monitoring.

Even some of the most pro-free-speech persons draw the line when the issue becomes one on a topic they consider sacrosanct for whatever reason. Eventually, it boils down to 'you can read or say anything as long as it is not . . .'. This is not as bigoted as it may seem; most of us consider some particularly hideous activities patently revolting and we really see no good reason why others should not too; what more effective way to ensure this than through legislation? No decent human being would tolerate the gleeful depiction of torture of handicapped elders or the vengeful desecration of whatever one has been raised to hold sacred.

One can have a lively intellectual discussion on the limits of free speech; as a US Justice once said, freedom of speech does not include the right to falsely yell 'fire' in a crowded theater and cause people to get killed as they stampede to escape the imaginary danger. But the fact remains that banning this or that Usenet newsgroup is censorship nonetheless; where does one draw the line?

If one takes the position that all adults should be free to see whatever they like, how does one ensure that impressionable children cannot do likewise and, in the process, form a distorted persona that will haunt them throughout life? Given that the world at large includes a fair share of individuals who are not mature or who are unstable, should the openly available Usenet newsgroups also include detailed information on how to make lethal poisons and explosives?

At the same time, the fact remains that laws do differ from country to country, and these differences have their roots in age-old social and religious backgrounds. Common law differs from the Koran, for example, and neither is about to change. A visiting business person in country X may have a very defensible and legitimate reason to want to obtain Usenet information on a topic which country X could consider taboo. Even an individual in a free democratic society may well want to ask for information on some medical condition that concerns him or her without permitting all his or her neighbors to know of this expressed interest.

It is reminded again that, pontifications by law enforcement to the contrary notwithstanding, the use of anonymous and pseudonymous speech played a vital role in the founding of the USA. When Thomas Paine's *Common Sense* was first released it was signed 'An Englishman'. Similarly, James Madison, Alexander Hamilton, John Jay, Samuel Adams, and others carried out the debate between Federalists and Anti-Federalists using pseudonyms. Finally the use of a pseudonym or 'nom de plume' in literature has a time-honored history (Mark Twain was Samuel Clemens, etc.,).

Even on the highest court of the land, US Supreme Court Justices have ruled in favor of anonymity:

> *Anonymity is a shield from the tyranny of the majority ... It thus exemplifies the purpose behind the Bill of Rights, and of the First Amendment in particular: to protect unpopular individuals from retaliation – and their ideas from suppression – at the hand of an intolerant society.*
> Justice Stevens, *McIntyre v. Ohio Elections Commission*, 1996

> *Anonymous pamphlets, leaflets, brochures and even books have played an important role in the progress of mankind. Persecuted groups and sects from time to time throughout history have been able to criticize oppressive practices and laws either anonymously or not at all.*
> Justice Black, *Talley v. California*, 1960

> *After reviewing the weight of the historical evidence, it seems that the Framers understood the First Amendment to protect an author's right to express his thoughts on political candidates or issues in an anonymous fashion.*
> Justice Thomas, *McIntyre v. Ohio Elections Commission*, 1996

In short, anonymous Usenet newsgroup access is legitimate in many cases. It is certainly defensible philosophically. This chapter is about 'how to go about it'.

It is interesting to ask, 'where are all the Usenet postings stored?' The answer, surprisingly, is 'wherever individual Usenet monitors feel like it, if at all'. There is no central Usenet depository nor authority. When a Usenet message is posted by anyone, it goes out worldwide; whichever entity with access to that 'wire' feels like capturing it can do so and can keep it for as little or as long as it likes. In fact, you can run your own Usenet server if you feel like it and if you have (and pay for) a connection to the Internet which is of high enough bandwidth to allow for the deluge of postings coming from some 100 000 newsgroups all the time. In fact, some people who wanted to 'spam' (to send unsolicited advertising) used to do just that. Realistically, running your own newsgroup server is highly impractical, not to mention attention-getting.

'Accessing' a Usenet newsgroup has two separate elements: viewing what others have said, and saying something (such as asking a question or expressing a view). Neither is anonymous unless one goes to considerable effort to make it so. Not surprisingly, anonymous viewing is easier to achieve than anonymous posting.

5.6.1   Secure Usenet viewing

The threats to anonymity here are from:

- one's ISP

- a phone tap

- screen-capturing software (commercially available; see Section 4.11)

- Van Eck radiation (see Section 3.2.7)

- the operator of the newsgroup server that one accesses; this may be the ISP or another server altogether

- every reader of a Usenet newsgroup posting

Before proceeding to take corrective actions, you should ask yourself just exactly what are you really trying to protect, from whom, and why; it may well be, for example, that Usenet viewing is not the best way to get the information you are looking for in the first place.

It must be realized that Usenet viewing is *not* a passive act. The mere process of selecting which newsgroups and which postings in each selected newsgroup to view is very much an active act and a very visible one at that. About the only substantive different between 'viewing' and 'posting on' newsgroups is that, in the latter case, you also risk antagonizing the viewers of what you post; as far as a local regime's censors are concerned, there is not much difference.

Also, keep in mind that, unless you take great lengths to prevent it [see the many subsection within this section (Section 5.6) that deal with the various individual threats], it is highly likely that the process of Usenet viewing will leave numerous traces on your hard disk that can subsequently be scrutinized by forensic analysis. Along those lines, it defies logic why most Internet users insist on using their Web browsers (which are notoriously full of security problems) for Usenet access. Do not! Use a dedicated Usenet software, instead, such as Gravity from http://www.microplanet.com/order If you leave the 'order' part off, you can download a free trial version.

To keep the local in-country ISP and a possible phone tap from observing your Usenet browsing, you can do the following:

- Use an encrypted (SSL) link to a newsserver that is unlikely to care about your viewing habits and one that is unlikely to be within the reach of your own country's legal reach; in short, one in another country with more freedom. Getting an encrypted connection to an out-of-country server is a separate step from getting Usenet access. The former can be done through http://www.rewebber.com in Germany, for example. Usenet access requires a separate subscription (since it is a for-profit service) to any of the following:

  - http://www.altopia.com

  - http://www.uncensored-news.com/

  - http://www.vip-news.com/

  - http://www.newsfeeds.com/

  and numerous others. A free one is available at http://news.cis.dfn.de/ but you have to sign up first to get a user ID and password. Keep in mind that:

  - the SSL anonymizer will know your IP address and is likely to record it;

  - the SSL anonymizer will want to get paid; this could further identify you to that anonynizer unless you take steps to prevent that;

  - the SSL anonymizer will know precisely what newsgroups and what posting in those newsgroups you are looking at;

  - unless you anonymize yourself from the SSL anonymizer (e.g., by accessing that service from someone else's computer and you pay for it using someone else's identity), you place a lot of faith in that anonymizing SSL.

- You can skip the encryption step and thumb your nose at local interception by accessing the newsgroups of your choice from someone else's computer. This clearly puts that 'someone else' at risk unless it is a public terminal (e.g., in a hotel, Internet café, public library, etc.,). In that case you must keep in mind that:

  o   public libraries and Internet cafés often require identification from their patrons that use the Internet; many also use video cameras to record the faces of their patrons.

  o   any online activity that antagonizes a local oppressive regime that monitor Internet usage could cause the enforcers to come within mimutes to the physical address of the 'public' establishment you patronize.

- You can bypass the entire local regime by connecting your computer to a system that accesses a satellite directly; options include Globalstar (slow), Inmarsat Mini-M, Starband 2-way satellite Internet access, etc (see Chapter 6).

5.6.2   Secure Usenet posting

In addition to the threats itemized listed above for viewing, one who posts has to contend with the following threats:

- keystroke-capturing software and hardware, commercially available (see Section 4.11),

- anyone and everyone who looks at the posted message or file in perpetuity.

Unless one has taken active measures to disguise one's identity well enough, it can readily be seen or it can easily be found if the disguise is nothing more than having changed the poster's name and e-mail address in the configuration settings of the newsgroup reading software prior to posting.[12] Even if years have elapsed since a message was posted and the message can no longer be seen on the newsgroup itself, numerous commercial and other organizations make a practice of saving them all

---

[12] Given the long list of security-related problems associated with Netscape and especially with Internet Explorer, do not use either of them for either e-mail or for Usenet access (reading or writing). For Usenet access, one should use, instead, software made just for Usenet access, such as Forte Agent from http://www.arrowweb.com/tecNovia/home.htm (among many other sources).

and of making those huge databases searchable on the basis of keywords, sender's name, date, topic, etc., Since it is inevitable that even the most innocuous phrase may irritate some one person somewhere on earth, common sense dictates that one should post pseudonymously or anonymously. Also, given the fact that a lot of junk e-mail ('spam') comes from senders who retrieve valid e-mail addresses from Usenet postings, one is again well-advised not to post Usenet messages with a valid name or valid e-mail address.

You may want to ask yourself, in view of all of the foregoing, at this stage, 'Why post anything on Usenet?'

- Is it to advertise something ('spam')? Don't do it. It is bad form. It is also illegal in increasingly more countries. It is also very annoying.

- Is it to proclaim to the world your views on something? Don't do it; nobody cares.

- Is it to proselytize others to your point of view? Don't do it; it won't work; anybody who gets convinced to a point of view merely by reading notoriously unreliable Usenet postings is not worth proselytizing.

- Is it to defame or libel someone? Do not do it. It is abuse of freedom of expression, bad form, and likely to get lawyers to subpoena numerous servers' logs (and possibly even your own computer, if you are a suspect) to try to identify you for civil action.

- Is it to communicate confidentially and discretely with a third party? Here you may have a point. Use innocuous and mundane postings if you must.

- Is it 'whistle blowing' to air a patently illegal act? This is not the best way to do it. Send you anonymous complaint only to the handful of persons who can do something about it.

Legitimate (philosophically, not necessarily legally) postings could be honest technical questions to others who are likely to know, for example: 'When is the best time to visit Upper Slobovia' (or whichever country you want to travel to), or 'Why does Windows crash when I do this or that?', and so on. Even then, do *not* use your true e-mail address or name, in order to reduce the amount of junk mail you will receive from advertising entities that look for real e-mail addresses.

Keep in mind that the server that you use to access Usenet will add a line of information to what you post (the NNTP header) over which you have no control[13] this should also stand as a reminder that anyone who sees your posted message will know which server it came from and could subpoena that server to find out (from that server's logs) which customer (you) made the posting.[14] Unless you have taken steps to preclude that, merely changing your username and e-mail address in your Usenet posting software is really no fig leaf at all.

No Usenet reading or posting software can alter your IP address you post from because none of them can change what they do not add in the first place. The IP address is added by the server you use for reading or posting Usenet messages.

The choices you have for anonymous posting to Usenet are the following:

1. Use COTSE's service (https://www.cotse.net), but keep in mind that the e-mail name of your account with that company will show up on the posting depending on how you have configured your service. This is nowhere near as secure as Mixmaster remailers [see item (4) below] but very convenient.

2. Use http://www.nymserver.com or http://www.mailanon.com but keep in mind that, since you have to 'sign up' with either, they will know who posted what to where and they can and will disclose that information if subpoenaed.

3. First install and use a proxy server that changes your IP address (see Section 5.3 on proxies), then set up a pseudonymous account with a free service such as http://www.hotmail.com or http://www.netaddress.com/, and, finally, after both of these are working, access news at http://newsone.net/nnr/browse.

4. First set up an anonymous remailer using any of the web-based anonymous remailers such as https://riot.eu.org/cgi/remailer.cgi, or best of all, use the Mixmaster remailers through Private Idaho, JBN, or QuickSilver (see Sections

---

[13] You can get around this by using a server that does not add this information, such as Altopia, Newscene, and Remarq (formerly Supernews). Altopia (www.altopia.com) costs around $6 per month ($12 per month if you want binaries, too) but has a poor retention of only 2–3 days and has very slow download speeds. Remarq (www.remarq.com) keeps Usenet messages longer but is alleged to be hard to deal with. Remarq and Newscene (www.newscene.com) have metered service of so many gigabytes of downloads per month. Some servers even add your IP address(!) to what you post; luckily most readers of Usenet postings do not know how to read the extended headers that come with the posted messages; servers that strip your IP address from the postings include www.cotse.com, www.hushmail.com, and others.

[14] This holds in spades if you use a high-speed connection to the Internet, such as through a DSL or cable modem, in which case you effectively have a static IP address for a long time; even if you are a dial-up customer to whom the ISP dynamically assigns an IP address, your ISP keeps logs of who had which IP address when, and can still track you down many days or weeks after the fact.

5.4.2–5.4.4), and then send your post as an e-mail using the e-mail-to-news gateways obtainable from http://www.duke.edu/~mg/usenet/mail-to-news.html. Keep in mind that those change all the time. Ones to try include:

- group.name@news.cs.dal.ca

- group.name@news.demon.co.uk

- group.name@alpha.jpunix..com

- group.name@dispatch.demon.co.uk

- group.name@brushtail.hna.com.au

- group.name@myriad.alias.net

- group.name@news.cs.indiana.edu

- group.name@undergrad.math.uwaterloo.ca

- group.name@magnus.acs.ohio-state.edu

- group-name-news@newsbase.cs.yale.edu

- group.name@comlab.ox.ac.uk

- group.name@ccs.uwo.ca

- group.name@julian.uwo.ca

- group.name@ug.cs.dal.ca (Limited newsgroups)

- group.name@usenet.ucs.indiana.edu (Preserves all headers)

- group.name@bull.com

- group.name@cass.ma02.bull.com

- group.name@paris.ics.uci.edu

The e-mail that you send to those gateways has to be addressed as follows, assuming for example that you are using the last gateway above and are posting to alt.security.pgp:

m2n-YYYYMMDD-alt.security.pgp@paris.ics.uci.edu

where YYYYMMDD is the current calendar date. Try it first with a mundane posting.

5. First, configure your newsreader software so that there is no indication of your identity in it; make sure you are not using a web browser as a newsreader. Second, download the SocksCap32 software from http://www.socks.nec.com/ so that it will change your IP address to is own. Finally, use a free 'socks' server that you can find at http://tools.rosinstrument.com/proxy/. Again, try it with a mundane test posting and look at the end result very carefully to make sure that it contains no identifying information; be aware that the 'looking' will readily show to someone who is watching your Internet connection (telephone tap or the ISP) that you are carefully looking at a specific anonymous posting after you were seen doing all of the above; this will strongly suggest that you are the author of that test posting.

5.7 Web Bugs to Track E-mail, Reading of Usenet Posts, and Website Visits

A 'web bug' is an html tag that is invisible (because it can be as small as 1×1 pixels) and is part of a website's image intended to track those visiting it. It is also known by such politically correct terms as 'clear gif', 'invisible gif', among others. This html tag is usually loaded into the web page from a different server from the rest of the page, when one visits such a website, that 'other' server is contacted and is provided with the visitor's IP address as well as with the standard information that is volunteered by web browsers, such as type of browser, previous website visited, previously set cookie values, etc.

To detect the web bug one has to view the html source code of the website being accessed (look for 'height' and 'width' parameter values of 1 and for that pixel being served by a different server.

The same technique is used with incoming e-mails; they can contain the same kind of html code that is invisible yet causes one's e-mail client software (if it is capable and enabled to handle html e-mail) to contact the Internet site affiliated with the web bug so as to notify it that the e-mail sent has been received and opened. This is of obvious use to bulk mailers of junk e-mail who want to know which of those e-mail addresses are valid. It is just as useful to any snoop. There were numerous Usenet postings in 2001 alleging that reputable companies as Barnes and Noble, eToys, Microsoft, and others (e.g., see also http://www.cexx.org/adware.htm).

Web bugs are also easy to place in Microsoft Word and some other Microsoft Office documents, as was demonstrated by The Privacy Foundation, an Internet privacy research foundation run by the University of Denver (http://news.cnet.com/news/0-1005-200-2652562.htm?tag=st.ne.ron.lthd.ni and http://www.privacy foundation.org/advisories/advWordBugs.html. Any portion containing that web bug that is Edit/pasted to another document will also be contaminated by that web bug.

When a web bug is hidden in a Microsoft Word document, the web bug can transmit secretly via the Internet:

- the full URL of the web bug image, which can contain any information the inserter of the web bug wants, such as a unique ID number for the document, the name of the person to whom the document was originally sent, etc.;

- an optional browser cookie;

- the IP address and host name of the computer that wants the web bug;

- an identification of the document that has the web bug.

Placing a web bug in a Word document is easy:

1. Insert/Picture/From File.

2. Type the URL in the 'File Name' field of the 'Insert Picture' dialog box.

3. Select the 'Link to File' option of the Insert button.

To track the movement of the web bug in this simple manner will require access to the sender's server logs.
   Note:

- web bugs have already caused a number of privacy-related lawsuits;

- web bugs cannot be removed from html pages.

The security threat is obvious and serious. A repressive regime can place web bugs in Usenet newsgroup messages that its citizens are not supposed to read and then obtain the e-mail addresses of those who read them, along with the time/date stamp that can be correlated with surveilled citizens' whereabouts.

For demonstration of a bugged Yahoo profile, one can visit http://profiles.yahoo.com/webbug2000, where the bug will show you the name of your own computer in addition to planting a cookie into your computer from www.privacycenter.du.edu (not a threat because everyone gets the same cookie and it expires within five days).

One particularly disconcerting application of web bugs is in bugging e-mail so that a third party will be notified every time an incoming e-mail is read, to whom it is forwarded (if it is forwarded), and even what comments were added by everyone who forwards it. This disastrous situation can occur with Outlook,[15] Outlook Express, and web browsers being used to read e-mail. A pictorial depiction of what is happening is shown in Figure 5.7.

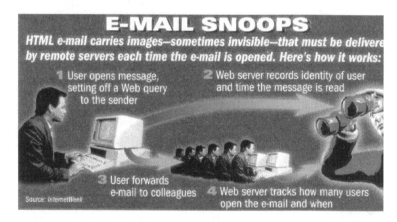

Figure 5.7   E-mail snooping through invisible html images; reproduced with permission from *InternetWeek*

Since this bugging technique uses html and since html e-mail can look quite 'normal', an easy way to detect if an incoming e-mail is html is to right click on its body; if an option that appears is 'view source', then it is html.

For a self-congratulatory text on all that can be done by web bugs by a company that provides that capability to those who pay for it, see http://www.doc-tracker.com. That company's tracking will work with Word, Excel, Power-Point, and html documents. The document can be tracked for ever as long as one pays the company to provide the information as to which document was accessed when and by whom.

---

[15] Use of Outlook and Outlook Express is now forbidden within some US companies for basically the reasons outlined in Microsoft's own website http://www.microsoft.com/technet/security/bulletin/MS01-012.asp.

5.7.1   Web bugs and AOL

As of 5 October 2001, AOL modified its privacy policy in a manner that clears the way for that company to use some online tracking tools (such as cookies and web bugs), according to CNET (http://news.cnet.com/news/0-1005-200-7421528.html). AOL spokesman Andrew Weinstein has stated that AOL would not track user behavior but would only use web bugs to track aggregates, such as how many users view a given ad.

5.7.2   Negating web bugs

1. In e-mail:

   (a) Disable html in your e-mail reader.

   (b) Do not read your e-mail when online. After downloading your e-mail, go offline and then read your e-mail.

   (c) Do not 'reply to' nor 'forward' e-mail if in doubt. Compose a new one instead.

   (d) Do not use a web browser to read your e-mail. Use an e-mail program and make sure you disable any html capability.

   (e) Do not use Outlook or Outlook Express as e-mail clients.

   (f) Disable Javascript.

   (g) Install and use Zone Alarm Pro (http://www.zonelabs.com). Go to the configuration panel for your e-mail software, such as Eudora, and click on the 'options' red button as shown in Figure 5.8.

   (h) Now select the 'ports' option and specify that you only want your e-mail reader to access the ports that e-mail software have a legitimate need for, such as pop and smtp server ports, as shown in Figure 5.9.

   This 'works' because most web bugs use port 80 to communicate out. Note: it is easier to opt, instead, for 'Allow access for any port EXCEPT for those checked below' where 'those checked below' should be the web port 80. Use the same technique for the whichever Usenet software you elect to use for

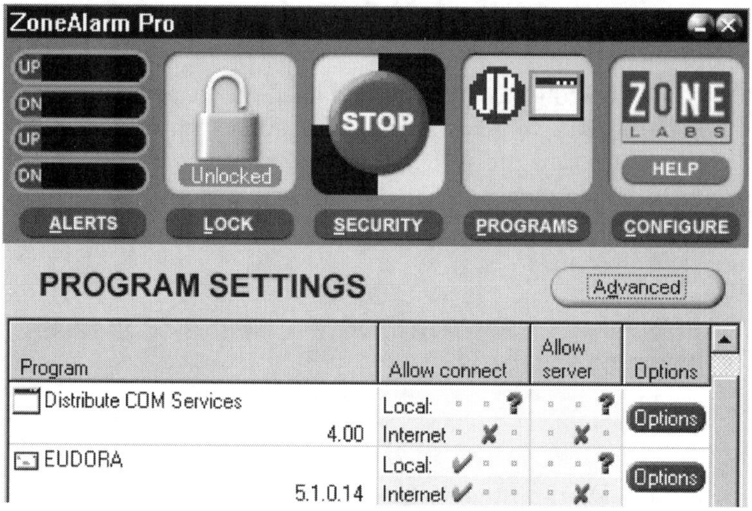

Figure 5.8   Setting up Zone Alarm Pro to defeat web bugs in e-mail

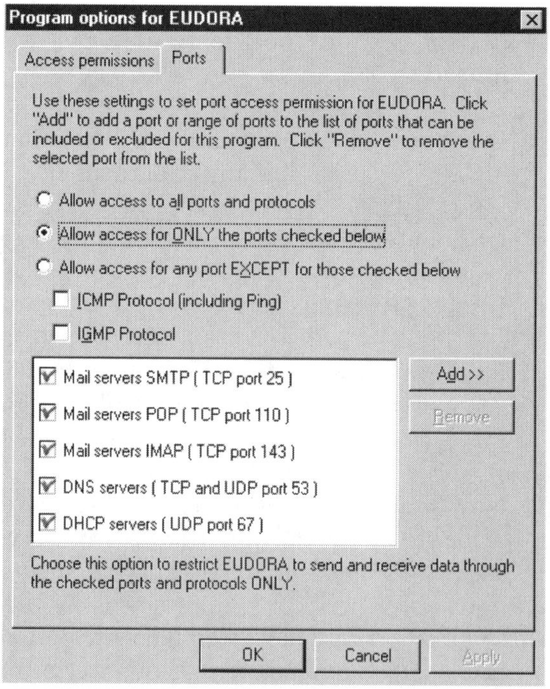

Figure 5.9   Preventing web bugs from accessing the Internet

reading Usenet posts so that your choices of what to read will not be broadcast to anyone snooping on your choices (see item (2) below).

2. In Usenet reading:

    (a) Do not use a web browser for Usenet access. Instead use a newsreader such as Forte Agent, referenced in Footnote 12. Keep in mind that the IP address of your postings is *not* added by your software and therefore; cannot be removed by tinkering with your newsposting software; you have to route your posting through anonymizing remailers, such as the Mixmaster types (see Section 5.4).

    (b) Do not read Usenet e-mail online. Download an entire series of messages and read them offline.

    (c) Do not use your ISP's Usenet servers. Use others that (one hopes) do not track your IP address, such as http://www.altopia.com. For good measure, access them through an anonymizer service.

    (d) Access Usenet only through anonymizers.

3. In web browsing:

    (a) Disable cookies.

    (b) Disable Java, Javascript, ActiveX, VBScript.

    (c) Use an anonymizing proxy such as Junkbusters (http://www.junkbuster.com) after you configure it properly for your web browser.

    (d) Do not use Internet Explorer.

5.8 Secure E-mail

5.8.1 What any encryption software will *not* do

Even the most unbreakable encryption in the universe will, in and by itself:

- *not* prevent you from leaving an unencrypted version on your hard disk,

- *not* prevent unencrypted data from leaking into the swap/Paging files if you use Windows,

- *not* keep you from selecting a poor key (such as your birthday) or passphrase (such as the first few words from a popular poem),

- *not* prevent a keystroke-capturing piece of software or hardware from stealing your encryption key and passing it to someone else,

- *not* prevent your computer from radiating anything going to its screen for commercially available systems to intercept across the street,

- *not* hide the e-mail connectivity of who is sending that encrypted file to whom,

- *not* hide the alerting fact that the file is encrypted,

- *not* prevent the intended recipient of your encrypted file from publicizing it to people that you did not want to see it,

- *not* prevent the intended recipient of your encrypted file from inadvertently quoting your decrypted message in an unencrypted reply,

- *not* protect you losing or otherwise compromising your encryption and decryption keys,

- *not* prevent you from being fooled by someone who claims to be Alice and who gives you what you naively believe to be Alice's encryption key, from being, in fact, Ted (The 'man-in-the-middle' problem).

The above cannot be emphasized enough. At the risk of being repetitious, but in the interest of preventing a potential calamity, it is stated yet once more that the process of actually encrypting a file is only a very small part of the overall process of hiding something from someone. It is really pointless to have a huge padlock on the front door when the backdoor and the windows are left wide open; in fact, it is worse than pointless because it allows one to hold the misconception that the house is more secure than without that padlock, which is not the case.

This having been said, and I hope that the reader takes the above message to heart and takes the appropriate measures discussed throughout this book that address all of the other parts of the overall process of hiding something from someone, we can now address the actual issue of encryption.

The best software for encrypting files to be e-mailed to someone else is PGP because:

- its source code has been out in the open ever since the project started many years ago and it has withstood the intense scrutiny of a large number of qualified cryptologists;

- the encryption algorithms that it uses are mainstream ones that have also withstood the intense scrutiny of a large number of qualified users;

- it is openly available worldwide to anyone at no cost; one does not need to send it to an intended correspondent;

- for those who suspect that their copy may have been modified, it is available from multiple independent sources online both in digitally signed machine language (executable) form and even in source code form that one can compile on one's own into an executable file;

- there is no evidence that it has ever been 'broken' through cryptanalysis by anyone;

- it uses public key encryption, which allows any two people who have never met and who may never have the luxury of a secure means to exchange encryption keys to communicate with encrypted messages.

The serious problem of authenticating the sender of encrypted messages

Far worse than not receiving a sensitive message is receiving one that appears to have been sent by the identified sender but was, in fact, faked and was sent by a third party. This can result in a disastrous situation because the recipient could end up acting on false information. If it is a financial matter (e.g., a falsified filing at the Securities and Exchange Commission), this could result in financial losses and a manipulated stock market. It could also result in the loss of life: imagine a forged e-mail to a police informant that appears to be coming from the police but is in fact coming from a drug cartel inviting that informant to a meeting.

Any encryption scheme, whether conventional (where the sender and the receiver share the same key) or public key (where the decryption key is different from the encryption key), have a fundamental logical weakness that has nothing to do with mathematics: the sender and the receiver must have some *totally independent* means of assuring each other that they are who they claim to be. In fact, the same need applies to the case of no encryption just as well: a stamped letter that claims that it came from Mary does not prove that it really came from her; the recipient needs some independent means of verifying it, such as the handwriting, the content that refers to information that only Mary could have known, etc. Unlike conventional mail, one cannot check handwriting in e-mail and the electronic return address can easily be faked.

In the case of conventional (symmetric) encryption where both sender and recipient use the same key, there is no proof that nobody else has that key, too. In the case of public key encryption (see Section 5.8.3), just because some server or database asserts that a public key belongs to the local police does not mean that it does not, in fact, belong to the local criminal, instead; a sender of e-mail would be a fool to e-mail sensitive information encrypted with that public key without independent corroboration of that key's ownership.[16]

Public key encryption is often – mistakenly – claimed to have solved the problem of allowing two people who have never met to exchange encrypted information that nobody else can read. In reality it has not because these two people still need some *independent* way of authenticating themselves to each other, and this is extremely difficult unless:

- there is some third party that is unquestionably trusted by both that can act as an official certifier ('Mr Smith, this is Mrs Jones; Mrs Jones, this is Mr Smith'), or

- the content of the electronic messages exchanged involves some 'challenge and response' such as 'if you are my brother, what happened seventeen years ago to Aunt Mary during her birthday?'

It is only after this independent authentication has taken place that the two individuals can trust each other's public key encrypted e-mail (subject to all the other 'ifs, buts, and howevers' of elsewhere in this section). They can never trust the confidentiality nor the authenticity of each other's *conventionally* encrypted e-mail because there is no logical way they can assure themselves that nobody else has stolen a copy of that same key.

---

[16] Falling victim to this impersonation would be as naive as the California bank customers who saw a sign over the bank's night deposit slot that read 'Out of order; please use temporary box to the right'. By early morning, that 'temporary box' had been removed by whoever placed it there, along with the deposits in it.

The foregoing is intended as yet another strong reminder that encryption in and by itself can lull one into a very dangerous complacency and false sense of security. Encryption can only be a part of an entire security process and never be a standalone solution.

5.8.2 Conventional (symmetric) encryption

In conventional encryption, the same key used to encrypt a file must be used to decrypt it. This is all well and good if there is some secure way that the sender and the recipient can communicate that shared key. Often, this is not possible.

Such encryption uses any one of numerous mathematical operations ('algorithms' or recipes) which take the unencrypted data (the 'palintext'), do something to it, and convert it into its encrypted version (the 'ciphertext').

The best such algorithms are: Triple-DES (also known as 3DES), Idea, Blowfish, Twofish, Cast, and Rijandel (which is the Belgian algorithm that was very recently selected as the new advanced encryption standard [AES] to replace DES). One can get into a heated debate as to which of the above is 'more secure'; the reality is that they are all unbreakable if properly implemented.

Idea is a 128 bit cipher and was developed by Xuejia Lai.[17] It requires a license for commercial use but is free for personal use. Even though it has a large number of keys that are 'weak',[18] the likelihood that one will pick one of those among all possible keys is infinitesimally small (2^{-77}) which is far smaller[19] than the chance of being hit by a meteorite on the head while walking to the beach.

Cast is a family of algorithms developed by C. Adams and S. Tavares. The PGP version of Cast has 128 bits and is also considered to be secure. It is the default algorithm in newer versions of PGP owing to the patent issues of Idea above. Although some Cast designs have been successfully attacked,[20] the version used in PGP has not been successfully attacked.

3DES is a triple sequential application of DES. It is considered secure.

Rijandel (or AES) is not yet implemented in PGP. It accommodates key lengths of 128, 196, and 256 bits. It is considered secure.

Twofish is an evolution from Blowfish. Both Blowfish and Twofish were dev-

---

[17] See X. Lai, 1991, 'Detailed Description and a Software Implementation of the IPES Cipher', Institute for Signal and Information Processing, ETH-Zentrum, Zurich, Switzerland.

[18] See J. Daemen *et al*,. 1993, 'Weak Deys for DIEA'.

[19] See A. J. Menzies *et al*., 1996, *Handbook of Applied Cryptograpbty*, CRC Press, Boca Raton, FL.

[20] See J. Kasey *et al*., 1997, 'Related-key Cryptanalysis of 3-WAY, Biham-DES, CAST, DES-X, newDES, RC2 and TEA'.

eloped by noted cryptologist Bruce Schneier. It is also considered secure. It has not had the benefit yet of a long time of being assessed, but there is no indication that it will not withstand such scrutiny. It was one of the five finalist contenders to become the AES (as decided by the National Institute of Standards in consultation with the National Security Agency).

Clearly, the longer the encryption key, the more possibilities there are for one that attempts to try every single possible key ('exhaustive cryptanalysis') to find it. Conventional encryption keys of length equal to or longer than 128 bits are considered unbreakable today and for the foreseeable future.

5.8.3 Public key encryption

Public key encryption is the brainchild of W, Diffie and Hellman. The idea in a nutshell is this:

1. You and I each get a copy of a software that implements it, such as PGP.

2. When we first 'run' the program we ask it to 'create keys'. It creates not one, not three, but always two keys. These keys bear a mathematical relationship to each other. The keys that you create and that I create will be totally different because they are based on some extensive randomness in our respective computers.

3. Each of us calls one of these two keys the 'public' key and the other the 'secret key'. PGP takes care of which one is called what.

4. We each publicize our respective 'public keys' to each other, or even to the whole wide world (though there is hardly a good reason most of the time for alerting the whole wide world that we are into encryption).

5. If I want to encrypt something to you, I use your public key. The resulting encrypted message can only be decrypted by you and by nobody else because only you have the dual of your own public key, namely, your secret key; not even I who encrypted it can decrypt it. Conversely, if you want to encrypt a message to me, you use my public key to encrypt it and the only way to decrypt it is by my secret key (which is the dual to my public key).

In short, a message encrypted with a public key can be decrypted only by the secret key that was created at the same time as the public key. The converse is also true: a message that is encrypted with my secret key (that only I have) can be decrypted only with my public key (that everybody has), thereby proving that I am the one who wrote it.

So far so good. But there is a fly in the ointment. If I receive a message (electronic or otherwise) that claims to have come from you and includes your public key, I really have no way of knowing if that message really and truly came from you and not from my worst enemy. As such, if I were to go on faith and encrypt a message with my most highly prized recipe for chocolate pie to what I thought was your public key, the message will be read by my nemesis and not by you. If that 'man in the middle' is smart enough, he can even forward my message to you after reading it first, by encrypting it with you real public key and really sending it to you; this way you will get the message that I sent you and neither of us will know that we have been 'had'. This applies to the converse path just as well.

In short, *whether using conventional symmetric encryption or public key encryption, you must have some independent way of verifying that an encryption key came from the person you think it came* and not from an enterprising go-between man-in-the-middle. This independent means can be whatever is appropriate for the situation at hand; it can be a voice conversation if you know the other person's voice, a personal meeting (which partially negates the advantages of public key encryption), and so on.

5.8.4 PGP

> *If all the personal computers in the world −* ∼*260 million computers −*
> *were put to work on a single PGP-encrypted message, it would still take an*
> *estimated 12 million times the age of the universe, on average, to break a*
> *single message.*
>
> Wiliam Crowell, Deputy Director of the National Security Agency

For the past decade or so, PGP has been the defacto standard for encrypting e-mail to others. The DOS versions of yesteryear are the most secure and are highly recommended instead of the Windows versions of today that are not recommended. Unlike the Windows-based versions that can be installed very quickly, however, getting the DOS versions installed properly can take up to an hour or two; this is done only once, though, and is well worth it in terms of security. If you do install and use the DOS versions, do not do so in a 'DOS window' of Windows but boot your computer with DOS from a floppy disk instead. Yes, it is a bit of a hassle the first time around but the security provided is incomparably higher and this is the whole point of using effective personal encryption in the first place.

An excellent tutorial on PGP can be found at http://home.mpinet.net/pilobilus/ ComSec2.htm. A more esoteric but excellent reference for the advanced user can be found at http://scramdisk.clara.net/pgpfaq.html. Excellent extensive information is also available at http://cryptography.org/getpgp.htm and at http://cryptography.org/getpgp.txt.

How PGP Works

Since public key encryption is way too slow compared with conventional encryption, PGP, as well as practically all public key encryption software, use conventional ('symmetric') encryption to encrypt the plaintext with an encryption key that is locally generated, on the spot, at the sending machine. It is that locally generated conventional encryption key that is then encrypted with public key encryption using the public key of the intended recipient. What gets e-mailed or sent to the intended recipient is both the conventionally encrypted message and the public key encrypted key for that conventionally encrypted message. This is all done in a single seamless operation that requires no action from the user.

At the receiving end, the process is reversed. The public key encrypted portion is decrypted with the intended recipient's secret key to reveal the conventional encryption key used to encrypt the plaintext into a ciphertext. The ciphertext is then decrypted and displayed to the intended recipient.

It is that simple!

Actually, PGP (and most public key encryption implementations) can perform two more useful functions:

- ascertain that the decrypted message you received from me has not been doctored while in transit;

- ascertain that the message you received was indeed from me and not from an impersonator (this is conditional on having precluded the 'man-in-the-middle' problem described above, which is done conclusively by having an independent means to assure oneself once and for all that a key came from the person who claims to have sent it).

Both of these functions are done in a single process, as follows:

1. My PGP takes a 'digital digest' (essentially a short digital summary of the message being sent); this digital summary is mathematically impossible to be the same if the message is altered;

2. my PGP then encrypts that digital digest with my *secret* key;

3. my PGP appends that encrypted output from step (2) above to that which is sent to you.

At your end, your PGP will first try to decrypt item (2) above by using my public key that you have. If it succeeds, it means that the message indeed came from me because my public key can only decrypt what was encrypted by my secret key that (hopefully) only I have.

Your PGP will then decrypt the message and, independently, generate a digital digest at your end just like I generated one at my end before sending it. If the two digital digests match 'to a t', then the message could not have been altered in public.

PGP messages to someone with no PGP

You have two choices:

- You use your PGP not to encrypt but merely to sign digitally (authenticate) your message to the recipient. This is routine and 'socially acceptable'; even Microsoft digitally signs (with PGP) its security bulletins that it e-mails to those who subscribe to them. Of course, for this to be of any use to the recipient, he or she must know a thing or two about PGP and bother to check your PGP digital signature; realistically, this means that the recipient might as well have an installed version of PGP to do this. Most people do *not* validate the authentication of a digitally signed message.

- You can encrypt your message into a self-decrypting file if you use PGP version 6.5 or higher and both you and the intended recipient use the same operating system. The practical problem then will be how to communicate the decrypting key (actually passphrase) to the intended recipient in a secure manner; the logical conundrum here is the fundamental problem with any conventional (nonpublic key) encryption system; namely, that if you find a secure way to communicate the decryption key, then you might as well communicate the entire message.

PGP use for the highest security

Anyone who wants to go through the process of encrypting with a serious encryption program such as *PGP* is assumed to be serious enough about it to forego conveniences that compromise security. This means *do not use any of the Windows-based PGP versions.*

Yes, it may be 'inconvenient' to use the DOS-based ones, but the inconvenience is fictional because it is more than made up for by not having to spend the vast amount of time to clean up after the security weaknesses of anything running on Windows.

The procedure below comes as close as possible to guaranteeing security in encryption:

1. Get a cheap computer. You should be able to get a free one.

2. Get rid of its hard disk. If possible, install a second floppy disk drive.

3. Make a bootable floppy disk with DOS version 6.22.

4. Create a RAM disk by entering the following line in the CONFIG.SYS file:

    DEVICE=C:\DOS\RAMDRIVE.SYS 4444/E

5. Get an old DOS version of PGP, such as 2.6.3a, or better yet, get version 2.6.3 iaMULTI[21] from http://disastry.dhs.org/pgp/263multi.htm and from http://www.ipgpp.com (this PGP version includes the option for long keys and for using the new encryption algorithms such as AES, Twofish, etc.,), or any DOS-based version, from CKT at http://www.ipgpp.com.

6. Do *not* run the DOS version of PGP from the DOS window of Windows, as this defeats the whole purpose of using the DOS version.

7. Install it on the floppy disk after reading the voluminous but very informative instructions. This will take a while but you do it only once. Do not forget to add the required line in the AUTOEXEC.BAT file as well as the required text change in the CONFIG.TXT file. Configure it to use the RAM disk created in (4) above for its scratch disk area.

---

[21] • Supports Idea, Cast5, Blowfish, Twofish, AES (Rijandel) and 3DES ciphers for encryption.

   • Supports MD5, SHA1, and RIPEMD160 message digest algorithms.

   • Supports RSA keys up to 4096 bit.

   • Does not choke DSS/DH signatures and keys found in key files.

   • Supports key expiration time.

   • Allows to change 'Version:' line.

8. Do *not* give in to the PGP prompt to identify your key with your name and e-mail address. Instead, enter a nondescript name and address such as 'John Doe IV' and *someone@somewhere.com*, or some such.

9. If you get a version that allows it, change the 'Version number' that your PGP version advertises in every message it creates; change it to some other version so as to confuse further a possible threat.

10. Create a keypair of the longest length that is supported by the version you got; make it no less than 4096 bits. Ignore the pontifications by those who claim that it is 'not needed'. It is! Ignore pontifications by others about 'compatibility' because you should not be exchanging encrypted mail with a cast of thousands that you have never met anyway, because of the 'man-in-the-middle' problem.[22] This can take the computer as long as a few hours if you use a slow old computer. That is fine. You will do it only once. Use a very long (at least 30 pseudorandom symbols) and a very unpredictable passphrase that includes upper and lower case, numbers, misspellings, and punctuation symbols. Make sure you can remember it after a few weeks. Do not write it down.

11. Make the DOS boot-up floppy read only.

12. Do not publicize your 'public' keys except to those with whom you communicate.

13. Regularly trash the previously generated keypair and create a new one. If it is a particularly sensitive communication, create a keypair just for that one and destroy it after you have received a reply.

14. Insist that the person you communicate with does likewise. Since you are personally far more liable for what you send than for what others send you, and since what you send is protected by the recipient's public key (and hence by the recipient's security), insist that the recipient is equally security conscious.

15. Store the PGP floppy disk in a secure but not obvious place. The 'safe' in which you keep family heirlooms is too obvious; some empty space in the kids' toys or the bottom of the sugar can that says 'coffee' on the outside may be better.

---

[22] As described above, the 'man-in-the-middle' problem is a logical problem that applies to all encryption, whether public key or conventional. It amounts, quite simply, to this: unless you have some foolproof *independent* means of verifying that a certain key does indeed belong to the person you think it does, you may end up communicating through a 'man-in-the-middle' who reads your encrypted e-mail before forwarding it to the intended recipient. Not a nice predicament to be in.

16. Do all of your encryption and decryption on that standalone old DOS computer that has no hard disk, using *only* the RAM disk for unencrypted text. Use DOS's own minimal text editors (such as EDIT.COM) for text entry. Store only encrypted files on the floppy disk. To send by e-mail, take the floppy disk and copy the encrypted files to the computer that is used to connect to the Internet.

17. If you live in a place that takes a dim view of encryption (all countries do), consider downloading the DOS utility Stealth v 1.1 by Henry Hastur. All it does is to remove the tell-tale header and footer of a PGP-encrypted message. Your correspondent should also have it so as to reinsert them prior to decrypting. After you have run your PGP-encrypted file through Stealth you can further disguise it with steganography (see Section 5.9), merging with another file, or what-not. Whatever you do, do not do it more than once or twice or it will become alerting. The utility Stealth is available from numerous sites, such as ftp.dsi.unimi.it, where version 1.0 is at subdirectory /pub/security/crypt/PGP/stealth.zip, and version 1.1 is available at subdirectory /pub/security/crypt/code/stealth.zip. Detailed information about how to use Stealth is available at http://www.infonex.com/~mark/pgp/s-readme.html. It is important to use Stealth with no hard disk as it tends to leave temporary files behind.

Less-secure (Windows-based) PGP

If you are totally unwilling to spend the mere couple of hours needed to learn the basics of using DOS and are willing to take the significant security risks involved with using encryption on Windows (which requires the hard disk), then at least get PGP version 6.02CKT build 7 from http://www.ipgpp.com. Again, you are taking *major* security risks by using Windows and a hard disk.

Positively do *not* use any of the version 7 PGP Security Suite products, and certainly not any post-7.3 version because NAI that made them stopped releasing the source code coincidentally with a few other concurrent events of concern (see http://www.McCune.cc/PGP.htm).

Also do *not* install trouble-prone PGPdisk nor PGPnet as part of the installation.

Practical aspects of installation and use

1. Get your PGP copy from a trustworthy source, such as:

    (a) the MIT distribution site at http://web.mit.edu/network/pgp.html,

(b) the CKT site http://www.ipgpp.com (for long-key versions).

2. Check the digital signature of that file to verify that it is legitimate.

3. Do *not* generate keys while online. In fact, do *not* install PGP or any other encryption software on a computer that *ever* goes online.

4. When installing it, specify that you want the keys to go to a floppy disk and *not* to your hard disk. Make a copy of that floppy disk and keep it in a very secure place.

5. When generating the keys, disable the 'fast key generation' option that uses precomputed primes. You can certainly afford to take a few more seconds to generate keys with decent security.

6. Select the longest key length that your version and that of your intended correspondent can handle. Long keys (e.g., >8,000 bit RSA keys) will take a long time to create, but they are highly preferable in the long term.

7. Use the longest passphrase you can remember but:

   (a) Make sure it contains more than just 'words', (i.e., numbers and symbols); if words, they should not be in a guessable sequence (e.g., a known poem) and should have unexpected intentional misspellings and midword capitalization;

   (b) include part of the passphrase, nonalphabetical symbols such as ALT+*xxxx* where *xxxx* is four numbers; this nice feature has been removed from the new versions 7.x by NAI, versions that are not recommended for numerous valid reasons anyway.[23]

8. Unless you want to put those you want to avoid on notice that you like encryption (a rather unwise action, given practically every government's virulent opposition to it), do *not* upload your public key into any database server, and do *not* enter your name and/or e-mail address as part of the PGP keys that will be created just because the software asks you for that. Enter, instead, something nondescript such as 'John Q. Public' for name and *someone@ somewhere.com* as the e-mail address. Of course, the person with whom you

---

[23] These reasons include no source code, PGP-guru Phil Zimmerman's departure from NAI, and what may be regarded as suspicious government contracts to NAI.

will be communicating should enter something different, though equally non-descript.

9. The longer you have and/or use a PGP keypair the more vulnerable it becomes. Get in the habit of deleting keys and creating new ones on a regular but not predictable schedule. For particularly sensitive communications create a new key for just that one communication and completely remove it ('wipe it') after it has been used once (i.e., after the incoming message to you encrypted to that new public key has been read).

10. To encrypt attachments, carry out the following:

    (a) Richt click on the file you want to encrypt (even machine language ones).

    (b) Use the 'copy' option.

    Proceed now as you would with any unencrypted text in the clipboard, that is:

    (c) Click on the PGP lock icon on the lower right corner of your screen.

    (d) Select 'encrypt clipboard'.

    (e) Select the intended recipient and drag that recipient's name on the lower side of the screen.

    (f) Choose OK. This will create an encrypted version of the file you want to encrypt and will save it in the same folder where the unencrypted one is.

    (g) Now proceed as you normally would have to write and encrypt the normal outgoing e-mail, [i.e., steps (a)–(f) above].

    (h) Use your e-mail software's 'attach file' feature to attach the encrypted file from above, making sure you are attaching the encrypted and not the unencrypted one. (Don't laugh; it has happened time and again.)

Security aspects of some technical details of PGP

Size of the public key encryption key   All else being equal, a brute force cryptanalytic effort on conventional symmetric encryption using a 128 bit key is generally accepted to be equivalent to the effort in attacking a 2304 bit key in public key encryption systems. As such, if a public key were to be used only once and never again then one would need a public key encryption key length at least that long. However, the vast majority of implementations use the same public key over and over, and a different 'session key' for the symmetric encryption; this means that whereas the compromise of a single symmetric key would affect a single message, the compromise of the public key encryption key would compromise all messages to that sender. It follows that the public key encryption key length should, therefore, be considerably longer. If 128 bit symmetric encryption is used (as was the case with most systems up to the establishment of the AES, a public key encryption key of no less than 4096 bits should be used. If 256 bit symmetric keys are used, then the public key encryption key length should be at least 8192 bits.

RSA versus DH   Everything else being equal (e.g., for a given length of key) use DH as long as you can protect your private keys.

DSS   This generates the digital digest of your outgoing message. Even though it has been reported to have an arcane weakness (subliminal channels), it is considered safe for another couple of decades.

Which encryption algorithm?   Idea, TripleDES, Blowfish, and, in recent unofficial implementations, Twofish and Rijandel are all very secure.

MD5 versus SHA-1   Use SHA-1. It is slower but theoretically more secure.[24]

Key revocation   It is not recommended that you publish your public key anywhere. If someone that you know wants to send you a PGP-encrypted message, then you can e-mail him or her your public key that you have just created for the occasion and for that person only. As such, the issue of revocation, the implementation problems of which plague large public key systems, does not apply here.

Mutliple encryption   All implementations of PGP accept anything for encryption; 'anything' includes a previously encrypted file. Is it worth the hassle if the same public key encryption key is used? The answer is 'probably not'; if a different public

---

[24] Although MD5 has some known weaknesses in its compression function (see http://home.clara.net/scramdisk/pgpfaq.htmlubMD5Broke) there has not been any case shown in the open literature where two messages had the same MD5 hash value or, equivalently, where one could create a message to have a given MD5 hash value.

key encryption key is used, however, then the fraction of a minute it takes to re-encrypt an already encrypted PGP file is probably worth it. Of course, if keystrokes are intercepted (see Section 4.11) then it is futile.

PGP-specific security weaknesses

Although PGP is arguably the best openly available software-based encryption there is, it does have its weaknesses over and above the security weaknesses inherent in any software encryption product as outlined at the very top of this section (Section 5.8). The most noteworthy ones are:

- A PGP-signed message may conceal a malicious .dll file which will be activated on verification of the PGP signature. This applies to Windows-based versions only. Go to http://www.securiteam.com, and read the section on 'Windows NT Focus'. A patch (pgpregfix) was made available at http://www.ipgp.com.

- The 'additional decryption key' (ADK) flaw applies to versions 5.5x through 6.5.3 only.

- A 'private key vulnerability' was discovered in March 2001 in the Czech Republic (see next section). For it to be exploited, the attacker has to get hold of your private key and you must sign your outgoing messages. *Never ever* place your private keys on a disk that is 'online'; protect your private keys with great diligence.

- It is possible to wrap a malformed ASCII-armored file around an arbitrary binary file. This means that you can get PGP to 'extract' whatever file you like, including a .dll. Because of the way that .dlls are loaded on the windows platform, it is possible to fool a number of applications (including PGP) into loading a malicious .dll extracted in this way. *Any* detached, ASCII-armored file can show this behavior (such as .asc files in public keys and .pgp files too, and not just .sig files. See http://www.atstake.com/research/advisories/2001/index_q2.html#040901-1 for a lot more detail on this, including which versions are vulnerable and where patches can be found.

The 'ICZ' vulnerability in PGP

On 21 March 2001 researchers in the Czech Republic announced a flaw in PGP that allwos one to impersonate another PGP user, but not to decrypt e-mail. For this flaw to 'work', the attacker has to:

- steal the target's PGP private key,

- modify it,

- reinsert it in the trarget's computer,

- wait until the target digitally signs an outgoing PGP message.

Although this is a threat to keep in mind, it underscores the importance of keeping one's private PGP keys private.

In practical terms, this vulnerability amounts to the following: if an attacker gets hold of your PGP's private keyring key file ('secring.pgp'), and if you subsequently digitally sign (as is customary and also necessary for sender authentication) an outgoing encrypted e-mail that the attacker intercepts, the attacker can subsequently impersonate you.[25]

On the surface it may appear that an attacker cannot get your secret key file and cannot intercept your outgoing e-mail. Both of these assumptions are usually false. In addition to some investigative arm of a government gaining routine surreptitious entry to your premises and copying your entire hard disk – including your PGP private keyring – this can usually be done online. Time and again it has been demonstrated that, unless one takes all of the many specific protective measures identified in this book to

- negate malicious mobile code (Java, Javascript, ActiveX, Virtual Basic Scritp, etc.),

- eliminate the likelihood that software has been installed (whether through physical access or merely over an Internet connection unbeknownst to you) that will capture and transmit any file in your computer, such as your PGP keys

any file in your hard disk can be retrieved or added without your knowledge. As far as intercepting your outgoing e-mail goes, that is almost to be taken as a given.

---

[25] For those who are technically inclined, the specifics of this vulnerability stem from the fact that a public key, including public parameters, is stored in both the public keyring and in the private keyring; the difference between the two places is that the public key and its parameters are digitally signed in the public keyring but are stored unsigned in the private keyring. The ICZ attack has three steps: it modifies the key parameters in the secret keyring (but not the key itself); it calculates the private key from the digital signature, the digitally signed text, and the key parameters; it replaces the original key parameters in the secret ring as a means of cleaning up after the attack.

It has been claimed that 'if an adversary can get your secret key from your online computer, that person can also get the actual files from your computer, so you might as well give up'. Not so! In the first place, your secret keys have no business being on the computer that you use to go online. Furthermore, you can invoke the many specific protective steps spelled out below.

Are there 'fixes' to this vulnerability (which Phil Zimmerman, the creator of PGP, perhaps rightly refuses to call a 'flaw' because it is a consequence of sloppy behavior on the part of the PGP user)? Indeed, there are:

- Never store your PGP keys (public or especially private) online. No, not even in encrypted form because they will be unencrypted and vulnerable when you do use them and are online. Instead, store them in an encrypted floppy disk that is kept in a physically safe place. No, the combination safe is not a 'safe place' because that is precisely where a physical intruder would look first; put it, instead, in the coffee can that says 'sugar' on the outside and that sits next to the salt and the flour.

- Never encrypt or decrypt online. Do so offline, preferably using a totally different computer that never gets connected to the Internet or any other network.

- Do not publicize you 'public' key. Instead, provide it only to the specific individual(s) that you communicate with. The rest of the world (including your adversaries) has no business benefiting from anything it can infer from it (a lot).

- Regularly scrap your PGP keypair and create a new one from scratch. In special cases, create one for a single message and then securely delete it (wipe it) immediately after you have received and read the message for which you created it.

- Given the vulnerability associated with authentication discussed, above, and given that authentication is still desirable, you can 'have your cake and eat it too' by using double PGP encryption: encrypt and digitally sign your plaintext; then re-encrypt but do not digitally sign the results of the previous encryption. This way the interceptor will not have the benefit of your digital signature on the inside layer because only your unsigned outer layer will be visible. Of course, this requires each person to have two PGP keypairs, which is no big deal anyway.

- As with all discrete activities, it serves no purpose to flaunt the use of PGP in public, especially since PGP-encrypted files advertise the fact that they are, well,

PGP encrypted files. As a minimum, put an outer layer such as zip compression (using WinZip, for example) on what is being sent. Better yet, use some steganography as the outer envelope (see Section 5.9) realizing, however, that most steganography packages available over the Internet today result in only a fig leaf of protection. Alternately, 'envelope' your message with an outer layer of conventional encryption (e.g., triple DES or other) to obscure the fact that there is PGP underneath (which spells out the intended recipient's nom de plume anyway) and then zip compress it. Yes, it is a hassle to do this if you are sending an encrypted Merry Christmas to Grandma, but not if you are sending the membership list of the human rights group in a totalitarian regime (which you should not be doing, anyway, because you cannot control what even the intended recipient will do with it; see Section 3.2.6).

As a philosophical comment, you may wish to reflect on the fact that it took many years of many expert review of PGP's open source code to identify the above vulnerability. You should therefore flatly refuse to use encryption that has not been subjected to thorough expert review and then some. And even then, for critical matters, you would be well advised to use two *different* encryption products (e.g., PGP and, say, a 3DES implementation of some repute) sequentially (i.e., to encrypt the encrypted) just in case one of them is discovered at some later time to have an exploitable flaw.

Encrypting files to oneself (local encryption) with PGP

Again it is assumed that you are serious enough to want the best confidentiality for the documents you want to protect and are willing to spend the extra effort to do things right. The recipe is pretty much the same as in the case of encrypting messages to someone else (see the section on 'PGP use for the highest security', pages 217–220), except that the someone else will be yourself. You may also want seriously to consider sending the encrypted documents on a routine basis to someone else in another country [say to the USA or to Switzerland], without necessarily giving him or her the decryption key; the idea here is to eliminate the chance of being compelled by an oppressive regime to 'decrypt these files in your possession or else!' The documents will not be in your possession and you should not volunteer the fact that you have the key if these encrypted documents are intercepted in transit to the intended recipient. In this case, the documents should be encrypted to a PGP key that should appear to belong to that 'someone else'.

As stated many times already, forget about Windows and follow verbatim the recipe shown above under 'PGP use for the highest security' (pages 217–220). If you are willing to take the risk of keeping your encrypted documents locally, then do so. If your security needs are minimal (e.g., if you are concerned only about the maid stumbling across your secret family recipe for Yorkshire pudding), you can then think about using the convenience and insecurity of Windows. The best choice then is Scramdisk, which creates an encrypted partition on your hard disk, described in detail in Section 4.10.1.

You should also give serious consideration to Scramdisk if you simply want to be nonalerting and have a need to travel with your laptop, since no self-respecting laptop uses DOS exclusively any more. With Scramdisk in the 'traveler mode' your laptop will have minimal indication that it has Scramdisk or any Scramdisk-created file in it. The business end of the encryption software will be in a floppy disk that you arrange to precede you or follow you in your travels into and out of oppressive regimes (or you can download or otherwise obtain the software in-country).

Government use of PGP in the United Kingdom

The UK government has been reported by *The Register* (http://www.theregister. co.uk/content/4/20037.html) to be planning to use a version of PGP for its own official needs; this version has been called PGP HMG. It is reported that this version of PGP will work only with Microsoft operating systems and the Microsoft web browser. If true, this suggests major security flaws in the decision to go along that route for the technical reasons outlined in this book about Microsoft's Internet Explorer.

GnuPG

In mid-July 2001 Imad Faiad, the creator of the long-key versions of PGP known as the CKT versions (http://www.ipgpp.com), abruptly removed all of these versions from his web page, stating, unconvincingly in the opinion of many, that the GnuPG (GPG) developments were overtaking his own CKT enhancements to PGP.[26] It did not help that some personal derogatory remarks were made about him in GPG newsgroup messages.

The fact remains that, as with all software, encryption software has been evolving as well and new features are inevitably incompatible with older versions.

---

[26] The Gnu Project was launched in 1984 to develop a complete Unix-like operating system which is free software: the Gnu system. (Gnu is a recursive acronym for 'Gnu's Not Unix'; it is pronounced 'guh-new'.) Variants of the Gnu operating system, which use the kernel Linux, are now widely used; though these systems are often referred to as 'Linux', they are more accurately called Gnu/Linux systems. The PG in GnuPG stands for 'privacy guard'.

Part of the evolution is the inevitable inclusion of 256 bit algorithms such as in some versions of the new advanced encryption standard – something that PGP does not handle (but there is no reason why it could not be upgraded to handle them).

The problem is that NAI, which made many of the versions of PGP up to October 2001, has not released the source code and versions 7.x.x cannot be independently checked. This, in and by itself, is a fatal flaw in encryption software. Additionally, the Usenet newsgroup rumor mill has had more than enough allegations of other reasons to suspect versions 7.x.x.

Yet the direction that software encryption is going is towards 256 bit encryption, even though it has been shown time and again that the 128 bit encryption of algorithms such as Idea and the encryption provided by true Triple-DES is perfectly impenetrable for the foreseeable future. Furthermore, the OpenPGP movement is also heading in the direction of adopting new encryption algorithms and so is GnuPG (http://www.gnupg.org), which is roughly 90 per cent–95 per cent compliant with OpenPGP (RFC2440). GnuPG is partially compatible with NAI's 7.x.x versions.

Although PGP and GnuPG are growing apart with increasing incompatibilities, one should ask oneself if this really matters; it should not. One-to-one encryption should never be used to communicate with total strangers in the first place because you never know it the stranger you are exchanging encrypted e-mail with is indeed the person you think he or she is; just because a key server says that a public key belongs to person X does not mean that this is true; similarly, just because an encrypted e-mail comes to you from someone claiming to be X and including a public key for X does not prove that it is true. In short, there is really no benefit and a lot of risk in exchanging e-mail (encrypted and unencrypted) with someone that you have no *independent* way of assuring yourself that he or she is the person that he or she claims to be.[27] As such, 'compatibility' of PGP keys with any other encryption software should never be a consideration; whichever person you want to communicate with and whom you have ascertained to be the person you think he or she is can always go and get a good copy of PGP.

Is GnuPG 'secure'?   GnuPG was intended as a complete and free replacement for PGP which, until recently, was heavily export-controlled by the US goverment.[28]

---

[27] This is to eliminate both the problem of impersonation and the problem of the 'man in the middle'.

[28] Or, at least, that was the official intent. In practice, it was available worldwide. Amusingly, this was legal because a loophole in US laws then permitted software to be exported in printed form but not in electronic form; accordingly, the source code of each new version was printed in the USA, legally sent overseas, optically scanned overseas, and converted back into electronic form.

Because it does not use the patented Idea algorithm (patented but free and legal to use for noncommercial use) it can be used without any restrictions.

The German Federal Ministry of Economics and Technology granted funds for the further development of GnuPG. Version 1.0.0 was released on 7 September 1999. The current version is 1.0.6.

GnuPG is open source, unlike NAI versions 7.x.x of PGP. A number of minor flaws have been found, but no major ones yet. A plug-in exists for the Idea encryption algorithm. It is certainly 'high risk' merely because it is too new (given that the yardstick of time needed to assess encryption software thoroughly is in units of many years). Given that there is no known reason to suspect the known and verified older algorithms such as Idea and Triple-DES, it is very hard to make a logical case for opting for the risk of new ones.

The Windows version of the GPG development reportedly uses Peter Gutman's 'cryptlib' for the essential random number generation. This code is generally respected as being secure. GnuPG for Windows is really a command line program using Win32. This is actually a security benefit since every interaction with Windows brings its own security problems. GnuPGshell is functional but is nowhere near as polished as PGP for Windows; it has difficulty with long file paths. GnuPG also has some other Windows graphical user interfaces, such as WinPT and GPA, but these are work-in-progress and are constantly being improved upon. As of August 2001 there is no real Windows Installer for GnuPG as there has been with PGP.

GnuPG is also incompatible with most remailers that use encryption, regardless of which side of the ocean they are located; remailers use PGP version 2.6.x in general.

The recommendation is to experiment with it, but for a few more years keep it at arm's-length for situations requiring high security until it passes the time-consuming scrutiny of many qualified reviewers.

A PGP vulnerability

Many PGP users feel the desire to 'publish' their public keys with one or more key servers; after all, this is one of the 'natural' options recommended by the PGP installation process. One reason given is that a PGP key is useless unless someone can find the public key. Do not publicize the keys! The reasons are as follows:

- The entire PGP public key server concept can come crashing down in a hurry if someone elects maliciously to post fake PGP keys there for you and for others. It will be a while before these servers revert back to earlier versions of the data, presuming that these earlier versions have not been compromised as well.

- There is no benefit to you to advertise to the world that you have a PGP key, other than helping an adversary or getting you on your home country's watch list.

- You really have no way of verifying that the PGP public key in a server really belongs to whomever it asserts that it belongs to.

In short, do not post your PGP public key anywhere; provide it only to whomever you want to hear from, and do so in a manner that ensures that the intended recipient will indeed be the recipient, and that he or she reciprocates in a manner that you yourself can be assured that it came from that person and not someone else.

5.8.5   ZixMail: fine for casual security

ZixMail (www.zixmail.com) is a user-friendly implementation of public key encryption, for a $24 per year fee (Figure 5.10). Its unique characteristic is that the intended recipient need not be a paying user, not even to reply to an incoming mail from a paying user. It is designed to work in conjunction with one's current e-mail

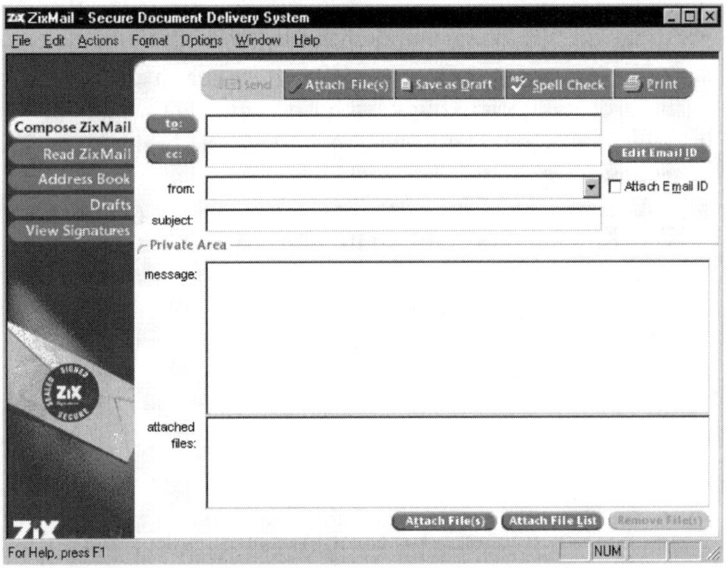

Figure 5.10   ZixMail

program, such as Microsoft Outlook, Netscape Communicator, Lotus Notes, and Qualcomm's Eudora, and it also works with web-based and proprietary e-mail systems such as Yahoo, Hotmail, and AOL.

The communication from the member sender to ZixMail is encrypted and hence not decipherable by one's local ISP or by a telephone-tap-based interception – assuming that the encryption is properly implemented. If the intended recipient is also a ZixMail paying user, the outgoing message (with attachments if desired) is encrypted to the intended recipient's public key. If the intended recipient is not a ZixMail subscriber, the outgoing message is actually sent to ZixMail, is encrypted with Zix company's public key (i.e., it is encrypted to be read by Zix company), and the intended recipient gets an e-mailed notification of mail waiting at the Zix server and how to retrieve it; the retrieval by the recipient who is not a ZixMail subscriber can be encrypted if the recipient uses an SSL-capable web browser.

For the majority of situations requiring confidentiality from casual interceptors over the Internet, ZixMail seems convenient and effective in its intended purpose. Of course, neither ZixMail nor any other secure e-mail software can protect a user from some other threats such as commercial keystroke-capturing hardware or software, nor from Van Eck radiation interception.

Given the security problems of Microsoft's Outlook (see http://www.cert.org), users are advised to use a different e-mail client software, with or without ZixMail, or ZixMail's own software – assuming that it does not share Microsoft Word's annoying propensity to make temporary unencrypted copies on one's hard disk behind one's back.

One inconvenience with using any secure e-mail that involves a go-between server (as opposed to, say, PGP, which is a direct user-to-user connectivity) is that the process of revoking keys has to involve that go-between server and cannot be done locally by a user since a portion of the keys resides with that go-between's servers.

Although a $24 per year fee is minimal, it applies to *each* e-mail address one uses with ZixMail. For those of us who have a number of those (e.g., a work-related, a personal, and a few free e-mail addresses for web-based e-mail) this can run up the yearly bill proportionately.

If one wants to use the same ZixMail account(s) on more than one computer (e.g., a desktop at home and a laptop while traveling), one needs to copy all files with a '.zky' suffix from the computer that was used to create those accounts to the corresponding folder of the computer that has a clean copy of ZixMail installed and no accounts. In Windows 2000 computers, for example, this folder is at

C:\DocumentsandSettings\"logon profile name"\ApplicationData\ZixIt\

In Windows 9x, the private key storage location is at

C:\Windows\Application Data\ZixIt\"user logon name"\

To be sure, one should look for '*.zky' using the 'Find Folders' command in the computer one is moving the files from, and for the 'ZixIt' folder in the computer one is copying the files to.

For casual users of e-mail encryption, ZixMail attempts to take the place of Verisign (which charges $10 per year for an essentially equivalent service, or is totally free if obtained from its newly acquired company Thawte).

For those living in oppressive regimes that forbid encryption and are likely to have local law enforcers break one's door down to demand to read the encrypted information, there are numerous serious concerns with using ZixMail:

- The secret keys of the public/secret key pairs of public key encryption can not be hidden away from one's hard disk because they are sought by the software in a specific location in one's hard disk. Unlike PGP, which allows one to store the keyrings on a floppy that can be stored safely out of harm's way, ZixMail does not permit that. This is a serious shortcoming.

- Since ZixMail is a for-profit company, the source code of its software is not publicly available for scrutiny by impartial cryptologists. One has to take it on faith that the software implementation of the encryption algorithms used is flawless. This requires a giant leap of faith given the recent (mid-March 2001) discovery of a vulnerability even in a highly reviewed open source code encryption program, PGP (see Section 5.8.4).

- It is not known if ZixMail software takes the initiative to overwrite any temporary files of plaintext (unencrypted) files that it handles at the sending or the receiving end. Of course, the security weaknesses of Windows such as the swap/Paging file are not unique to nor the fault of ZixMail.

- Since ZixMail is the go-between in any communication from a sender to a receiver, access to its servers can be blocked by a regime that may be sufficiently hostile to encrypted e-mail regardless of the content of the message. Since one cannot 'envelope' the uploaded message in an innocuous cover using steganography, any message to or from ZixMail can only be encrypted.

- Even though ZixMail between two subscribing users does not actually go through ZixIt company, the sender has to access ZixIt company when sending the mail so as to obtain the public encryption key of the intended recipient; as such, ZixIt can keep a record of who sent ZixMail to whom and when.

- As with any reputable corporation, ZixMail, too, has to comply with any legal order by a US court to 'preserve' all communication to and from a particular user. Although ZixMail asserts that it does not normally retain any data from past traffic – and indeed it has no commercial incentive to do so – a court order to preserve and retain all *future* traffic has to be complied with; this is not unique to ZixMail but applies to any secure e-mail that involves a 'go-between' server such as ZixMail. By comparison, Zero Knoweledge Systems (www.zeroknowledge.com) asserts that its architecture is such that it physically cannot comply with any similar court order.[29] For example, it is certainly technically possible for any host such as ZixMail to collect and retain the IP addresses used by a user at each and every connection; although ZixMail may have no commercial incentive to do so, it would have to comply to a properly served court order or subpoena.

- Unlike PGP (or any other secure e-mail option that does not involve a go-between server that stores parts of one's encryption keys), one cannot make keys disappear on a moment's notice if an overzealous investigator is knocking on the door.

5.8.6 Easy-to-use anonymizers

Zero Knowledge Systems' "Freedom 2"

Zero Knowledge Systems, a Canadian firm that offered commercial anonymity for the masses, abandoned its Freedom network of anonynizing remailers as of mid-October 2001. This is likely to be the result of financial difficulties, although the timing of the announcement (shortly after terrorist attacks on the USA on 11 September 2001) and the short notice given to its subscribers is deemed by many to be a little suspect.

The best alternative is the use of Mixmaster remailers and of such free software as Private Idaho, JBN, and QuickSilver (see Section 5.4). Alternatives that are far less secure but much easier to use the first time around include:

---

[29] The concern here is not about a US court order for a suspected violation of US law. The concern is about the likely ramifications of the Council of Europe's International Treaty on Cybercrime (see Chapter 7) which will make it possible for any of the 43 member nations to compel US law enforcement authorities to serve a warrant on any US company, such as ZixMail, to retain and produce data in connection with acts that may not be a crime in the USA at all.

- http://www.privacy.li: this one deals with 'e-gold', which has a black cloud over it because of legal problems in the USA, according to http://www.wired.com/news/politics/0,1283,42745,00.html.

- http://www.mailvault.com: for free pseudonymous mail. It, too, is totally web-based (you will need 128 bit SSL) and uses open PGP. The new user connects through an SSL-encrypted connection, picks an e-mail name of his or her choice, and even allows that server to generate PGP keys that can be used to encrypt mail to that user; of course, one would be wise not to depend on that server-provided PGP and to use one's own and merely to Edit/Paste the encrypted ASCII text onto that server's message window.

- http://www.IDZap.com: IDZap offers two versions: a free one, which does not use an SSL-encrypted connection (and that hence can be readily monitored by one's ISP, employer, local telephone taps, etc.), and one which does use SSL encryption.

- http://www.cryptoheaven.com/UserGuide/UserGuide.htm: Cryptohaven is selling a service using its own free encryption software. To ensure that users of its free software pay for the service, the software works only with that service; one cannot send encrypted e-mail to a non-cryptohaven customer.

- https://homesteads.lfcity.com/Painted_Desert/PrivateSea_Corp/: this offers two services: a 'basic' one for $8.50 per month, and a 'premium' one for $18.50 per month. The latter uses encrypted tunneling to that server and is therefore unreadable by one's ISP, local telephone taps, etc.,

- https://www.cotse.net: this one costs $5.95 per month and provides anonymous web browsing (through an SSL-encrypted connection) and anonymous e-mail and Usenet posting and reading. The e-mail anonymity is largely fictional as the 'from' header of e-mail sent shows as the fixed subscriber-chosen e-mail address.

All such services provide anonymity from the website being browsed. They should never be depended on for anonymity from the eyes of the state as they can and most likely do keep records of the true IP address that you access them from and will have no choice but to provide all such information in response to a court order, subpoena, or even a police request.

5.8.7 'Safelt' and other services

About once per month a new service comes up that promises free and 'safe' e-mail. One that was announced in late June 2001 is SafeIt at http://safeit.com. One cannot help but wonder about the business model behind anything free. Some companies start free and then switch to a 'for-pay' mode after enough users have been accustomed to the use of the service; this is understandable. What is not understandable and is highly suspicious is the small number of companies that really and truly do not charge anything for a long time.

'Proprietary' encryption is a contradiction in terms. If it is proprietary it is not open to review and hence it is totally untrustworthy; period. Thus, SafeIt is *not* recommended, nor are ZixIt or other schemes that provide their own 'proprietary' encryption.

If you do use such suspect services, whether for free or for pay, follow the following rules:

- Pre-encrypt your e-mail with your own encryption (e.g., PGP) and merely Edit/Paste your own-encrypted message into the outgoing mail window of such services. This way you do not depend on their unknown encryption.

- If you have reasons to be concerned about the connectivity (who sends e-mail to whom) becoming visible, then:

  - log in to the encryption service through a proxy or anonymizing remailer to hide your own IP;

  - make sure that the intended recipient's identity is also protected; his or her PGP public key should not identify him or her, and neither should his or her e-mail address.

- Never patronize 'safe' e-mail services that require you to have Java/Javascript or ActiveX enabled in your computer (such as www.safeweb.com) as you never know what they will do with the access you provide them into your computer.

- Make sure that the web browser profile that you use does not have any identifying information in its configuration.

5.8.8 Which is really the best algorithm among the five finalists for becoming the 'advanced encryption standard'?

In terms of resistance to cryptanalysis, they are all – Triple-DES, Idea, Blowfish/ Twofish, Cast, and Rijandel (Section 5.8.2) – perfectly secure and more-or-less equivalent. The decision of which to select as 'the' AES involved considerations in addition to (not in place of) encryption strength, however; such other considerations included which algorithm is fastest to execute and under what conditions, which one is most economic to implement in hardware, etc., As such, while Rijandel has been selected as 'the' AES, all the other four finalists are equivalently secure as far as personal encryption is concerned.

5.9 Steganography: Hiding in Plain View

5.9.1 A double-edged sword

In a nutshell, steganography is the process whereby a message is hidden in an overt act that can be seen by many and that is not alerting. That same act when seen by the person that the hidden message is intended for conveys the hidden message. Steganography is at the heart of the commercial technique known as Digital Watermarking, which attempts to create invisible marks on copyrighted files (images, sound files, etc.,).[30]

Scratching one's nose or ear as a discrete signal to the auctioneer in an auction is a form of steganography, and so is a pretty maiden's knowing sweet glance towards a youth who is courting her, and so was the microdot of World War 2 fame, and so is the use of openly available software to hide a document inside another file (typically inside an image or sound file), and just about any technique one can dream up for hiding a message.[31]

---

[30] In fact, the vast majority of watermarking techniques, notably including the latest Secure Digital Music Initiative, have failed in their intended purpose. Watermarks on images can be 'washed off' with some software, such as StirMark (http://www.cl.cam.ac.uk/users/fapp2/steganography/image_water-marking/stirmark/) and UnZign (http://www.stealthencrypt.com/watermk.html). See the end of this chapter for literature references on the weaknesses of digital watermarking schemes.

[31] A summary of many information-hiding techniques can be found in 'Information hiding; a survey', by Fabian Peticolas *et al*, in *Proc. IEEE*, Special Issue on Protection of Multimedia Content, as well as in the proceedings from the annual Workshop on Information Hiding, published by Springer-Verlag.

Figure 5.11

There is a vast number of ways that individuals have thought of over the years whereby a hidden message can reside within an innocuous-looking other message, event, or act; often the message is in the *absence* of an act. Intentional failure to say 'good night' could mean 'I am angry with you'; to an accomplice, failure to turn the living room light off at night could mean 'I am in trouble; meet me at Joe's at noon' – or anything else that has been pre-agreed.

The points being made are the following:

- It is ludicrous to make the often-heard statements nowadays that 'steganography can be detected' without specifying exactly which implementation one is talking about and who the detecting entity is and under what conditions. What these statements allude to (and very correctly at that) is that steganography using run-of-the-mill computer-aided steganographic tools in open existence around the world today can, indeed, be detected if the interceptor has:

  ○ a reason to test the files in question for steganographic content,

  ○ The technical capability to do so.

○   It is ludicrous for regimes to believe that steganography can be banned, since any human act (or absence of it, as per above) can have a pre-agreed steganographic meaning.

- You – and everyone else who is so inclined – can dream up a large number of novel *new* ways of hiding a message in something that is nonalerting. The more you use and reuse that same way, the more likely that you will attract attention, that your scheme will be scrutinized, and that the presence (though not necessarily the content) of a hidden message will be found. Conversely, if you use a novel scheme only once, chances are that nobody will catch on to your scheme; but this takes much more work.

- The larger the size of the hidden message that you want to convey (compared with the size of the overt message that is used to obscure the hidden message), the more likely that a determined interceptor will figure out that the overt message 'looks funny'. This is merely a rearticulation of the conventional wisdom of the proverbial 'needle in the haystack'; if the haystack consists of a single straw, the needle will be easy to spot. At the same time, if you are a fisherman, it would look very odd if you were to be seen carrying a large haystack – with or without a needle in it. In short, the observable act must be nonalerting and must fit naturally with your lifestyle.

- Do not openly use available steganography software as most of them have been analysed enough to have resulted in technical means for detecting if a file has a steganographically hidden message in it. Such openly available software for implementing steganography use rather simplistic concepts; for example, altering the least significant bits in a sound file may seem all well and good until one realizes that it is the wrong thing to do *if* that portion of a CD sound file that has *no* sound in it to begin with (i.e., digital silence); this is so because 'all zeros' gets replaced by the pseudorandom bits introduced by the simplistic steganography software.[32]

---

[32] As a minimum, the steganography software must adapt to the information content (or lack thereof) of the 'carrier' (i.e., the file used to hide the message); openly available software that do this include Jsteg (http://www.tiac.net/users/korejwa/jsteg.htm), jphs (http://the.wiretapped.net/security/steganography/jphs/), GzSteg (http://linkbeat.com/lb/files/), MP3Stego (hppt://www.cl.cam.ac.uk/~fapp2/steganography/mp3stego/), Outguess (http://www.outguess.org), Texthide (http://www.texthide.com), White Noise Storm (see http://www.inetone.com/cypherpunks/dir.1997.08.141997.08.20/msg00004. html). Even these software products are not recommended, however.

5.9.2   When would it make sense to use steganography?

If what you want is to send a message to someone else that no third party can read, and if you do not mind someone observing the fact that you want to send a message to that particular recipient, then encryption is the way to do it; not steganography.

If you *also* want to hide the fact that you are sending a message to that particular person but you do not mind that the communication is an encrypted one going to a remailer, then you can use remailers (e.g., Mixmaster remailers as per Section 5.4). This will hide both the content and the connectivity *but not* the fact that you are sending encrypted traffic to a hidden recipient. Still, steganography is not desired here. Alternatively, you can post a PGP encrypted message to one of the many Usenet newsgroups that cater to this activity (such as alt.anonymous.post) and only the intended recipient will be able to decode it; of course, the intended recipient's PGP key should not identify the recipient's identity.

If encryption is not allowed where you live, you may want to consider connecting to an anonymous remailer that is out of your country's legal reach *and* that has SSL enabled; this will give you end-to-end encryption to that site and you can then do whatever you want. Of course, the local regime will be able to see the SSL connection and may consider this an affront. Better yet, you can use the 'ultimate' privacy approach discussed in Section 4.1.2 that involves the combined use of anonymizing encrypted remailers and an SSH-encrypted Telnet connection to a remote server under your control.

If you want to encrypt something to yourself in your own computer, you can again use encryption; this is fine as long as encryption is tolerated where you live or travel. You can use PGP or, better yet, ScramDisk (see Section 4.10.1).

Steganography comes in handy when *both* of the following conditions are met:

- You are in a situation where the use of *any* encrypted connection between you and another server is likely to get you in trouble with the local repressive regime.

- You need to communicate a message to another person via the Internet, or you need to store data in your computer in a manner than does not look like you have encrypted files in the computer (e.g., traveling into or out of a country that takes a dim view of encryption in travelers' laptops).

5.9.3   Do's and don'ts if you must use steganography

- Do *not* under any circumstances use any of the openly available software that claim to do steganography. They each leave their respective signature on their steganographically 'hidden' output that can be readily detected (see for example Sections 5.9.1 and 5.9.2).

- Do come up with a number of your own creative *new* ways of doing steganography, and use each sparingly. As an amusing example of such creativity, consider a software program called 'Spam Mimic' from http://www.spamMimic.com. This free service lets you encode messages in spam-like e-mails. The recipient can then decode the message using the same service (and so can an interceptor). The message 'Hide a message in Spam' encoded as follows:

"Dear Friend , Especially for you – this breath-taking news ! If you no longer wish to receive our publications simply reply with a Subject: of "REMOVE" and you will immediately be removed from our club ! This mail is being sent in compliance with Senate bill 1626 , Title 4 ; Section 309 ! This is not multi-level marketing ! Why work for somebody else when you can become rich in 70 days . Have you ever noticed more people than ever are surfing the web and how many people you know are on the Internet . Well, now is your chance to capitalize on this . WE will help YOU decrease perceived waiting time by 110% & use credit cards on your website ! The best thing about our system is that it is absolutely risk free for you . But don't believe us ! Mr Anderson who resides in Connecticut tried us and says "My only problem now is where to park all my cars" . This offer is 100% legal ! We IMPLORE you – act now . Sign up a friend and your friend will be rich too . Thanks . Dear Salaryman , We know you are interested in receiving cutting-edge information . This is a one time mailing there is no need to request removal if you won't want any more ! This mail is being sent in compliance with Senate bill 1621 , Title 6 ; Section 308 ! This is NOT unsolicited bulk mail ! Why work for somebody else when you can become rich inside 38 weeks ! Have you ever noticed most everyone has a cellphone and how long the line-ups are at bank machines ! Well, now is your chance to capitalize on this . WE will help YOU increase customer response by 120% and process your orders within seconds . You can begin at absolutely no cost to you ! But don't believe us . Ms Simpson who resides in Arizona tried us and says "I was skeptical but it worked for me" ! We are licensed to operate in all states . DO NOT DELAY – order today ! Sign up a friend and your friend will be rich too . Best regards ! "

- Do spend *a lot* of effort in ensuring that the observable portion of whatever you end up with (and either save on disk or e-mail or otherwise communicate to the intended recipient) is not alerting and fits in with your personality and lifestyle. Expect to be confronted and have a ready explanation *before* you are confronted; do not wait to be confronted by an oppressive regime to find one while you are nervous. If you plan to hide data in images or sound files (not a good idea, anyway, because everyone is doing exactly that) at least be a photographer or a musician by profession or hobby.

- Adversaries are not stupid. Do not assume that they will only question this or that aspect of your computer activities. Make sure you have a good explanation about the presence of software that does data hiding of some sort; even if you deleted it or even 'wiped' it, chances are that it can still be found with use of computer forensics. Are all of your backups suspicion-free, too? How about all of your printouts that you threw in the trash over the last year? So the paper was shredded, eh? Why is it that a person like yourself would buy and use a paper-shredder?

5.9.4   Using existing steganography tools: *Not* a good idea

If, despite the strong admonitions above, you still want to use openly available software tools for doing steganography – and it strains the imagination to conceive of any good reason to risk life and limb by so doing – then the technical information below should be of use. Realize, however, that doing so is, well, foolish because:

- your computer will likely have forensically obtainable evidence that you have been using steganographic software,

- even if the computer is 'clean', the signatures of outputs generated with openly available steganographic software are well known and can be detected.

In short, you will end up taunting a repressive regime to catch you; this is a very unwise course of action in any regime.

Some have argued that the sheer volume of image files and sound files on the Internet is such that it is highly unlikely that an interceptor will zero in on *your* file and subject it to steganalysis. This argument is logically flawed because:

- if you are indeed nobody that an oppressive regime would ever suspect of irreverence, then you hardly need to use steganography in the first place,

- if you are somebody that an oppressive regime would likely suspect of harboring any seditious thoughts, then what is created by your computer is not 'just any file in a sea of files' but a file coming out of a suspect's computer, in which case the presence of another trillion files out there is irrelevant.

If all you want to do is to have fun with the modern equivalent of writing messages with lemon so that the recipient will read them by going over the paper with a warm iron used for ironing shirts, then you can experiment with the openly available steganographic tools mentioned in this section, keeping in mind that they do not provide any security and may be alerting. (If you live in a repressive regime, it is *not* recommended that you start browsing the Internet looking for everything there is to find on steganography, as this would be a quick way to get yourself in the 'to be watched' list – if you are not there already.) For additional information on commercial steganography and its detection, see http://members.tripod.com/steganography/stego/info.html.

5.10 Advanced Security Risks and Countermeasures

5.10.1 NETBios security risks

Network Basic Input/Output System, (NETBIOS), is the software that allows applications on different computers communicate within a local area network; it does not 'work' on larger networks (e.g., the Internet) because it does not have a means to route traffic; as such it needs a wide area network's data transport infrastructure and protocols (such as TCP/IP) to 'work' over such networks NETBIOS uses ports 137–139.

NETBIOS does not provide a standard frame or data format even for local area network (LAN) transmission; that is done by the NETBIOS Extended User Interface (NETBEUI). In that sense, NETBIOS is the payload and NetBEUI is the transportation vehicle, just like TCP/IP.

NETBIOS over TCP/IP allows resources such as printers, disk drives, etc., to be shared over the Internet. This means that someone a thousand miles away can print on your printer (and you on his or her printer) and also that he or she can wipe your hard disk (and you, his or her hard disk). When one installs the TCP/IP protocol, Windows automatically installs the 'NETBIOS over TCP/IP' protocol too! If you want the TCP/IP protocol, but not 'NETBIOS over TCP/IP' (because you are worried, as you should be, about security), you should uncheck 'Files and Printer Sharing' in the Bindings tab of the TCP/IP entry in Network Configuration.

For an in-depth technical overview of NETBIOS, the interested reader is referred to http://support.baynetworks.com/library/tpubs/html/router/soft1200/117358AA/ B_39.htm and also to http://patriot.net/~carvdawg/use_netbios.txt as well as to http://cable-dsl.home.att.net/netbios.htm.

For NETBIOS to be a security threat, *both* of the following conditions must be met:

- File-sharing and printer-sharing for Microsoft Networks have been installed, enabled, and have been 'bound' to TCP/IP.

- Passwords have either not been set or weak passwords have been chosen.

Since Microsoft 95/98/Me have been found to have a security vulnerability especially (but not exclusively) when 'Scope ID' has not been set, one is strongly advised to install a Microsoft-provided security patch from http://www.microsoft. com/technet/security/bulletin/MS00-072.asp.

In the vast majority of cases, one can safely disable NETBIOS over TCP/IP or, better yet, remove NETBIOS altogether unless you have a small network inside your house or office to which your computer is connected to (a very bad idea for secure computing in the first place).

An additional step to take is to block ports 137 through 139, used by NETBIOS over TCP/IP, for either TCP or UDP traffic.[33] A computer that has those ports open can be readily accessed by clicking on 'Network Neighborhood'. Issuing the

NBTSTAT

command against a targeted remote system will be informative; if one gets the hex code 20 in the center column back then that means that the system is capable of sharing some of its resources.

Any decent firewall can block TCP/IP and UDP ports for you. To confirm that this has been done, use any of the following utilities:

---

[33] TCP was developed by the Department of Defense (DARPA) as a protocol for sending data in packets and is the way how all Internet traffic is handled. A useful tutorial can be found at http:// www.yale.edu/pclt/COMM/TCPIP.HTM.

UDP (user datagram protocol) is defined to make available a datagram mode of packet-switched computer communication in the environment of an interconnected set of computer networks. This protocol assumes that the Internet Protocol (IP) is used as the underlying protocol.

- NBSTAT −n: lists your NETBIOS names;

- NBSTAT −s: lists current NETBIOS sessions;

- NETSTAT −a: lists all listening ports and connections;

- NETSTATE −n: lists addresses and port numbers in use;

- NET VIEW: a network command if you are in a network; will list all available computers with NETBIOS support in the network.

If you absolutely have to have NETBIOS enabled over TCP/IP (and it strains one's imagination as to why you would even think of doing anything secure in such a computer setup), then make sure you use a strong 'Scope ID', which is *not* set by default. For information on how to do that, see page 5 of 'File and printer sharing. Fact and fiction', at http://cable-dsl.att.net/netbios.htm.

Disabling NETBIOS is not a cure-all; nothing is. All it does is to remove that particular security threat.

5.10.2   The RPCSS and DCOM program security risks

Microsoft's Remote Procedure Call Service program, rpcss.exe, is a 53 kB program installed by some Microsoft products, such as MS Visual Studio, Visual C++, Visual Basic, Interdev, J++, and others. It takes it upon itself to open ports on your computer (usually port 135 and random ports in the low 1000s) and tries to access the Internet. With the exception of Windows NT, RPCSS does not seem to do anything useful and can be removed.

Besides deleting rpcss.exe, you should turn off 'remote connections' in Windows 95/98 by setting the Registry keys

EnableRemoteConnect

and

EnableDCOM

to N in HKEY_LOCAL_MACHINE\SOFTWARE\Microsoft\OLE. This can be done through REGEDIT as per above, or by running DCOMCNFG, clicking on the Default Security tab and unchecking the 'enable remote connection' option. Alternatively, a process manager approach for the same thing can be found at http://atm.idic.caos.it/higheng.html. Of course, if you do need to have remote connections enabled,[34] the foregoing should be disregarded. Again, do not disable or remove RPCSS in Windows NT because your computer will not function after so doing.

Similar comments apply to Microsoft's Machine Debug Manager, mdm.exe, which, by the way, executes the above-mentioned rpcss.exe. Although mdm.exe does not seem to connect to the Internet, it is ill-behaved in that it leaves numerous temporary files all over one's hard disk that it does not delete. Although it can be useful to software developers and some 'power users', its security shortcomings make it an undesirable program to have around, and even Microsoft provides instructions for its removal, at http://support.microsoft.com/support/kb/articles/ q221/4/38.asp. Basically, you must remove any reference to mdm.exe from the list under the registry keys

HKEY_LOCAL_MACHINE\Software\Microsoft\Windows\CurrentVersion\

RunServices

and

HKEY_LOCAL_MACHINE\Software\Microsoft\OLE

If you are using Internet Explorer version 5 or later (not a good idea from a security perspective to begin with; see http:www.cert.org), turn off the script debugging option (in the Tools menu, click Internet Options; on the Advanced tab under Setting, make sure that 'Disable script debugging' is selected.); if you do not, you will get error messages.

Furthermore mdm.exe has also been found to be the culprit when numerous files whose names start with 'ff' start appearing in your Windows folder after installing Office 2000.

In the case of Windows NT/2000, use Zone Alarm Pro firewall and set it to deny access to Distributed Services, although there have been indications that this may not always succeed.

5.10.3 The wireless threat: 802.11b

It is increasingly common for individual users to install a wireless connection between their high-speed modem (xDSL or cable modem) and their laptop or other

---

[34] Distributed COM (see http://packetderm.cotse.com/mailing-lists/bugtraq/1999/1343.html) first appeared in Windows NT 4.0 and has since propagated to Windows 95/98. There have been unsubstantiated allegations by an alleged former Microsoft employee that DCOM services were intended to profile product key and other registration data as a future means of enforcing software piracy laws.

transportable computer around the house or office; the price of the hardware is tolerable [about $400 for the 'base end' ('access point') and another $200 or so for each wireless remote ('client')], and the convenience of having high-speed access anywhere within a house is unparalleled.

The advertised range of these devices is around 100 feet. However, they often cannot even handle 50 feet inside a house. As any telecommunications engineer knows, however, 'range' is highly dependent on:

- what is between the two communicating stations,

- what kind of antenna is used at either or both ends.

This writer, being an electrical engineer by training, built a simple parabolic antenna at the frequency of these devices (2.4 GHz), placed the standard home 'base end' of the wireless system next to the window, and drove a measured 4 miles away to a high elevation spot having a direct view to that window. The signal received at that distance on a commercially available receiver was perfectly adequate to demodulate (i.e., to read, in plain English) the data being radiated by the '100 foot range' home system.

In practice, since all of these devices operate in the same radio frequency band, the ultimate limitation to the interceptor will not be range but the interference caused by all other such systems used that may be of no interest to an interceptor; this can easily be taken care of with highly directional antennas, though.

Additionally, in early 2001 there were detailed technical descriptions posted on the Internet that exposed a significant security vulnerability in the protocol used by early versions of these systems. These devices come with no encryption enabled as a default; as an option, most allow the use of 40 bit encryption, which is laughable because of its insecurity. Independently, they use only a 24 bit initialization vector, which is totally inadequate. As if all that were not bad enough, their handshaking protocol is also very vulnerable (see http://www.cs.umd.edu/~waa for the full details). The bottom line is that currently-sold devices are hopelessly insecure; it will take a major upgrade in the hardware to fix the existing security holes, and this is unlikely to happen for at least another year.

It has been reported that a number of enterprising hackers have been known to be driving around town ('war driving'[35])with the 'remote end' of such commercial systems until they are close enough to a house or office that has a complete such system installed with the default no-encryption mode, and availing themselves of free Internet connectivity – and snooping at the unsuspecting users' data while at it, as well.

---

[35] This is a reference to 'war dialing', (i.e., the standard process of dialing a large number of telephone numbers sequentially until one – or more – is answered by a modem; this term seems to have been coined in the movie 'War Games' from about a decade ago.

There is an additional threat that you should be aware of. Many individuals have availed themselves of releatively inexpensive hardware that allows them to share a single high-speed Internet line (e.f. xDSL or cable modem) among many computers in the house; all that this requires is a 'switch' (not a physical switch but a standard electronic box sold in most computer stores for around $20–$100). One of the receptacles on the back of this 'switch' box can be connected to a standard 'wireless access point'(WAP), which is also available at almost any computer store for about $150; it amounts to a transmitter/receiver that complies with the above-mentioned 802.11b standard, and it 'talks to' a matching PCI card that one can install in one's desktop computer or to a PCMCIA card that one can install in one's laptop. This way, one can get high-speed internet coverage with one's laptop in bed, on the sofa, etc. An example of such commercially available set of hardware is D-Link's DWL-1000AP for the access point and DEL-650 for the PCMCIA card.

In the 'out-of-the-box' default state these wireless devices do not have any encryption enabled. If all the computers in one's house are turned off, the worst that can happen is that a passerby will be able to access your Internet account; at best, the intruder will run up your bill; at worst, the intruder can access sites whose content is illegal in your country and you may well end up in jail as a result because it will be next to impossible to convince a 'technically challenged jury' that your Internet account was not used by you, especially if you happened to be at home when this occurred.

If one or more of your computers are turned on, however, and you have enabled file sharing among them so that you can, well, share files among them the easy way, then the wireless outside intruder will also be able to share those same files since the outsider intruder is now a part of your network. Not a happy scene.

As a minimum, if you do install such a wireless link in your home LAN, make sure that you configure it to use 128 bit encryption; even though it has been shown to be compromised, it is far better than no encryption at all; not all hardware allow this. Better yet, make sure that you have not enabled file sharing.

Appendix G has technical detail on the security shortcomings of the 802.11b wireless LAN protocol and implementations.

Better yet, forege devices that comply with 802.11b, and use, instead the new ones that comply with 802.11a.

5.10.4 Packet sniffing to defeat keystroke capturers that send captured data through a network connection

Detecting commercial keystroke-capturing software or hardware can range from easy to near impossible, depending on how sophisticated the software or hardware is and on how adept at cyber detective work one is. By far the safest and easiest way out is to prevent the installation of any keystroke capturing by following the advice under 'starting clean' in Section 4.3 and the advice in Section 4.11.

Software-based commercially-sold key capturers may be detected by on or more of the following:

- Resident software, such as WinPatrol from http://www.billp.com/winpatrol, which detects if a new program is trying to run in the background and informs the user; of course, the installer of the keystroke-capturing software is likely to see such detecting software and appease it by telling it that it is OK to run the keystroke-capturing software (which will likely show up with an innocuous nondescript name such as 'Microsoft such-and-such', so as to fool the user into letting it run;

- the use of Windows own software, which lists what all is running in the background; in the case of Windows 95/95, type 'Ctrl-Alt-Delete' – in Windows NT and 2000, type Cntrl-Shift-Esc – and the list of software that is running will show up. Since no self-respecting keystroke-capturing software will show up by that alerting name, the only way to detect one is to know which software should be running in the background under normal circumstances; most people do not know that and will therefore be unable to spot an additional one with an innocuous name.

Hardware-based commercially-sold key capturers can be detected only through physical examination. This presumes that one knows what the unmodified hardware looked like when it was bought, and most users do not bother to check and record that, let alone to mark it in a way that they can tell, later on, if any of it has been changed. There should be no adaptors on keyboard cables (see Figure 4.12, page 127). If the device is embedded in a modified connector or in the keyboard itself, as is the case with 'Keyghost' (Section 4.11.1) (commercially available at http://www.keyghost.com), chances are that one will not find it. If in doubt, spend the $20–$50 needed to replace the keyboard with another one.

Both software and hardware commercial keystroke capturers need to send their collected information out to the entity that installed them. In almost all case this is done while the user is connected to the Internet anyway, in which case Zone Alarm Pro should catch the attempt and ask the user for approval. Again, it is highly unlikely that the user will be faced with a question like 'Do you approve keystroke capturer to send your surreptitiously collected keystrokes to such-and-such?' The request will most likely be nonalerting, such as 'Do you approve antivirus services to connect to the Internet?' or something equally sacrosanct that is likely to evoke a knee-jerk approval response from most people.

By far the most effective way to catch a surreptitious transmittal of information through the Internet out of your computer is by using a packer sniffer; in other words, by recording and poring over the recorded data of all that went out of your computer to the Internet. This can be done with simple software that stay resident within your computer, such as the ones described below. The problem is twofold. First, this is a very boring task that most people will not do. Second, if the keystroke-capturing system is any good, and some commercial ones are, the information going out will be encrypted and nonalerting. This leaves only the destination of the data packets as the sole suspect data to ponder over, and that is unlikely to be too obviously alerting. Even so, this is the ultimate means of confirming a surreptitious transmission of data out of one's computer to the Internet.

One must realize, of course, that this is *not* the only way that data can leave one's computer. It can also leave by being physically retrieved by whoever installed the keystroke-capturing capability, and it can also leave by radio; the latter requires that the intended receiver be in the neighborhood.

Two free software packages that do packet sniffing are:

- Ethereal, from http://www.Ethereal.xing.org. It is available for Windows NT and 2000 (not for Windows 95/98) as well as for various versions of Unix, Linux, FreeBSD, and Solaris.

- Windump, from http://www.netgroup-serv.polito.it/. It works in DOS, in Windows 95/98 but not with Windows NT/2000.

Both use the same packet-capturing driver (from http://netgroup-serv.polito.it/winpcap/ that must also be downloaded and installed. To install that driver:

1. Right click on 'Network Neighborhood' and select 'Properties'.

2. Select 'Add', then 'Protocol', then 'Add' again, then 'have disk'.

3. Point to the directory where you put the 'packet.inf' file from the winpcap driver downloaded above.

4. Reboot the computer.

5. Right click again on 'Network Neighborhood' and select 'Properties'. The list should now contain 'Network Packet Driver ...'. Select it, and the description 'Network Capture Packet Driver for NDIS adapter' should appear.

To install the actual Ethereal software:

1. Create a new folder called Ethereal in C:\Program Files (or wherever you want).

2. Create another folder where you will store the captured data and give it any name you like.

3. Unpack all of the files from the Ethereal download in the Ethereal folder created two steps earlier.

4. The executable to be run is the one called 'ethereal.exe'.

To capture data:

1. Either access the menu option 'Capture' or push ctrl-K.

2. Enter the amount of data you want captured – 65 kilobytes is typical; if you want more, keep in mind that you will have to go through it all if it is to do you any good.

3. Make sure that 'Update list of packets in real time' is selected.

4. Select 'Enable Name Resolution' if you want to see the name rather than merely the IP address of the server.

5. Click OK. Do not close the window; minimize it if you want.

6. Start the network connection (if it is not ongoing already). You will see considerable activity on the Ethereal window.

Now starts the tedious part of reading and interpreting the data captured. This requires an amount of training that is beyond the scope of this book. You can teach yourself most of it from the following sources:

• Contact info@hazeleger.net and ask them for the PS-CC file and any additional tutorial material. The web page is at http://www.hazeleger.com.

• http://www.decodes.com has examples of analyzed network protocols.

• http://www.robertgraham.com has an FAQ section on network sniffing.

- http://www.3com.com/nsc/501302.html explains IP addressing.

- http://www.charm.net/ppp.html http://www.protocols.com and http://www.radcom-inc.com explain Internet protocols and PPP.

- http://packetstorm.security.com/sniffers   and   http://www.cyberport.com/~tangent/programming/winsock/resources/debugging.html   discuss   network packet sniffers.

5.10.5   Peekabooty and M-o-o-t

Interception of Internet-based traffic is based on the premise (which characterizes practically all of *today*'s Internet traffic) that the way that the Internet works is the only way it can possibly function. The key premise of all of today's interception schemes, including those deployed by repressive nation states, is basically that there are a few 'choke points' that all data passes through. These are:

- the user's path to the Internet; this is usually the phone line or some alternative to it (satellite link, cellphone, network connection, etc.);

- the domain name server (DNS); this is where each user's computer 'goes to' in order to find where to send outgoing data (and 'outgoing data' include the process of contacting a remote website for the purpose of merely browsing it).

But what if one or both of those assumptions were rendered false?

Similarly, the fundamental premise of computer forensics is that one has a hard disk in one's computer and, most likely, uses Windows (or, to a lesser extent, MacOS or a Unix variant) as the operating system. If one's computer were not to use any media to store anything, then computer forensics would be about as useful as a refrigerator to an Eskimo in an igloo.

This is where cDc (Cult of the Dead Cow, an irreverent group of computer-literate individuals) and M-o-o-t (a UK-headquartered group of computer professionals united by their opposition to the British RIP Act) come in. Oddly, M-o-o-t has been, well, rather quiet about the progress of this effort as of late.

Peekabooty works in a peer-to-peer mode in a manner similar to controversial Napster and Gnutella, using no central servers; rather than fetching music, Peekabooty will fetch web pages. It will also use encryption.

CDc's Peekabooty (http://www.thekult.org/forum.php3?newsid=3073&filter=2, and http://www.vnunet.com/News/1121286) was demonstrated on 4 July 2001 with a release to follow in the near future, and M-o-o-t is ostensibly in continuing development at http://www.m-o-o-t.com.

5.10.6 Network sniffing

Numerous software and hardware tools exist the overt purpose of which is to allow a company to debug its own networks by monitoring every data packet that goes through. The same tools can monitor data packets to and from the Internet.

One such example is NetIntercept by Sandstorm Entreprises Inc. in Boston, MA. Curiously, the chief technology officer of the company that makes this product is the same Simson Farfinkel who wrote *Database Nation: The Death of Privacy in the 21st Century* in 2000. He is quoted in the *Boston Globe* of 15 October 2001 to have stated that 'This product is more pro-privacy than other network monitoring systems', while candidly also saying that 'this is a rationalization we needed to make early on if we wanted to sell this product' (http://www.boston.com/dailyglobe2/288/business/Send_in_the-Cuber_G-men+.shtml). As with practically all network sniffers, it collects data about all users whose data passes through the interception point.

5.11 Excellent Websites with Current Information on PGP

Tom McCune's FAQs: http://www.mccune.cc/PGP.htm.
PGP Users' mailing list: http://cryptorights.org/pgp-users/.
Cypherpunks Home Page: ftp://ftp.csua.berkeley.edu/pub/cypherpunks/Home.html.
An excellent UK site: http://www.users.globalnet.co.uk/~firstcut/.

5.12 References on Cryptography and Security

An excellent current list of many Internet-accessible documents on security and steganography is available at http://www.intelinfo.com/newly_researched_free_training/Security_Cryptography.html. This site also offers a free CD ROM; the reader is advised to be careful about asking for it because the site appears to require Javascript and is hosted and supported by advertising companies.

5.13 References on Digital Watermarking

Peticolas, F.A.P. *et al.*, 1998 'Attacks on Copyright marking Systems', in David Aucsmith, Information Hiding Second International Workshop, IH'98, Portland, Oregon, USA, 15–17 April 1998, Proceedings, LNCS 1525, Springer-Verlag, ISBN 3-540-65386-4, pp. 219–239.

Peticolas, F.A.P. and Anderson, R.J. 1991, 'Evaluation of Copyright marking systems', in *Proc. IEEE Multimedica Systems (ICMCS'99)*, 7–11 June 1999, Florence, Italy, Volume 1, pp. 574–579.

6

Encrypted Telephony

Having a confidential oral conversation is *very* difficult. Unless you whisper sweet nothings in your beloved's ears, today's technology makes every other form of oral communication loaded with the risk that it can be overheard, taped, and used against you; this is a lesson that many a powerful person learned the hard way, including the UK's Prince Charles, the US former Speaker of the House Newt Gingrich, and numerous others.

On 21 May 2001, the US Supreme Court decided that *even when a private telephone conversation has been intercepted by illegal means*, a journalist has the right to broadcast it if he or she did not do the intercepting; the rationale given was, amazingly, that the public's right to know supercedes any privacy considerations even if criminality was involved in the interception.[1] In short, telephone privacy is not protected under US law, and you have to rely on your own resources to keep conversations private.

So where can you have a confidential communication? This is one situation where 'intuition' leads the person with a nontechnical background to precisely the wrong conclusions – sometimes at considerable peril.

6.1 Confidential Conversations in Person

Common sense would dictate that being far away from other people would provide the desired privacy. But we have all watched television crews covering sports events from the bleachers (stands) being able to aim directional microphones at the players on the field and let us listen in on what these players are actually saying. Similarly,

---

[1] This case concerned an illegally intercepted cellular telephone conversation between a union leader and an associate of his during some tense negotiations. The interception was made by parties unknown and the taped intercepted conversation was placed in a reporter's mailbox who subsequently broadcast it.

nature-lovers' magazines, as well as magazines catering to private investigators, are full of setups peddled to listen to the birds far away and to others' conversations, respectively. The technology is openly available commercially.

We can easily hear each other talk softly across quite a distance inside a quiet church, yet we cannot hear each other across the dinner table in a noisy restaurant; the reason is the presence of interfering noises.

Realizing the above, it now becomes plausible that the locations offering the most privacy for oral communications from undesired snooping could be the places with the most noise and commotion–as long as we do not yell to overcome the ambient noise but talk into each others' ears, of course.

Try to place yourself in the shoes of the local birdwatcher or private investigator. The ideal scenario for him or her is to set up shop someplace and sit back and relax while listening in. If you are so inconsiderate of the snoop's tranquility that you elect to go to a very noisy place and also to keep moving while you are talking, you end up with a very frustrated snoop. Ergo, go to the central market, to the local flea market, or to an outdoor cocktail party.

But businesspeople, while on travel, do not normally conduct meetings at the zoo nor at the local flea market; it is just 'unbecoming'. One will have to use some ingenuity in coming up with locales that are both conducive to business and not conducive to compromises in confidentiality.

6.2 Confidential Conversations at a Distance

Despite the advances of technology, very little can compete with childhood's 'two cups connected with a tight string' for confidentiality. Governments consent (reluctantly, perhaps) to the confidentiality of conversations where two people are separated by a couple of inches, but the same governments (all of them) have eloquent verbal gymnastics to justify their 'right' to listen in on the very same conversations if that distance increases from a couple of inches to 'beyond shouting distance'.

As of a few years ago, it has become technically possible – and inexpensive – for any two people to converse with full confidentiality across any distance. All it takes is an Internet-connected PC at each end and the use of a free and openly available software known as 'Speak Freely'. It is available from http://www.speakfreely.org and it includes the option of encrypting the conversation with strong encryption. A lesser-used alternative (not recommended) is 'PGPfone', available from numerous sources on the Internet, such as http://www.ipgpp.com.

As with the use of any encryption for text messages and files, the user of voice encryption is again cautioned that encryption is only a small portion of the solution to the overall problem of implementing confidentiality. Unless all of the other portions of the solution are attended to, one is likely to end up with a false sense of security, and that is far worse than no security at all because a false sense of security will lull one into disclosing information that would not have been disclosed if one knew that there was no security.

The specifics that have to be attended to are:

- make sure that the room itself that is being used at either end for the 'secure conversation' has not itself been compromised with the presence of some other means of audio interception. This is very hard to do. Enough said. To be on the safe side, assume that the room *has* been compromised and:

  - use headphones, instead of a loudspeaker, to listen to the other party;

  - speak softly in the presence of background noise;

  - use a laptop, rather than a desktop, and use a different room each time.

- If you use 'Speak Freely', as recommended in Section 6.5.1 below, get it from the source identified above and not from an untrusted go-between.

- Before using it in the encrypted mode, establish some way securely to agree on the encryption password(s) to be used with the other person. This is obvious but hard to do (a classical 'Catch 22' situation) since it implies having a different secure channel to begin with. If you know the person you will be communicating with, you could agree on the password by openly referring to something that only the two of you would know, such as 'the fourth and fifth words of the fifth page of the business document we got from Joe last week'.

- Do not use the same encrypted password for every conversation.

6.3 Anonymized Telephones

Regardless which encryption and/or anonymizing schemes one uses (see repeated earlier admonitions in Chapter 4 about using *any* such schemes because they raise one's profile), the fact remains that–unless one uses wireless of some sort–one connects to the Internet through either a telephone line (whether conventional,

ISDN, or xDSL)[2] or through a hard-wired network connection (e.g., a 'cable modem'); both are readily and rapidly identifiable as to their exact physical location. The old movie scenes where a policeman is trying to keep the caller on the phone long enough to allow telephone company employees to 'trace' the call are not true any more; calls have been traceable instantaneously ever since 'Signaling System 7' became the norm across the world.[3] Even if a telephone number at location X is registered to one's parent company in location Y that gets the bill, the phone company knows the physical location X.

Dialing *67 in the USA or 141 in the UK (or whatever the local code is to disable the caller's phone number from being displayed at the called party's 'caller ID box') achieves absolutely nothing in most cases as the phone company still knows and records who called whom and when. Also, some called numbers (such as emergency services and all toll-free numbers in the USA) get the caller-ID information regardless, using a technology known as automatic number identification (ANI).

Using a cellphone that is registered to someone else provides no additional privacy or anonymity. One exception is the increasing use of cellphones bought at local convenience stores that include a prepaid amount of air-time usage; in this case, oppressive regimes cannot know who a phone belongs to, but this is true only *until the very first phone call is made to a known telephone number under surveillance*.

Regardless of which type of cellphone is used, it can be geolocated very quickly.[4] Attempting to maintain Internet connectivity with a cellphone while one is driving

---

[2] ISDN stands for Integrated Services Digital Network. It is much more common in Europe and Japan than in the USA, where ineffective marketing and exorbitant rates turned potential buyers off. Some scoffingly refer to ISDN as standing for 'I Still Don't Need it'.

DSL stands for Digital Subscriber Line and is the telephone companies' answer to cable modems. It uses the existing conventional cables; the data rates that can be accommodated decrease as one moves further away from the telephone company's nearest local switching office.

[3] In the 'old' telephone system, the information about what number was dialed was being sent down the same path as the actual communication. This allowed the 'blue boxes' of yesteryear to exist; these were generators of the precise audio tones used by the telephone companies for signaling and billing, and their specifications were publicly available. Signaling System 7 (SS7) is a digital system; the voice is digitized as soon as it reaches a subscriber's local switching office, is mixed with other digital datastreams from other subscribers, and is transmitted as a sequence of ones and zeros through physical paths that may change in response to the loading of different pathways numerous times during a single phone call; the dialing information (who is calling whom) is sent through a physically separate path. SS7 allows such popular features as 'Caller ID', 'Call rejection', 'Call forwarding', 'Caller ID blocking', and so on.

[4] CALEA, (Communications Assistance to Law Enforcement) in the USA is the name of the Federal law that compels cellular telephone service providers to have installed the technology whereby any cellular phone they service can be geolocated within about 100 feet. This was done ostensibly to help stranded motorists having a heart attack, although one wonders why it has been sponsored and furiously lobbied by Federal law enforcement and not by any health-minded civic organization.

is almost guaranteed to fail very fast; as one drives about, transmission problems which are tolerable and may not even be noticeable in voice communications are enough to cause an Internet connection to terminate.

The only other remaining ways to connect are through a host of wireless services that differ from country to country and even within any one country, and include the following:

- Inmarsat M+; these are briefcase-size self-contained satellite telephones with digital data ports. They can be bought or leased (hence be traceable to an individual or company) and, like any radio transmitters, can be intercepted if an adversary feels strongly enough about so doing. Although legal in many countries, unless a user's business involves a lot of traveling, he or she may have to do some explaining as to why he or she is using one when there is a perfectly functioning regular telephone a few steps away that costs less too. A typical user's Inmarsat Mini-M terminal is shown in Figure 6.1, the older Inmarsat M terminal is shown in Figure 6.2 below.

Figure 6.1   Typical Inmarsat Mini-M user terminal

- They can be used in most areas on earth as per the coverage map in Figure 6.3.

- Globalstar: this is a satellite-based personal communication like Iridium. Unlike Iridium, which was purchased by the US Department of Defense after it declared bankruptcy, Globalstar is still functioning. The handset is depicted in Figure 6.4. Coverage is depicted in Figure 6.5.

- Ricochet: this was a US-only wireless scheme that runs at up to 128 kbps. It was no more anonymous than a registered cellphone because each modem has its own electronic address and can be pinpointed to within about 1000 feet. It

Figure 6.2   Inmarsat M user terminal

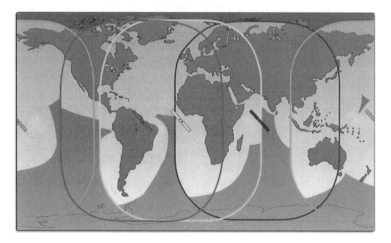

Figure 6.3   Inmarsat coverage

was available in select metropolitan areas in the USA. As of mid-2000, Ricochet went into bankruptcy, with a debt allegedly approaching $1 billion. It is no longer available.

- Palmnet and assorted other wireless networks that services Palm Pilot VII units in the USA: these palmtop devices, such as that pictured in Figure 6.6 are also

Figure 6.4   Globalstar user equipment

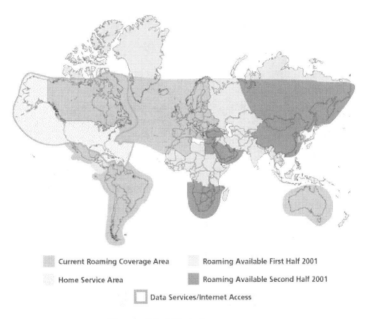

Current Roaming Coverage Area   Roaming Available First Half 2001

Home Service Area   Roaming Available Second Half 2001

Data Services/Internet Access

Figure 6.5   Globalstar coverage

individually serial numbered and registered and billed to someone's credit card every month.

- Orbcomm: this is a network of low-flying satellites with nearly-worldwide coverage. Individual users' units look like walkie-talkies, (Figure 6.7) sport a

Figure 6.6   Palm Pilot VII device for wireless access to select Internet services

Figure 6.7   Magellan unit for accessing the Internet through Orbcomm

50 cm long vertical antenna, and have to be within unobstructed view of the sky. Each unit has its own Internet address (and associated billing and identifying information). Unlike Palm Pilot devices and Ricochet modems, they work worldwide.

- StarBand and numerous radio-based schemes that require a fixed installation (Figures 6.8 and 6.9) these require directional antennas of about 20 inches in diameter to be aimed accurately at the satellite that provides the corresponding service. As such, their location is readily known.

Figure 6.8   Satellite terminal for two-way Internet access to the Starband satellite system

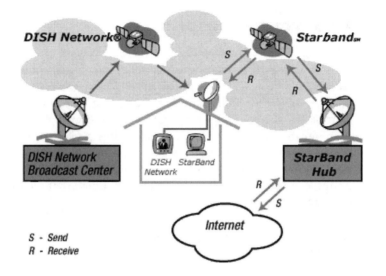

Figure 6.9   Starband satellite system for two-way Internet access

The upshot of all the above is that it is extremely difficult to hide one's whereabouts when connecting to any network, such as the Internet. Partly to ensure that local telephone companies (and the country's tax revenues) are not reduced, and partly for other reasons, most countries have always taken a dim view of unauthorized transmissions from their land, and are usually able and willing to devote resources to find out who is transmitting from where and why; this is difficult to do if one makes a single such wireless connection but becomes increasingly easy if the same person (or radio) makes a sequence of such connections – even if spread over a period of days or weeks.

This underscores yet once more the point of this book encryption is all well and good but:

- it is alerting, and

- it is only a small part of the overall process of hiding a communication.

Since mid-2001, a new Dutch company, Aramiska, backed by venture capital firm Whitney & Co., has been offering a 'first two-way open standard broadband connectivity service'. Independently, Tiscali Co. announced on 17 June 2001 that it will be offering a pan-European two-way satellite Internet service from Gilat Satellite Networks Ltd., starting in the autumn of 2001. This service is also now available (see http://www.net4nowt.com/comments/1005111692, 57886,.shtml).

6.4 Anonymized Cellphones

Most countries that use the GSM cellphone system (and that is just about every country in the world except for the USA, which uses AMPS, CDMA, DAMPS, TDMA, and other incompatible systems; the U.S. does use GSM at 1900 MHz, in contrast to the standard 800 MHz used everywhere else) sell prepaid cellphone usage in the form of cards.[5] The user buys a GSM phone and a card for a fixed prepaid amount of usage; when that amount gets used up, one can buy another card, and so on. These phones are anonymous as nobody knows who the buyer is–until the buyer calls a telephone (such as 'home') that identifies the cellphone to any intercepting authorities once and for all.

The same concept is becoming increasingly popular in the USA as well, where cellphones with a prepaid amount of air time can be bought anonymously with cash at assorted convenience stores. In the USA, you can also go to a '7–11' convenience store and give cash to obtain a 7–11 credit card (actually a debt card; see http://www.seveneleven.com/internetcard); it is limited to $2000, which is enough for most minor transactions that one wants to keep anonymous.

One additional interesting option is for one to buy an anonymous GSM card from a foreign country. This gets around two practical problems of cards sold over the counter in-country:

- sellers of cards sold over the counter in-country often require the buyer to show some identification, which is recorded.

- such cards are usually limited to in-country use.

---

[5] AMPS (advanced mobile phone service) was the first cellular system to come into existence. It is an analog voice scheme and it is still used in many parts of the world. It has been superseded by digital systems because the cellular telephone service providers can accommodate more subscribers within the allocated portion of the radio spectrum, and hence derive more revenue.

There are numerous mutually imcompatible digital cellular systems:

- GSM was the first and is used all over the world. It stands for 'Global System Mobile'. It was the first-generation digital cellular system.

- DAMPS stands for 'digital AMPS' (discussed above).

- CDMA stands for Code Division Multiple Access. It is used extensively in the USA, where it is marketed by Sprint PCS Co.

- TDMA stands for Time Division Multiple Access. It is also used extensively in the USA, where it is marketed by AT&T.

One can buy GSM cards registered to the United Kingdom or to the Czech Republic *with* international roaming through http://www.reputablefirm.com/GSM5000.htm. Another source is http://www.foreverfree.net/gsm.html, which promises to provide an anonymous GSM card for $99 and includes a prepaid credit of CHF 50.

6.5 Encrypted Telephony Over the Internet

Unencrypted telephony over the Internet has been around for years in numerous software packages, some (like Netscape) for free and others for a fee. Encrypted telephony has also been around for a number of years dating back to the DOS days (e.g., PGPfone, NAUTILUS.zip and others). As of the past few years, a free piece of software, 'speak freely', has been popularized worldwide and it is highly recommended.

It is amusing that, whereas security-minded computer users have spent enormous efforts improving software products for encrypting e-mail and documents, most are unaware that they can have encrypted voice just as well and that encrypted voice has a fundamental security advantage over encrypted e-mail: the encryption key is different for each communication and will disappear for ever if one turns the power off; as such, it cannot be surrendered on demand.

6.5.1 Demystifying the Use of 'Speak Freely'

Speak Freely (Figure 6.10) is an amazingly useful piece of free software obtainable from anywhere through http://www.speakfreely.org. It allows any two individuals on the Internet to communicate by voice with full end-to-end strong encryption. It defeats any and all interception means, including computer forensics, subject to the qualifications and warnings at the end of this section. To obtain this service, follow the instructions below.

1. Install the software on a computer that either has a microphone and speaker(s) (or earphones), or receptacles to which external microphones and speakers can be connected.

2. Under the Options pull-down menu, the only item that should be checked is 'GSM compression' (Figure 6.11). Specifically, 'Voice Activation' should have the 'none' option selected and 'Jitter Correction' the '1 second' option.

Figure 6.10   Speak Freely freewave software

Figure 6.11   Speak Freely: pull drop-down Options menu – the only item checked in this menu should be GSM Compression.

3. Under the Help pull-down menu, select 'Local Loopback'.

4. Place the cursor inside the small new window that will appear and click once in it. If the cursor looks like a handset, push the space bar once; the cursor should change into an image of an ear.

5. Speak a few words and click on the space bar again. Your voice should come out of the loudspeaker (or headphones) a few seconds later. If not, check your computer's audio settings (unrelated to the Speak Freely software) by right-clicking on the speaker icon in the lower right-hand corner of the screen and selecting the 'adjust audio' option. If all works OK, close the small window that opened after step (3) above.

6. Under the Connection pull-down menu, select the 'New' option and type the following in the resulting window that opens: echo.fourmilab.ch

7. Place the cursor inside that window and click once. If the cursor is a handset, push the space bar once and it should become an ear.

8. Speak a few words into the microphone and push the spacebar once again. The cursor should become a handset. Wait 10 seconds and you should hear your own words repeated. If you do not the problem is Internet-related; make sure that any firewalls you might be using do not block incoming or outgoing data.

9. If all works OK – and as chances are that will be the case – you are ready for an actual online voice communication.

The above steps must be done only once when setting up Speak Freely and never again. The three steps below are the only ones that must be taken to set up and carry out a voice communication.

1. Contact the person you want to communicate by some means [preferably a secure means, such as PGP-encrypted e-mail (see Section 5.8.4) if you plan to used Speak Freely for what it is really intended, namely, encrypted voice communications]. Arrange for a mutually convenient time as well as 'who is going to call whom' as well as up to *three* encryption words that others would not be able to guess. Let us assume you do the calling of the other person. Instruct the other person [who must have gone through the identical one-time ritual above (which, remember, will never have to be repeated)] a few minutes before the agreed communications time to:

(a) Go to the phonebook pull-down menu and select 'Edit Listing';

(b) enter a unique e-mail address that does *not* have to be a true one; that person must tell you what that e-mail address will be; that person should also check the 'Exact match only' box. That person should enter the server name. lwl.fourmilab.ch

2. When the agreed on communications time comes, you, the caller, should go to the phonebook pull-down menu and select the 'Search' option. Enter the same server name (lwl.fourmilab.ch) and the same e-mail address that the other person has said he or she will use in (item 1b) above; check 'Exact search only'. Push the 'Search' key and Speak Freely will find the 'other' person's IP address, pass it to your copy of Speak Freely, and automatically start the connection between you and the other person. To do so move the cursor to the window which opens as soon as the connection is established, and click on it; if it takes the shape of a headset, push the space bar (which will change the cursor to one looking like an ear) and speak; *remember to push the space bar again to be able to listen.*

3. It is only *after* the communication has been established that you can activate encryption, as follows:

(a) Recall the three encryption words agreed upon (confidentially, in an encrypted e-mail) in step (1) above.

(b) Tell the person you are communicating with that you will now both switch to encrypted communications by using one, two, or all three pre-agreed encryption words in the Options pull-down-menu 'Connection' option for the DES key, Idea key, and Blowfish key, respectively. Clearly, both of you have to enter the same encryption word in the same box (e.g., the DES key) for the encrypted connection to work.

(c) If the above step is done correctly by both people, subsequent communication will be fully encrypted end-to-end and uninterceptable by anyone else. If it not done correctly, you will hear an ugly buzzing sound instead of a voice; return to the unencrypted mode by deleting all encryption keys and ask the other person to do the same. Note that an unencrypted transmission from you *will* be heard clearly by the other person even if he or she has encryption enabled.

Some words of caution on security issues that you *must* keep in mind are in order:

- All the encrypted communication in the world will do you no good if your room where you speak (or that of the other person) has an audio 'bug' in it. The problem is compounded if you and/or the other person is using a loudspeaker rather than earphones. To the extent possible, make sure the room is not bugged; since this is next to impossible to do, use earphones instead of a speaker, speak softly into the microphone, and have some cassette player playing something noisy in the background.

- You can control – to some extent – things at your own end only, not at the other person's end. Do you trust the other person? Watch what you say, and assume the other person is tape-recording you – perhaps against his or her will.

- Recall from item 3(c) above that Speak Freely is (unfortunately) configured so that even if you have the encryption keys set, you can still hear unencrypted voice coming out of the other end. As such, you really cannot tell for sure if the other person's transmission to you is encrypted at all. Again, trusting the other person is important (or, better yet, be extra cautious just in case).

- The communication that established the encryption keys to be used should be secure (encrypted e-mail, in-person face-to-face contact, or a reference to some words that you and the other person would know but nobody else would–such as Joe's phone number at his house five years ago, followed by the name of his cat then and our third-grade teacher's first name – if all else fails).

- Wipe(see Section 4.4) all places where the agreed encryption keys above could have been stored (e.g., in e-mail) *before* the encrypted voice communication starts (which means you will have to remember them or jot them down on paper in some cryptic manner) so that you cannot be compelled to produce them even a short time after the encrypted voice communication. As an ancient Greek fellow who was being ferried to Hades (hell) told the boat man in response to the latter's request for money, 'Ουκ αν λαβης παρα του μη εχοντος' which means 'You cannot get something from someone who doesn't have it.

- Speak Freely hides the content of a communication. It does not hide who is communicating with whom (as evidenced by the IP addresses that have to be known so that the data packets can go back and forth). If the situation is one where the identification of the 'other' party can be incriminating (e.g., a US-sympathizer in a repressive regime overseas communicating with, say, an employee of the US Department of Justice), then one must take additional steps to launder this connectivity.

6.5.2 Other voice encryption software

PGPfone is widely available[6] on the Internet but is not recommended because of software flaws. Older DOS-based voice-encryption software such as NAUTILUS[7] are also not recommended because of annoying quirks; unlike document encryption which should be done under DOS in order to get away from the numerous security problems of Windows (discussed in Chapter 4), this issue does not apply to voice encryption much because there is no unencrypted file that could end up on a hard disk.

6.5.3 Encrypted voice communications over cellphones

A respected German company (Rhode and Schwartz; http://rhode-schwartz.com) is now selling for about $3000 a GSM cellphone (a model Siemens S35i) with built-in encryption capability. A similar capability cellphone has been marketed by Swiss firm CryptoAG (http://www.crypto.ch) for at least three years, but is not being sold to individuals.

Not surprisingly, law enforcement is not pleased with the availability of encryption. 'Encryption, whether data or voice, impedes investigations', said Glenn Nick, assistant director of the US Customs Cyber Smuggling Center in Fairfax, VA. 'It is debatable what public good it presents' (http://detnews.com/2001/technews/0106/20/b04-238328.htm)

An example of such a cellphone is illustrated in Figure 6.12.

---

[6] PGPfone can be downloaded from

- http://web.mit.edu/network/pgpfone/ and

- http://www.pgpi.org/products/pgpfone/, among other places.

[7] Nautilus can be downloaded from http://www.lila.com/nautilus.html, http://sss.sevelocks.com/SWVoiceEncryption.htm and http://www.ensta.fr/internet/dos-windows/Nautilus.html, among other places.

Figure 6.12   GSM phone with built-in encryption

7

Legal Issues

7.1 Reasonable Doubt

Laws do not prosecute computers; laws prosecute people. Eventually a court of law has to be convinced – in theory, beyond reasonable doubt – that the accused individual is the one who did what he or she is accused of.

The existence and discovery in a computer of digitized contraband, be that bomb-making plans, stock-market-manipulation schemes or what-not, does *not* prove that any given person did it even if the computer is owned by that person. Unless the accused makes a voluntary confession that holds up in court, an accused and his or her defense counsel can plausibly claim that:

- Others, such as visitors and friends had access to the use of that computer.

- The computer (or at least its hard disk) was purchased used and, therefore, any incriminating information found may well have been the result of the activities of the previous owner(s).

Furthermore:

- It has been shown time and again that if one's computer is left out of one's physical control for some time, another person who can obtain temporary physical access to that computer can modify its contents at will, including changing date/time stamps that could be incorrectly claimed by the prosecution to 'prove' something.

- As many know, when the computer is also used to go online:

  ○ when one receives incoming mail with attachments, these attachments get saved on the disk even if one deletes the unsolicited e-mail that brought them;

○ when one is web browsing, one is often bombarded with unsolicited images that are parts of the advertisements that support a website being browsed (intentionally, as a result of mistyping an URL, or even as a result of a hacked DNS server that misdirects a legitimate URL into a pornographic one); these images related files are stored in one's cache even though one never sought them.

○ time and again it has been shown that, unless one has taken extreme security precautions that few people actually take, remote websites can maliciously add just about any digital file into one's computer, alter existing ones, and delete others.

○ in the case of wireless networks, LANs, etc., there are even more opportunities for a computer to be hacked into, as was recently made public by the disclosure of serious flaws in the popular 802.11b standard (see Section 5.10.3 and Appendix G).

It follows that even if an accused states that he or she is the sole owner of a computer and even if the accused stated that he or she has purchased it new, proving that the evidence could only have been placed in it by the accused is a very difficult task if the defendant's counsel – or his or her expert witness – is well versed in computers.

In common law countries, such as the USA, the prosecutor has to be prepared to show convincingly that:

• the accused is the sole user of that computer and has always been the sole user, *and*

• the computer in question has never been exposed to anyone else who could have walked into the premises of the accused, *and*

• the hard disk in question was bought new, *and*

• the computer has never been used to connect online to the Internet or any other network, *and*

• the computer has never been connected to a wireless modem (e.g., 802.11b, Ricochet, or other), whether or not there was an active network connection on the other end.

These are very hard items to prove. Whereas few defense attorneys today are qualified enough to raise the above outlined defense issues, this should not be viewed as carte blanche by unscrupulous prosecutors to mislead juries into believing something which simply is not true.

7.2 The Impossibility of Uniformizing Cybercrime Laws Around the Globe

Laws are the consequence of societal needs, and different societies have different needs that are shaped by geography, population, history, religion, etc. In an extreme case, the laws of the Jamamani tribe in Brazil are obviously quite different from those of France. In a less extreme case, the laws in the United Kingdom are vastly different from those in the USA. For example, the Regulation of Investigatory Powers (RIP)Act that was enacted in the United Kingdom in 2000 gives many British law enforcement officials the power to demand that an individual provide the decryption keys to an encrypted file in his or her possession under penalty of a two-year jail sentence. By comparison, the US Constitution's Fifth Amendment permits a 'US Person'[1] to refuse to incriminate himself or herself by surrendering a decryption key that resides in his or her head. Unless the US Constitution is amended, this is unlikely to change.

Similarly, countries whose laws are based on the Koran, for example, criminalize different acts from those criminalized in the laws in the USA, for example; it is highly unlikely that Koran-based laws will be changed to accommodate the USA, or vice versa.

Of course, acts that are considered to be crimes under most countries' legal systems, such as murder, are in no need of uniformizing; even then, however, the fact that penalties differ for the same crime will continue to be an issue; one recalls, for example, the many cases when foreign countries with no death penalty have refused to extradite to the USA a person accused of what is crime in both countries until and unless the USA provides assurances that the accused will not be executed.[2]

---

[1] A 'US Person' is not only a US citizen; the term also includes any person legally residing in the USA as well as people in some other categories. The Fifth Amendment states that 'No person ... shall be compelled in any criminal case to be a witness against himself'.

[2] For example, (see http://www.usatoday.com/news/attack/2001/10/03/extradite-usat.htm, or http://www.washingtonpost.com/ac2/wp-dyn?pagename=article&node=&contentId-A31065-2001(Nov28).

For crimes that are clearly far less serious than premeditated murder, such as when a teenager experiments with a computer virus and inadvertently unleashes it on the Internet, many countries do not have laws criminalizing it yet because the need has not yet been felt for such a law. The recent case of the alleged creator of the 'I Love You' virus in Manila, Philippines, is a typical example; in that case, the Philippines passed a new law making that a crime henceforth.

Then there is the issue of whether an act constitutes a criminal wrongdoing or is a civil wrongdoing, or is neither even though it may be 'unethical'. Some acts are civil wrongs in one country and criminal wrongs in another and merely unethical in a third country.

The Proposed Convention on Jurisdiction and Foreign Judgments in Civil and Criminal Matters of the Hague Convention on Private International Laws is interesting as a theoretical piece of work (see http://www.cptech.org/ecom/jurisdiction/hague.html. A list of different countries' agencies that are representing those countries in the above Convention can be found at http://www.hcch.net/e/members.html.

Finally, the innocuous-sounding term 'harmonization of laws' should raise a flag because it often stands for the desire of special interests to enact multinational deals, to prevent competition in both commerce as well as in ideas, and to impose restrictions on citizens under the guise of 'having to abide by the treaty that resulted from the effort to harmonize our laws with those of other nations'.

7.2.1   South Africa's and other countries' internet crackdown

Even before the terrorist attacks that resulted in the tragedy of 11 September 2001, the Internet has been demonized by most every government in the world, including democratic ones as well as totalitarian ones.

Typically, in mid-2001, new censorship laws to control and monitor all Internet (and postal) communications were being pushed by president Thabo Mbeki through the South African parliament by the ruling African National Congress party.

Similar laws have been passed in such diverse countries as China, the USA (after the 11 September tragedy), the United Kingdom, Cuba, Iraq, New Zealand, and others. In the United Kingdom, for example, section 12 of the infamous RIP Act that sets out the 'reasonable interception capabilities' of telecommunications and postal services lists the following requirements (paraphrased):

- Provision of a mechnism for intercepting the entire contents of the communications, with transmission to the government or intercepting agencies in 'near real time';

- minimization of the risk that the warranted person becomes aware of the interception;

- the operation of a system of clandestine opening, copying, and resealing of any letter carried for less than £1.

The consultation document can be found at http://www.homeoffice.gov.uk/ripa/section12.htm and at http://www.legislation.hmso.gov.uk/acts/acts2000/20000023.htm

In Hong Kong, the government wanted Internet service providers (ISPs) to retain subscriber records and files for six months and to gain access to encryption used by individuals over the Internet. Putting momentarily aside the practical impossibility of so doing, the Honk Kong Internet Service Providers Association (HKIPSA) asked for judicial scrutiny if this were to become the norm (http://www.theregister.co.uk/content/6/17704.html).

7.2.2 'Recording' of instant messaging

Is instant messaging 'similar' to a telephone conversation as far as the legalities of recording it are concerned? The State of New York does not require one to ask permission before recording a telephone conversation. Maryland does. It is not clear to what extent the laws that were developed for the telephone carry through to 'telephone-like communications' over the Internet. When the instant messaging communication crosses national boundaries, then it is anyone's guess as to whose laws apply to the recording of such message exchanges.

7.3 Attempts to Form International Cybercrime Treaties, and Their Shortcomings

The Seventh United Nations Congress on the Prevention of Crime and the Treatment of Offenders took place in 1985. Computer crime was discussed in paragraphs 42–44 of the Secretary General's report titled 'Proposals for Concerted International Action Against Forms of Crime Identified in the Milan Plan of Action' (see http://www.uncjin.org/Documents/EighthCongress.html).

The 12th plenary meeting of the Eighth Congress in 1990 included a draft resolution introduced by Canada on computer-related crimes. This was adopted in the 13th plenary meeting and calls upon member states to intensify efforts to combat computer crime.

Interestingly, 'computer crime' has not been defined in a global manner; this is unlikely to change because what a 'computer' is and what it can do has been rapidly evolving. Computer 'abuse' (or 'misuse') is not necessarily a crime; it can be accidental, it can be negligent, or it can be intentional. An employee given a password that also happens to access files that an employer would not want the employee to access (but has forgotten to so inform the employee) cannot be held accountable for accessing such files.

The common types of computer activities that are generally viewed as illegal are:

- fraud by computer manipulation; this includes a very large collection of situations;

- forgery (modification of documents, creation of false documents, etc.);

- damage to or modification of computer data or software; this includes all sorts of malicious mobile code (viruses, trojans, worms, etc.), logic bombs, etc.;

- deliberate unauthorized access to computer systems and services; the motives can range from curiosity, to sabotage, to theft, and the means for gaining such access can be numerous and include remote access from different locations;

- unauthorized reproduction of legally protected software.

In addition, different countries consider different activities to be illegal; one country may consider any use of a computer to generate, copy, or transmit criticism of its leaders to be illegal; another may have laws making it illegal to use a computer to modify or even display text or images having local religious significance, and so on.

More recently, the Convention on Cybercrime has been proposed as a treaty by the Council of Europe, a 43-nation public body.[3] Interestingly, its primary architect is the US Department of Justice even though the USA is not a member of the Council of Europe (which was created after World War II). Signatories are expected to cooperate 'on the basis of uniform or reciprocal legislation and domestic laws to the widest extent possible'. Signatories 'shall adopt such legislative and other measures as may be necessary to oblige [anyone in control of computer data] to preserve and maintain the integrity of that computer data for a period of time as

---

[3] For example, see http://conventions.coe.int/Treaty/EN/projets/FinalCybercrime.htm, http://www.coe.int/T/E/Communication_and_Research/Press/Themes_Files/Cybercrime/, and http://press.coe.int/cp/2001/646a(2001).htm.

long as necessary' and 'Each party shall adopt such legislative or other measures as may be necessary to oblige the custodian or other person who is to preserve the data to keep confidential the undertaking of such procedures'. This appears as a possible end run around the normal practice of obtaining a warrant *before* intercepting anything. Finally, in a paragraph that parallels the UK RIP Act, the document states that:

> *each party shall adopt such legislative and other measures as may be necessary to empower its competent authorities to order any person who has knowledge about the functioning of the computer system or measures applied to protect the computer data therein to provide, as is reasonable, the necessary information.*

In short, to force a person to decrypt files he or she has the decryption key for.

According to numerous quotes on the Internet, the intent of this is suspected to be an effort by law enforcement in the USA (where the Fifth Amendment protects one from being forced to provide decryption keys) to make an end run by forcing the US Congress to allow the forced production of decryption keys as a consequence of being a signatory to this international treaty.

The minimum list of activities involving a computer that are proposed to be criminalized by the above treaty includes the following:

- computer fraud;

- computer forgery;

- damage to computer data or computer programs;

- computer sabotage;

- unauthorized access;

- Unauthorized interception (naturally, interception by governments is allowed!);

- unauthorized reproduction of protected computer programs;

- unauthorized reproduction of a topography protected by law (e.g., topography of a semiconductor product).

The list of optional additional activities is the following:

- alteration of computer data or programs (without the right to do so);

- computer (industrial) espionage;

- unauthorized use of a computer (or network) that either (can cause) a significant risk of loss to the person entitled to use the system or harm the system or its functioning, or is made with the intent of causing loss or harm, or actually causes loss or harm;

- unauthorized use of a protected computer program (that is protected by law).

The above list has been rightly criticized. For example:

- it does not criminalize the trafficking of wrongly obtained passwords or the distribution of viruses;

- it does not define many terms (such as what is 'unauthorized access') accurately enough.

It must also be realized that, as with conventional crime that does not involve computers, what is 'legal' and what is not is constantly changing; typically, until less than a decade or two ago, the notion of a 'computer virus' was an abstraction and a curiosity and there was no need then for any laws pertaining to such an abstraction. Conversely, connecting one's personally owned telecommunications equipment to national (and, in many overseas countries, government-owned) telephone networks was illegal but is legal now.

   Although a US person can understand and even sympathize with the US desire to create an infrastructure that favors the interests of the US Department of Justice to extradite and prosecute foreign nationals for certain US crimes, the other edge of the same sword is that the same powers are handed over to the 43 nations of the Council of Europe, including Azerbaijan, Bulgaria, Romania, and others for acts which are *not* a crime under US laws. German authorities, for example, could invoke that proposed treaty to attempt to extradite to Germany and prosecute a US citizen for, say, selling pro-Nazi memorabilia over the Internet, by framing the warrant in terms of 'suspected terrorist activity'.

   The supporters of this cyber treaty include the Motion Picture Association of America, the Recording Industry of America Association, the Business Software Alliance, and others with an interest in easing the prosecution of individuals accused of copyright violations; they see in it a more streamlined version of the 1996 Intellectual Property Treaty of the World Intellectual Property Organization, drafted largely by Bruce Lehman, who was the then head of the US Patent and Treaty Office. Shortly after that treaty was signed and ratified, Congress created the Digital Millenium Copyright Act to implement that treaty.

   There are numerous critics of the 'Convention on Cybercrime'. According to Stewart Baker, a former general counsel at the National Security Agency and recipient of the Department of Defense Medal for Meritorious Civilian Service, and now a partner at the Washington, DC, legal firm of Steptoe & Johnson, 'The [cybercrime] treaty was written by government bureaucrats for government bureaucrats. The process was entirely dominated by one viewpoint: criminal enforcement'.[4] Jeffrey Pryce, of the same legal firm, has stated that 'industry and civil liberties groups are remarkably aligned' in their opposition to this treaty, especially in the areas of due process protection.[5]

It would seem that AT&T Corporation and other high-technology firms have been trying to stop or at least to soften this treaty; even, it would appear, the US Chamber of Commerce and the Information Association of America oppose it. Indeed, US businesses are now starting to appeal to foreign businesses to oppose this treaty; amusingly, since the treaty is available only in French and English, individuals who speak neither of these two languages are likely to be unaware of what it says.

Although the aspects of this treaty that require member nations to treat unauthorized computer intrusion, the distribution of child pornography, and the release of viruses are uncontroversial, its effort to make copyright infringement and what is called 'virtual child porn' criminal acts (both of which are under constitutional challenge in the USA) are contested. Equally contested is the proposed requirement that nations will have to share electronic evidence across borders about matters that have nothing to do with cybercrime and that may not even be a crime in the USA.

This treaty will also require member nations to develop procedures to order the 'freezing' of data on any computer, to capture network traffic (including telephone networks) in real time, and even to intercept the content of communications. This means that US telephone companies and ISPs would have to meet the demands of foreign investigators, with no compensation for so doing.

Some view this treaty as intended as an effort by the Department of Justice to complement the Communications Assistance to Law Enforcement Act (CALEA) of 1994 (which does not cover Internet services) by importing this provision as a 'treaty' commitment to be approved by Congress. It will be interesting to test in court of law what happens when an individual in the USA is told to surrender

---

[4] See http//www.law.com/cgi-bin/gx.cgi/AppLogic+FTContentServer?pagename=law/View&c=Article&cid=ZZZD3WRL5LC&live=true&cst=1&pa=0&s=News&ExpIgnore=ture&showsummary=0. ALSO QUOTED VERBATIM IN http://www.scuadvocate.org/apr01_6.html.

[5] See http://www.law.com/cgi-bin/gx.cgi/AppLogic+FTContentServer?pagename=law/View&c=Article&cid=ZZZD3WRL5LC&live=true&cst=1&pc-0&pa=0&s=News&ExpIgnore=true&ashowsummary=0, and http://WWW.GOOGLE.COM/search?hl=en&q=%22Industry+and+civil+liberties+groups+are+remarkably+aligned%22&btnG=Google+Search.

his or her decryption keys on the basis of this treaty (if it is signed by Congress) and if that individual invokes his or her Fifth Amendment rights against self-incrimination.

In summary, the concern with this treaty is that it submits USA citizens and companies to foreign criminal process.

7.4 Computer Laws and Privacy Laws

Unlike the theft of physical property, the theft of a copy of information stored in computers does not deprive the original owner of the use that original information. Indeed, before computers became popular, the theft of information was a very uncommon matter and it was not commonly litigated. With the popularization of computers and information, societies have had to deal with the notion of privacy.

For historical reasons, the USA Constitution has concerned itself with what the government may not do to its citizens and not to what these citizens may not do to each other (with the exception of slavery, which is banned outright). By and large, legal privacy protection in the USA can come only from property laws on the premise that what is taken belongs to the person it was taken from. Such laws vary from State to State and from one local jurisdiction to another. The issue is not that the USA is not concerned with privacy; it is very concerned with it, as evidenced by a large number of bills presently pending before the US Congress (see http://www.epic.org/privacy/terrorism/). The problem is twofold:

- Private data, like most anything else, are viewed in the USA as a commodity that can be bought and sold at a profit. Whereas individuals may want their privacy, numerous groups want to buy and sell it; such groups include insurance companies, marketers of assorted commercial products, and marketers of databases (such as CDB Infotek in Santa Ana, CA, which also admits to collecting and selling such data to assorted components of the US Government in what seems like an end run around laws that prohibit the US government from collecting and storing personal information beyond strictly prescribed limits).

- The First Amendment to the US Constitution, which establishes the freedom of speech, is often (ab)used by those that sell personal data; they basically claim that freedom of speech includes the right to 'speak' such data, and Federal Courts have sided with that interpretation.

7.4.1 Employee monitoring in the workplace

Since laws vary from country to country, and since an exhaustive presentation of all countries' laws on the subject is beyond the scope of this book, this section will be limited itself to the situation in the USA and the United Kingdom.

In the USA and the United Kingdom, an employer is legally allowed to monitor any employee's use of employer-provided resources; this specifically includes the monitoring of employee e-mail and web browsing. The rationale is easy to see: US employers do not want the legal liability of being sued by employees who alleged that the employer 'did not take adequate means to prevent harassment by e-mail'; employers also want to ensure that employees do not spend their time at work web-browsing sites that are not work-related.

On the other side of the coin, employee morale predictably plummets when employees know (or believe) that they are being watched all the time; this results in frequent resignations to accept other jobs where the employer may have a policy of not monitoring employee use of e-mail and/or web browsing. Additionally, when employers keep such records of e-mail usage by all employees, they become vulnerable to lawsuits for wrongful termination[6] as well as to numerous subpoenas for such records.

7.4.2 Is industry self-regulation (for privacy) viable?

Faced with an unprecedented number of bills pending before the US Congress that want to put some penalties for abuse of consumer privacy, especially online, US industry has been orchestrating a massive public relations campaign to convince the public:

- that many limitations on what liberties industry can take with individuals' privacy will be very expensive and that these costs will be passed on to the consumers (this is the 'stick' portion of the carrot-and-stick approach);

- that industry can regulate itself;

- that nobody wants the government to poke its nose into citizens' rights. This final point is intended to appeal to the libertarians. It is also amusing in view of

---

[6] See, for example, the wrongful termination alwsuit by Michael A. Smith v. The Pillsubry Company, C.A. No. 95-5712 heard in the US District Court for the Eastern District of Pennsylvania. The Court stated that *the e-mail belonged to the employer even though the employee may have used encryption to protect it from the employer.*

the same industry's support of unprecedented government intrusion in what suits the industry, namely, the Digital Millennium Copyright Act (see Section 7.10).

In fact, industry cannot regulate itself, for the following reasons:

- Profits: US industry has realized the profits that result from directed marketing (made possible by tracking individuals' preferences in anything and everything). Private information is bought and sold like a commodity. Asking private industry voluntarily to forgo profits is about as likely to succeed as asking a small child to volunteer not to eat candy.

- Common sense: it is no more likely for industry to regulate itself not to profit from privacy abuses than it is for individuals to regulate themselves not to download music from Napster; yet industry wants the former but not the latter.

7.4.3 European trends

The British Regulation of Investigatory Powers Act has already been enacted to give law enforcement the power to intercept communications and to demand that individuals surrender their decryption keys under penalty of a two-year jail sentence.[7]

Responding to a National Crime Intelligence Squad (NCIS) report, a new initiative in a draft proposal from the European Commission on the processing of personal data in electronic communication, if adopted, will allow the police to demand the recording of all telecommunications data (specifically including all

---

[7] The United Kingdom has the dubious reputation as 'the most monitored land of all' (http://msnbc.com/news/577446.asp?0nm=T13O&cp1=1). The state has poured millions into closed-circuit TV systems for surveillance of public places; the Newham Borough of London has been using Visionics software in camera surveillance systems since autumn of 1998; many Britons will never forget the shopping mall images of a Liverpool toddler, James Bulger, being taken to his death by two ten-year-old boys some eight years ago. Most Britons accept this use of surveillance. By comparison, USA police caused quite a stir when it was disclosed that they filmed all patrons of a Superbowl game in Tampa, Fl. in early 2001. Even so, the USA is not far behind Britain; Jersey City proudly announced in late May 2001 that it had installed multiple video cameras in public places and that these cameras are monitored; also, on 3 July 2001, Tampa police installed 36 cameras to cover a 16-block area in Ybor city district for images to match against a database that will eventually include 30 000 records, according to detective Bill Todd (http://www.civic.com/civic/articles/2001/0702/web-tampa-07-03-01.asp).

e-mail and all records of Internet usage) for an unprecedented seven years.[8] European Council ministers have already agreed to support this initiative. The Council of the European Union represents the 15 member governments. This is a proposal that was reportedly designed with the US Federal Bureau of Investigation (FBI) approximately six years ago.

For the proposal to be accepted, a joint decision is needed between the European Council of Ministers and the European Parliament. If it is enacted into law, it will amount to an overthrow of Europe's privacy protections and it will fly in the face of the Council of Europe's conventions on data protection (http://europa.eu.int/comm/internal_market/en/media/dataprot/inter/con10881.htm#HD_NM_10) and the human rights rulings by the European Court of Human Rights (http://www.echr.coe.int/)

This proposal affects companies as well in that it places on them the burden of storing such data for seven years just in case the police might want to look at them. Not surprisingly, business groups (who would have to foot the bill for this) and privacy watchgroups, such as 'Statewatch', have formed a marriage of convenience to fight it: 'The fact that it is being proposed in the "democratic" EU does not make it any less authoritarian or totalitarian', according to Tony Bunyan, editor of Statewatch, (http://www.statewatch.org/news/2001/may/03Genfopol.htm).

Three European governments – those of the United Kingdom, France, and Belgium – have already pressed ahead with requiring the retention of telecommunications data for 12 months, despite the conflict with EU law on data protection and privacy (http://www.statewatch.org/news/2001/may/03Genfopol.htm), according to the EU Police Cooperation Working Party (24 April 2001). This effort includes an attempt to end user anonymity (e.g., Internet cafes) by stating that 'It is also imperative that a solution be found to the problems raised by the various forms of anonymity on the World Wide Web, the most significant example being cybercafes'.

The European Union has a bit of a contradictory perspective on encryption. On the one hand, it is giving unprecedented powers to the police to intercept and force the decryption of private files,[9] and, on the other hand, the new European Parliament document recommends that all European citizens should encrypt their e-mail and steer clear of closed-source software (http://www.newscientist.com/dailynews/news.jsp?id=ns9999789).

---

[8] Although such a 'resolution' will have no legal force, it would provide guidelines on what European Union members will be expected to request from their respective providers of telecommunication and internet services. Current EU legislation requires law enforcers to obtain permission every time they want to tap electronic communications; these same current laws also restrict the amount of time that communications firms can keep data and records before destroying them.

[9] By Thomas C. Greene, 'Cyber-crime justifies world government', (see http://www.theregister.co.uk/content/6/1 9321.html).

This amusing contradiction, which amounts to 'hide it from everyone but not from me', is because of persistent European fears of US and United Kingdom interception. This has also been pointed out by the 'father of the Internet', Vince Cerf, who stated in Brussels on 31 May 2001 that the EU's plans for new rules to fight crime on the web risk clashing with existing EU privacy regulations. (http://www.zdnet.com/zdnn/stories/news/0,4586,2767085,00,html).

7.5 US Federal Search and Seizure

According to the 'Computer Crime and Intellectual Property Section' document published by the US Department of Justice (made publicly available by that government organization at http://www.cybercrime.gov/searchmanual.htm#lc), the federal government has vast powers to seize and search computers; these include 'no-knock searches' (i.e., breaking the door down). The reader is referred to that document for the details and the legal justification behind them.

7.5.1 Exactly what are the applicable US laws on computer crime?

The Electronic Communications Privacy Act (ECPA) covers the following.

Title I: capture of live electronic communications

It is illegal for anyone to intercept wire and electronic communications while these are being transmitted. It is also illegal to disclose the contents of unlawful interceptions. Exceptions are made in the case of:

- the system operator (sysop); the sysop can provide intercepted evidence and can continue so doing, usually for 5–10 days; law enforcement has to be careful not to make the sysop its agent;

- consent to intercept;

- consent for interception by persons not related to law enforcement;

- information readily accessible to the public;

- court orders.

Title II: accessing of stored communications

It is illegal for anyone to access a wire or electronic communication while it is in electronic storage, without authorization. However, system providers can disclose contents of a stored communication under three conditions:

- the sysop acting in an authorized capacity;
- through the consent of the sender or the intended recipient of the communication;
- through a subpoena or court order.

ECPA Title II:

- applies to public providers;
- is limited to the content of the communication;
- deals with voluntary disclosures that the sysop wants to make;
- does not suppress evidence on violation.

Subscriber information (name and address, local and long-distance billing records, telephone number or other subscriber number or identity, length of service, and other types of service) requires a subpoena. Connection logs and records require a court order under paragraph 2703. Everything else requires a warrant. Under paragraph 2703, government access to e-mail it requires a warrant if e-mail is stored for 180 days or less; if the e-mail is stored for 181 or more days it requires a warrant if no notice is to be given to the subscriber, a subpoena, or a court order if prior notice is given. To preserve existing and future potential evidence for 90 days, paragraph 2703[f] requires a letter to the entity having such evidence.

Title III: use of trap and trace devices

18 USC 3121 prohibits the use of trap-and-trace devices unless:

- it is done in the normal course of business;
- the user has provided consent;
- a court order has been obtained; court orders are given if the information to be obtained is likely to be relevant to an investigation.

It must be realized that pen registers do not capture content.

The Privacy Protection Act

The 1980 Privacy Protection Act (PPA) covers seizing the work products of a publisher. It was originally devised to protect traditional publishers but is now interpreted to protect computer publications as well. Violation of the PPA Act carries civil damages.

The PPA Act requires the use of a subpoena, rather than a search warrant, except if:

- the person with the material has committed a crime;

- immediate seizure will prevent death or injury;

- immediate seizure will prevent the loss of the materials;

- a subpoena was issued but did not work.

18 USC 1030

This is the primary law covering hacker activities such as the following.

- Espionage (Section 1). This covers:
  - classified material and material related to atomic weapons;
  - acts that cannot be accidental but purposeful.

- Accessing protected financial records. (Section 2). This:
  - applies both to authorized and to unauthorized users;
  - covers private information involved in interstate or foreign commerce; reading the information constitutes a violation.

- Committing computer trespassing (Section 3). Here:
  - no damages are required;
  - it applies only to unauthorized users and not to internal hackers;
  - it applies to any 'nonpublic' computer;

- it prohibits computer fraud limited intent: damage less than $5000 in one year;

- it prohibits computer damage to a protected computer (knowingly, reck-lessly, or unintentionally).

- Trafficking in passwords (Section 6). In this case there must be intent to defraud.

- Computer Extortion (Section 7). This covers:

  - threat to cause damage;

  - intent to extort.

18 USC 1029

This act makes it a felony to possess, traffic, or use:

- an unauthorized or counterfeit device, knowingly and with intent;

- 15 or more cracked passwords;

- 'device-making equipment' which can be hardware (e.g., a machine that makes credit cards) or software (e.g., a cellphone-cloning program);

- 'illegal access devices' (the currency of hackers).

18 USC 2252 and 2252A

This act makes child pornography (transmission, reception, or possession of) a prosecutable offense.

7.5.2 The 'Patriot Act' and other laws after the 11 September 2001 tragedy

Understandably, the USA as well as many Western countries passed a flurry of new laws in an effort to react to the 11 September 2001 tragedy. Contrary to popular belief, however, most of those laws do not expire four years later; this 'sunset clause' applies only to a smally portion of the huge 'Patriot Act'. The bottom line is that the Judiciary, one of the three pillars of power under the US Constitution, is bypassed in numerous actions by the police. In summary:

- Police now have the *permanent* ability to conduct Internet surveillance without a court order in some circumstances and to search homes and offices secretly and without notifying the owner (Section 213).

- Any investigations under way by December 2005, and any future investigations of crimes that took place before that date, are also exempted from the four-year sunset clause.

- Whereas prior to this law there were strict legal restrictions governing the use of federal interception devices, now any US attorney or state attorney general can order the installation of the FBI Carnivore surveillance system and record addresses of web pages visited and e-mail correspondents – without going to a judge.

- Any person who scans in an image of a *foreign* currency note or e-mails or transmits such an image 'with intent to defraud' can go to jail for up to 20 years (Section 375).

- A foreign citizen accused of terrorism who cannot be deported can be held for an unspecified series of 'periods of up to six months' with only the attorney general's approval (Section 412).

- Internet service providers and telephone companies must turn over customer information, including phone numbers called, with no court order required if the FBI claims the 'records sought are relevant to an authorized investigation to protect against international terrorism'. The ISP or telephone company so contacted is not allowed to 'disclose to any person' that the FBI is doing such an investigation (Section 505).

- Credit-reporting firms must disclose to federal police authorities any information that agents request in connection with a terrorist investigation – without the police needing to seek a court order first. Prior to the passage of this new law, this was permitted only in espionage cases (Section 505).

- Terrorism is radically expanded to include acts such as hacking a US government system or breaking into and damaging any Internet-connected computer, actions that were mere 'computer crimes' prior to this law (Section 808). A new crime of 'cyberterrorism' is added, which covers hacking attempts causing damage 'aggregating at least $5000 in value' in one year, any damage to medical equipment or 'physical injury to any person'. Prison terms range between 5 years and 20 years (Section 814).

More specifically:

- Section 202 (authority to intercept voice communications in computer hacking investigations) amends 18 USC paragraph 2516(1) and adds felony convictions; this will 'sunset' in 4 years;

- Section 209 (obtaining voice mail and other stored voice communications) places stored wire communications under the same rules as stored elecronic communications; police can now obtain these with a search warrant, without needing a wiretap order;

- Section 210 (scope of subpoenas for electronic evidence) expands the list of records that police can obtain with a subpoena to include IP addresses and 'means and source of payment' to identify individuals who signed up using a false name, to an ISP;

- Section 211 (clarifying the scope of the Cable Act) allows cable internet providers to be covered by the ECPA provisions; this is not subject to the four-year sunset provision;

- Section 212 (emergency disclosure by communications providers) permits (but does not compel) ISPs to disclose customer records with or without e-mail content in emergencies to police; ISPs may be liable for civil damages, however;

- Section 213 (authority for delaying notice of the execution of a warrant) authorizes delayed notice not only of seizures but also of searches;

- Section 216 (pen register and trap-and-trace statute) applies now to a broad range of communications technologies, including cellular paths, Internet paths, the to/from data from e-mail, etc., but not the content of the communication; it makes the cooperation of providers of communications services compulsory;

- Section 217 (intercepting communications of computer trespassers) allows police to intercept communications of a computer trespasser to or through any protected computer; this provision expires in four years;

- Section 220 (nationwide search warrants for e-mail) allows police to obtain records outside the district where the court is located; this will 'sunset' in four years;

- Section 814 (deterrence of cyberterrorism) increases hacking penalties from 10 years to 20 years; hackers need not cause damage but only to intend to cause damage to be covered under this law.

The above is only a partial list of the many provisions of the new law. Given that it was drafted, voted on, and passed within about a month from the date of the tragedy of 11 September it is reasonable to infer that most of it had been drafted long before 11 September and was waiting for an opportunity to be submitted to a sympathetic Congress and that the immense tragedy of 11 September provide that opportunity.

In the United Kingdom, the Anti-Terrorism, Crime and Security Bill was introduced in the House of Commons on 12 November 2001.

Internationally, 30 countries have signed the 'cybercrime treaty' (http://www.securityfocus.com/news/291), and most have expanded it with post-September-11 provisions that essentially give unlimited powers to their respective security services to monitor anything and everything they possibly can.

7.6 Admissibility of Computer-based Evidence

This depends very heavily on the existing fundamental rules of evidence in effect in each country. It differs, for example, in civil law countries compared with common law countries, not to mention Islamic law countries.

In civil law countries, any evidence can be introduced for free evaluation, and it is up to the judge to decide how much weight, if any, can be placed on such evidence.

In common law countries, where the 'best evidence' rule generally requires that originals, rather than copies, be introduced as evidence, there are exceptions for 'business records' and 'photographic copies'; whether or not computer data fall under either of those two exceptions has been extensively debated by legal scholars; usually, computer printouts have been accepted as falling within the 'business records exception'. Different countries have different rules on copies of magnetic media.

In Islamic law countries, where computer crime comes under the area of *taazir* offenses, procedures as to the admissibility of computer evidence are similar to those of civil law countries, where anything can be admitted into evidence and it is up to the judge to assess that evidence.

7.7 Jurisdictional Issues

Most laws evolved to address a world where crime was local; they cannot handle transnational crime. Who is going to prosecute a hacker in country A who launders his or her data packets through countries B, C, and D in order to attack computers of a multinational company having a presence in countries E and F? And what if some of those countries (A through F) do not have diplomatic relations with each other as a result of age-old animosities?

Recently, Italy's Supreme Court opined that it has the jurisdictional power over any country that harbors an individual or company that maligns Italian equities (in this case it was an Israeli group that was taking issue with some Italian adoption proceedings). Other countries could claim something analogous, and indeed the USA did so in the case of Panamanian former leader General Noriega and in the case of a Mexican Dr Alvarez who had been an active participant in the torturing of a drug enforcement administration (DEA) agent in Mexico a few years earlier. Regardless of how justified a country's indignation is – as was the case against Alvarez – this opens the door to international kidnappings by states as a way of doing business; this evokes images of some 40 years ago when some non-US countries resorted to capturing dissidents, stuffing them in suitcases in the USA, and shipping them to other countries for prosecution (actually for execution); this is clearly an unacceptable way of international conduct.

Some countries' legal systems place more emphasis on the location of an offense; others place more emphasis on other aspects of an act, such as whether the act involved facilities owned by a country, or persons who are citizens of that country, and so on. Depending on each country's relative emphasis on the different aspects of a transnational computer act, may different countries' existing legal systems can claim extraterritoriality.

Common law countries' legal systems usually take the position that a transnational crime has to be dealt with by the country in which the damage is done. An often conflicting legal principle, the 'ubiquity doctrine', holds that a transnational act should be dealt with in the country where 'one of the constitutive elements of the offense, or the ultimate result', occurred. A still different, conflicting, doctrine, the 'active nationality principle', holds that jurisdiction in transnational crimes rests with the country of citizenship of the accused. This, clearly, can result in double and triple jeopardy.

Related to the jurisdictional issues above is the issue of whether one country can search databases in another without the consent of the latter. A practical situation that can motivate this is in the case of multinational corporations that centralize data for all countries they have a presence in, in a single database in a single country; can criminal investigators from a third, affected, country search that database? A possible reason for such stealthy access could be that formal international procedures for requesting that same information through official channels can take longer than it takes an accused to erase the data sought.

Although this may sound like music to law enforcement ears, it is highly unlikely to become a reality because of the difficulty of:

- ensuring that what is retrieved remotely is all relevant to an ongoing criminal investigation,

- ensuring that no more than what is specifically needed is retrieved,

- protecting corporate proprietary data from transnational data theft,

- instituting 'bullet-proof' auditing to ensure that all such access is not abused under the guise of law enforcement by countries where, for example, there is a totalitarian regime looking for ways to identify critics.

A typical example is the case of Frederick Tobern, who was born in Germany but is now an Australian citizen who lives and works in Australia. In December 2000, Germany's highest court found that Tobern's Australian website, which promulgates a revisionist view of the holocaust, violated Germany's laws and upheld a 10-month jail sentence against Tobern. In another example, in November 2000, a French court ordered Yahoo (that has a site in French as well as employees in France) to block French nationals from viewing or buying Nazi paraphernalia in Yahoo's auction sites, regardless of whether these nationals used the French or the US portal of Yahoo.

Independently from criminal law, civil law complexities are just as much of a thorn in the side of companies doing electronic business across national lines. A European Union proposal, the 'Rome II Green Paper', proposes that the law in the consumers' country should apply in disputes between citizens of EU countries and global Internet companies. According to Stuart Baker, a lawyer at the Washington-based legal firm of Steptoe and Johnson, 'Companies on the Internet that sell a few products to someone in Greece are going to discover that Greek consumer protection laws will apply to them' (http://www.washtech.com/washtechway/2_9/techcap/9555-1.html). The USA position is that 'the European rule on jurisdiction should not [be used] because it is inconsistent with settled US law and is unlikely to be broadly acceptable in the US', according to a spokesman for the State Department (http://www.washtech.com/washtechway/2_9/techcap/9555-1.html).

In summary, the legal aspects of handling transnational crime are extremely complex in that they involve deeply held religious, societal and fundamental constitutional and other legal differences between different countries; differences that are unlikely to be uniformized beyond a superficial level. National pride and issues of sovereignty play no small role.

7.8   For the Law Enforcer: Arrest or Observe?

Any nation's system of justice has an interest in two complementary aspects of justice: prosecution and collection of information. In national security matters, for example, such as in the case of accredited diplomats from other nations, prosecution is not an option, and the collection of information about the activities of one or more individuals is of great interest.

Even in the case of clear criminality, such as drug distribution, money laundering, organized crime, etc., arresting a low-level functionary may again be the most unwise course of action if by so doing it deprives the Department of Justice from such more important options as:

- observing the identified law breaker (say, a low-level drug pusher) to identify his or her sources, networks, modus operandi, etc., so as to disrupt the entire network as opposed to alerting it by arresting a low-level functionary;

- coercing the identified law breaker to turn into 'State's evidence' and help arrest and convict individuals with much more serious criminal activity up the chain of command of organized crime.

The foregoing cases apply to computer forensics and to network forensics much more so than do say, shoplifting or assault cases. It is, therefore, important for the National Institute of Justice (NIJ) to articulate to the agencies it serves the fact that computer and network forensics do not come 'cost free' but have consequences that should be carefully evaluated before computer – and network forensics activities are undertaken. The following are examples of such tradeoffs that must be assessed:

- By seizing a person's computer's storage media one alerts those with whom that person had been communicating to wipe their hard disks, disable their encryption keys, and change their modus operandi. Even the mere appearance of any law enforcement interest could have the same effect.

- Unless network forensics is done in a manner that is unobtrusive enough to a suspect, that suspect is likely to hide his or her tracks at the slightest suspicion of a threat; as a minimum, that suspect is likely to abstain from any further hacking. Given that most cyberattacks have been done by insiders, being 'unobtrusive enough' to an insider (such as *the* system administrator) is extremely difficult. If the hacker is not an insider (and this is impossible to tell a priori), then a forensics investigator has a little more leeway, but not much because remote hackers are often better versed in the details of the networks they attack than the administrators of the networks themselves.

Even after a computer forensics examination has started, there are numerous options that may be mutually exclusive. Examples are as follows:

- Magnetic forensic microscopy, which always requires that a hard disk case be opened and major hardware changes be made, should be done *after* and not before an exact copy has been made of the hard disk for conventional forensics.

- Pulling the plug off the wall for a computer that is 'on' will remove all data in RAM. Keeping it 'on' allows for the likelihood that some data on the disks will be irretrievably overwritten.

- Turning a seized computer 'on' in order to accommodate an operationally urgent need to retrieve some information from it before the disk is copied will likely make the data on the diskinadmissible as evidence because the process of booting the computer can be reasonably claimed to have altered the contents of the disk in a manner that the prosecution cannot describe.

The much publicized case of Kevin Mitnick contains much self-serving fiction written by Dr Shimomura, who wrote an entire book (*Take Down*) in which he prides himself on how he tracked Mitnick against seemingly overwhelming odds (see http://www.takedown.com); see also (http://www.sdsc.edu/SDSCwire/v2.2/1105.tsutomu.html). The fact is that Dr Shimomura had the uncommon luxury of standing on the shoulders of cooperating giants, namely, having had the benefit of massive human and equipment resources from local, State, *and* Federal law enforcement, telephone companies, *and* private companies, all working together. This is an exception rather than common practice, as anyone in law enforcement will attest. It is also noteworthy that Mitnick's encrypted hard disk was never decrypted despite the obviously concerted law enforcement effort to do so; this points out that computer forensics is far more effective against someone who is not knowledgeable enough about the intricacies of computers.

7.9 Legal Defense for Responsible Professionals in Oppressive Regimes

It is dangerous to be right when the government is wrong.

Voltaire

Clearly, the legal systems in different countries are is different and no single set of guidelines can apply to all. In a totalitarian system, no amount of legal steps of arguments can exonerate one from the wrath of the regime.

In civilized countries, especially ones with a written constitution, the rule of law usually (but not always) protects an innocent person from malicious prosecution. This presumes, of course, that the innocent person has the wherewithal (for this, read 'nearly limitless funds') to hire competent legal defense and to pursue appeals up the legal chain all the way to the Supreme Court if necessary. The annals of justice are full of documented cases where court-appointed legal defense was inept, asleep, drunk, or otherwise ineffective. It behooves one to know which potholes to avoid up front in connection with the use of a computer rather than to have to extricate oneself out of a legal pothole placed in front of one by unscrupulous prosecutors and overzealous law enforcers.

The reader is cautioned once again abut the importance of the golden rule that permeates this book: 'above all, do not pop up on a government's radar screen'. This has nothing to do with 'justice'; it has everything to do with human nature and the assertive and self-righteous nature of those who have been attracted to seek positions in law enforcement and prosecution in any regime or political system. In short, 'it's an ego thing'.

Sadly, even in what can be seen as the country with the highest degree of protection for one's civil rights, the USA, there have been numerous documented cases of gross abuse of authority by assorted law enforcers and prosecutors over the years; human nature is the same across the globe. Ensuring the privacy and confidentiality of your files from prosecutorial abuse is, therefore, important within the USA as well.

Even if you live in the USA, therefore, do not depend too much on the protection against self-incrimination offered by the Fifth Amendment to the US constitution thinking that it will always support you in a refusal to provide a court-ordered decryption key. A miffed judge could claim that 'decrypting your hard disk is not testimony against yourself but is more like being compelled to open your safe in your office that may contain evidence; preventing that is an obstruction of justice and contempt of court'. Although you could appeal this to higher courts if you have the vast sums required to do so, you will likely do so while waiting in jail.

Along those lines, do not even think of using the 'I forgot the decryption password' line. The burden is on *you* to *prove* that you really and truly cannot come up with the password. A judge will decide the 'balance of probabilities' as to whether your claim is believable (by him or her) or not; and since that will be the same judge as the one who issued the original order for you to provide the password, chances are that he or she will not side with you.[10]

Interestingly, entrusting a password only to memory may work *against* one, even in the USA where there is Fifth Amendment protection against self-incrimination, and especially in countries *without* such protection, precisely because the 'I forgot it' argument is not believable. A far more convincing argument is

> *the password was in the particular order that my books [or papers or whatever] were stacked, but the police ransacked my property and destroyed that order which contained my password that can now never be retrieved again. I would have and could have complied, but it is now physically impossible for me to do so, much as I wanted to.*

And do not take the adage 'innocent until proven guilty' in any country that has it too literally; if it were true, no innocent person would even have been convicted in such countries, yet many have, as proven by numerous documented cases where courts exonerated formerly convicted (and in some cases executed) individuals after new evidence came to light.

In general, any prosecutor has to establish that what was done with a computer (whether online or offline) was done by the person being accused. This is a very difficult element to establish unless the accused obliges by so stating. An investigator will first ask, ever so gently, 'is this your computer?', and 'are you the only user?', in an effort to get one to admit that nobody else has used that computer.

---

[10] A renowned legal case of judicial imposition of contempt-of-court charges (and jail time) to defendants who claimed they 'could not comply' is the case of the Federal Trade Commission (FTC) versus the defendants Michael and Denyse Anderson (FTC v. Affordable Media, No. 98-16378, D.C. No. CV-98-00669-LDG, filed 15 June 1999). The defendants were accused of placing profits from an allegedly fraudulent telemarketing campaign in a foreign (Cook Islands) 'asset protection trust', and claiming that they could not repatriate those profits even after a US judge ordered them to do so. In fact, the accused sent repeated notices to their trustee ordering it to repatriate the trust assets, as the US judge had ordered. The trustee refused to do so citing the terms of the trust. The 9th Circuit Court of Appeals stated clearly in its opinion that, indeed, 'inability to comply with a judicial order constitutes a defense to a charge of civil contempt' but that the accused in this case had not demonstrated that inability sufficiently well. The fact that the accused blatantly admitted that the trust was part of an 'asset protection plan' intended to frustrate creditors and US courts did not help the accused. Similarly, if a password is demanded by a court to decrypt files suspected of containing evidence of illegal action, the court is unlikely to be too sympathetic to any attempts to prevent that unless one can prove that one cannot comply despite one's best efforts. Such best efforts, for example, could be repeated and credible attempts by one to remember the password; attitude is the key here.

Once this admission has been documented, the niceties are likely to go out the window.

If you live in an oppressive regime, do not ever state that you are the only user of any one computer. Quite the contrary, take pains to allow others to use your computer *under your direct supervision*, and document the times and dates of such usage so as to bring them up to support your defense.

If you live in an oppressive regime, do not ever state that your hard disk was purchased new. Quite the contrary, make a point of buying a used hard disk and documenting that fact; a competent defense lawyer can then show a jury that what is on a hard disk is not only the result of the actions of the last user.

If you live in an oppressive regime, document examples of Internet connectivity to some legitimate website that flash unsolicited and inappropriate images on one's screen as part of advertising revenue, and show how those images get 'cached' in one's hard disk without you having ever solicited them. A competent defense lawyer can then show a jury that what is on one's hard disk may have nothing to do with a user's intent.

If you live in an oppressive regime, try not to use the internet when you are the only person in the house (or office). Instead, make it a point to use the Internet for anything that might upset the regime (e.g., sending or receiving encrypted data, accessing a human-rights website, etc.) either not at all or when visitors are also at home, preferably ones who are just passing by and are unlikely to be summoned back by the regime to testify. When you are the only person in the house and you have Internet connectivity, use it to access only the most suitable websites that praise the regime; and make a record of that.

Create a legitimate reason for computer security consciousness. This is important if you do not want your security consciousness to be used against you. Consider teaching local charity groups or schools about the virtues of computer security, and document that.

Answer police questions only in the presence of your lawyer and not in your house. Police work, like all human endeavors, is done by human beings. Although most police employees are individuals with integrity, it is inevitable that some are not; this is just human nature. Since the consequences of police misconduct are far more serious to you than the consequences of, say, ice-cream parlor employee misconduct, you have to avail yourself of all the legally allowed rights you have.

Do not allow police onto your premises without a warrant. If they knock on your door and want to 'just ask a few questions', politely but firmly advise them that you are very busy but that you will be happy to arrange for a time to talk with them at the police station *with your lawyer present*; have your lawyer's name and phone number handy to give out. In their eagerness to make a case or obtain a warrant, police may glance at technical books on your shelf and call them 'hacking tools'. Be very polite and appear to be cooperative but do not answer *any* questions without your lawyer present nor let police in your house without a warrant.

Establish a professional connection with a computer-savvy defense lawyer, just in case. Most lawyers today are not well-informed about computers; you want one who is, and you do not want to look for one from the inside of a detention facility. A competent defense attorney will know, for example, that:

- files in your computer may have been placed by hackers unbeknownst to you;

- images in your computer are automatically placed there by normal web browsing even though you never solicited them; the same goes for unsolicited incoming e-mail with attachments that stay long after the unsolicited e-mail is deleted;

- the now popular wireless home LANs (802.11b standard) allows anyone passing by outside your house to access your Internet connection as if it were you; the lack of security of these wireless home LANs is well documented;

- older versions of Netscape Messenger could not be configured to restrict e-mail relaying and were used extensively by spammers to send out e-mail that appears to have come from you when in fact it did not;

- use of the popular ICQ software allows remote persons to expose one to objectionable and illegal material which, under some circumstances, ends up being stored in one's hard disk even though one never solicited or wanted it in the first place; this is stated very clearly in the ICQ Inc. License Agreement version 99b, 10 August 1999 (http://home.mpinet.net/pilobilus/CS07.html).

The reader should not misinterpret the flavor of the above to be pro-accused. It is not. It is pro-justice and pro-privacy, as opposed to pro-prosecution and pro-'jail-for-good-measure'.

Privacy is the cornerstone of individuality and freedom. Even what *you* might think is legally privileged information may not be; some USA judges have even ruled that conversations with one's lawyer – long considered sacrosanct in the popular literature – are *not* necessarily privileged. The lawyer has to be serving as your attorney and not as your partner in crime.[11]

---

[11] Some organized crime figures carefully included their lawyers in their meetings just in case they were bugged by law enforcement; when that bugged conversation was brought into court, the defendants tried to suppress it by claiming that it was privileged attorney – client communication. The courts admittced the evidence none-the-less.

Justice is emphatically not synonymous with arrest and incarceration; just ask the legions of people who were falsely arrested, falsely imprisoned, and even falsely executed. Given that the resources of any individual are always dwarfed by the resources of the state, the individual needs all the help he or she can get in seeking justice.

7.9.1 Should you bet your life on assuming legal police conduct?

In mid-June 2001, the US Supreme Court decided that it is illegal for police to use intrusive modern technology, such as thermal imaging, to collect evidence through a house's exterior walls.[12] This new rule covers

> *obtaining by sense-enhancing technology any information regarding the interior of the home that could not otherwise have been obtained without physical intrusion into a constitutionally protected area at least where (as here) the technology in question is not in general public use.*

This apparent protection to individual privacy in one's home seems to disappear just as soon as the relevant technology becomes 'in general public use' – whatever that means. Is a thermal imager, which can already be bought over the counter around the world, 'in general public use'? How about a light-amplification night-scope that can be bought anywhere for a couple of hundred dollars? How about the standard laboratory equipment that is used to intercept Van Eck radiation from computer terminals?

There is a misconception outside police circles that just because any evidence that has been collected by the police illegally may be thrown out of court such evidence is useless to the police and that the police will therefore not bother to collect it. Even in highly democratic societies that are renown for their professed respect for the letter of the law, this is not true for the following reasons:

In Canada, one has to have a plausible legal 'presentation' reason for having a legally privileged relationship with a lawyer. In fact, Canadian tax laws have been changed to make lawyers, accountants, and other professionals liable for any planning advice they give. Not surprisingly, the Ontario Bar Association objected very strongly.

[12] See http://cryptome.org/tempest-scotus.htm, http://www.wired.com/news/politics/0,1283,44444,00.html, http://www.nytimes.com/2001/06/12/national/12STEX.html, http://www.nytimes.com/2001/06/12/national/12SEAR.html. This decisions appears to be applicable to TEMPEST technolog and is the first instance to make use of this technology illegal. For comprehensive information on TEMPEST, see Section 3.2.7 and http://www.eskimo.com/~joelm/tempest.html.

- Even though the police information may be inadmissible in court, it is still very useful to the police. Once they have the information, all they need to do is to find an alternative, legally admissible, means of obtaining the same information as well.

- Even though the police information may be inadmissible in court, it is still very useful to the police in focusing their search for additional evidence that *will* be admissible.

- This writer has attended a class by a law enforcement person who simply advised his law enforcement audience to:

  - obtain the evidence sought, even by knowingly illegal means;

  - purchase personal liability insurance in case the defendant sues (from jail!).

- Although there are exceptions, many in law enforcement eventually develop a self-righteous siege mentality of them against (what they perceive to be) a world of criminals; police use of illegal means to obtain a conviction is rationalized in their minds as being in support of a worthy cause. In so doing, they set themselves up as judge and jury as well.

It follows that you have every reason to assume that any technology and procedure can be used against you, and that fairness or legality has nothing to do with it. This applies in spades, of course, to police in repressive and totalitarian regimes, where the police do not even have to bother with the pretense of legality.

In practical terms, this means that, if there is any reason why your computer-related activities may be targeted by the local prosecutors or security services, you *do* have to protect yourself from high-technology intrusive threats discussed in this book, such as Van Eck radiation detection, remote theft of data from your computer, keystroke interception, etc., as well as from low-technology threats such as warrant-less entries to plant just about anything into your room or computer, warrant-less searches under some contrived pretext, etc.

And this does not even get into the sad subject of corruption and criminality by police. Although the overwhelming majority of police in civilized nations are honorable professionals, there are far too many documented cases of police criminality even in civilized nations, let alone in less democratic regimes.

It should be evident yet once more that it is far, far more difficult to protect oneself effectively from *all* of these threats than simply not to have popped up on the radar screen of law enforcers and security services wherever you live or work.

7.10 US Service Provider Liability Under the Digital Millennium Copyright Act and the Death of the Internet for the USA

The US District Court of Appeals for the Fourth Circuit ruled in early 2001 that if an Internet service provider (ISP) is informed that its system is being used to infringe on a third party's copyright, it has an obligation to 'substantially comply' with the request to stop this from happening in the future.[13] Although this sounds laudable on the surface, it means that every ISP has to preclude access to any and all Usenet newsgroups and web pages for which any third party asserts that it carries copyrighted material.

The particular case involved Usenet newsgroups carried on RemarQ Communities Inc. internet service that included alt.als. The plaintiff asserted that the newsgroups mere name (als) was a registered trademark and that the newsgroup itself carried allegedly infringing works that were posted there by individuals around the world. ALS invoked title II of the Digital Millennium Copyright Act (DMCA; passed by US congress) and required RemarQ to remove those newsgroups from its system.

RemarQ's legal reply was to the effect that the plaintiff had to identify specifically which of the thousands of messages posted contained the alleged copyright infringements, by stating that the DMCA's 'safe harbor' provision protected it from liability. The Fourth Circuit Court, however, decreed that it the burden was on RemarQ to investigate the claims of the copyright holder and to show 'substantial compliance'.

It is not hard for anyone to see how a similar allegation of copyright infringement can be used by anyone about any of the nearly 100 000 Usenet newsgroups and millions of web pages around the world. Under the DMCA, every US based ISP that is 'notified' of an alleged copyright infringement in any of them will have to investigate individually and 'substantially comply' with demands to prevent further access to that website or Usenet newsgroup. The alternative is to risk expensive litigation, which no ISP can afford.

Unless the DMCA is repealed or substantively modified, this may well spell the end of the Internet (web access and Usenet access) in the USA. This could cause a shift towards databases being kept away from the USA and access to them through remailers that may also have to be physically located on non-USA soil. Alternatively, the future of the Internet may well be in peer-to-peer networking that is inherently immune to conventional interception and controls, such as through the

---

[13] This information is based on work by attorney and author David J. Loundy of Chicago, IL. See http://www.Loundy.com/ALSScan.html.

use of cDc's Peekabooty or through the British m-o-o-t approach (see Section 5.10.5).

As of October 2001, the DMCA has faced increasingly tough challenges in US courts as to its constitutionality. The interested reader will find a wealth of legal information on Internet-related issues at: http://www.Loundy.com/InternetLaw Books.html and at http://www.Loundy.com/ComputerCrimeBooks.html.

7.10.1   The Digital Millennium Copyright Act is an international matter

Although the DMCA is on the surface a US law, the corporate funding behind it is concerned with international protection of US copyrights. For example, New Zealand has been formally asked by Micosoft to protect further its (Microsoft's) digital copyrights by updating New Zealand's Digital Technology Copyright Act of 1994. The US Electronic Frontier Foundation (EFF) has been trying to convince New Zealand not to pass a law similar to the US DMCA (http://www.newsbytes. com/news/01/171435.html).

An activist Recording Industry Association of America (RIAA) had been considering such offbeat schemes as software to masquerade as a file-swapper online (see http://www.theregister.co.uk/content/6/22327.html); once it places itself in a computer that offers copyrighted music to others, that software would try to block others from downloading that song. Such software would not be confined to within the USA, of course. Amusingly, this technique would run foul of new antiterrorism bills in the USA. Also, since such software could cause damage to the computer it finds its way into, RIAA has lobbied for legal protection from any damage done by the software to such computers. In short, RIAA wanted legal license to attack file-swappers' computers without incurring any civil liability. We refer to it as 'license to virus', according to a congressional staffer (http://www.zdnet.com/zdnn/stories/news/0,4586,2818064,00.html).

In mid-2001, at the request of Adobe Corporation in the USA, the FBI arrested 27-year-old Dmitry Sklyarov, a Russian who had come to the USA to deliver an academic presentation and charged him with crimes under the DMCA. He was not accused of any copyright infringement but of writing software that enables purchasers of electronic books to view their e-Books; such software is legal in his native Russia where he developed it. What is banned by the DMCA is the act of providing the technology. Sklyarov made the mistake of revealing weaknesses in an encryption scheme that Adobe employs in its electronic book-reading programs and was arrested for composing the software to unlock the Adobe e-Book reader encryption system. Sklyarov's company was selling copies of the decryption software for $99 through his Ecomsoft Company. The specific violation of the DMCA was in circumventing any protection measure that a copyright holder puts around digital files to regulate access. As a result of intense pressure by Adobe product customers, Adobe subsequently asked that Sklyarov be released, and refused to prosecute him (http://www.cryptome.org/dmitry-eff.ag.html).

At about the same time, Edward Felten, a Princeton University professor of computer science, was threatened with criminal prosecution after he announced his intent to discuss the findings of his encryption research that dealt with digital watermarking of music files. As a result, many US conferences with cutting-edge technical content may move offshore or to Canada.

7.10.2   The Uniform computer information transactions act (UCITA)

In a nutshell, the Uniform Computer Information Transactions Act (UCITA) is a piece of highly controversial US State (as opposed to federal, as the DMCA above) legislation that has been sponsored and promoted by software-makers and has been opposed by users. It was designed as an update to the Uniform Commercial Code to include the concepts of computers and software.

Unfortunately, it gives all rights to software-makers and none to software users. For example:

- software users are not allowed publicly to complain about faults in the software they have purchased;

- software-makers are allowed to disable users' software remotely if the software--makers feel that the users are not abiding by the software-makers' terms of use;

- it allows software-makers to disclaim warranties;

- it allows new software to be sold with no warranty so the buyer cannot get his or her money back if the software does not work or if it gives buyer's system a virus.

Some 26 State Attorneys general, the insurance industry, libraries, consumer protection groups, and large technology users such as Boeing Corp. and Phillips Petroleum have opposed UCITA and so has the USA Instititute of Electrical and Electronic Engineers (IEEE). According to the IEEE president, Ned Sauthoff, 'The failure of UCITA proponents to secure passage in any state this year, coupled with the ABA's decision to take a critical look ar UCITA, signals the legislation's dim future, at least in its present form' (See http://www.ieeeUSA.org/forum/POSITIONS/ucita.html).

The States of New York, North Dakota, Iowa, and Oregon have introduced anti-UCITA legislation intended to negate UCITA in those States. Also, UCITA is widely opposed by the Americans for Fair Electronic Transactions (AFECT), formerly known as 4CITE.

7.11 The Landmark Decision of the US Supreme Court on Evidence Collected Through Intrusive Technical Means

In June 2001 the US Supreme Court decided that

> *where, as here, the government uses a device that is not in general public use, to explore details of the home that would previously have been unknowable without physical intrusion, the surveillance is a 'search' and is presumptively unreasonable without a warrant (see http://www.supreme-courtus.gov/opinions/00pdf/99-8508.pdf)*

This decision arguably makes it illegal for US law enforcement to monitor emanations from computers. House majority leader Dick Armey (Republican, Texas) sent a letter to attorney general Ashcroft arguing that this decision may also make the use of FBI's DCS1000 (also known as Carnivore) illegal unless a specific court warrant has been issued (see http://www.freedom.gov/library/technology/ashcrofletter.asp).[14]

In practical terms, this Supreme Court decision has minimal impact, for two reasons. First, technology-augmented surveillance is legal if the technology is using a device that is 'in general public use' – whatever that means. As discussed in Section 7.9.1 is a light amplification (night-imaging) device, that is sold in most sports and boating stores, 'in general public use'? How about a thermal imager that has been commercially available worldwide during the past decade? How about detection of emanations from a computer using laboratory equipment that has been available publicly worldwide for many years? Second, law enforcement may not be able to use such illegally obtained evidence in a US court of law, but it can be tipped by that information to find other, legal, means for collecting the same evidence in a

---

[14] On 23 July 2001, the US House of Representatives passed an amendment offered by Congressman Bob Barr (Repulican, Georgia) requiring the Justice Department to disclose use of the Department's Carnivore (DCS1000) surveillance system, an eavesdropping mechanism designed to monitor Internet traffic. Barr's amendment, which was offered to address citizens' growing privacy concerns, passed as part of the annual Department of Justice appropriations bill.

legally admissible manner (Section 7.9.1). All that the Supreme Court warrant states is that a court warrant is required prior to the use of the intrusive technology. Law enforcement officers have long been known to apply for such warrants to judges known for their pro-prosecution mindset and never be turned down.

7.12 The Huge Societal Costs of Excessive Lack of Privacy for Easy Law Enforcement

> *You already have zero privacy – get over it*
> Scott McNealy, Chief Executive Officer Sun Microsystems

> *Even the Four Horsemen of kidporn, dope dealers, mafia and terrorists don't worry me as much as totalitarian governments. It's been a long century and we've had enough of them.*
> Bruce Sterling

James C. Scott, a Yale political scientist, has written in *Seeing like a State: How Certain Schemes to Improve the Human Condition Have Failed* (1998, Yale University Press) that 'the modern state, through its officials, attempts with varying success to create a terrain and a population with precisely those standardized characteristics that will be easiest to monitor, count, assess and manage'. This is really what Aldous Huxley's *Brave New World* is all about.

If you live in a technologically backwards society, count your blessings as far as privacy is concerned. If you live in a technologically advanced society today, hardly anything can be kept private. In fact, the US Supreme Court has asserted that the much heralded US Constitutional protection against unreasonable searches may not apply when citizens have no reasonable expectation of privacy. As more and more technologies make it easy for us to be recorded when online, viewed through thermal imaging behind walls, and geolocated when we use cellphones, it appears that what used to be 'unreasonable' search in the past will soon be 'reasonable' simply because technology makes it easy to do.

Private diaries are no longer off limits to others, as Senator Packwood and others have found. The principle that private diaries cannot be subpoenaed as 'mere evidence' has withered away. The inclusion of sexually explicit speech as evidence of sexual discrimination and gender discrimination has made it very difficult to make a distinction between coercion and consensual relationships.

In an 1877 Supreme Court decision, it was stated that postal inspectors needed a judicial search warrant to open first-class mail even if it had been sent from one's office. Today, searches of employee e-mail by employers is routine and requires no search warrant even though the search covers every single keystroke by an employee. (It will be interesting to see a court case of what happens if an employee is telecommuting from home; would the employer be deemed to have the right to see anything that the employee writes and reads from home while 'on the clock'?)

As a minimum, one must therefore be aware of what is no longer private. E-mail is at the top of the list because it has blurred the distinction between oral and written gossip and many treat it as private when in fact it is anything but. It has the informality of a chat by the water fountain, but the permanence and retrievability of the best that humankind has ever come up with.

The real problem is not so much the visibility of our lives but that the intimate details are brought out of context and are misjudged and misinterpreted by people who do not know us. A casual remark by Auntie Martha, who is known among her friends and family to have a sailor's mouth, will be judged totally differently by those who know her than by a jury convinced by a skillful opposition attorney that the same Auntie Martha was 'obviously a hostile person who assaulted my client'.

Since there is a vast amount of information passing through telephone and Internet channels these days, law enforcement organizations are increasingly resorting to wholesale interception and automated filtering to do the data reduction; this is based on the false premise that a human being can be abstracted in a few snippets of information. A classical example is the surreptitiously recorded (by a Canadian security organization) conversation of a high-school student's mother to the effect that her son had 'bombed' in his school theatre play. One should not be too ready to dismiss this on the assumption that it would be 'obviously' cleared up and dismissed in any court of law, for two fundamental reasons:

- If a skillful but unethical prosecutor were selectively to collect out of context a number of snippets from any one of our lives, such a prosecutor could easily 'substantiate' an assertion that we are anything he or she wants to portray us to be. An impressionable jury would see an 'obvious pattern'; never mind that a collage of different out-of-context snippets from the same person's life could just as easily 'substantiate' (in the minds of the same impressionable jury) exactly the opposite pattern.

- It is ever so easy for anyone who wants to do so to collect vast amounts of personal information about any one in the USA or, to a far lesser extent, in other industrialized countries. Information is a commodity that is collected, stored, sold, traded, and used as anyone feels. We really are not too far off from the caricature of 'The Truman Show' where every aspect of the hero's life was monitored and displayed to the world without his knowledge or consent.

Those in favor of transparency for ease in law enforcement might argue, 'So what? It is all for a good cause'. But is it really? Openly available information about any of us has been used for cyberstalking (which has already resulted in at least one murder). Readily obtainable information about any of us has been used for identity theft, extortion, blackmail, fraud, and just about every conceivable crime one can think of. Most important is the huge loss to society of the creativity that gets suppressed when we all realize that we live in a fishbowl viewed by assorted carnivores. We will then (those who have not already) go into the mode where our only acts will be those intended for public consumption; there will be no private persona, which will atrophy and die. Yet the most creative moments in anyone's life have always been associated with privacy and solitude. Study after study has shown that we are most creative during daydreaming. Even Einstein is quoted to have said that imagination is the most difficult and most worthwhile human mental function.

Sadly, the acceptance of the dollar as the ultimate yardstick of value and self-worth has caused many to be willing even to surrender what little privacy they could opt for in exchange for money. We gladly allow detailed information about our grocery shopping habits in exchange for a minuscule discount. We gladly provide personal information in exchange for 'a chance to win a sawing machine'. How long until we all allow a camera in our bathrooms?

But who is really the adversary? It is us! Leaders of oppressive regimes have always appreciated the immense benefit to their longevity of having vast numbers of informants; every oppressive regime in history has encouraged and rewarded informants, and there are chilling documented cases of children 'reporting' their parents to the authorities, of parents reporting their children, of spouses reporting spouses, and all this in exchange for some 'favor' from the regime.

Sadly, democratic regimes have also caught on to the benefits of this blood-stained tool; the pivotal trick has been for democratic regimes to make the citizens feel that it is their duty to do such reporting, and also to capitalize on most citizens' fear of their neighbor being 'different' or, God forbid, better off in any way. The Internet makes it very easy for everyone to keep tabs on everybody else. Anybody, anywhere in the world, can now find just about anything on every American through the Internet;[15] combine this with some mass-hysteria-of-the-month that news media are expert at generating and you have a nation of snitches on a crusade.[16]

---

[15] There is a dark human side to this that commercial television has recently come to exploit: the voyeurism by many people that enjoys 'reality TV' such as one can find in the increasingly popular 'Survivor' shows, and shows where camera-toting news media have been invited by publicity-seeking police to accompany the police to actual raids in suspects' houses.

[16] *Snitch Culture*: *How Citizens Are Turned Into The Eyes And Ears Of The State* (ISBN: 0-922915-63-6), by Jim Redden.

Then there is a far more serious issue that possibly could have implications that could affect the survival of the species. Humankind has survived not because of the labor of docile or subjugated good citizens but because of the major contributions brought in by great minds: the discovery of antibiotics; the discovery of vaccinations; the recipes for peaceful social coexistence advocated by the revered leaders of the most influential religions of the world. If dinosaurs became extinct as a result of a the impact of a major asteroid with the earth, as is believed to have been the case, humankind's hope for survival may well be in the hands of the creative minds that will find a way to prevent the next major asteroid from hitting the earth and killing all life; it will come from creative minds that do not mind challenging the status quo, and not from the docile Johnny-be-goods that governments and law enforcers like to have as citizens.

DNA profiling is already here with the human genome project, which is promising to find the genetic causes and cures for some of humankind's medical problems. Yet it is the same DNA that is also largely responsible for intellect, irreverence towards established falsehoods (such as the pre-Galileo religious belief that the earth is the center of the universe, or the pre-Einstein erroneous principles of physics). It will be very tempting for governments to engage in a reasoning along the lines of:

- Social order is good.

- Therefore, anyone upsetting the social order is bad.

- Therefore, since DNA manipulation can change a baby's DNA to one where he or she will not challenge the status quo, this should be done 'for the good of society'.

This will ensure that humankind will never allow into existence the future Galileos or Archimedeses, or Feynmans.[17] And in so doing, humankind will sign its own death warrant as a species, 'for the good of society' as narrowly perceived by some of the world's law enforcers.

This is not 'futuristic'; researchers at the Institute for Reproductive Medicine and Science of Saint Barnabas in West Orange, NJ, have already achieved 15 births by changing the DNA of a baby to contain DNA from two women instead of just one (see http://www.wired.com/news/medtech/0,1286,43579,00.html); the researchers performed this work in 1997 and 1998 using a technique called ooplasmic transfer

---

[17] The late Dick Feynman is reported to have testified at a court hearing convened by the city of Pasadena on whether or not to close down a strip tease parlor. Prof. Feynman testified that he found the establishment to provide intellectual food for thought, and the judge was compelled not to shut it down, to the great annoyance of the local police there.

to take mitochondria from donor eggs, inject them into the recipient woman's eggs in a petri dish, and place the resulting eggs back inside the womb. In March 2001 they published the results of DNA tests that confirmed that the babies' DNA contained DNA that was not inherited from either parent. Although mitochondrial DNA is not believed to have a significant impact on individuals' personality, the technique could be used with DNA that does.

Parents in the USA can already avail themselves of embryo screening to 'build a new child', as was reported by Rick Weiss in the June 30 2001 issue of the *Washington Post*. New tests, referred to as pre-implantation genetic diagnosis (PGD), allow parents to tell which of their embryos are likely to have a particular detectable disease so that only those that are free of the faulty gene can be transferred to the mother-to-be's womb. Today the faulty gene has to do with a bona fide disease; tomorrow it could be the gene found to be responsible for not being a good docile and obedient little citizen.

The pendulum is swinging – not of its own natural periodicity but as a result of concerted pushing by those who have something to gain from such a swing – in favor of a transparent society of transparent – and empty – individuals.[18] This places an enormous new responsibility on law enforcement agencies that they never had to shoulder before: to use this awesome new power maturely and wisely and not to abuse it as would a magician's apprentice, merely to secure a conviction at all costs including the very high societal cost of forcing society to adapt and become a society of content-free automata that evokes images from Aldous Huxley's *Brave New World* or of the *Stepford Wives*.

7.13 Is Law Enforcement Making Information Infrastructure More Secure or Actually *Less* Secure by Targeting Teenage Hackers?

Nearly all men can stand adversity, but if you want to test a man's character, give him power.

Abraham Lincoln

On the surface it may seem ludicrous even to conceive of any possibility whereby enforcement of laws against hacking can make a nation's information infrastructure

---

[18] 'Those with nothing to hide have nothing to offer'.

less secure. After all, we reason that if more teenage hackers are thrown in jail, there will be fewer of them left and the rest will be dissuaded from even trying.

This may well be true but it is logically false to infer that 'therefore the nation's computers will be more secure', because the real threat to a nation's computers is not the teenage hackers – also known as 'script kiddies' – that amount to ankle-biters, but foreign nation states. If country X wants to cripple country Y's computers it will obviously not be deterred by country Y making this illegal nor by country Y having placed its teenage hackers in jail. Indeed, if country Y places its teen hackers in jail and scares the rest of them into abstaining from finding security holes in its own computer systems, the peacetime rate of computer attacks from within the country will drop, misleading the local leaders in the mistaken belief that the nation's computers are more secure than they are, and not taking any actual technical measures needed to protect the same computers from a foreign adversary.

This is not to mention the societal cost. A 13-year-old boy, Shinjan Majumder, of New Jersey, USA, committed suicide by hanging himself, blaming his suspension from Grover Middle School, New Jersey, after being accused of hacking into the school district's computer in May 2001 (http://www.register.co.uk/content/8/18932.html).

Pontifications of commercial companies notwithstanding, the real threat to a nation's computer networks is not from in-country teenage peacetime hackers but from foreign nation states during war. Jailing the local teenage hackers – an easy way for law enforcement to get positive public relations exposure in the local press – leads to a false sense of national security because the resulting reduction in hacking incidents removes the motivation to take the necessary technical measures to prevent the real threat; that is, a savvy foreign nation state from doing the same on a grand and professional scale.

This truth has finally been accepted by key elements in the US Government which, until recently, was subscribing to and in many cases actually fueling the mass hysteria[19] about teenage hackers that was self-servingly supported by US commerce (that would occasionally lose a dollar or two to hackers) and law enforcement (that found an easy way to get positive public relations coverage from the easy task of catching teenagers). Senator Robert Bennett (Republican, Utah) dismissed hackers in late June 2001 as 'nothing more than a nuisance' during a hearing titled 'Wired Worlds: Cyber Security and the US Economy' (http://www.wired.com/news/print/0,1294,44742,00.html). The same URL reference quotes Lawrence Gershwin, a senior science and technology specialist at the

---

[19] Witness the official line in June 1998 when then deputy Secreteray of Defense John Hamre described a teen's (the 'Analyser's') attacks as highly disturbing, 'organized and systematic' and launched the alarmist prose about an 'electronic Pearl Harbor'. See http://www.soci.niu.edu/~crypt/other/modolts2.htm. and http://www.infowar.com/iwftp/c4i/022698.txt.

National Intelligence Council, as stating that even 'tech-savvy' terrorists still pose 'a limited cyber threat' compared with enemy nations; he added that 'for the next 5–10 years or so, only nation states appear to have the discipline, commitment and resources to fully develop capabilities to attack critical infrastructures'.

For a well reasoned discourse on this issue, see http://www.wired.com/news/technology/0,1282,49096,00.html. For a satirical look at law enforcers' obsession with the easy target that teenage hackers provide, see http://www.satirewire.com/news/0112/uh_oh.shtml.

8

In Conclusion

If McDonalds offered a free Big Mac in exchange for a DNA sample, there'd be lines around the block.

Bruce Schneier, noted cryptographer

It is human nature to have double standards; babies do it in a crude way, and (some) adults do it with more finesse. With regard to privacy, we want others to know as little as possible about us, yet we want to know as much as possible about our neighbors and those we deal with.

It is also human nature to want others to act in accordance with our wishes; controlling others requires knowing enough about them to squelch dissent and subversion before it reaches a magnitude of any consequence (i.e., we must remove their privacy). Although individuals cannot do this on any large scale as individual citizens, individuals in positions of authority can.

Technology today makes it easy and relatively inexpensive to monitor most any citizen's activities: how much one earns and from where, detailed buying habits (credit cards and 'preferred customer' cards), circles of friends and associates and what is discussed with them (monitoring of telephones and of Internet messages), location at any one time (through the individual's use of cellphones, telephone calling-cards, 'frequent flier' accounts, credit cards, street traffic cameras that look at license plates, GPS-enhanced bracelets for indigents and select convicted law violators), medical history, current appearance (through an increasing number of cameras in public places, and so on). Red-light cameras are proliferating, ostensibly to discourage traffic violators; in fact they are a cost-effective means for local municipalities to collect revenue when they are placed at intersections where the amber light lasts for too short a time, such that it is impossible to stop before the light turns red for a driver who entered the intersection with a green light.

Monitoring of online activities is even easier than is the monitoring of 'normal' activities. One no longer has to search for the person being monitored because the person is 'online'. Since we have the illusion, when 'online' from the 'privacy of our home', that nobody is watching us just because there is no live body sitting behind us, we tend to allow a lot more to be disclosed than if we realized that someone were sitting behind us taking notes for everything we do or do not do.

To be sure, we only have ourselves to blame for a lot of this disappearance of privacy.

- We willingly signed up for the neighborhood supermarket's 'preferred customer card' (or the frequent flier card, or what-not) because we were lured by financial benefits.

- We willingly used our credit card to buy things instead of using anonymous cash because the credit card is more convenient and does not feel like 'real money' that we pay.

- We willingly gave our name, address, phone number, and other information when we filled out that lottery ticket form where 'the lucky winner' would win a car or a trip to somewhere.

- We willingly put up with practically every company we deal with whose telephone greeting up front is that 'this call may be monitored or recorded for quality assurance'; what quality assurance? Do you seriously think that the recording is for the caller's benefit?

- We willingly accepted 'caller ID' that allows us to see who is calling us on the phone before we answer, forgetting that the same technology allows others to do the same and it also allows the phone company and the government to keep long records of who called whom and when.

- We applauded the use of technology for law enforcement to pinpoint the location of every cellphone that is 'on' because we swallowed the amusing propaganda that this is motivated by an overwhelming desire by law enforcement to bring the ambulance to us if we have a heart attack while driving, as if law enforcement was in the health-service-delivery business.

- We applauded having open access to information about every arrest made, even though many do not result in convictions, with the nebulous belief that this pertains only to criminals and that if they were innocent they would never have been arrested; so much for 'innocent until proven guilty'.

- We applauded having easy access to all public information, such as everyone else's residence address, history of employment, addresses of their relatives, details about any legal matters such as divorce and custody matters and small claims cases; then one day someone else found everything there is about us, stalked us, and even killed some of us, but by then it was too late to change the trend.

- We accepted the law enforcement view of the world that they are always beyond reproach; we forgot the hair-raising 'incident' when a handcuffed person in custody was shot in cold blood by Los Angeles policemen a couple of years ago and was framed for another murder he never committed, assuming that it was not the tip of an iceberg.

- We accepted the law enforcement view of the world that they are merely apprehending 'criminals', and never gave a second thought to the fact that, even in the society most respectful of due process and civil rights, numerous executed 'criminals' were posthumously proved by DNA tests not have been criminals at all and to have been totally innocent.

It is all too easy to allow the all-too-natural human yearning for peace and safety to want to sacrifice some liberty for some peace, especially since we reach the autumn and winter of our lives. But let us not forget Ben Franklin's admonition that 'Those who are willing to sacrifice a little more liberty for a little more security deserve neither'.

Technology is making wholesale surveillance and tracking easy and inexpensive. It is even easier and even less expensive when one is online.

Governments have always had the desire to control their citizens; now they can and they do. In addition to the actual benefits to any government of knowing what citizens are up to, there is a vast psychological benefit to governments derived from the fact that citizens themselves *know* they are under constant surveillance. This was appreciated even a couple of hundred years ago when Jeremy Bentham (1748–1832), a theorist of British legal reform, proposed the 'Panopticon', a round-the-clock surveillance prison where a prisoner would never know if he or she was being surveilled; the mental uncertainty itself being a crucial instrument of discipline.

Independently, commercial entities have always had the desire to maximize profits by targeting their advertising to those they know (from snooping) to be most likely to buy what is being peddled. Now they can, and they do. Employers and medical insurers are increasingly able legally to track our medical conditions so as to deny insurance coverage or employment.

None of these trends is about to change. If anything, privacy will be a fond memory, or maybe even a subversive impure thought in this 'Brave New World'. We are already in the middle of galloping Orwellism.

As we entrust more and more details of our daily lives to our computers, and as we conduct more and more of our daily affairs online, we can at least level the playing field by denying others the ability to snoop into our lives.

This book has shown that the process of reclaiming our privacy is not a simple matter of using encryption; if anything, the willy-nilly use of encryption will make things worse for us by attracting unwanted attention, not to mention the false sense of security that results from sloppy use of encryption. The *only* effective way to reclaim computer privacy is to understand the many threats that one is faced with so as to protect ourselves from them. This is what this book was all about. The price of freedom is knowledge and courage; it always has been.

Appendix A

A.1 Eudora E-mail Reader Security Fixes

Go to Tools/Options and:

1. Under 'attachments', change it to anything *other* than the default, after having created such a folder (e.g., C:\junk\abracadabra), preferably with a name that cannot be guessed by someone else. This prevents a documented Eudora security weakness from being exploitable (see Figure A.1).

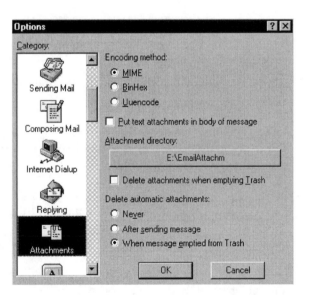

Figure A.1 Eudora e-mail attachments setting vulnerability

2. Under 'viewing mail', uncheck the 'use Microsoft viewer' option, so as to prevent another known security weakness in Eudora (Figure A.2).

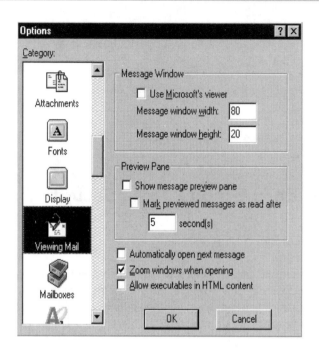

Figure A.2   Eudora message view vulnerability

3. Under 'viewing mail', disable the option that allows executables in html content (Figure A.2).

4. Under options, uncheck the 'automatically download HTML graphics', as shown in Figure A.3. This is a major security threat that distinguished Eudora from Outlook and Outlook Express, which do not permit one to do so.

5. By the way, you may elect to opt for having all incoming and outgoing e-mail copies stored in a fully encrypted 'volume' rather than being in the open for the world to see. To do this you must first create such encrypted volumes (Section 4.10, for example, that discusses ScramDisk, which uses encrypted volumes).

Caution: users of Eudora version 4.3 and version 5 should be advised that it 'calls home' (it calls the Eudora server) every so often and behind the user's back; the manufacturer claims that this is done merely to find if there is a new version of the program available. Regardless, users would be well advised to disable this dubious 'feature'; the Eudora website has instructions on how to do so. To disable

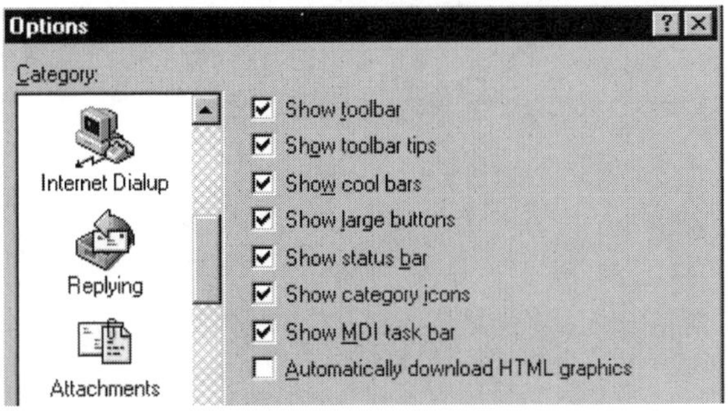

Figure A.3   Disabling html graphics in Eudora

this 'feature', copy and paste the following text into the message window of a new message in Eudora 4.3:

<x-eudora-option:DontShowUpdates=1>

This text will show up in blue as an URL. Hold down the Alt key and click on the URL; a window will appear asking one to click 'OK'. Click 'OK'.

Caution: users of PGP encryption should *not* use the PGP 'plug ins' for either Eudora or Outlook/Outlook Express; instead, encrypt the clipboard and cut and paste the ciphertext into the e-mail software program's window. The danger is that the 'Out' mailbox saves on the hard disk – under some conditions – both the plaintext and the ciphertext; this is about the worst scenario from a security perspective.

Appendix B

B.1 Secure Socket Layer Encryption

SSL (secure socket layer) is a protocol developed by Netscape that allows end-to-end encryption between one's browser and the website one visits. Since the recent change in US export policy, practically anyone can have legitimate access to the 'high-security' 128-bit key versions of SSL offered by both Netscape and Microsoft (for its web browser, which is not recommended because of numerous security problems related to the fact that it is too intimately connected to the operating system).

To make sure that you have an SSL connection, look at the little lock icon on the lower left-hand side of Netscape, as shown in Figure B.1, and make sure that the lock icon (lower left) is that of a closed lock and not an open lock as shown in Figure B.1.

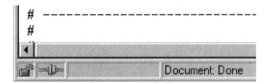

Figure B.1   Visual indication of the absence of secure-socket-layer-encrypted connection

'Out-of-the-box', web browsers allow you to connect with end-to-end encryption to whichever site is on the other end that also supports such connections; the content of the connection is invisible to the ISP and to anyone else along the way. However, you are strongly cautioned that:

- the remote site you are connected to knows both who you are (your IP address, unless you have gone through the elaborate schemes discussed in Chapter 5 to hide it) and what you are looking at;

- the ISP as well as the local regime, if it elects to, can see that you are using end-to-end encryption and to which remote site; if this is not to its liking, you could end up with someone knocking on your door or breaking your door down to obtain the tell-tale evidence that will be in your computer for the benefit of forensics investigators (unless you have taken the extensive countermeasures detailed in Chapters 4 and 5).

The process of using web-browser encryption to send and receive encrypted e-mail is quite straight forward from within either Netscape's or Microsoft's browser:

1. You connect to any one of a handful of popular 'certificate' issuing organizations, such as Verisign (www.verisign.com) which charges about $10 per year, or to Thawte (www.thawte.com), which gives free certificates even though it has been bought out by Verisign, or by PrivacyX (www.privacyX.com).

2. After installing this 'certificate', you can subsequently exchange encrypted e-mail with others who have also gone through the same ritual.

You are strongly cautioned that:

- SSL mail does not encrypt the 'from whom and to whom' information, nor the 'Subject' line.

- Also, outgoing SSL-encrypted e-mail is encrypted so that *the sender* can read it, too, after it has been sent; it follows that a sender can be compelled by local authorities to decrypt that mail; by comparison, a user of PGP (which is highly recommended as a superior alternative for e-mail encryption; see Section 5.8.4) cannot decrypt outgoing e-mail encrypted for some intended recipient who is the only one that can decrypt it.

In short, use SSL for web browsing subject to the warnings above, but not for e-mail.

Creating your own SSL certificate is straightforward; see http://www.openssl.org for details and download the software to do it. Whichever remote site you plan to communicate with has to be convinced to accept it; this is easy if you are planning to exchange SSL-encrypted mail with an associate, but then again SSL for e-mail encryption is far less secure than use of PGP.

Appendix C

C.1 Setting up Your Win95/98 Computer to Overwrite the Swap File Effectively: A One-Time Step-by-Step Setup Procedure

Note: Windows NT and 2000 do not need this, as they appear to wipe their own swap file *if* you follow the steps below:

1. Use Regedit and go to HKEY_LOCAL_MACHINES\System\Current ControlSet\Control\Session Manager\Memory Management.

2. Find ClearPageFileAtShutdown REG_DWORD.

3. Set it to 1.

Even so, security conscious users are strongly advised to use BestCrypt, version 7, which allows one the option of routinely encrypting the entire swp file as a background operation; this is important because there is no documentation as to just exactly how good (or bad) is Microsoft's 'wiping' of the WinNT/2000 swap file (see Section 4.3.2).

For Win95/98, follow the steps given below.

1. Create a DOS boot disk (if you do not have one already); this is important for numerous other uses, so you should do it regardless.

2. Place in that disk the files ATTRIB.EXE and EDIT.COM as a minimum. You would be well advised also to place there FDISK.EXE, FORMAT.COM, and SCANDISK.EXE. All of them should be available within your Windows computer; to locate them, Run COMMAND and then type DIR ATTRIB.EXE /S (in the case of ATTRIB.EXE).

3. Obtain SCORCH.ZIP from any one of many sources on the Internet, such as directly from its author (iolo@iname.com, iolo@tesco.net).

4. Unzip and extract its files into the root (C:\) directory.

5. Under ControlPanel/System/Performance/VirtualMemory, uncheck the default 'Windows will choose' and set both the minimum and the maximum Virtual Memory to the same large value such as 200 (this is in megabytes). When prompted to restart Windows, select 'yes' and place in the drive the bootable floppy disk created above.

6. You are now facing the A:\ prompt after rebooting. Type:

   A:\ATTRIB C:\WINDOWS\MSDOS.SYS –H –R –S

7. *If you use Windows 95*, type:

   A:\EDIT C:\WINDOWS\MSDOS.SYS

   In the window that comes up, use the up/down arrows and change the line from

   BootGUI=1

   to

   BootGUI=0

   The above line changes the boot sequence so that the computer does not go straight into Windows.

   If you use Windows 98, change MSDOS.SYS from

   BootGUI=3D1

   to

   BootGUI=3D0

For both Windows 95 and 98, check if there is also an MSDOS.SYS in the root directory C:\. Since the file is normally invisible, you must first make it visible to see if it exists, by typing:

A:\ATTRIB C:\MSDOS.SYS –H –R –S

If it does exist, do the same changes to BootGUI as shown above. Now, for both Windows 95 and 98, add the line

Logo=0

to get rid of the initial 'Starting Windows . . .' splash screen and replace it by a short flash. Push Alt+S to save and Alt+X to exit the editor.

8. Type:

A:\EDIT C:\AUTOEXEC.BAT

Just above the ECHO line, use the arrow keys and enter the line

C:\SCORCH [C:\WIN386.SWP]/THREE

exactly as shown above, specifically including the square brackets. This command will cause your swap file to be wiped three times on startup and for you to see that, but it will not delete the overwritten file. Now place the cursor at the end of the file and add the line:

C:\W.BAT

Push Alt+S to save and Alt+X to exit the editor.

9. Type:

A:\EDIT C:\W.BAT

In the window that opens, type the following lines exactly as shown:

CD\WINDOWS

Win

Mode co80

CD\

C:\SCORCH [WIN386.SWP]/ THREE/ NODEL/ VALID

The 'Mode co80' gets rid of the patronizing 'its OK to shut down your computer' message. Push Alt+S to save and Alt+X to exit the editor. This step has created a file that will cause your swap file to be overwritten on shutdown (which is more important than on boot up, which was provided for earlier for good measure). The intent of the '/NODEL /VALID' options is twofold:

(a) to allow you to see for yourself that the file has been overwritten;

(b) to retain the overwritten file so that the scorch command on bootup, discussed above, will find a file to overwrite; having a scorch function on bootup as well is an insurance measure just in case something goes wrong during shutdown and the file is not overwritten (e.g., an abnormal termination or crash).

10. If you are using a laptop with Windows 98, go to the SETUP upon bootup and change 'Automated Power Management' to 'disabled'.

11. Remove the floppy from the drive and push Alt+Cntrl+Del to restart the computer. The second time you boot up the computer (not this time) you will see the swap file overwriting at work. The reason you will not see it this time is because Windows may still think that the swap file is of variable size.

12. That's it. You are done.

While you are at it, remember that scorch can also clean up the trails left by specific software such as Microsoft Internet Explorer, which takes great liberties with users' privacy (see Appendix F for more).

To wipe the index.dat files, enter:

scorch [c:\windows\tempor~1\content.IE5\index.dat]/three

scorch [c:\windows\history\history.IE5\index.dat]/three

scorch [c:\windows\cookies\index.dat]/three

Appendix D

D.1 Downloading Hard-To-Find Files on the Internet

Most commercial – and some freeware – files are often available through websites; these can be found most easily through any of the 'search engines' such as http://www.google.com. Most of the useful free software, however, cannot be found in this manner, unless you are willing to go through a number of such search engines. The files are mostly available in databases that are simply not accessible through most of the search engines. One has to do things the old-fashioned way, which is through the use of Archie. Here is how.

1. Go to http://archie.emnet.co.uk/services.html; this will give you a list of numerous 'Archie Servers'. Pick one, such as the one at the University of

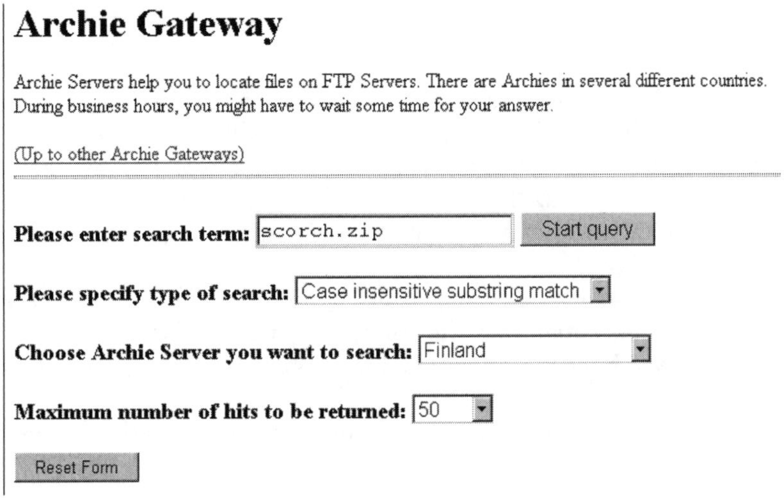

Figure D.1.   Archie search for SCORCH.ZIP

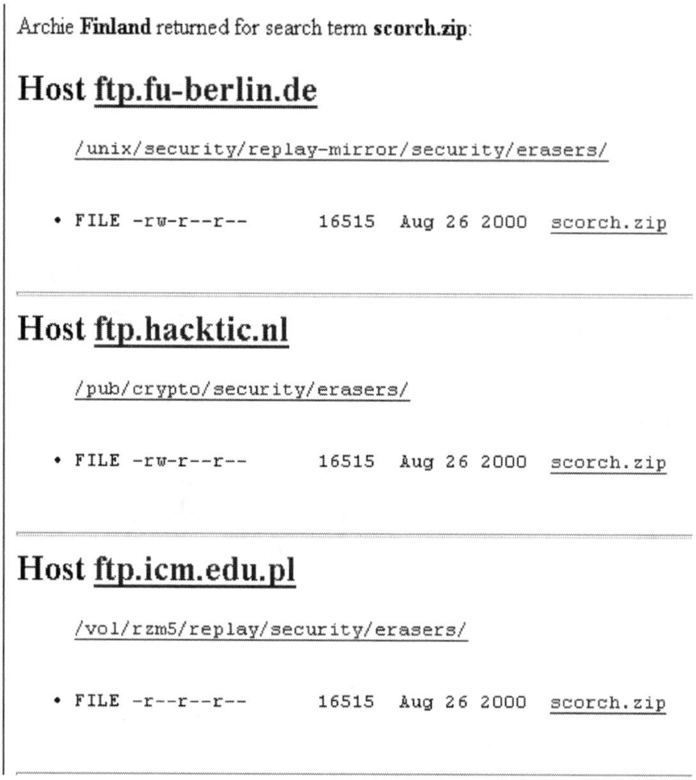

Archie **Finland** returned for search term **scorch.zip**:

Host ftp.fu-berlin.de

`/unix/security/replay-mirror/security/erasers/`

• `FILE -rw-r--r--    16515   Aug 26 2000   scorch.zip`

Host ftp.hacktic.nl

`/pub/crypto/security/erasers/`

• `FILE -rw-r--r--    16515   Aug 26 2000   scorch.zip`

Host ftp.icm.edu.pl

`/vol/rzm5/replay/security/erasers/`

• `FILE -r--r--r--    16515   Aug 26 2000   scorch.zip`

Figure D.2. Partial Archie search results

Oldenburg, Germany, at http://marvin.physik.uni-oldenburg.de/Docs/net-serv/archie-gate.html and go to it. You will be presented with a 'form' you can fill out with whatever you are looking for. Let us say you are looking for 'SCORCH.ZIP', which was discussed at length in Appendix C and which is hard to find with conventional 'search engines'. Enter the data as shown in Figure D.1.

2. Upon submitting the form, you will get back a long list of databases from which the file you are looking for can be downloaded, as shown in Figure D.2.

3. You then go to the site of your choice, click on the file, and it will download.

Appendix E

E.1 Encryption and Hashing Algorithms

RC4
http://www.cypherspace.org/~adam/rsa/rc4.html
http://www.cypherspace.org/~adam/rsa/rc4c.html
http://www.cypherspace.org/~adam/rsa/rc4.c

Seal
http://tirnanog.ls.fi.upm.es/Servicios/Software/ap_crypt/disk3/seal.zip

MD2
http://community.roxen.com/developers/idocs/rfc/rfc1319.html

MD4
http://community.roxen.com/developers/idocs/rfc/rfc1320.html

MD5
http://theory.lcs.mit.edu/~rivest/rfc1321.txt
http://theory.lcs.mit.edu/~rivest/md5
http://www.cypherspace.org/~adam/rsa/md5.html

RIPEMD-128
http://www.esat.kuleuven.ac.be/~cosicart/ps/AB-9601/

RIPEMD-160
http://www.esat.kuleuven.ac.be/~bosselae/ripemd160.html

SHA-1
http://csrc.nist.gov/cryptval/shs.html
http://home.earthlink.net/~neilbawd/sha1.html
http://csrc.nist.gov/encryption/shs/sha256-384-512.pdf
http://www.itl.nist.gov/fipspubs/fip180-1.htm

Tiger
http://citeseer.nj.nec.com/anderson96tiger.html

Blowfish
http://www.counterpane.com/blowfish.html

Cast
ftp://ftp.isi.edu/in-notes/rfc2144.txt

DES and 3DES
Paper at http://csrc.nist.gov/publications/fips/fips46-3/fips46-3.pdf

Idea
https://www.cosic.esat.kuleuven.ac.be/nessie/workshop/submissions/idea.zip

RC5	http://www.cypherspace.org/~adam/rsa/rc5.html http://www.cypherspace.org/~adam/rsa/rc5.c
Safer K-64	https://www.cosic.esat.kuleuven.ac.be/nessie/workshop/submissions/ safer++.zi
Safer K-128	ftp://ftp.isi.ee.ethz.ch/pub/simpl/safer.V1.0.tar.Z
Safer SK-64	http://home.ecn.ab.ca/~jsavard/crypto/co0403.htm
Shark	ftp://ftp.esat.kuleuven.ac.be/cosic/rijmen/shark/paper.ps
Square	http://www.esat.kuleuven.ac.be/~rijmen/square/index.html
Misty	https://www.cosic.esat.kuleuven.ac.be/nessie/workshop/submissions/ misty1.zip
SSL	http://home.netscape.com/eng/ssl3/ssl-toc.html http://developer.netscape.com/docs/manuals/security/sslin/index.htm ftp://ftp.psy.uq.oz.au/pub/Crypto/SSL/
PEM	http://community.roxen.com/developers/idocs/rfc/rfc1423.html
RC6	http://www.rsasecurity.com/rsalabs/rc6/index.html ftp://ftp.rsasecurity.com/pub/rsalabs/rc6/rc6v11.pdf
Rijandel	[the new advanced encryption standard or (AES)] http://fp.gladman.plus.com/cryptography_technology/rijndael/ aes_code.zip http://www.esat.kuleuven.ac.be/~rijmen/rijndael/
Serpent	http://www.cl.cam.ac.uk/~rja14/serpent.html http://www.ftp.cl.cam.ac.uk/ftp/users/rja14/serpent.pdf
Twofish	http://www.counterpane.com/download-twofish.html http://www.counterpane.com/twofish.html
S/Mime	http://www.imc.org/rfc2311 ftp://ftp.ietf.org/rfc/rfc2630.txt http://www.rsasecurity.com/standards/smime/resources.html
SSH	http://www.snailbook.com/docs/protocol-1.5.txt http://www.ietf.org/internet-drafts/draft-ietf-secsh-filexfer-00.txt http://www.ietf.org/internet-drafts/draft-ietf-secsh-architecture-07.txt http://www.ietf.org/internet-drafts/draft-ietf-secsh-transport-09.txt

	http://www.ietf.org/internet-drafts/draft-ietf-secsh-userauth-09.txt
	http://www.ietf.org/internet-drafts/draft-ietf-secsh-connect-09.txt
RC6	https://www.cosic.esat.kuleuven.ac.be/nessie/workshop/submissions/ rc6.zip
Frog	http://www.tecapro.com/aesfrog.htm
	http://196.40.15.121/Encryption/frogc.zip
Tea	http://www.ftp.cl.cam.ac.uk/ftp/papers/djw-rmn/djw-rmn-tea.html
	http://vader.brad.ac.uk/tea/source.shtml#powerpc
	ftp://ftp.rpini.com/pub/cryptocd/source/cyphers/tea/c/tea.c
AES-HPC	http://www.cs.arizona.edu/~rcs/hpc/
	http://www.cs.arizona.edu/~rcs/hpc/hpc-spec
AES-MARS	http://www.research.ibm.com/security/mars.pdf
	http://www.research.ibm.com/security/mars.html
Loki 97	http://www.adfa.oz.au/~lpb/research/loki97/
	http://www.adfa.oz.au/~lpb/research/loki97/cref.zip
Solitaire	http://www.counterpane.com/solitaire.html
	http://www.counterpane.com/solitaire.c
Ike	http://www.cisco.com/univercd/cc/td/doc/product/software/ios113ed/ 113t/113t_3/isakmp.htm#xtocid105340
	http://xml.resource.org/public/rfc/html/rfc2409.html
	http://www.cis.ohio-state.edu/cgi-bin/rfc/rfc2409.html
MS-PPTP	http://community.roxen.com/developers/idocs/rfc/rfc3078.html
CS-Cipher	https://www.cosic.esat.kuleuven.ac.be/nessie/workshop/submissions/ cs-cipher.zip
Hierocrypt-L1	https://www.cosic.esat.kuleuven.ac.be/nessie/workshop/submissions/ hierocrypt-l1.zip
Khazad	https://www.cosic.esat.kuleuven.ac.be/nessie/workshop/submissions/ khazad.zip
Nimbus	https://www.cosic.esat.kuleuven.ac.be/nessie/workshop/submissions/ nimbus.zip

Anubis	https://www.cosic.esat.kuleuven.ac.be/nessie/workshop/submissions/anubis.zip
Grand Cru	https://www.cosic.esat.kuleuven.ac.be/nessie/workshop/submissions/grandcru.zip
Hierocrypt-3	https://www.cosic.esat.kuleuven.ac.be/nessie/workshop/submissions/hierocrypt-3.zip
Nuekeon	https://www.cosic.esat.kuleuven.ac.be/nessie/workshop/submissions/noekeon.zip
Q	https://www.cosic.esat.kuleuven.ac.be/nessie/workshop/submissions/q.zip
SC2000	https://www.cosic.esat.kuleuven.ac.be/nessie/workshop/submissions/sc2000.zip
Shacal	https://www.cosic.esat.kuleuven.ac.be/nessie/workshop/submissions/shacal.zip
Nush	https://www.cosic.esat.kuleuven.ac.be/nessie/workshop/submissions/nush.zip
BMGL	https://www.cosic.esat.kuleuven.ac.be/nessie/workshop/submissions/bmgl.zip
	https://www.cosic.esat.kuleuven.ac.be/nessie/workshop/submissions/bmgl4.pdf
Leviathan	https://www.cosic.esat.kuleuven.ac.be/nessie/workshop/submissions/leviathan.zip
Lili-128	https://www.cosic.esat.kuleuven.ac.be/nessie/workshop/submissions/lili-128.zip
	https://www.cosic.esat.kuleuven.ac.be/nessie/reports/extwp3-001-2.pdf
Snow	https://www.cosic.esat.kuleuven.ac.be/nessie/workshop/submissions/snow.zip
Sober-T16	https://www.cosic.esat.kuleuven.ac.be/nessie/workshop/submissions/sober-t16.zip
Sober-T32	https://www.cosic.esat.kuleuven.ac.be/nessie/workshop/submissions/sober-t32.zip

Two-Track-Mac	https://www.cosic.esat.kuleuven.ac.be/nessie/workshop/submissions/twotrackmac3.zip
UMAC	https://www.cosic.esat.kuleuven.ac.be/nessie/workshop/submissions/umac.zip
Whirlpool	https://www.cosic.esat.kuleuven.ac.be/nessie/workshop/submissions/whirlpool.zip
GPS	https://www.cosic.esat.kuleuven.ac.be/nessie/workshop/submissions/gps.zip
Ace Encrypt	https://www.cosic.esat.kuleuven.ac.be/nessie/workshop/submissions/ace.zip
ECIES	https://www.cosic.esat.kuleuven.ac.be/nessie/workshop/submissions/ec.zip
Epoc	https://www.cosic.esat.kuleuven.ac.be/nessie/workshop/submissions/epoc.zip
PSEC	https://www.cosic.esat.kuleuven.ac.be/nessie/workshop/submissions/psec.zip
RSA-OAEP	https://www.cosic.esat.kuleuven.ac.be/nessie/workshop/submissions/rsa-oaep.zip
Acesign	https://www.cosic.esat.kuleuven.ac.be/nessie/workshop/submissions/ace.zip
ECDSA	https://www.cosic.esat.kuleuven.ac.be/nessie/workshop/submissions/ec.zip
Esign	https://www.cosic.esat.kuleuven.ac.be/nessie/workshop/submissions/esign.zip
Flash	https://www.cosic.esat.kuleuven.ac.be/nessie/workshop/submissions/flash.zip
Quartz	https://www.cosic.esat.kuleuven.ac.be/nessie/workshop/submissions/quartz.zip
RSA-PSS	https://www.cosic.esat.kuleuven.ac.be/nessie/workshop/submissions/rsa-pss.zip

SFlash	https://www.cosic.esat.kuleuven.ac.be/nessie/workshop/submissions/sflash.zip
KCS 1	http://community.roxen.com/developers/idocs/rfc/rfc2313.html http://community.roxen.com/developers/idocs/rfc/rfc2437.html
PKCS 5	http://community.roxen.com/developers/idocs/rfc/rfc2898.html
PKCS 7	http://community.roxen.com/developers/idocs/rfc/rfc2315.html
KCS 9	http://community.roxen.com/developers/idocs/rfc/rfc2985.html
F8 F9	http://www.etsi.org/dvbandca/3GPPSPECIFICATIONS/3GTS35.201%20ver1.2.pdf
Kasumi	http://www.etsi.org/dvbandca/3GPPSPECIFICATIONS/3GTS35.202.pdf
Cauley-Purser	http://www.cayley-purser.ie

<h1>Appendix F</h1>

F.1 Cleaning After the Litter in Internet Explorer, Outlook, and Outlook Express

The information in this appendix is an edited version of a longer file from the Usenet and is copyrighted by 'The Riddler', who permits its copying and dissemination.[1] Only the technical portions of this material are included. No agreement with 'The Riddler's' opinions is implied.

F1.1 Summary

There are folders on your computer that Microsoft has tried hard to keep secret. Within these folders you will find two major things: Microsoft Internet Explorer has been logging all of the sites you have ever visited – even after you've cleared your history – and Microsoft's Outlook Express has been logging all of your e-mail correspondence – even after you've erased them from your Deleted Items bin (this also includes all incoming and outgoing file attachments).

These files are hidden. If you do not have any knowledge of DOS then do not plan on finding these files on your own. These files/folders will not be displayed in Windows Explorer at all – only DOS (even after you have enabled Windows Explorer to 'view all files'). And to top it off, the only way to find them in DOS is if you know the exact location of them. Basically, if you did not know the files existed then the chances of you running across them is slim.

Microsoft has gone to great lengths to create files in your computer that are related to your online activities with Internet Explorer, Outlook, and Outlook Express that are impossible to find from within Windows, and still very hard to find even within DOS unless you know the files' names and locations. These files store a

---

[1] 'Microsoft's Really Hidden Files: A New Look At Forensics (v2.5b)', by 'The Riddler', 14 October 2001 (v2.0 finished 16 May 2001; v1.0 finished 11 June 2000).

record of your online activities and, in the case of Internet Explorer, are not removed merely by opting to 'Clear History' or 'Clear Cache'.

F.1.2   Microsoft Internet Explorer

If you own a copy of Microsoft Internet Explorer:

1. Shut your computer down, and turn it back on.

2. While your computer is booting keep pressing the [F8] key until you are given an option screen.

3. Choose 'Command Prompt Only'. This will take you to real DOS mode. ME users must use a bootdisk to get into real DOS mode.

4. When your computer is done booting, you will have a C:\> followed by a blinking cursor. Type the following hitting enter after each line (explanations are given in parentheses and are not for typing):

    C:\WINDOWS\SMARTDRV (loads smartdrive to speed things up)

    CD\

    DELTREE/Y TEMP (this line removes temporary files)

    CD WINDOWS

    DELTREE/Y COOKIES (this line removes cookies)

    DELTREE/Y TEMP (this removes temporary files)

    DELTREE/Y HISTORY (this line removes your browsing history)

    DELTREE/Y TEMPOR~1

    If this last line does not work, then type:

CD\WINDOWS\APPLIC~1

DELTREE/Y TEMPOR~1

If this does not work, then type:

CD\WINDOWS\LOCALS~1

DELTREE/Y TEMPOR~1

Older versions of Internet Explorer keep them under '\windows\content\'. This last step will take a very long time to process because there is a ton of semi-useless cache stored on your hard disk.

Clearing your registry from Internet Explorer history data

It was once believed that the registry is the central database of Windows that stores and maintains the operating system configuration information. Well, this is wrong. The registry maintains a lot of information that has absolutely nothing to do with the Windows configuration, such as your typed URLs. These are stored in:

HKEY_USERS/Default/Software/Microsoft/Internet Explorer/TypedURLs/

HKEY_CURRENT_USER/Software/Microsoft/Internet Explorer/TypedURLs/

These 'typed URLs' come from Internet Explorer's autocomplete feature. It records all URLs that you have typed in manually in order to save you some time filling out the address field. By typing 'ama' in the address line the autocomplete feature might bring up 'amazon.com' for you. Although for some it can be annoying, some people prefer this feature. One thing is for sure, however – it is an obvious privacy risk. You would not want a guest to type 'ama' and have it autocomplete 'amaturemudwrestlers.com' now would you?

You can clear your 'typed URLs' out of your registry by going to Tools/Internet Options/Content/AutoComplete and finally 'Clear Forms' under Internet Explorer. If you do not like the AutoComplete feature then uncheck the appropriate boxes here.

F.1.3 Microsoft Outlook and Outlook Express

Microsoft's e-mail clients *do not* delete your messages until:

- you really know how, and

- you go through the redundant process.

And besides this, there are the glaring e-mail virus problems (against which virtually all other e-mail clients are immune).
   My suggestion?

- Install another e-mail program such as Eudora (http://www.eudora.com) or Pegasus Mail (http://www.pmail.com). Make sure everything is setup correctly (www.eudora.com/www.pmail.com)

- Backup any e-mail and address books that you wish to save by making use of the export – import features.

- Uninstall Outlook.

Caution: simply uninstalling Outlook does not erase any of your e-mail correspondence. The database files are still there on your hard drive. To find them, open up a DOS window and type this:

dir *.mbx /s/p

The files you are looking for are:

PINBOX.MBX

OUTBOX.MBX

SENTIT~1.MBX

DELETE~1.MBX

DRAFTS.MBX

If these files come up they should be listed in either of these folders:

C:\Windows\Application Data\Microsoft\Outlook Express\Mail\

C:\Program Files\internet mail and news\%USER%\mail\

Now type either of the following (depending on the location of your .mbx files):[2]

CD\WINDOWS\APPLIC~1\MICROS~1\OUTLOO~1

DELTREE/Y MAIL

or

CD\PROGRA~1\INTERN~1\%USER%

replacing '%USER%' with the proper name. Then type:

DELTREE/Y MAIL

If you have newer versions of Outlook or Outlook Express the databases are *.dbx, or *.pst files: five times as 'creepy' as the *.mbx files. I recommend that you take a look at them yourself.

F.1.4   But I like Internet Explorer and/or Outlook Express

If you insist on using Microsoft Internet Explorer then I strongly recommend that you check out at least one of these programs:

- PurgeIE (www.aandrc.com/purgeie),
- Cache and Cookie Cleaner for Internet Explorer (www.webroot.com/washie.htm),
- Anonymizer Window Washer (www.anonymizer.com/anonwash).

And if you insist on using Outlook or Outlook Express then you should get in the habit of compacting your mailboxes. You can do this by going to

File/Folder/Compact All

---

[2] Remember that this will erase all your e-mail correspondence so backup what you want to keep. By now you should already have imported your mail into Eudora or Pegasus Mail.

if you have Outlook Express, or

Tools/Options/Other tab/Auto Archive

if you have Outlook. Make sure to set things up here.

F.1.5   Step-by-step guide through your hidden files

This next section is for those readers who are interested in learning the ins and outs of their computers. This section is intended for the 'savvy' user.

The most important files to be paying attention to are your 'index.dat' files. These are database files that reference your history, cache, and cookies. The first thing you should know about the index.dat files is that they do not advertise their existence, so you will not automatically know they are there. The second thing you should know about them is that some will *not* get cleared after deleting your history and cache. The result? There is a log of your browsing history hidden away on your computer after you thought you had cleared it away.

To view these files, follow these steps:[3]

1. First, drop to a DOS box and type this at prompt (all in lower-case) to bring up Windows Explorer under the correct directory:

    c:\windows\explorer /e,c:\windows\tempor ∼ 1\content.ie5\

    You see alphanumeric names listed under 'content.ie5?' (left-hand side). That is Microsoft's idea of making this project as hard as possible. Actually, these are your alphanumeric folders that were created to keep your cache. Write these names down on a peice of paper. (They should look something like this: 6YQ2GSWF, QRM7KL3F, U7YHQKI4, 7YMZ516U, etc.) If you click on any of the alphanumeric folders then nothing will be displayed. Not because there are not any files here, but because Windows Explorer has 'lied' to you. If you want to view the contents of these alphanumeric folders you will have to do so in DOS. (Actually, this is not always true. *Sometimes* Windows Explorer will display the contents of the alphanumeric folders – but mostly it will not.)

---

[3] In Internet Explorer 5.x you can skip the first step by opening Internet Explorer and going to Tools/ Internet Options/Settings/View Files. Now write down the names of your alphanumeric folders on a peice of paper. If you cannot see any alphanumeric folder names then start with step (1) above.

2. Then you must restart in MS-DOS mode. (Start/Shutdown/Restart in MS-DOS mode; ME users use a bootdisk.) Note that you must restart to DOS because windows has locked down some of the files and they can only be accessed in real DOS mode.

3. Type this in at prompt:

    CD\WINDOWS\TEMPOR~1\CONTENT.IE5

    CD %alphanumeric%

    replacing the '%alphanumeric%' with the first name that you wrote down in step (1). Then type:

    DIR/P

    The cache files you are now looking at are directly responsible for the mysterious erosion of hard disk space you may have been noticing. One thing particularly interesting is the ability to view some of your old e-mail if you happen to have a hotmail account. To see them for yourself you must first copy them into another directory and then open them with your browser. A note about these files: these are your cache files that help speed up your internet browsing. It is quite normal to use this cache system, as every major browser does. However, it is not normal for some cache files to be left behind after you have instructed your browser to erase them.

4. Type this in:

    CD\WINDOWS\TEMPOR~1\CONTENT.IE5

    EDIT /75 INDEX.DAT

    You will be brought to a blue screen with a bunch of binary.

5. Press and hold the 'Page Down' button until you start seeing lists of URLs. These are all the sites that you have ever visited as well as a brief description of each. You will notice it records everything you have searched for in a search engine in plain text, in addition to the URL.

6. When you get done searching around you can go to File/Exit.

7. Next you will probably want to erase these files by typing this:

    C:\WINDOWS\SMARTDRV

    CD\WINDOWS

    DELTREE/Y TEMPOR|~1

    replacing 'cd\windows' with the location of your TIF folder if different. This
    will take a seriously long time to process, even with smartdrive loaded.

8. Then check out the contents of your History folder by typing this:

    CD\WINDOWS\HISTORY\HISTORY.IE5

    EDIT /75 INDEX.DAT

    You will be brought to a blue screen with more binary.

9. Press and hold the 'Page Down' button until you start seeing lists of URLS
    again. This is another database of the sites you have visited.

10. Now type this:

    CD\WINDOWS\HISTORY

11. If you see any mmXXXX.dat files here, then check them out (and delete them).
    Then type:

    CD\WINDOWS\HISTORY\HISTORY.IE5

    CD MSHIST~1

    EDIT /75 INDEX.DAT

    You will see more URLs from your Internet history. There are probably other
    mshist~x folders here.

You can repeat these steps for every occurrence of a mshist~x folder. Type:

CD WINDOWS

DELTREE/Y HISTORY

You may also want to take a look at your *.mbx files if you own Outlook (dir *.mbx/s). All your e-mail correspondence and file attachments are located within these database files. More detailed information is covered in the next section.

F.1.6   A look at Outlook Express

Would you think twice about what you said if you knew it was being recorded? E-mail correspondence leaves a permanent record of everything you have said – *even after you have told Outlook Express to erase it*. You are given a false sense of security since you have erased it twice – so surely it must be gone? The first time, Outlook simply moves it to your 'Deleted Items' folder. The second time you erase it Outlook simply 'pretends' it is gone. The truth is your messages are still being retained in the database files on your hard drive. (The same is true of your e-mail attachments.)

For earlier versions of Outlook Express, they will be located in either of the following folders:

c:\program files\internet mail and news\%user%\mail*.mbx

(replacing '%user%' with the name you use), or if you are lucky,

c:\windows\application data\microsoft\outlook\mail*.mbx

At this point you have two choices.

- get in the habit of compacting your folders all the time;

- import the data into another e-mail client such as Pegasus Mail or Eudora and then delete the mbx files (and thus all your e-mail correspondence) by typing this:

cd\windows\intern~1\%user%\mail

deltree/y mail

or

cd\windows\applic~1\micros~1\outloo~1\

deltree/y mail

Typing in the above commands will 'kill' all your e-mail correspondence.
   Caution: do not follow these steps unless you have already exported your e-mail and address book!

F.1.7   How Microsoft does it

Study this section of this appendix if you would like to learn how to obscure your files using Windows's own built-in mechanisms.

How does Microsoft make these folders and files invisible to DOS?

The only thing Microsoft had to do to make the folders and files invisible to a directory listing is to set them +s[ystem]. That is it. As soon as the dir/s command hits a system folder, it renders the command useless (unlike for normal folders). A more detailed explanation is given in Section F.1.8.

How does Microsoft make these folders and files invisible to Windows Explorer?

The file desktop.ini is a standard text file that can be added to any folder to customize certain aspects of the folder's behavior. In these cases, Microsoft utilized the desktop.ini file to make these files invisible. Invisible to Windows Explorer and even to the 'Find/Files or Folders' utility (so you would not be able to perform searches in these folders!) All that Microsoft had to do was create a desktop.ini file with certain CLSID tags and the folders would disappear like magic.
   To show you exactly what is going on, in the c:\windows\temporary internet files\desktop.ini and the c:\windows\temporary internet files\content.ie5\desktop.ini you will find the following text:

[.ShellClassInfo]

UICLSID={7BD29E00-76C1-11CF-9DD0-00A0C9034933}

and in the c:\windows\history\desktop.ini and the c:\windows\history\history.ie5\ desktop.ini one find the following text

[.ShellClassInfo]

UICLSID={7BD29E00-76C1-11CF-9DD0-00A0C9034933}

CLSID={FF393560-C2A7-11CF-BFF4-444553540000}

The UICLSID line cloaks the folder in Windows Explorer. The CLSID line disables the 'Find' utility from searching through the folder. (Additionally, it gives a folder the appearance of the 'History' folder.)

To see for yourself, you can simply erase the desktop.ini files. You will see that it will instantly give Windows Explorer proper viewing functionality again and the 'Find' utility proper searching capabilities again. Problem solved, right? Actually, no. As it turns out, the desktop.ini files get reconstructed every single time you restart your computer!

Luckily, there is a work-around that will keep Windows from hiding these folders. You can manually edit the desktop.ini files and remove everything except for the '[.ShellClassInfo]' line. This will trick windows into thinking they have still covered their tracks, and wininet will not think to reconstruct them. Windows actually makes sure the files are hidden and in place on every single boot. No other files or folders get this kind of special treatment.

F.1.8   +S means [S]ecret, not [S]ystem

Executing the 'dir/a/s' command from root *should* be the correct command to display all files in all subdirectories in DOS. However, doing so will not display the index.dat files. This is because when DOS tries to get a list of the subdirectories of any +s(system) folder it 'hits a brick wall'. No files or folders will be listed within any system folder. Not only does this defeat the whole purpose of the '/s' switch in the first place, but I would say it looks like Microsoft took extra precautions to keep people from finding the files. Remember: the only thing you need to do to obscure a file in DOS is to mark the parent directory +s.

But, would you consider your temporary Internet files to be 'system files?' It would seem that your TIF folder appears to be marked +s for no good reason at all. Just because. Same with your history folder. Just because. It appears that Microsoft marked the folders as +s solely to hide any directory recursal from DOS.

Here is a small experiment that will show you what is meant. Since the content.ie5 and history.ie5 subfolders are both located within a +s folder, we will run the experiment with them. The proper command to locate them *should* be this:

CD\

DIR *.IE5 /as/s

The problem is that you will receive a 'No files found' message. Since we already know there is a content.ie5 subfolder located here, why is it giving the 'no files found' message? But there is a way to get around this 'brick wall'. That is, once you are inside the system directory, then it no longer has an effect on the dir listings. For example, if you enter the system folder first, and *then* try to find any +s directories you can see them just fine:

CD\WINDOWS\TEMPOR~1

DIR *.IE5 /as/s

Now you will get a '1 folder(s) found' message (but only after you knew the exact location). In other words, if you did not know the files existed then finding them would be almost impossible.

And, by the way, to see the 'bug' in progress, type:

CD\

DIR *.IE5 /as/s

It will echo 'no files found'. Now, just take away the system attributes from the parent directory:

CD\WINDOWS

ATTRIB -S TEMPOR~1

And retry the test:

CD\

DIR *.IE5 /as/s

It will echo '1 folder(s) found.'

F.1.9 The truth about find fast

Have you ever wondered what that 'Find Fast' program was under your control panel? Here is a hint: it has *nothing* to do with the 'Find/Files or Folders' utility located under the Start menu. Find Fast actually does serve some purpose.

Interestingly, Find Fast is scanning every single file on your hard drive In Office 95, for example, the Find Fast Indexer had an 'exclusion list' comprising .exe, .swp, .dll, and other extensions, but the feature was eliminated! If you were a programmer would you program Find Fast to index every single file, or just the ones with Office extensions?

For your information: if you have ever had problems with scandisk or defrag restarting because of disk writes, it is because Find Fast was indexing your hard drive in the background. It loads every time you start your computer up.

Now, here is a good example of the lengths Microsoft has gone through to keep people from finding out Find Fast is constantly scanning and indexing their hard drives. Look at the snippet taken from microsoft.com reproduced here in Box F.1.

Box F.1 Find Fast: quote from http://microsoft.com

When you specify the type of documents to index in the Create Index dialog box, Find Fast includes the document types that are listed in the following table.

Document type	File name extension
MS Office and Web Documents	All the Microsoft Excel, Microsoft PowerPoint, Microsoft Project, and Microsoft Word documents listed in this table. Microsoft Binder (.odb, .obt) and Microsoft Access (.mdb) files. Note that in .mdb files, only document properties are indexed.
Word documents	.doc (document), .dot (template), .ht* (Hypertext Markup Language document), .txt (text file), .rtf (Rich Text Format) files, Excel workbooks .xl* files
PowerPoint	.ppt (presentation), .pot (template), .pps (auto-running presentation) files
Microsoft Project files	.mpp, .mpw, .mpt, .mpx, .mpd files
All files	*.* files

Notice the 'All files' entry at the end of the table. Find Fast indexes Office Documents, Web documents, Word Documents, Power Point files, Project files, and *every other file on your computer.*

Actually, the good news is that this is not neccessarily true. In another statement, Microsoft claims that if Find Fast deems the file 'unreadable' then the file will not be included in the index. For example, your command.com probably would not get indexed because it does not have a lot of plain text – mostly binary.

Every single file that has legible text is going to be included in the Find Fast database. In short, *all text saved to your hard drive is indexed.* Do you see the forensic capabilities now? And do not forget 'all text' also means previously visited webpages from your cache. See for yourself. Open up a DOS window and type

CD\

then

DIR FF*.*/AH

which will bring up a list of the Find Fast databases. Then type

EDIT /75%ff%

replacing %ff% with any of the names that were listed. Do you notice the incredible amount of disk accesses to your cache and history folders? Why do we need two indexes?

Removing the Find Fast program

You can remove Find Fast using your Office CD, but I recommend you do it manually:

1. Reboot your computer in MS-DOS Mode.
2. Delete the findfast.cpl file from c:\windows\system\
3. Delete the shortcut (.lnk) under c:\windows\start menu\programs\startup\
4. Delete the findfast.exe file from c:\progra~1\micros~1\office\
5. Delete the find fast databases in your root, by typing

cd\

deltree ff*.*

You can also safely delete FFNT.exe, FFSetup.dll, FFService.dll, and FFast_bb.dll if you have them.

Feel free to check out the ffastlog.txt (which is the Find Fast error log). It is a +h(hidden) file under c:\windows\system\.

Recommended reading

http://www.theregister.co.uk/content/4/18002.html
http://www.findarticles.com/m0CGN/3741/55695355/p1/article.jhtml
http://www.mobtown.org/news/archive/msg00492.html
http://194.159.40.109/05069801.htm
http://www.yarbles.demon.co.uk/mssniff.html
http://www.macintouch.com/o98security.html
http://www.theregister.co.uk/content/archive/3079.html
http://www.fsm.nl/ward/
http://slashdot.org
http://www.peacefire.org
http://stopcarnivore.org
http://nomorefakenews.com
http://grc.com/steve.htm#project-x

Acknowledgements

Special thanks to Concerned Boss, Oblivion, and the F-Prot virus scanner.

References

http://support.microsoft.com/support/kb/articles/Q137/1/13.asp
http://support.microsoft.com/support/kb/articles/Q136/3/86.asp
http://support.microsoft.com/support/kb/articles/Q169/5/31.ASP
http://support.microsoft.com/support/kb/articles/Q141/0/12.asp
http://support.microsoft.com/support/kb/articles/Q205/2/89.ASP
http://support.microsoft.com/support/kb/articles/Q166/3/02.ASP

http://www.insecure.org/sploits/Internet.explorer.web.usage.logs.html
http://www.parascope.com/cgi-bin/psforum.pl/topic=matrix&disc=514&mmark
  =all~http://www.hackers.com/bulletin/
http://slashdot.org/articles/00/05/11/173257.shtml
http://peacefire.org

Copyright information

The information in this appendix is copyrighted by 'The Riddler'. The author of
this book assumes no responsibility for the information in this appendix.

Appendix G

G.1 The Security Flaws of the IEEE 802.11b Wireless LAN Implemenation[1]

Anyone with a wireless local area network (LAN) card complying with the 802.11b specification and with some custom software[2] who elects to drive around town within radio range from an existing wirelss LAN 802.11b network will notice the service set identifiers (SSIDs), MAC address, and WEP usage displayed in the screen[3]. This is information that is identifying information that is broadcast by existing wireless networks, and its reception may be perfectly legal since it is a broadcast.

What is illegal is to exploit this signal in order to gain unauthorized access into the network associated with the wireless LAN. But it is just as illegal for a burglar to pick a lock to get into a private property, or even to enter a private property whose owner forgot to lock the front door; the illegality of the act is of little consolation to the owner of the burglarized property (or of the private wireless network); what is important is to make it technically impossible for a trangressor to gain uauthorized access; sadly, the 802.11b standard does not do that, for the following technical reasons:

- It implements encryption in a manner that has been demonstrated to be easily breakable. In the 2001 Black Hat conference, Timothy Newsham (http://www.atstake.com) showed a tool that could crack the encryption keys used by this scheme within less than a minute–often within less than a second! Although RC4 encryption, if implemented properly, can be solid, the implementation in the present standard is about as strong as a wet paper bag.

---

[1] See http://www.cs.umd.edu/~waa/wireless.html and http://www.eyetap.org~rguerra/toronto2001/rc4_ksaproc.pdf

[2] See http://www.starkrealities.com/shipley.htm, and http://sourceforge.net/projects/wepcrack.

[3] See 'Wireless Security: A Contradiction in Terms', by Rik Farrow, *Network Magazine*, December 2001.

- Most vendors' products have a default configuration that has disabled both encryption and access control. Anyone within radio range can connect—no questions asked.

- The LAN-carried traffic itself is vulnerable to unauthorized decryption. A variety of techniques was demonstrated by Ian Goldberg of the University of California at the same 2001 Black Hat conference.

- It has been demonstrated that it is possible for a malicious attacker to change encrypted messages without even knowing the encryption key or the keystream while concurrently modifying the integrity checksum so that all appears correct when that integrity is checked; this can be quite disastrous in a financial transaction.

To be sure, the IEEE 802.11b committee (http://standards.ieee.org/catalog/IEEE802.11.html) is working to fix the above problems. In the mean time, the following recommendations should be observed:

- All data going over the 802.11b path should be superencrypted (i.e. encrypted over and above any protection offered by the 802.11b network; for example, the data could be VPN-encrypted).

- All data going over the 802.11b path should be treated as vulnerable to malicious attack and be routed through a firewall as if it were coming from the Internet at large. In network security terms, it should be in the DMZ outside the firewall.

- When setting encryption keys in the 802.11b LANs, enter those in hexadecimal form, rather than strings that are later converted to hexadecimals.

- Locate the wireless access points in locations with the minimum exposure to the outside of a building, preferably behind walls with metal content (such as aluminum siding or California-style stucco with chicken wire in it in the case of houses), deep inside the facility, away from windows, and preferably at the ground floor.

Glossary

Biometrics: the collection of science based techniques that abstract a biological characteristic of an individual's (such as fingerprint, retinal pattern, voiceprint, palmprint, etc.) for the purpose of ensuring authentication.

BIOS: shorthand for 'basic input—output system'. It is the set of instructions, stored in a computer 'chip' (integrated circuit) that is used by the computer to interface the hardware with the operating system and facilitate the 'boot-up' (starting, after power is applied) process.

Booting up: the sequence of steps involved in getting a computer to become functional after it is turned on. Some of these steps are automated (e.g., ones stored in CMOS, others on disk) and some are manual (e.g., entry of passwords).

Caller-ID: a service offered by many telephone companies worldwide, made possible by the widespread use of a protocol called 'signaling system 7' that sends the telephone number of the calling party to the called party. Most countries' telephone companies have this and use it for internal purposes, even though they may not offer it to their customers.

Cluster: a collection of a number of disk sectors that forms a disk's 'allocation unit' for storing data; this is the smallest unit of storage that is handled by the particular operating system and disk being used.

CMOS memory: a small amount of battery-backed electronic memory in a computer circuit that stores a computer's configuration so that the computer can be started merely by pressing a switch.

Cryptography: the process of converting a message into an equivalent version that is not understandable by unauthorized viewers (encryption), and the converse process of making it understandable (decryption).

E-mail: shorthand for 'electronic mail', (i.e., the creation, transmission, reception, and viewing of messages with use of computers).

Firewall: generic name for any technique (software, hardware, or both) intended to reduce a network-connected user's vulnerability to security threats associated with being on that network (such as the Internet).

FTP: shorthand for 'file transfer protocol' for transferring files over the Internet or other network using TCP/IP.

Hacker: initially, the term denoted a competent computer programmer. The term has degenerated to denote a person who performs a programming act that is illegal.

Hashing: the software-based mathematical process of creating a short collection of digital symbols in connection with a digital file so that if that file were to be modified a different set of digital symbols would result. Intended to ensure that digital files cannot be altered undetectably.

ICQ: short for 'I seek you'. Israeli-developed software protocol (now acquired by AOL) for teleconferencing over the Internet. Allows 'chatting' (actually typing back and forth), e-mail, and even transfer of files. Its main claim to fame is that it alerts one that someone else in one's list is 'online'.

Internet: a large network of smaller networks that was originally developed for the US Advanced Research Projects Agency as a network intended to survive almost any attack of any of its portions. Now it is the global network that links all countries for data communications.

NetBIOS: the standard networking protocol for DOS and Windows. It facilitates a programming interface for computer programs ('applications') for networking purposes over, for example, TCP/IP.

PGP: short for 'pretty good privacy'; a hugely popular encryption software using a combination of public and conventional key encryption that is considered very secure if used properly, originally developed by Phil Zimmerman.

Public key cryptography: an encryption method using two keys (either one of which cannot be inferred from the other) whereby a file encrypted with one of these two keys can only be decrypted by the other. A user typically publicizes one key (labeled as the 'public key') so that anyone can encrypt files to that user that only that user can decrypt with the other key that is labeled 'secret'.

Registry: a database file in a computer using Windows 95/98/NT/2000 that contains large amounts of information about a computer's entire configuration (including hardware and software).

Sector: a portion of a track.

Slack: the colloquial commonly-used term to denote the portion of a track of a disk that contains data after the 'end of file' and before the 'end of cluster'.

SSL: short for 'secure socket layer'; a protocol developed by Netscape Co. that uses public key encryption in conjunction with a browser that allows end-to-end encryption between an Internet user's browser and the web site with which that user is communicating.

Steganography: the process of hiding the existence of a sensitive file by using any one or more of a large collection of computer-related techniques. It is the modern-day equivalent of the microdot of World-War-2 fame.

Swap file: a file on a computer disk created by Windows and used as virtual (make-believe) memory; usually intended to allow a computer with limited conventional electronic volatile memory (RAM) to accommodate software that has higher RAM requirements.

TCP/IP: shorthand for 'transmission control protocol/Internet protocol'; a protocol developed for the US Department of Defense that has become the worldwide standard for data telecommunications; it includes functionality to ensure that the data arrive at their destination (as opposed to UDP, that does not).

Track: a concentric circle on a computer disk that is intended to store data. On magnetic tape, tracks are parallel to each other or, in some cases, such as with videocasette recorder (VCR) tapes, helical.

VPN: short for 'virtual private network'; a way to enjoy private communications as if one had one's private network but by using a public network such as the Internet.

Web (or www or World Wide Web): a user-friendly graphical way of connecting to other sites on the Internet for the purpose of receiving and sending information.

'Wiping': rendering data recorded on a disk unreadable by any known technical means intended to retrieve it.

Index